RACISM:
THE AUSTRALIAN EXPERIENCE
A STUDY OF RACE PREJUDICE IN AUSTRALIA

VOLUME 2
BLACK VERSUS WHITE

VOLUME 1
PREJUDICE AND XENOPHOBIA

VOLUME 3
COLONIALISM

DU 120
R282
v. 2

RACISM:
The Australian Experience

A STUDY OF RACE PREJUDICE IN AUSTRALIA

Edited by
F. S. STEVENS

VOLUME 2
BLACK VERSUS WHITE

TAPLINGER PUBLISHING COMPANY
NEW YORK

JUN 7 1976

193924

First published in the United States in 1972 by
TAPLINGER PUBLISHING CO, INC
New York, New York

Copyright © 1972 by Australia and New Zealand Book Company Pty Ltd
except as otherwise acknowledged
All rights reserved

No part of this publication may be reproduced or transmitted in any form
or by any means, electronic or mechanical, including photocopy, recording,
or any information storage and retrieval system now known or to be
invented, except by a reviewer who wishes to quote brief passages in
connection with a review written for inclusion in a magazine, newspaper
or broadcast

Published simultaneously in the Dominion of Canada by
Burns & MacEachern Ltd, Ontario

Library of Congress Catalog Card Number: 70-179992

ISBN 0-8008-6581-4

PREFACE

With the object of assisting in the celebration of the United Nations International Year for Action to Combat Racism and Racial Discrimination, an *ad hoc* committee of interested individuals was formed in Sydney in October, 1970. Under the chairmanship of Hyam Brezniak, Editor of *The Bridge*, journal of the Australian Jewish Quarterly Foundation, the committee was limited to a small, but balanced representation of university and community leaders. These included:

>Sol Encel, Professor of Sociology, University of New South Wales
>Frank Engel, Secretary of the Australian Council of Churches
>Peter McGregor, Secretary, The Australian Citizens Campaign to Overcome Racial Discrimination (A.C.C.O.R.D.)
>Frank Stevens, Senior Lecturer in Industrial Relations, University of New South Wales

After consideration of various ways in which the most direct contribution to discussion of the subject of race prejudice might be made, the committee decided to produce an anthology on the subject, contributed to by people working in the field of race relations.

As a statement of policy, the committee determined that the question of the existence of racism in Australia was to be an open matter and that contributors invited to participate in the series should be selected, not for their opinions on the matter, but on their standing in the field. In all, some ninety invitations to contribute were extended, and approximately one third of the recipients accepted the opportunity. Their contributions are published in full, without any attempt to achieve a strict editorial format tied to the general terms of reference of the main or subsidiary titles of the volumes.

F.S.S.

Kensington

June 71

The publication of this book has been sponsored by the
United Nations Association of Australia
and the
Australian Committee to Combat Racism
and
Racial Discrimination

CONTENTS

AUTHORS

E. T. BRASH

> Department of English
> University of Papua and New Guinea
> Boroko, Territory of Papua and New Guinea.
> *(Chapter 3)*

J. CAWTE, M.D., B.S.(Adel.), D.P.M.(Melb.), Ph.D.(U.N.S.W.),
F.A.N.Z.C.P.

> Professor, School of Psychiatry
> University of New South Wales
> Prince Henry Hospital, Little Bay, N.S.W.
> *(Chapter 4)*

BARRY E. CHRISTOPHERS, M.B., B.S., B.Sc.(Melb.)

> 366 Church Street, Richmond, Victoria.
> *(Chapter 12, co-author)*

A. DOOBOV, B.Sc.(Qld.)

> A.B.S.C.H.O.L. Education Officer, University of Queensland,
> St. Lucia, Queensland.
> *(Chapter 11, co-author)*

RUTH DOOBOV, M.A.(Qld.)

> Assistant A.B.S.C.H.O.L. Education Officer,
> University of Queensland, St. Lucia, Queensland.
> *(Chapter 11, co-author)*

ELIZABETH M. EGGLESTON, LL.B.(Melb.), Ph.D.(Monash)

> Director, Centre for Research into Aboriginal Affairs,
> Monash University, Clayton, Victoria.
> *(Chapter 7)*

M. C. HARTWIG, B.A., Ph.D.(Adel.)

> Senior Lecturer,
> School of Historical, Philosophical and Political Studies,
> Macquarie University, Ryde, New South Wales.
> *(Chapter 1)*

√ J. HORNER

> General Secretary,
> Federal Council for the Advancement of Aborigines and Torres Strait
>   Islanders,
> 5 Chester Road, Turramurra, New South Wales.
> *(Chapter 14)*

√ LORNA LIPPMAN, B.A.(Melb.)

> Research Officer,
> Centre for Research into Aboriginal Affairs,
> Monash University, Clayton, Victoria.
> *(Chapter 2)*

J. LITTLE, LL.B.(Melb.), LL.M.(Michigan)

> Junior Counsel in the Yirrkala Land Rights Case,
> 29 Mortimer Street, Moorabbin, Victoria.
> *(Chapter 6)*

FRANCES H. LOVEJOY, B.Sc., B.Com.(Qld.)

> Senior Tutor, Department of Economic Statistics,
> University of New England, Armidale, New South Wales.
> *(Chapter 12—Statistical Appendix)*

JOE McGINNESS

> President,
> Federal Council for the Advancement of Aborigines and Torres Strait
> Islanders,
> 10 Gough Street, Cairns, Queensland.
> *(Chapter 12, co-author)*

BRUCE McGUINNESS

> Aboriginal Leader and Field Officer,
> Aboriginal Advancement League,
> 56 Cunningham Street, Northcote, Victoria.
> *(Chapter 10)*

PETER M. MOODIE, M.B., B.S., D.T.M. & H. (Qld.)

> Medical Officer (Research),
> School of Public Health and Tropical Medicine,
> University of Sydney, Sydney, New South Wales.
> *(Chapter 16)*

A. BARRIE PITTOCK, B.Sc., M.Sc., Ph.D.(Melb.)

> Advisory (non-Aboriginal) member of the executive of the National
> Tribal Council, and Councillor for Land and Legislation,
> 38 Yackatoon Avenue, Aspendale, Victoria.
> *(Chapter 13)*

F. S. STEVENS, B.A.(Syd.), M.A.(Stan.)

> Senior Lecturer, Department of Industrial Relations,
> University of New South Wales, Kensington, New South Wales.
> *(Editor, Introduction, Chapter 9)*

C. M. TATZ, M.A.(Natal), Ph.D.(A.N.U.)

> Professor of Political Science,
> University of New England, Armidale, New South Wales.
> *(Chapters 8, 18)*

CLIVE TURNBULL

Author,
18 Yarra Grove, Hawthorn, Victoria.
(Chapter 15)

REVEREND E. A. WELLS

Superintendent Minister, Balmoral Methodist Circuit,
22 Nuttall Street, Bulimba, Queensland.
(Chapter 17)

INTRODUCTION

F. S. Stevens

In the first volume of this series (*Racism: The Australian Experience;* Volume 1, Prejudice and Xenophobia) Professor S. Encel developed the semantic differences between the terms 'racism' and 'racialism'. The first, in that writer's opinion, refers to the ideology of race prejudice whilst the second covers the practice and system of discrimination and repression amongst human groups. On the other hand, it was shown that the World Council of Churches and U.N.E.S.C.O. use a classificatory and functional definition of racism in which they emphasise both biological differences and the objective of the exclusion of one group from the other on these grounds.

It was the feeling of the present writer, expressed in that volume, that our search for evidence of racism in the inter-personal relationships of Australian European society was unsuccessful, whereas racialism was marginally recognised. On reflection, it could be that the two terms are complementary; one cannot exist in its developed form without the other. Indeed, in all systems of race prejudice the two might be witnessed at the same time. The descriptive material in Banton's study *Race Relations*,[1] from which Encel drew his definitions, indicates the interchangeability of the two concepts. At the edges, the semantic differences between ideology and action become irrelevant. It is in the dual state that a racist society functions. If this fundamental proposition is accepted, one might consider the position of Aborigines in Australian society.

From the broadest construction of the term 'racist', down to the inter-personal relationships between Aborigines and Europeans in Australian society, it is difficult to deny that prejudice exists and that this prejudice, over the years, has been erected into a functional system. The external manifestations of prejudice might be witnessed daily throughout the country. The relative situation and standing of the indigenous community also demonstrates that Australians of European origin are prepared to employ a different standard of social, political, economic and legal behaviour when applied to individuals of different genetic origin from that which they would apply to people 'of their own kind'. The duality of standards is most noticeable in economic relations but it runs through the whole pattern of the individual's complex association with his external world. Only recently, for example, have Australians come to recognise that Aborigines are subject to different standards of medical and legal care.[2] To date, so few have been concerned, that no positive action has been taken to redress these injustices. In the meantime, Aboriginal children have died of malnutrition, contributing to 'one of the highest infant mortality rates in the world';[3] Aboriginal leaders have been harassed[4] and wrongfully imprisoned[5] to serve the short-run purpose of administrative convenience. This has led to a sub-system of control and jurisprudence based on skin colouration and social habit.[6] Indeed, so entrenched are these actions at official level that, in an attempt to remove the external manifestations of prejudice, the nation's Prime Minister has been called upon to act against the most intransigent States.[7]

The compass of this volume, then, deals with racism in its most patent form—discrimination between people, based on biological grounds. To this writer, the evidence in support of the charge of racism, when applied to Australian relationships with the original inhabitants of the continent, is overwhelming. Douglas Lockwood, a journalist of national repute, recently described one such situation in the Northern Territory as containing 'meanness and malevolence and lack of charity equalled in few civilised countries'.[8] This is a description, however, which might be applied to the majority of race contact situations affecting Aborigines throughout the continent. The pattern of prejudice is not recent nor is it isolated. As Merv Hartwig adequately shows in his introductory essay to this volume, failure to recognise prejudice has not willed it away. He concludes: 'Racism is an attitude of mind, and it is by no means clear that, in absence of any great challenge, it has not become habitual'.

Hartwig's thesis is adequately supported by the following essays. Lorna Lippman demonstrates the inter-relationship between prejudice, action and response arising from ignorance and isolation on both sides. She believes it to be a social gap well on the way to being bridged in Australia. Brash, on the other hand, delves into the past and witnesses the character-forming role of literature on the question of race prejudice, particularly where Aborigines are concerned. Like Lippman, he witnesses a change for the better through the virtual disappearance of prejudice in contemporary writing, and expects an upsurge of tolerance in a new era of Australian literature contributed to by indigenes. Cawte, however, sees the situation as needing fundamental change before there is any real improvement. This is a theme reflected by most of the other writers in the volume. The need, Cawte believes, lies in the improvement of the physical conditions of the Aborigines before any spectacular advance can be made in their physical and mental health. The radical new step might be found in *Marginal Estate Legislation*. Other writers feel differently.

Relocation and design of physical areas is not sufficient in itself. Tobin shows the institutionalisation of prejudice in its broadest sweep, ranging over States and towns alike—from the colonial practices of control through to the administration of coercion as part of the technique of modern European legal practice. In Tobin's study, the walls are down but the gaol remains, resting, as Little points out, in the inherent depersonalisation of Aborigines at law; a fundamental basis for the administration of segregation and *apartheid*. In Eggleston's terms—'It is doubtful whether Aborigines will ever be truly equal before the law until their social and economic status has been raised to a level comparable to that of the rest of the community'. A long haul indeed!

Colin Tatz takes up the need for the development of Aboriginal legal rights, but places it firmly in the context of political action. The combination of effective democracy with the development of personal rights is presented as an indispensable requirement for the avoidance of violence in a situation which has been marked, up to date, by official ambiguity, if not duplicity.

In my own essay, I endeavour to trace the formulation of policy through several of the more important legislatures, noting the prejudiced, thoughtless and ill-conceived notions of the average elected member when it comes to the delicate question of race relations. This was the foundation for the creation of the administrative structure to contain 'the Aboriginal problem'. It is little wonder that civil servants have continued to press European advantage in open breach of their trust.

The economics of this advantage is clearly shown in the two studies of the Queensland system of native affairs. The broad consideration of the workings of the Queensland Aboriginal and Torres Strait Islanders Affairs Act completed by Alan and Ruth Doobov shows how totally confining are its provisions. In Queensland, people 'under the Act' are depersonalised both in law and practice. If any doubt is left about this, the study by Barry Christophers and Joe McGinness of the iniquitous manner in which Aborigines' personal earnings are administered should remove it. Pittock, in turn, inspects our record in relation to Aboriginal land rights and finds Australia sadly wanting in adjusting the situation, even by the standards of other countries frequently considered to be more racist than our own.

Prejudice at the official level has been matched by brutality and lack of compassion on an inter-personal basis. One aspect of this, the extermination of the Tasmanian Aborigines, stands as a ghoulish national monument. Clive Turnbull's treatment of this subject clearly demonstrates this. However, the more subtle forms of prejudice and discrimination against individuals is of greater concern today. Peter Moodie demonstrates how this takes place even amongst Australia's highly educated and otherwise liberal medical fraternity. He calls for the removal of 'the remaining discriminatory practices' in Aboriginal medical services so that a more vigorous attack might be made on those diseases which reinforce discrimination and prejudice. Possibly the continuation of prejudice amongst groups subject to the Hippocratic oath is the real touchstone of Australian racism! But intolerance, lack of compassion and neglect is not an isolated experience in Australia for Aborigines. The passing of some ninety Aboriginal tongues and tribes is adequate evidence of the widespread nature of the cruel impact of European society on the indigines.

Jack Horner, in his article on 'Brutality and the Aboriginal People', traces part of this history throughout both the country and time. He found, as did Lockwood and the present writer, that Aboriginal-European relationships have been marked by meanness and lack of personal consideration almost unequalled in the world. A patrol officer of the Department of Native Welfare of Western Australia, in 1951, compared his experiences in India in the following way:—

'In India . . . where extremes of wealth and poverty are to be found, there is no parallel to the wretched living conditions of the natives (of my) district. Even the lowest caste and class of India, the Domes, who represent the poorest and most looked-down-on section of the community—their task is the removal of corpses and dead bodies of animals from the village confines—are housed in huts which most of our natives would be glad to occupy'.[9]

Although it is recognised that considerable attention has been given to Aboriginal housing in recent years, it has been calculated that an immediate investment of over $250,000,000 is needed to overcome the back-log in accommodation, without taking into consideration the rapid expansion of the Aboriginal birthrate.[10] The Aboriginal artist and poet, Kevin Gilbert, who was released from gaol recently after a sojourn of some fourteen years, has claimed that he is unable to witness any change in the material conditions of his people in that time.[11] It would be hard to make a similar comment about the environment of European Australia. Indeed, the direct product of Australians' racist attitudes towards the original inhabitants of the continent is forcing the gap to become wider. There is no integrated plan to assist

Aborigines. At best, the work of the recently created Commonwealth Office of Aboriginal Affairs can only be thought of as another exercise in paternalism and palliative treatment. In the words of *The Bulletin* (Sydney) (quoted in my chapter) it might be considered as an extension of the historic attempts of the pastoral lobby in Australia 'to keep Aborigines in a state of subjugation'.

Australian native policy can only be described as a complete and abject failure. Even conceding official goodwill, and noting the increased sums being spent on Aboriginal welfare, it is obvious that the social, economic and political gap between the two communities is not being closed. Any reasonable explanation of these disparities must include a consideration of the ability and intention of the administrators who direct and run these programmes. The essay by the Reverend Edgar Wells, on his experiences in remote mission stations, outlines some of the personal attitudes restricting accomplishment. But the problem is greater than the personal disposition of junior officers and functionaries. The attitudes of intolerance permeate practically every level of administration. The writer, in common with most research workers, journalists and writers interested in Aboriginal affairs, has been subject to restrictions on freedom of movement and the collection of data through which the current situation might be analysed and improved.[12] This has taken place in face of the administrators' statutory obligations to preserve and improve Aboriginal social and political rights.

Whilst present administrative attitudes to Aboriginal affairs remain, it is questionable whether any real improvement will be made, regardless of the sums spent. Indeed, political control of the interests of any subordinate group within society would seem to preclude development of the personal initiative and confidence necessary to overcome the multiplicity of problems of adjustment. As shown by Tobin and others, today the system runs against Aborigines. It is a matter of devising means whereby the programmes will not impede Aboriginal development through being imposed on them by outside agencies, but will arise in response to their own felt needs. This should be the case at present, but the administrations have rarely had the humility to sit down with the people they control and consult with them. A recent example of this attitude was the formation of a virtually all white committee of enquiry into conditions of Aborigines working on Northern Territory cattle stations. It is even more significant that trade union representation was omitted. In these circumstances, the political orientation of the committee seems obvious. The voice of the lone Aboriginal representative is hardly any match for the representatives of the Northern Territory Pastoral Lessees Association, the Northern Territory Welfare Branch (controlled by a Country Party Minister), the appointees of the Liberal-Country Party coalition Government and their directly nominated expert associates. If only to masquerade due process, one would have thought that the Commonwealth Government might have been able to find one or two more indigenes who understand the conditions of employment. But then again, as illiteracy amongst Aborigines on the cattle stations is still virtually universal, they could have hardly been expected to contribute to a report in the measured tones of the civil servants and lobbyists. The objectivity of the report will be, of course, another matter.[13]

The general problem, in short, seems to revolve around the necessity for devising means whereby the programmes will not impede and restrain Aboriginal development but provide the effective tools of participation for

Aborigines to determine and accomplish their own destiny. Tatz, in the final essay in this volume, makes some provocative suggestions in this regard. However, as a starting point it is well to recall the conclusion to his Ph.D. thesis, written in 1964:—

> 'Will persons engaged in Aboriginal administration alter their procedures, practices and attitudes ... ? Will ... legislative change be accompanied by changes in administrative machinery? ... Sweeping changes in legislation, however liberal in spirit, have little or no meaning for Aborigines unless there is a drastic revision of relations between agents of policy and the internal organisation of the agencies themselves. If there is corresponding "sweeping reform" in the machinery, the stage may be set for the beginning of the implementation of the policy of assimilation.'[14]

The past history of Aboriginal affairs clearly shows that it is based on racist assumptions. There is no indication that the situation in 1971 has changed. Until the administrative environment is purged of prejudice and political opportunism there will be no real accomplishment.

REFERENCES

1 BANTON, MICHAEL. *Race Relations,* Social Science Paperbacks. London, 1967.

2 See generally the two essays on the subject in this Volume.

3 LANCASTER JONES, F. *A Demographic Survey of the Aboriginal Population of the Northern Territory, With Special Reference to Bathurst Island Mission,* Australian Institute of Aboriginal Studies, Canberra, 1963, p. 96.

4 DOWNING, J. 'Consultation and Self Determination in the Social Development of Aborigines', a paper presented to the 41st A.N.Z.A.A.S. Conference, Adelaide, August 1969, p. 15.

5 STANNER, W. E. H. *After the Dreaming,* The Boyer Lectures, 1968, A.B.C. Sydney, 1968, p. 46. See also the arrest and imprisonment of Aboriginal leader Dexter Daniels on fabricated charges of vagrancy, *Sydney Morning Herald,* 6 December 1967 and *Canberra Times,* 7 December 1967.

6 See generally EGGLESTON, E. M. 'Aborigines and the Administration of Justice', unpublished Ph.D. thesis, Monash University, 1970.

7 See article 'Keeping Blacks Second Rate', ROPER, TOM, *The Sunday Review,* Melbourne, 18 April 1971, p. 794 and 'We Shall Overcome (by 1972)', *The Bulletin,* Sydney, 21 March 1970, pp. 19-20.

8 LOCKWOOD, D. 'Goodbye to God's Country', *Sydney Morning Herald,* 2 November 1968, p. 19.

9 Report of the Commissioner for Native Welfare, Western Australia, 1951, p. 7.

10 *The Bulletin,* Sydney, *op. cit.*

11 Interview on A.B.C. television programme, *This Day Tonight,* 12 July 1971.

12 See 'The Unpermitted Man', *The Territorian,* Darwin, December 1967.

13 Circular letter from the Chairman, 7 June 1971.

14 TATZ, C. M. 'Aboriginal Administration in the Northern Territory of Australia', Ph.D. thesis, Australian National University, 1964, p. 304.

THE PARAMETERS OF CONFLICT

1

ABORIGINES AND RACISM; AN HISTORICAL PERSPECTIVE

M. C. Hartwig

Writing as recently as 1961, Russel Ward argued that, while racist attitudes were prevalent in Australia for some ninety years after 1851, especially during the few decades before and after the turn of the century, they were virtually absent in the period prior to 1851, and that, since 1939, most Australians have ceased to be racists. Various evidence was cited in support of this contention, but the main argument seems to have been that racism is logically and emotionally incompatible with a fundamental component of our national legend, namely, belief in the 'essential brotherhood and equality' of all men.[1]

There will be reason to revert to the question of the relationship between egalitarianism and racism later in this essay. Meanwhile, it is worth noting what Ward had to say about Aborigines in his discussion of Australian racism. He mentioned them twice, once to cite the post-1930 movement for their assimilation as evidence for the waning of 'racist delusions' (the undiscussed implication being that previous policy was grounded on such delusions); and a second time in context of an argument that racist attitudes became prevalent after 1851, initially because of the arrival on the goldfields of large numbers of Chinese, differing greatly from British colonists in language, customs, and culture.

> 'Before the Gold Rush there were, after all, few foreigners of any one race in Australia—except for the Aborigines, if we may, sheepishly I hope, call them foreigners after a manner of speaking. And no one who knows anything of Australian history needs to be reminded of how our ancestors regarded and treated them!'[2]

Obviously some sort of mental block was at work here—the development of racism depended on the presence of large numbers of foreigners leading a different way of life. Before 1851 there were such large numbers of Aborigines (larger numbers, both proportionately and absolutely, than the Chinese ever attained to), and yet no racism. Again, 'no one who knows anything of Australian history needs to be reminded of how our ancestors regarded' the Aborigines. How, if not as inferior beings, incapable of 'improvement' and destined to extinction?[3] Either it was not appreciated that these attitudes were racist, or what was believed about Aborigines somehow did not count.

This sort of mental block is, of course, by no means peculiar to Russel Ward.[4] Neglect of Aborigines, though the position is rapidly changing now, has been a feature of Australian historiography, and it is not enough to say that this is because historians have felt that Aborigines were so few in

9

number, and the structure of their society and the nature of their culture
such, that they could not possibly be relevant to the major theme which all
general historians of Australia must take, namely, the coming of Western
civilization and its modification and development here. For it does not
explain why, unlike the history of indigenous minorities in comparable situations, the history of Aborigines, as distinct from what white Australians have
done to or thought about them, has scarcely begun to be written; and in the
almost total absence of inquiry it remains an unproven assumption. Even
where Aborigines have played a significant, albeit indirect, role in important
political events—for example, in the defeat of Gipps' squatting proposals of
1844—that role has tended to be overlooked.[5] And, while the best of the few
historians who have made the history of our attitudes to and ideas about
Aborigines the subject of specialized monographs and articles have documented the prevalence of racism, they have been capable of doing so without
employing the term—let alone posing or exploring such questions as whether
prejudice against immigrant groups, the development of the White Australia
policy, the 'paternalism bordering on mania'[6] of our officials in New Guinea,
and our external alignment with white colonialism in Africa and elsewhere
have been related to our prior experience of contact with Aborigines.[7]

Neglect of this proportion can be explained only by the truism that
historians tend to reflect the society that produces them. Two long-standing
popular assumptions seem pertinent. First, that the Australian story has, by
and large, been one of social and political improvement; second, that
Aborigines are not deserving of respect. Radical historians have recently been
accused of attempting to minimize the significance of racism because it conflicts with their view of nineteenth-century Australia 'as a vast spawning
ground of all that is politically democratic, socially egalitarian and economically non-competitive', and of a nationalism that was 'anti-imperial and anti-
militarist'.[8] Some have conceded that the charge is not entirely without
foundation.[9] But there is no reason why this sort of criticism should be confined to radical historians. Writing in 1962, A. W. Martin criticized such
historians for assuming that 'it is possible to discern in a society's history
some crucial single line of progress' and that 'a certain group or body or
movement acts historically as the bearers or agents of the line of progress',
but conceded 'the plain fact of . . . political advance—towards wider
democracy and a greater degree of social justice'. Most Australian historians,
he went on to suggest, have taken this 'plain' fact for granted.[10]

Uncritical acceptance of a concept of progress in one form or another,
it seems probable, has prevented most historians from appreciating the racist
character of Australian society, especially since racism was most prevalent
and intense at the very time when most 'progress' is believed to have taken
place. It might even be that historians have reflected the racism they have
tended to overlook. W. E. H. Stanner has demonstrated how, in the case of
Aborigines, historians have reflected 'something like a cult of forgetfulness
practised on a national scale'.[11] It would not be difficult to show that this has
been grounded on a cult of disrespect. Disrespect is implicit in the many
historians whose brief accounts of the moral and political issues involved in
the occupation of a continent and the destruction of a culture 'read like
ancient history',[12] and it is quite explicit in the work of others. S. H. Roberts,
for example, in *The Squatting Age in Australia 1835-1847*,[13] substantially
identifies with the squatters' derogatory view of the Aborigines; and Barry
Bridges, in 'The Aborigines and the Law: New South Wales 1788-1855',

expounds the advantages that a legal system of coercion 'for the pacification of the dispossessed and for the imposition of a satisfactory adjustment to the destruction of their way of life'[14] would have had in early New South Wales.

For these, and, no doubt other reasons, Australian historiography is still at the stage (recently arrived at) of debating whether or to what extent Australian society, even in the late nineteenth century, was racist; the primary task of the historian, to answer the question 'why', remains largely unattempted. In the debate on the origins of the White Australia policy,[15] for example, earlier historians were often concerned to show that 'the racial factor' was less important than the 'economic factor' or 'the desire to preserve British-Australian nationality'. The issue having been cast in these terms, and the effort of perception being, perhaps, so great, those who have glimpsed the importance of racism have replied that 'the racial factor' was more important than 'the economic factor' or that 'racial as well as economic factors' were involved. Racism having thus been separated from other factors, there has been no thoroughgoing attempt to explain it; indeed, it has sometimes been treated as external to society, something 'given' or 'instinctual', *requiring* no explanation.[16] The tendency of modern social science, it seems necessary to point out, is in the opposite direction. 'Race . . . has no objective reality independent of its *social* definition.'[17] ('Race', in the sense of subspecies of *homo sapiens,* may or may not have objective reality; in either case it may be disregarded as having no social significance.) Race, in its social scientific sense, refers to human groups that are *socially* defined but on the basis of real or imagined physical characteristics which are believed to be both innate and intrinsically related to moral, intellectual and other non-physical attributes and abilities. Racism is the perception of race in this sense and hence that it is the legitimate basis of invidious social distinctions. Race and racism are thus special cases of more general social facts and must be explained in terms of 'the total institutional and cultural context of the society studied'.[18]

A full understanding of the 'total context' of Australian racism plainly cannot be arrived at from the sole vantage point of the interior perspectives which have prevailed in Australian historical study, and which have contributed above all else to neglect of racism. Australia is a product of Western expansion, and its history spans the coming of age of modern Western racism in the second quarter of the nineteenth century and the apparent beginning of its decline a century later. The limitations of the interior perspective can be transcended only by the adoption of an international and comparative perspective.

❋   ❋   ❋   ❋

As soon as we begin to develop such a perspective we can see that, in spite of the silence of historians, it would be surprising if racist attitudes towards Aborigines had *not* been prevalent from early times. For all the important forces that seem to have given rise to racism elsewhere in the modern era were operative in Australia from the outset; and Australians had the added incentive of the spectacular failure of Aborigines (in comparison with most other non-Western peoples) to adjust to European intrusion in a way that Europeans could regard as very successful.

In discussing the origins of Western racism it is useful to distinguish, following van den Berghe, between necessary antecedent conditions and efficient causes:—

'The most important necessary . . . condition for the rise of racism is

the presence in sufficient numbers of two or more groups that look
different enough so that at least some of their members can be readily
classifiable [as belonging to races]. In addition to their physical differences, these groups also have to be culturally different (at least
when they first met) and in a position of institutionalized inequality
for the idea of inherent racial differences to take root.'[19]

No one would want to deny that these conditions have obtained in Australia
since shortly after 1788. But they are not sufficient conditions for the rise of
racism. They are necessary antecedent conditions, in that it is difficult to
think of any case in which racism developed when they were not met, but
there have been many cases in which they were met but in which racism did
not develop to any marked extent.

What, then, have been the efficient causes of Western racism? Until very
recently hardly any worthwhile studies had been devoted to this question,
probably for reasons similar to those which have inhibited inquiry into the
origins of Australian racism; in addition, in the social sciences, which have
tended to pre-empt the field of race relations, questions about origins have,
until recently, lacked intellectual respectability. In the absence of sustained
rigorous inquiry, a wide variety of fragmentary answers has been suggested.
There is, however, considerable agreement about four, which stand out as
most important—to anyone, that is, who adopts the view that no monocausal
theory is likely to suffice for so complex a phenomenon, and who attempts a
sociohistorical rather than a psychopathological explanation. And there are
various reasons why it seems legitimate to do that. Most importantly, while
there is unquestionably a psychopathology of racism—while some people are
racists because they have 'frustration-aggression' complexes or 'authoritarian
personalities'—it is very much less likely that most people in racist societies
are 'sick' in this sense, than that they conform to social norms and historically
derived patterns of thought and behaviour.[20] On this assumption, the efficient
causes of Western racism appear to have been the need to rationalize dispossession and/or exploitation of non-European peoples; extreme ethnocentrism, which is to be accounted for in terms of a complex range of factors,
important among which is the idea of social development, biological
evolutionism, and egalitarianism.

*   *   *   *

The need to rationalize dispossession and exploitation of Aborigines
(especially the former, and the use of force and the devastating effects on
Aboriginal society that settlement entailed) has obviously been felt in Australia from the outset. For the colonist participating in the process of dispossession, it was psychologically desirable, at the very least, to persuade
himself that Aborigines were inferior beings, pests and nuisances who
deserved their fate. That is why intensity of racist feeling against Aborigines
has tended to be directly related to the scope and intensity of conflict and
dispossession on the frontier. Except during the few decades before and after
the turn of the century, it was the squatter and his men, the men on the spot
doing the actual dispossessing, and the killing that it entailed, who were most
ready to deny Aboriginal humanity. 'Before they are made Christians you
must make them men', wrote a Murrumbidgee squatter in 1838, when conflict on the New South Wales frontier was at its height, '. . . every man of
common experience knows that the aboriginals of my native country are the
most degenerate, despicable and brutal race of beings in existence . . .—a

scoff and a jest upon humanity—they are insensible to every bond which binds man to his friend—husband to wife—parent to its child—or creature to its God.'[21] Almost inevitably, since the overriding concern in a colony of settlement must be that, where there is a conflict of interest, the interest of the settler will prevail, the settlers who conquered Australia bit by bit were given official encouragement, except during a brief period in the 1830s and 1840s when humanitarian sentiment prevailed in the Colonial Office, in the belief that killing Aborigines was no crime. Thus the 'punitive expedition' (still a popular euphemism for 'act of conquest'; 'pacification' is another) and vigilante traditions, with the authorities deploying the military, or the police in a paramilitary role, or encouraging or allowing settlers to defend their lives and property by killing if need be, were established in Australia at the time of Governor Phillip and continued until conquest was all but complete in the late 1920s. And it is probably no coincidence that, with the failure in the 1840s of the efforts of the Colonial Office at protection, it was only after Aboriginal resistance had all but ceased to present obstacles to settlement that some systematic measures for the relief of the physical destitution of the detribalized remnants left in the wake of the expanding frontier were reinstituted in each colony—in Victoria first, in South Australia with her vast frontier in the Northern Territory last.

Nor did dispossession operate only in this direct way to foster racism. Expropriation was justified also on the grounds that Aborigines had no government, law or society and therefore no title to land; that they did not improve the land by Lockean labour; and that in any case nothing must be allowed to stand in the way of 'progress' as represented by British Christian civilization. In these ways, dispossession enhanced the already extreme ethnocentrism of white Australians, which, as will be shown, also helped to foster racism.

The need to rationalize exploitation of Aborigines (as distinct from exploitation of the land) was probably less important, but where extensive use was made of cheap Aboriginal labour, as in the predominantly pastoral northern and central regions, it certainly played a part. In the earlier settled southern regions, there was at first an abundance of cheap convict labour. When shortage of labour became a problem, this coincided with rapid squatting expansion and hence with extensive Aboriginal resistance, while the small, dispirited tribal remnants left in the wake of conquest offered no adequate solution. In the more sparsely settled northern and central regions, once the resistance of Aborigines had been quelled, their labour potential was considerable and a dearth of other workers forced settlers to avail themselves of it on a scale that had not been possible in the south, so that 'the Aboriginal labour camp [became] an essential adjunct of the station economy'.[22] With the settlers in a small minority and united in an unequal exploitative symbiosis with Aborigines whose traditional economy had been undermined or abandoned, race relations in these regions came to resemble, in many respects, van den Berghe's 'paternalistic' or 'master-servant' model, the 'purest' examples of which are the systems of race relations to be found in pre-abolition times in northeastern Brazil, the Western Cape Province of South Africa, the West Indies, and the southern United States.[23]

The various station and, occasionally, farm communities were stratified into two racial castes separated by a wide gap in status, living standards (except during the early years of settlement in some areas), legal rights, and cultural traditions. Intercaste mobility thus seldom, if ever, occurred, and the spatial mobility of the subordinate group, for various cultural, economic and sometimes legal reasons, was severely limited. Anthropologists who have worked in these regions over the years have testified that, 'generally speaking', Aborigines were in a 'weak and helpless position',[24] that 'working natives were [in some cases] virtually peons',[25] and that 'station managers regarded their Aboriginal workers as part of the property, and treated them as dependent children who could not be expected to assume individual responsibilities.'[26] Division of labour, sex and age divisions aside, tended to be along racial lines, with Aborigines performing manual work and whites, supervisory and managerial functions. Spatial segregation, while prominent, was reinforced as a mechanism of social control by considerable social distance, which was symbolized by an etiquette of subservience and dominance as well as by the gap in culture, living standards and legal rights. In the following description of intercaste etiquette in the southern United States prior to the Civil War, 'Aborigines' may be substituted for 'slaves' without doing great violence to the facts:—

> 'Slaves were expected to behave submissively through self-deprecatory gestures and speech, the frequent use of terms of respect toward whites, self-debasing clowning, and general fulfilment of their role-expectation as incompetent and backward grown-up children. Conversely, masters addressed slaves familiarly by their first names, sometimes preceded by the term "uncle" or "aunt" . . . .'[27]

In Australia, it should be added, first names (bestowed by whites) were often highly derogatory. Since social distance was so great, physical segregation, which, in any case, was dictated by the subordinate group's cultural tradition and the dominant group's desire for privacy as much as by its convenience as a mechanism of social control, could be relaxed as occasion demanded. Miscegenation in particular, between Aboriginal women and white men, was not uncommon, and, as in other paternalistic systems, was accepted by the dominant group 'as another of its legitimate prerogatives and forms of exploitation'.[28] Most importantly for our present purposes, the settlers rationalized their exploitative dominance in an ideology of paternalism and racism, regarding Aborigines as inferior, unintelligent, lazy, irresponsible grown-up children, acceptable and even lovable, as long as they were ' "kept in their place" '.[29]

Such a system of race relations, as van den Berghe has demonstrated, possesses an inherent stability. The converse of the paternalism of the dominant caste is accommodation of the subordinate group to its inferior status, which it may even internalize;[30] and, while stability derives in part from coercion, it is at least as importantly the product of 'close, intimate, albeit highly unequal symbiosis. The very asymmetry and complementarity of economic ties between racial castes makes for a tightly integrated pattern of economic interdependence. In addition, miscegenation and other forms of unequal but intimate social relations create powerful affective (although often ambivalent) bonds across caste lines'.[31] But the inherent stability of the system is 'accompanied by inherent inflexibility and inadaptability; that is, when the system is attacked from the outside . . . or when internal developments such as industrialization are incompatible with paternalism, the whole system collapses altogether or evolves into a competitive situation'.[32] The system in northern and central Australia has always had some external pressure brought to bear upon it, and, today, is undoubtedly breaking down as the pastoral economy is diversified by mining and industrial enterprises, as Aborigines are brought within a system of award wages, as legal rights are equalized and as Aborigines themselves increasingly demand an end to it. But one result of this unprecedented challenge to unequal status is that anti-Aboriginal feeling is probably nowhere more intense. Thus, a North Queensland grazier could publicly state on an ABC television programme in 1970:—

> 'I look on the Aboriginal as being a sort of link between the upper and the lower forms of the animal kingdom. I don't think they'll ever be the equal of the white man and therefore I say it's dangerous to put him into society' [*sic*].[33]

Aborigines should be put out of society, he said, into Cape York Peninsula.

＊　　＊　　＊　　＊

The need to rationalize dispossession and exploitation is, however, hardly a sufficient explanation of either the development of racist attitudes towards Aborigines, since vilification of Aborigines reached a crescendo in the late nineteenth and early twentieth centuries when dispossession was virtually complete, and exploitation not significantly more extensive than hitherto, or of modern racism generally, since in countries such as Latin America, an unusually brutal form of dispossession, exploitation and even slavery was accompanied by only mild forms of racism. But if racism is not implicit in colonial situations as such, a heightened form of ethnocentrism does seem to be. The very fact that a people is prepared to come unasked to a country, appropriate it and alter and disrupt the indigenous way of life presupposes that they believe their own culture to be superior, and that they constantly reassure themselves on this score. It does not necessarily presuppose, though, a fundamental disregard for the indigenous people themselves, for they can persuade themselves that any hurt their intrusion may occasion will be more than offset by the gift of their culture. However, while the distinction here drawn between racism and ethnocentrism[34] is thus analytically useful, it is well to remember that, in practice, this sort of distinction has seldom been clearly made, and that, in the context of the Western tradition especially, extreme contempt for a culture all too readily leads to contempt for the mental capacity of the people who produced it, and extreme confidence in the superiority of one's own culture all too readily leads to contempt for the capacity of the people who fail to accept it.

Of the many factors, apart from the psychology of colonial situations which have worked to enhance Western ethnocentrism, probably none has been more important than the idea of social development. As Robert A. Nisbet has recently demonstrated, social developmentalism is profoundly rooted in the Western tradition, and its nineteenth century version, the theory of social evolution, was not, as is commonly supposed,[35] 'simply an adaptation of the ideas of biological evolutionism, chiefly those of Charles Darwin, to the study of social institutions. While one must admit immediately that the ideas of social evolution acquired a certain lustre from about 1859 on as the consequence of the immediate popularity of Darwin's work, they did not depend on it'.[36] They were built upon a model of organic growth which has nothing in common with Darwin's chief contribution to the theory of evolution, the idea of variation as a result of natural selection—as were the eighteenth century theory of natural history, the seventeenth century theory of intellectual progress, the Augustinian epic and Greek and Roman theories of cyclical change. When Herbert Spencer wrote that 'the analogy supplied by the individual life yields the true conception [of social evolution]'[37] he was using an analogy that had been employed repeatedly for more than two millennia; and when he and his contemporaries, combining comparison with developmentalism, asserted that specific historic or contemporary societies represented 'stages' in the evolution of 'society', they were making assumptions equally as old, and which had attained 'immense popularity'[38] already in the eighteenth century. Not surprisingly, in spite of the circularity of reasoning involved, the standards of comparison employed were Western ones, the direction of change found was always towards a set of qualities possessed by Western Europe alone, and those peoples—such as Aborigines—whose societies differed most from Western society were assumed to be at the 'lowest stage' of development. When the logic of this mode of reasoning was called into question in the late nineteenth century, the anthropologist Tylor 'literally created the idea of survivals as a form of counter-attack.'[39] One could be sure that change in time was progressive, and that the world's cultures could be arranged in correct order by the comparative method because of the 'survival' of 'primitive' elements in Western society, which closely resembled elements which were integral parts of the culture of one or the other 'preliterate' people. It followed, Tylor argued, that Western society had once known a stage where these surviving elements were integral to its own culture. Thus, by further circular reasoning, was the theory of social evolution reinforced, and contemporary non-literate peoples, most notably the Aborigines, came to be regarded widely as 'our contemporary ancestors', 'fossilized societies', or (to cite Baldwin Spencer on the Tasmanians) 'living representatives of palaeolithic man, lower in the scale of culture than any human beings now upon earth'.[40]

This is not to imply that the Darwinian theory of biological evolution did not make important contributions of its own to modern racism. But it was what it was congruent with that made it important. As has often been pointed out, it dovetailed with nineteenth century economic liberalism. The poor were poor, Negroes were slaves, indigenous peoples were doomed to extinction, it was argued, because of the process of natural selection which, in an ideal society, would not be interfered with. '[W]e invoke and remorselessly fulfil the inexorable law of natural selection', wrote an ardent Australian defender of laissez-faire in 1876,

> '... when exterminating the inferior Australian and Maori races .... The world is better for it; and would be incalculably better still, were we loyally to accept the lesson thus taught by nature, and consistently to apply the same principle to our conventional practice; by preserving the varieties most perfect in every way, instead of actually promoting the non-survival of the fittest by protecting the propagation of the imprudent, the diseased, the defective, the criminal. Thus we surely lower the average of, and tend to destroy, the human race almost as surely as if we were openly to resort to communism.'[41]

Those who were inclined to 'resort to communism' could reply that society interfered with natural selection by (for example) sanctioning the inheritance of wealth and that 'survival of the fittest' was impossible without a radical programme of state intervention. More importantly, since the Darwinian theory allowed for interspecific as well as intraspecific selection, it could be appealed to as supporting struggles between nations and races as well as individuals. It thus dovetailed also with the aggressive nationalism and imperialism of the age.

But its impact on racist thought probably depended most of all on social developmentalism. It provided a ready 'explanation' of what had long seemed obvious: that some 'races', mainly by virtue of their 'low level' of civilization, were/ inferior in mental capacity to others. There was little in biological evolutionism and the theory of natural selection to indicate which peoples were at which stages of physical evolution—to suggest that Negroes or Hottentots or Aborigines were at a lower stage than whites (and not vice versa). What, above all, suggested that, and suggested it powerfully, was the conviction that these people were at a lower stage of social evolution and that Western European culture represented the most advanced stage. Darwin himself, it is true, was not entirely averse to the extension of 'the preservation of favoured races [i.e., varieties or species]' to human 'races', 'these being as much subject to the struggle for existence and survival of the fittest as plant and animal varieties'.[42] But even for him, how they fared in the struggle, which races were fitter than others, was indicated by their performance in history and degree of civilization.[43]

It is important to remember, moreover, that biological evolutionism supplanted already existing theories which had served the purpose of explaining physical and mental differences among races almost equally as well. The most important of these was the idea of a 'great chain of being', an idea which was first generated in Greek philosophy and which achieved its widest diffusion and acceptance in the eighteenth century, remaining popular until the second half of the nineteenth century.[44] All creatures in the universe, according to this theory, were arranged in linear gradation in a continuous 'scale of nature', from the smallest conceivable being to God himself. Since every creature in the scale was held to differ from the one immediately above it and the one immediately below it by the 'least possible' degree of difference, it followed (for those who cared to draw the conclusion) that the mental and physical differences between man and the higher apes were infinitesimal. There was, therefore, every incentive to dwell on differences within humanity and to search for 'missing links' in the chain between man and the apes, and, from the seventeenth century on, the new knowledge of non-European peoples provided ample materials. By the late eighteenth century the notion of a 'scale of humanity' had come to be widely accepted, with Aborigines and Hottentots competing for the lowest place and, thus, for the status of 'connecting links' between man and the monkeys. (In Australia in the first half of the nineteenth century, the prize was almost invariably awarded to Aborigines.[45]) Since 'reason' or 'intelligence', above all, differentiated man from the apes, position on the scale tended to be determined by the degree of these qualities, which in turn was determined chiefly by the 'different progress' of peoples in 'civilization'. Here again social developmentalism was of crucial importance.

Of course, since the influence of any idea depends largely on its social context, it was what it was congruent with that made social developmentalism important too. Ethnocentrism is universal, and it is likely that any human group that accepted the idea of social development would have assumed that it was in the vanguard of progress, and judged the 'stages' other peoples had arrived at by its own values and standards. But the wide acceptance and popularity of the idea in the West in the era of modern racism would need to be traced to a complex of forces which placed Western Europe in a position of undisputed dominance over the rest of the world. Suffice it to say here that, shortly after Australia was colonized, the British, their industrial, commercial and naval supremacy firmly established, and professing a religion that was thought to be inextricably linked with their supremacy and which tended to regard pagan cultures as moral evils fit only for destruction, took the idea and their vanguard status for granted.

In Australia, one result of this confidence in the material and spiritual superiority of British Christian civilization was that few colonists investigated or came to respect the culture of the Aborigines. It tended to be dismissed as a product of depravity[46] or as virtually non-existent and possessing no validity of its own. There was, in particular, a tendency to judge it by its technology and material accomplishments. William Dampier was by no means the last to draw the conclusion that, since Aborigines had few material possessions, 'setting aside their humane shape, they differ but little from Brutes'. And when Aboriginal culture did come to be seen as possessing some validity of it own and attracted the attention of the new science of anthropology, it was studied for many years as an interesting 'survival' from the Stone Age. Thus the argument used in respect of Aborigines to gain support for the establishment of the first department of anthropology in an Australian university in 1925 was that 'one of the lowest types of culture' should be recorded while this was still possible.[47] The assumption of Aboriginal mental inferiority remained unchallenged.[48]

❖   ❖   ❖   ❖

But perhaps the most important force in the rise of modern racism was that very egalitarianism which, Russel Ward argued, militated against it. There was, indeed, a logical and emotional contradiction involved, but it could be resolved by restricting the definition of humanity:—

> 'The egalitarian and libertarian ideas of the Enlightenment spread by the American and French Revolutions conflicted, of course, with racism, but they also paradoxically contributed to its development. Faced with the blatant contradiction between the treatment of slaves and colonial peoples and the official rhetoric of freedom and equality, Europeans and white North Americans began to dichotomize humanity between men and submen (or the "civilized" and the "savages"). The scope of applicability of the egalitarian ideals was restricted to "the people", that is, the whites, and there resulted what I have called "*Herrenvolk* democracies",—regimes such as those of the United States or South Africa that are democratic for the master race but tyrannical for the subordinate groups. The desire to preserve both the profitable forms of discrimination and exploitation and the democratic ideology made it necessary to deny humanity to the oppressed groups.'[49]

The full importance of egalitarianism becomes clear if we compare what happened in societies founded in feudal times, such as those in colonial Latin America. Louis Hartz has argued convincingly that the main reason why the lot of the slave and the Indian was typically better there, was that it was possibly to admit them into society without in any way conceding equality; and, this being done, there was no compulsion to deny essential humanity.[50] Thus the 'whole drift' of these colonies 'was to constitute their class identity out of the very material of the new races'.[51] The main question concerning the Indian and the Negro tended to be, not a racial one, but whether their status should be lower or higher, and they benefited from currents of social reform. But, in societies espousing egalitarian ideals from the outset,[52] the question was very different. In their case, a human being was entitled to full equality, so that if he was to be enslaved or exterminated or dispossessed or treated in some other radically unequal way, his very humanity had to be denied and he tended to be excluded from society. By the same token, the egalitarian ideology provided a set of ideals that could eventually be used to challenge the racial *status quo*. Hartz seems to follow Myrdal in locating the focus of this ideological contradiction within the dominant group. Van den Berghe is probably more correct in believing that the 'ideological dialectic has operated primarily *between* the conflicting racial groups.'[53] But the point is the same: the Enlightenment imposed a 'moral polarity', an 'oscillation between exclusion and inclusion' on the issue of race. 'We are dealing with nothing less than Civil Wars and Great Treks, radical overturns in outlook.'[54]

Nothing so dramatic, of course, has happened in Australia. We have avoided our Civil Wars, as Hartz himself points out, by the accident of having had limited contact with African slavery and Aboriginal subordination, and by excluding cheap coloured labour. But there has been a tendency to oscillate between including Aborigines in Australian society and separating them off. During the period down to about 1850, the aim of official policy was on the whole—insofar as there was a policy—to include them. This was probably not unrelated to the sort of society envisaged for Australia—a replica, in essentials, of British class society. It was easy for the Colonial Office and governors on the spot to concede the humanity of Aborigines and implement measures for their inclusion, because this involved finding a place for them only among the 'lower orders' of society.[55] But while official policy was, on the whole, inclusionist during this period, the climate of opinion among the colonists was predominantly and increasingly in favour of exclusion. And, from the 1850s, when control of policy passed into the hands of settler democracies (except in Western Australia) and there began to emerge a middle class hegemony which could 'rely on a consensus about a typically Australian set of values and institutions', including 'emphasis on . . . racial and social homogeneity, and the avoidance of ethnic and social classes',[56] the basic feature of policy until recent times has been its separatism. (Its counterpart has been 'the spirit of egalitarian apartheid'[57] expressed in the restriction of coloured immigration.) It is true that the 'protection-segregation' policies of this era were not separatist and racist *insofar as* it was assumed that Aborigines would eventually achieve equality and be assimilated into Australian society. But policy was sometimes based on segregationist motives (the desire to lock away a racially inferior social nuisance on reserves or in institutions), especially where Aborigines or part-Aborigines showed signs of increasing rapidly and competing for a place in society.[58] And, in practice, at the administrative level in particular, it was assumed that paternal supervision, tuition and control would go on indefinitely or until Aborigines died out. Policy, that is to say, was grounded on lack of faith in the capacity of Aborigines to achieve equality. And it is well to remember that the distinction often drawn between paternalism and racism, while analytically useful, is by no means clear—indeed, is usually not evident at all —to the victims of paternalism.

❋   ❋   ❋   ❋

Lack of faith in the capacity of Aborigines stemmed partly from the way in which they responded to European settlement. Hence the suggestion made earlier, that Australians have had a special incentive to be racist in their attitudes towards Aborigines: Aborigines have not been able to adjust to European intrusion in a way that Europeans could regard as at all successful. Initially, this was largely owing to what may be termed their powerlessness in the context of Western invasion—powerlessness deriving chiefly from their dispersal in small, fluid groups over a vast country; from the acephalous nature of political organization within these groups and the absence of military organization; and from a dearth of economic assets which might have induced the intruders to facilitate their survival as autonomous societies. Aboriginal powerlessness permitted an unusually rapacious form of colonization which took 'all the land and [often] only the *land*',[59] leaving (especially in the earlier settled southern regions) demoralized and resentful tribal remnants lacking that degree of autonomy without which constructive adjustment to change is impossible. Hence a racist syndrome emerged very early in Australia. Aboriginal 'incompetence' and 'apathy' reinforced the racism implicit in the colonial situation and the European tradition; and racist and ethnocentric attitudes and practices helped to ensure the continuance of retreatist, unconstructive behaviour on the part of Aborigines. Where Aboriginal societies were not destroyed as functioning entities by settlement, as in some parts of northern and central Australia, similar attitudes and practices, together with loss of autonomy, contributed to similar results.

That Aboriginal 'incompetence' has reinforced racism is evidenced most strikingly by the fact that, even in informed circles, it has often been explained at least partly by 'race'. Thus as late as 1936 A. P. Elkin could advance the Lamarkian proposition that

'It may be that his [the Aboriginal's] present adjustment [to his environment] has become part of his very nature—biological—and that he cannot become adapted to the environmental changes [wrought by Europeans] and so . . . is doomed to extinction . . . so far the aborigines have not shown themselves capable of adapting to the new . . . . The mere fact that half-castes are said to be superior to the full-bloods, and yet are only seldom successful in adaptation, makes the matter all the more serious for the latter.'[60]

It is only fairly recently that a 'cultural' explanation, which stresses the persistence of Aboriginal values, has displaced the racist one, and only very recently indeed that a 'sociohistorical' explanation which stresses that Aborigines have responded to settlement in much the same way as any other people would have responded in a comparable situation has even been advanced.[61]

*   *   *   *

It would be nice to conclude on an optimistic note. Certainly, by the logic of the argument here presented, Australians ought to be less racist in their attitudes to Aborigines than they used to be, for all efficient causes of racism seem to be less efficient now. But, by the same token, most of them are still operative.

Aborigines themselves have been able to do more than previously over the last forty years to dispel the myth that they are an incompetent race. But their position in Australian society (outside it, in some cases) still tempts easy rationalization in terms of innate inferiority. Australians are, perhaps, no longer such naive believers in progress as they used to be, but a sophisticated version of social developmentalism still suffuses most social scientific thought; and it is to be doubted whether there are many Australians who do not believe that Aboriginal culture is 'primitive' and Western culture 'advanced' or who can see that there is no valid way of judging any culture to be 'superior' or 'inferior' to any other. Again, at the level of official policy, the pendulum has swung once more towards including Aborigines in Australian society and, over the last few years, more determined efforts than ever before have been made in this direction. But, since the currents of social reform were not previously related to Aborigines, the task is huge. A prevalent individualist ethic seems to prevent most Australians from appreciating that, without rights in property, indigenous groups tends to remain sullen and apart, and the role envisaged for Aborigines in Australian society is seldom higher than that of propertyless labourers. And, at the administrative level, there is often still the same old assumption that tuition and control must go on indefinitely.

Moreover, while it cannot be maintained that Australian racism is as overt and intense as it was when 'nationalized' at the turn of the century, it may be that, just as there was an easy triumph and traditionalization of liberal democracy in Australia in the absence of an aristocracy, so there has been an easy triumph of racism. It has perhaps seemed self-evident to most Australians, isolated from contact with other non-Western peoples (or isolating themselves), that Aborigines are inferior: given that the causal factors here discussed were operative, this could, as it were, simply be taken for granted. Because of the easy elimination of Aborigines and the exclusion for long periods of those who survived, and because of the exclusion of other coloured people, opportunities for explicit racist expression have always been limited; but racism is an attitude of mind, and it is by no means clear that, in the absence of any great challenge, it has not become habitual.

REFERENCES

1 WARD, RUSSEL. 'An Australian Legend', *Royal Australian Historical Society Journal and Proceedings*, 47:6 (December 1961), 335-51. See also the same author's *The Australian Legend* (Melbourne, 1958), 120-3, 239.

2 *Ibid.*, 344.

3 That such beliefs were prevalent in New South Wales long before 1851 has since been amply demonstrated by R. H. Reece in 'The Aborigines and Colonial Society in New South Wales before 1850, with Special Reference to the period of the Gipps Administration, 1838-1846' (unpublished M.A. thesis, University of Queensland, 1969). Cf. Ward's own statement in *The Australian Legend* (186), that 'the usual overt attitude to Aborigines continued to be almost as brutal and contemptuous at the end of the nineteenth century as it had been earlier'.

4 Even Humphrey McQueen (*A New Britannia* [Melbourne, 1970] 42), who has been concerned to show that racism is an important component of the Australian radical tradition, can state that 'neither were there many coloureds before 1850'.

5 Cf. Reece, *op. cit.*, xvii-xix, 6; Barry Bridges, 'Sir George Gipps and William Lee's Squatting Licence 1842', *Teaching History*, 3:2 (September 1969), 32.

6 The phrase is Allan Healy's ('The Intercultural Problem: Isolated Australians', *Meanjin Quarterly*, 29:1 [1970], 64).

7 ROWLEY's, C. D., *The Destruction of Aboriginal Society* (Canberra, 1970) is a recent exception to this statement. Apart from this, the best published works on the subject are Paul Hasluck, *Black Australians: A Survey of Native Policy in Western Australia 1829-1897* (2nd edition, Melbourne, 1970) and D. J.

Mulvaney, 'Australian Aborigines: Opinion and Fieldwork, 1606-1929' in J. J. Eastwood and F. B. Smith (eds.), *Historical Studies: Selected Articles* (Melbourne, 1964), 1-56.

8 McQUEEN, *op. cit.*, 15, 42.

9 E.g. Robin Gollan in his review of K. D. Buckley, *The Amalgamated Engineers of Australia* in *Historical Studies*, 14:55 (October 1970), 468. See also his 'An Inquiry into the Australian Radical Tradition—McQueen's "New Britannia"', *Arena*, 24 (1970), 36, and Russel Ward 'Home Thoughts From Abroad; Australia's Racist Image' *Meanjin Quarterly*, 2 (1971) 149-156.

10 MARTIN, A. W., 'The Whig View of Australian History'. Australian Association for Cultural Freedom, Seminar, August, 1964.

11 STANNER, W. E. H., *After the Dreaming* (The Boyer Lectures, Sydney, 1968), 25.

12 ENCEL, SOL, 'The Racialist Society', *The Sunday Review*, 16 May 1971, 900.

13 ROBERTS, S. H., *The Squatting Age in Australia 1835-1847* (rev. edition, Melbourne, 1964).

14 BRIDGES, BARRY, 'The Aborigines and the Law: New South Wales 1788-1855', *Teaching History*, 4:3 (December 1970), 70.

15 For a bibliography of the relevant literature, see A. T. Yarwood, *Attitudes to Non-European Immigration* (Melbourne, 1968), 146.

16 E.g. *ibid.*, 1 ('Was it rather a primordial instinct for race purity . . .?'); Humphrey McQueen, *op. cit.*, 46 ('pure racism').

17 VAN DEN BERGHE, *Race and Racism: A Comparative Perspective* (New York, 1967), 148. Emphasis added.

18 *Ibid.*, 6. The above definitions closely follow those given by this author. Cf. Philip Mason, *Race Relations* (London, 1970), 162; Michael Banton, *Race Relations* (London, 1967), 5.

19 *Ibid.*, 13.

20 Cf. *ibid.*, 18-21.

21 Cited in Brian W. Harrison, 'The Myall Creek Massacre and its Significance in the Controversy over the Aborigines during Australia's Early Squatting Period' (unpublished B.A. Hons. thesis, University of New England, 1966) and R. H. Reece, *op. cit.*, 113. It would be difficult to find a statement made before the last quarter of the nineteenth century by someone not personally involved is dispossession to match this intensity of racist feeling. That many of the colonists on the New South Wales frontier were convicts or ex-convicts is probably important. Attitudes to (and treatment of) Aborigines were not significantly different in South Australia, where there were no convicts, or in Western Australia before convicts were introduced: and Hasluck (*op. cit.*) has shown that when they were introduced in Western Australia no important changes resulted.

22 ROWLEY, *op. cit.*, 68.

23 VAN DEN BERGHE, *op. cit.*, 28 and *passim*. See also the same author's *Race and Ethnicity: Essays in Comparative Sociology* (New York and London, 1970), Chapter 1, 'Paternalistic versus Competitive Race Relations: An Ideal Type Approach'. I am indebted to these works for the framework of the following analysis. A. P. Elkin's analysis of race relations in these regions in terms of 'dependence' on the part of settlers and 'intelligent parasitism' on the part of Aborigines ('Reaction and Interaction: A Food Gathering People and European Settlement in Australia', in Paul Bohannan and Fred Plog [eds.], *Beyond the Frontier: Social Process and Cultural Change* [New York, 1967], 43-70) is inadequate, for it assumes a roughly *equal* symbiosis; indeed, insofar as any group is said to be dominant, it is the Aborigines. A very different picture is presented in the earlier works of this author cited hereafter.

24 ELKIN, A. P., 'Aboriginal Evidence and Justice in North Australia', *Oceania*, 17:3 (March 1947), 175.

25 STANNER, W. E. H., 'Industrial Justice in the Never-Never', *Australian Quarterly*, 39:1 (March 1967), 41.

26 FINK, RUTH, 'The Changing Aborigines of Western Australia', *Transactions of the New York Academy of Science*, Series II, 20 (1957-1958), 651.

27 VAN DEN BERGHE, *Race and Racism, op. cit.*, 81.

28 *Ibid.*, 27.

29 ELKIN, A. P., *Citizenship for the Aborigines: A National Policy* (Sydney, 1944), 31. See also, e.g., A. P. Elkin, 'Aboriginal Evidence and Justice', *op. cit.*, 173-176; R. M. and C. H. Berndt, 'A Northern Territory Problem: Aboriginal Labour in a Pastoral Area' (unpublished MS, 1948); Frank Stevens, 'Aboriginal Labour', *Australian Quarterly*, 43:1 (March 1971), 70-78; and the novels of Conrad H. Sayce (e.g. *Golden Buckles*, Melbourne, 1920), and Mrs. Aeneas Gunn. The paternalistic model could clearly also be used fruitfully to explore race relations in most government and mission institutions for Aborigines.

30 For evidence that Aborigines often internalized their subservient status see, e.g., A. P. Elkin, 'Aboriginal Evidence and Justice', *op. cit.*, 174 and *Citizenship for Aborigines, op. cit.*, 27 ('To regard a native [or any] people as inferior or as a child "race" almost inevitably results in inferior or child-like work. This is part of their accommodation to what they sense and infer is expected of them.'); also Ruth Fink, *op. cit.*, 651.

31 VAN DEN BERGHE, *Race and Racism, op. cit.*, 29.

32 VAN DEN BERGHE, *Race and Ethnicity, op. cit.*, 26.

33 'Four Corners', 21 February 1970 (transcript supplied by courtesy of the A.B.C.).

34 Hence also between 'race' (a group socially defined but on the basis of *physical* criteria) and 'ethnic group' (socially defined but on the basis of *cultural* criteria). As originally formulated by W. G. Sumner and by G. P. Murdock the concept of ethnocentrism was broad enough to include the notion of 'racism'. It is employed here in its narrower sense to mean the tendency of human groups to believe in the unique value and rightness of their own ways and to judge the culture of other groups by their own concepts and standards.

35 E.g. by F. W. Gossett in *Race: The History of an Idea in America* (New York, 1965), 144 ('Acceptance of the Darwinian theory of evolution led to the acceptance of the idea of evolving institutions and civilizations . . . .').

36 NISBET, ROBERT A., *Social Change and History: Aspects of the Western Theory of Development* (Oxford, 1969), 161.

37 Cited in Gossett, *op. cit.*, 147.

38 NISBET, *op. cit.*, 194.

39 *Ibid.*, 203.

40 SPENCER, BALDWIN, *Guide to the Australian Ethnographical Collection in the National Museum of Victoria* (Melbourne, [1901]), 8.

41 RUSDEN, H. K., 'Labour and Capital', *Melbourne Review*, 1 (1876), 78; cited in Craufurd D. Goodwin, 'Evolution Theory in Australian Social Thought', *Journal of the History of Ideas*, 25:1 (January-March 1964), 399-400.

42 HIMMELFARB, GERTRUDE, *Darwin and the Darwinian Revolution* (New York, 1968), 416.

43 See the letter cited in *ibid.*

44 See Arthur O. Lovejoy, *The Great Chain of Being: A Study of the History of an Idea* (New York, 1960).

45 REECE, *op. cit.*, 101. I am indebted also to Ann Curthoys for this point which she develops in the first chapter of her forthcoming Ph.D. thesis on British attitudes to Aborigines and Chinese in New South Wales (Macquarie University).

46 On the important role of evangelical Christian missionary enterprise in promoting this attitude see, e.g., D. J. Mulvaney, *op. cit.* But while the overall impact of Christianity in Australia has probably been to promote racism by fostering ethnocentrism it must be said that Christians have always been foremost among those who have stressed the essential humanity of Aborigines. They have tended to be respecters of persons, that is, but not of cultures.

47 ELKIN, A. P., 'Changing and Disappearing Cultures in the Australian Region', *International Social Science Bulletin*, 9:3 (1957), 340.

48 For how long may be adduced from the fact that Ronald M. and Catherine H. Berndt devoted a section of their *The World of the First Australians: An Introduction to the Traditional Life of the Australian Aborigines* (Chicago, 1964) to proving that Aborigines 'are not survivals with a stone-age culture' but 'our contemporaries' (8).

49 VAN DEN BERGHE, *Race and Racism, op. cit.*, 17-18.

50 HARTZ, LOUIS, *The Founding of New Societies: Studies in the History of the United States, Latin America, South Africa, Canada, and Australia* (New York, 1964).

51 *Ibid.*, 54.

52 On the notion that the southern United States and South Africa prior to the abolition of slavery are *not* included among these see, e.g., *ibid.*, 58-60 and Philip Mason, *op. cit.*, 108-11.

53 VAN DEN BERGHE, *Race and Racism, op. cit.*, 126.

54 HARTZ, *op. cit.*, 51.

55 Cf. HASLUCK, *op. cit.*, 58 and ROWLEY, *op. cit.*, 24, 87.

56 IRVING, TERRY, and BERZINS, BAIBA, 'History and the New Left: Beyond Radicalism', in Richard Gordon (ed.), *The Australian New Left* (Melbourne, 1970), 82.

57 The phrase is Louis Hartz's, *op. cit.*, 51.

58 See, e.g., Peter Biskup's account of policy towards part-Aborigines in 'Native Administration and Welfare in Western Australia, 1897-1954' (unpublished M.A. thesis, University of Western Australia, 1965).

59 ROWLEY, *op. cit.*, 16.

60 ELKIN, A. P., 'Native Education, with Special Reference to the Australian Aborigines', *Oceania*, 7 (1936-7), 470, 472, 497.

61 By C. D. Rowley (*op. cit.*).

2

ABORIGINAL-WHITE ATTITUDES: A SYNDROME OF RACE PREJUDICE

Lorna Lippman

Introduction

Since modern industrial societies have incorporated into the body politic the working class, which, by and large, shares its aims and values, class differences have become less apparent. Social stratification now is by a new status order—by occupation, life-styles, education, value systems. Judged by these criteria, ethnic minorities are often placed low in the stratification order. Aborigines, indeed, may find themselves outside the stratification system altogether, unemployed or in jobs not acceptable to the white worker, in housing not wanted by the general population, with education of a low standard or with none at all, and a value system at variance with the rest of society.

Studies of part-Aboriginal communities[1] have emphasized this low socio-economic status and difference in values. Forming their own sub-culture, with adherence to an ethic of mutual aid, which denies upward social mobility, their members have strong affiliation to the area of origin with social interaction largely among kin. De facto and unstable marriages are frequent, and there is more emphasis on the extended and less on the nuclear family than in the general society. Group integration, on the whole, is high and there is a strong feeling of separate identity. All these features tend to make their fellow-Australians view Aboriginal communities as deviant—as socially different and socially sick. Even the anthropologist, trained as he is to regard social differences in a sympathetic light, is yet forced to see Aboriginal groups as weak, chronically in need of assistance, permanently on the bottom socio-economic rung. The modern industrial complex achieves its aims by imposing its needs and values, its goals and work disciplines on society as a whole, by the use of normative sanctions, but it can survive without small minorities, who tend to get swept out of sight as non-contributors to the economic whole.

But there is an important reason for considering racial attitudes—not just to give Aborigines pride in their culture, not just to allow white liberals to wallow in guilt, not just to use sociology as a substitute for higher taxes, but to lessen the emphasis on and glorification of common ideals and values in Australian society, and to consider those whom our democracy passes over as unequal.

The gradually increasing interest in Aboriginal attitudes in recent years has been accelerated by world-wide concern with race relations, by the social scientists' dissection of Aboriginal communities, and by liberal whites in the Advancement organisations who assisted Aborigines to formulate their aspirations and become more vociferous in their demands. The mass media have also given sympathetic consideration to Aboriginal affairs, bringing them to the forefront of the national consciousness, though this publicity may sometimes rebound to increase prejudice. This was shown in the Survey of Race Relations in Selected Country Towns[2] (hereafter referred to as the Country Towns Survey), where many interviewees who had seen the same television programme showing substandard living conditions for an Aboriginal community had their prejudices reinforced. Those with originally favourable attitudes blamed poor environment; those unfavourably inclined saw the scene as an indication of Aboriginal inability and unworthiness. Sarnoff and Katz[3] have argued that information which is unacceptable is apt to be rejected and can result in increased aggression if, factually, the subject is proved wrong.[4]

Since the takeover of most Advancement organisations by Aborigines in 1969-70—a rapid and Australia-wide phenomenon—Aboriginal attitudes to specific political issues are gradually coming to the surface and being given a voice which is more militant and more demanding on the subject of land rights and equality, and more positive in evaluation of the indigenous culture. A case could possibly be made out to indicate that these organisations are not representative of rank-and-file Aboriginal opinion, particularly not of the opinion of distant full-blood communities whose life-style precludes militancy. But then, many white organisations do not represent majority opinion. Their role is to educate the public and to influence the government. The all-Aboriginal Advancement organisations, linked as they are to the National Tribal Council, offer some opportunity for the expression of Aboriginal opinion. They cannot be said to be a coherent political movement but, like Black Power in the United States, form an emotional safety valve for the humiliations and tensions of black minority life. Such acts as a petition to the United Nations for large sums of reparations for land appropriated (September 1970) or a 'sit-in' in the recreational area of Sherbrook Forest in Victoria (February 1971) indicate anger and frustration rather than an intimate knowledge of political realities. Further concurrence is gradually being achieved as to Aboriginal needs, but there is still a considerable lack of expertise, due to long and enforced dependency on whites, as to how to enjoin those needs.

The Country Towns Survey embraced four towns in Victoria and New South Wales, towns with few economic problems (beyond a shortage of employment for adolescents and females) and where the percentage of Aborigines to the whole was low, ranging from 0.6 per cent to 1.9 per cent. These were town-dwellers, living (geographically) among whites, most working among whites, in States where there are no discriminatory laws but where special government agencies purport to assist them. On the surface, conditions are good. But Aborigines are beginning to ask, 'If we're so free and equal, why are we so poor?' They do not equate their poverty with that of poor whites, since the big majority of Aborigines in the survey (some 507 in all) regard themselves as of separate group identity and have always been treated as separate by the general community. Their physical integration has been only of short duration since many of them have, until recent years, been Reserve dwellers, and living in the general community is a new and uneasy experience.

Aboriginal disabilities

In a poignant essay entitled *Fear and Doubt*, Huey P. Newton describes the American Black male as 'a man of confusion. He faces a hostile environment and is not sure that it is not his own sins that have attracted the hostilities of society . . . His attitude is that he lacks innate ability to cope with the socio-economic problems confronting him . . . in a desperate effort to *assume* self-respect, he rationalizes that he is lethargic: in this way he denies a possible lack of innate ability . . . Society responds to him as a thing, a nonentity, something to be ignored or stepped on . . . He is confused and in a constant state of rage, of shame and doubt . . . The parents pass it on to the child and the social system reinforces [it] . . . He is dependent upon the white man to feed his family, to give him a job, educate his children, serve as the model that he tries to emulate. He is dependent and he hates "THE MAN" and he hates himself'. A similar struggle against a feeling of inferiority and its attitudinal consequences have been discussed recently in differing contexts by two part-Aborigines. Mr. Bruce McGuinness of Melbourne contends that 'the discrimination [practised in his home town during schooldays] was the worst I have ever seen. I didn't have one white friend . . . I was good at my school work . . . But the other kids were always setting me up for trouble'.[5] Now, when Bruce McGuinness returns to that town, he stays 'at the top motel or hotel and I deliberately talk down to the Europeans. It's a fixation with me. I just can't help myself'. Part-Aboriginal Pastor David Kirk reacts to the constant emotional pressure under which his people feel themselves to live by asserting:[6] 'Aborigines must stop hating and resenting whites. We have a massive inferiority complex. If we think inferior, we are inferior. Aborigines must snap out of their apathy and stand up for themselves'. And later, in the same interview: 'I hated all whites. This hatred is something Aborigines everywhere feel constantly.'

These men are among the leaders. Many of the rank-and-file, while filled with the same resentment, feel themselves incapable of retaliatory action and take refuge in anti-social conduct which appears to be increasing among the full-blood groups also. Closer contact with whites over the last few years, bringing with it a realisation of their own depressed living conditions and lack of opportunities, has caused the dissatisfaction of the Ngatatjara Aborigines of the Warburton Ranges to grow rapidly 'to Western proportions',[7] while begging and thieving, unknown in the traditional society, grow with them. A strong sense of disillusion prevails in tribal areas like Yirrkala,[8] where, not alone, is there a disparity between the white man's egalitarian and Christian precepts and his often unequal and unChristian practice, but where the Aborigines finds himself castigated for espousing this same 'Christian' morality of sharing and brotherhood, even at the expense of personal advancement. At the same time, there is a continuous pull between the material ease of Western society, with all its power, and the emotional satisfaction which tribal life traditionally brought.

The inferiority of their social position has forced Aborigines to accept special help—though often reluctantly. On the one hand, even those living in cities or towns are largely outside the cultural mainstream and are not accustomed to using the institutions of the major society. Indeed, they are frequently not aware of their existence, and therefore require assistance from specialized agencies. On the other hand, they resent this special assistance as yet a further form of enforced degradation, a further statement of the white man's superiority. As one mother in the Country Towns Survey expressed it: 'We don't want to cry our way into the schools' (a reference to the provision of special scholarships and living allowances for Aboriginal students). Commenting on constant newspaper publicity on Aboriginal 'problems' an

Aboriginal High School student commented tartly, 'We are fed up with being solved'. This resentment is coupled with an innate suspicion that, in any case, whites are likely to take the action favoured by themselves rather than by their Aboriginal clients (a contention often born out in fact).

Aborigines who look thoughtfully at their freedom to act find themselves circumscribed by a variety of disabilities, the most evident of which is poverty, in which the majority live in varying degrees. A psychiatrist,[9] discussing their situation has stated: 'Poverty is a yoke that the most capable may not throw off. After repeated attempts at betterment, frustrated by debts, family expenses and uncertain employment, even the best-organized personality gives up'; and poverty, together with dearth of numbers, ensures lack of political power. In any case, the culture of the group does not encourage the individual to believe in the possibility of manipulating the physical and social environment to his advantage.[10]

Nominally, Aborigines in States other than Western Australia, Queensland and the Northern Territory have no legal disabilities. Yet there is evidence that their involvement with the criminal law is out of all proportion to their numbers, and their participation in civil proceedings, particularly as plaintiffs, is slight.[11] Attitude to law and its enforcement officers varies from those to whom a trip to a distant gaol is by nature of an excursion,[12] to those whose defiance of the law enhances prestige in their own community or whose ethos enjoins keeping out of trouble.[13]

A further disability is caused by chronic ill-health which, even though accepted as inevitable, adds to the difficulties of competing. There is research evidence from all States and from the Northern Territory that the Aboriginal health and nutritional level is so low as to prevent normal functioning in employment, education or social interaction.[14]

Historically, Aborigines have been excluded from Australian life, and most have been banished to remote areas. Even those who are no longer spatially remote still do not take part, nor are they expected to take part, in public affairs. They are low in personal resources, having insufficient education and information (a further bar to competitiveness) and are well aware that they have never counted socially. Though constantly adjured to take advantage of the educational opportunities offering, looking at their peers who have secondary education, they realize that it has not automatically provided a rung to mount the stratification ladder, as would be the case for the children of, say, migrants. Statistics bear out this contention. An analysis of the 1966 census has shown that of thirty-seven Aboriginal women with matriculation, fourteen were employed in personal or domestic service; of 103 males similarly equipped only nine were in the top seven categories of occupation. For Aborigines, then, 'education is not the determinant of job status',[15] since, frequently, there is a lack of employment in areas where they live, and just as frequently, prejudice exists against them as being unreliable, of 'going walkabout'. This usually mythical 'walkabout' is a stereotype, often accepted by Aborigines themselves, but which includes, in fact, visits to relatives or search for seasonal work. For a few it represents the vagabondage of the social isolate.

Aboriginal assets

The Aborigine sees himself, at the same time, through the eyes of his own community and through those of the general society, and has to achieve a satisfactory balance in identifying with these two major cultural reference groups. His own community is not bereft of strengths which, though not always visible to the white observer, help govern his attitudes and behaviour. The social organisation of both part- and full-blood Aboriginal communities along kinship and area-of-origin lines ensures economic and emotional support. A poor Aborigine is not usually as isolated as a poor white, though, if he is considered too deviant socially, community backing can dry up.

Even among the young and better-educated, even among many part-Aborigines who could pass for white, the feeling of group identity is strong and there is a slowly increasing mood of self-confidence and pride in ancestry. One of a band of young Aboriginal students recently interviewed on an Australian Broadcasting Commission programme[16] stated that 'the young are now beginning to find self-respect and, to people like myself, this means a hell of a lot'. Another declared, 'We intend standing up for our own rights. Up till now, Aborigines have taken on a defensive attitude; but not any longer. It takes a lot of assertion for young Aborigines to get there, but we'll make it'. A third chimed in, 'We don't want to be patronised by whitey in so-called Aboriginal organisations any longer. It's a case of the father who can't bear to see his children growing up. The white man can't understand what it's like to be black. He thinks we want to be like him—but that's a fallacy'. And a bitter final comment: 'You can bust your guts, but if you're black you won't get anywhere'. A similar sentiment is expressed in:[17] 'We Aborigines have yet to be restored to the personal dignity with which we once roamed the lands of Australia. Our government speaks of equal rights for all men, yet treats the Aboriginal race as though they are children. They pat us on the head, speak fine words and talk about what should be done . . . Once given the opportunity we will prove ourselves capable of standing on our own two feet . . . and becoming responsible upright citizens'. This mood of bitter assertiveness is coming to the forefront among the young particularly, though many still remain passive and inarticulate.

Coupled with assertion is a growing pride in Aboriginal ancestry, especially among those part-Aborigines who have had no knowledge of their traditional culture. A young Aboriginal mother on this same radio programme felt that she had 'a special sympathy and understanding of Aboriginal music and would like to learn an Aboriginal language'. Professor Elkin has stated that this interest in the traditional culture was not uncommon as far back as the 1930s among the part-Aboriginal groups in New South Wales whom he was studying. The Department of Adult Education, University of Sydney, which supports Aboriginal Family Education Centres, reports today a growing demand for classes in Aboriginal language, myths and bark painting, even though the latter often depart from the traditional subject-matter to express present-day living.

In one area of northern New South Wales, eighteen months ago only 20 per cent of the Aboriginal population admitted to a knowledge of the indigenous language, since it was felt to be a matter of backwardness and shame in white eyes. Now, with the upsurge of interest among both black and white, 60 per cent of this same group profess knowledge of their own language.[18]

Government Aboriginal agencies, which exist in each State save Tasmania, are regarded with ambivalent feelings by the communities they are intended to serve. The Country Towns Survey indicated that, historically, they have been seen as instruments of oppression of the major society. In recent years, with the government tendency to employ better trained and

more sympathetic staff, Aboriginal attitudes in the southern States have
changed—from the outright suspicious to the wary. Individual officers who
have merited it can gain their clients' trust. Knowledge of the special facili-
tities available to Aborigines is gaining ground. But grumbling against
authority and, in particular, the Aboriginal agencies, has long been a
favoured emotional outlet which the mere employment of some Aboriginal
officers in minor posts has still not mitigated. The vice-president of the
Townsville Aborigines Advancement League, until recently an inhabitant of
Palm Island, commented[19] that those Queensland Aborigines who were classified under *The Aborigines and Torres Strait Islanders' Affairs Act* 1965-1967
as assisted people were governed by police, by racial prejudice and by
bureaucracy and were subject to an arbitrary authority. 'I think Aborigines
are the most kept down of all the coloured races', she added. 'Among my
people they sort of lose faith in themselves. They are promised a lot of things
and they expect things to happen in a few months or a few years. When it
doesn't they think, what's it matter? It's no use telling anyone else our
problems because nothing is ever done'.

Judicious use of the mass media for political pressurizing has tended to
increase Aboriginal confidence, and their leaders, realizing that reports of
injustices against a coloured minority make news, have not hesitated to take
advantage of this new-found strength. Well-publicized reports of malnutrition or infant deaths will bring some government response, even if only of a
token kind. No doubt even the threat of such adverse publicity must constitute effective armoury in Aboriginal hands.

Finally, the realisation that they are not alone has added to Aboriginal
assertiveness. Through local and Australia-wide organisations such as the
Federal Council for the Advancement of Aborigines and Torres Strait
Islanders and the National Tribal Council, Aborigines have become aware of
each others' presence, each others' problems. Through the mass media they
know they are part of a world-wide group of downtrodden coloured people.
Direct contact with other groups has heightened the feeling of solidarity.
Visits to Aboriginal areas by Maoris, American Indians and a West Indian
Black Power leader, and the journey in 1970 of five Aboriginal leaders to a
Black people's conference in the United States have made the Aboriginal
advancement movement more confident, more militant.

Yet, even this cursory glance at the situation indicates that Aboriginal
liabilities far outweigh assets in terms of capability of assertion of equality.

White Attitudes

Public opinion polls concerning Aboriginal questions conducted in 1954,
1961 and 1965 revealed generally favourable public attitudes. A national
referendum conducted in May 1967 gave a resounding majority of 89.3 per
cent to a proposition that Aborigines be included in the census and that the
Federal government be given power to legislate on their behalf. More
detailed questioning, however, has brought forth less favourable response.

In the Country Towns Survey, white respondents were at no stage asked
to mention attributes which they considered characteristic of Aborigines in
general. However, 52 per cent spontaneously did so. All attributes referred
to were unfavourable, all were of the type commonly ascribed to black
minorities. Most frequently employed was 'dirty', followed by 'drunken',
'irresponsible' and 'inferior'. Aborigines, then, are commonly believed to
violate the conventional codes of cleanliness, work and sobriety. In a com-

parable study by Taft[20] in 1968 concerning the attitudes of Western Australian whites, most traits selected from a given list as being typical of Aborigines were unfavourable: 'wasteful with money' came first, selected by 50 per cent of respondents, 'dirty and slovenly' (28 per cent), and 'drunken' (26 per cent). Twenty-one per cent of whites in a city and a small country town in New South Wales surveyed by Western[21] in 1969 agreed with the statement 'The incorporation of Aborigines into our communities could well lower our standards of hygiene'. Dark skins, poor living conditions and dirt are again synthesized in the white mind.

The Country Towns Survey was marked by a willingness (ranging from 92 per cent to 99 per cent) to generalize on all questions asked about Aborigines, as to their abilities, disadvantages and acceptability.[22] This contrasts markedly with similar English and American surveys where there has been an increasing refusal to apply stereotypes. Banton, for instance, reports that 59 per cent of an English sample declined to categorize about coloured minorities.[23]

The lack of contact between whites and Aborigines living in the same country town is striking. Of all the whites questioned, none stated that they had had a 'great deal' of contact with Aborigines and only 12 per cent had had 'a fair amount'. Fifty-one per cent had had no contact whatever.[24] A favourability scale was devised on the basis of replies to a structured questionnaire[25] which disclosed that 40 per cent of the sample were either favourable or tolerant in their attitudes towards Aborigines while the remaining 60 per cent were, in varying degrees, unfavourably disposed. Only 4 per cent of the total were actively favourable and 6 per cent very unfavourable, these small percentages representing the lack of interest of the majority, as much as tolerance. Williams has commented[26] that 'the great majority of prejudiced persons carry prejudice at a low temperature, and much of their discriminatory behaviour reflects relatively passive conformity to taken-for-granted patterns prevalent in the social groups which give them their statuses and sense of belonging'. Yet, though racism is not as a rule virulent in Australia, there is an overall belief in the inferiority of Aborigines, of their intrinsic inequality—a belief similar to that concerning the poor of the last century, whose proverty was seen as accusatory and, at the same time, constituted an affront to middle-class sensibilities.

Conclusion

The remarkable lack of contact between Aborigines and whites (encouraged on either side) both gives rise to, and results from a lack of awareness, on the part of the whites, of Aboriginal existence. One is reminded of the third form isolationist who wrote, in response to a request for an essay on the Chinese: 'I don't think anything about the Chinese. I never will have nothing to say about them . . . or ever have said anything about them'.[27]

On the other hand, the expectancy of Aborigines, based on long experience, is to be despised and rejected or, what is even worse, ignored, which results in a distrust of whites and an acute sensitivity to slight, real or imagined. Partly because they have incorporated the white view into their self-image, this Aboriginal distrust has been directed not just to the major society, but also to their own. However, changes in the varied Aboriginal viewpoints are rapidly being wrought. No longer are they content to have whites as their spokesmen; no longer are their leaders afraid to speak out.

Their increasing bitterness and militancy have never been expressed so loud
and clear as in very recent years and, in the last few months, manifestations
of solidarity with other oppressed minorities have been made publicly on at
least four occasions.[28]
Once again the syndrome of Aboriginal-white attitudes is apparent:
Aborigines are becoming more outspoken in their demands because they
sense some increase in white support, while white interest and sympathy are
slowly broadening in response to Aboriginal demands.

ACKNOWLEDGEMENT

The material contained in this chapter is partly based on A Survey of Race
Relations in Selected Country Towns, Lorna Lippmann, 1970, roneod, Centre
for Research into Aboriginal Affairs, Melbourne (in press, Penguin Books, 1971)
and refers mainly to part-Aborigines, with passing reference to full-blood
communities.

REFERENCES

1 BARWICK, DIANA E., 1963: A Little More Than Kin, unpublished Ph.D. thesis,
Australian National University, Canberra; BECKETT, JEREMY, 1958: Mixed-
Blood Aboriginal Minority in the Pastoral West of New South Wales, un-
published M.A. thesis, Australian National University, Canberra; BELL, J. H.,
1961: "Some Demographic and Cultural Characteristics of the La Perouse
Aborigines", Mankind, 5:425-438; CALLEY, MALCOLM J. C., 1959: Social
Organisation of Mixed-Blood Communities in North-Eastern New South Wales,
unpublished Ph.D. thesis, University of Sydney; FINK, RUTH A., 1955: Social
Stratification: A Sequel to the Assimilation Process in a Part-Aboriginal Com-
munity, unpublished M.A. thesis, University of Sydney; FINK, RUTH A., 1957:
"The Caste Barrier: An Obstacle to the Assimilation of Part-Aborigines in
North-West New South Wales", Oceania, Vol. XXVIII, No. 1; GALE, FAY,
1960: A Study of Assimilation: Part-Aborigines in South Australia, Ph.D.
thesis, University of Adelaide; INGLIS, JUDY, 1961: "Aborigines in Adelaide",
Journal of the Polynesian Society, 70: 200-218; REAY, MARIE, 1945: "A Half-
Caste Aboriginal Community in North-Western New South Wales", Oceania,
15:296-323; REAY, MARIE, 1963: "Aboriginal and White Australian Family
Structure: An Enquiry into Assimilation Trends", The Sociological Review,
11:19-47.
2 LIPPMANN, LORNA, 1970: op. cit., p. 79.
3 SARNOFF, J. and KATZ, D., 1954: "The Motivational Bases of Attitude Change",
Journal of Abnormal and Social Psychology, Vol. 49, pp. 115-124.
4 In this context it is worth noting that increased assistance to or consideration
for Aborigines can produce articulate prejudice. For example, during the
flood emergencies in northern New South Wales in February 1971, a considerable number of white small town residents expressed their resentments—in
newspaper letters and on radio and television—at the "higher" standard of
flood and food relief for Aborigines. That Aborigines were getting more than
other residents is doubtful, but it was perceived as such by some white towns-
people.
5 As reported in the Melbourne Herald, 12 December, 1970.
6 As reported in The Australian, 21 December, 1970.
7 GOULD, RICHARD A., 1969: Yiwara: Foragers of the Australian Desert, Collins,
London.
8 Private communication from the Reverend Ronald Croxford, former head
teacher at Yirrkala and one of the instigators of the movement to contest the
validity of mineral leases granted to private companies in that area.

9 CAWTE, J. E., 1969: Paper presented to the World Psychiatric Conference, Melbourne.

10 *Cf.* 'Minority Children have less chance to control their environment than do the majority whites'—COLEMAN, JAMES S. & ASSOCIATES, *Equality of Educational Opportunity*, U.S. Government Printing Office, Washington, 1966.

11 EGGLESTON, ELIZABETH M., 1970: *Aborigines and the Administration of Justice*, unpublished Ph.D. thesis, Monash University. For example, this author cites the case of Western Australia, where Aborigines constitute 2.5 per cent of the population. However, this percentage is convicted of 11 per cent of all offences and constitutes 24 per cent of the prison population (1965). In a survey of 10 towns in 1965, she found that 14.3 per cent of Aborigines arrested were released on bail as opposed to 33.6 per cent of whites; further, 42.6 per cent of Aborigines sentenced were imprisoned, compared with 19.6 per cent of whites.

12 GOULD, RICHARD A., 1969: *op. cit.*, p. 186.

13 LIPPMANN, LORNA, 1970: *op. cit.*, p. 85.

14 *The Medical Journal of Australia*
1967, 1:46. ELLIOTT, R. B. and MAXWELL, G. M.: 'Lactose Maldigestion in Australian Aboriginal Children'.
2:237. GANDEVIA, BRYAN: 'Chronic Respiratory Disease in Pintubi and and Walbiri Aborigines'.
1968, 2:990. MAXWELL, G. M., ELLIOTT, R. B., McCOY, W. T. and LANGSFORD, W. A.: 'Respiratory Infections in Australian Aboriginal Children'.
1969, 1:180. MOODIE, P. M.: 'Mortality and Morbidity in Australian Aboriginal Children'.
2:1005. KIRKE, D. K.: 'Mortality and Morbidity in Australian Aboriginal Children'.
2:1026. 'Symposia: Aboriginal Health'.
1970, 1:345. 'The Health of Aboriginal Children'.
1:349. JOSE, D. G. and WELCH, J. S.: 'Protein-Calorie Malnutrition in Australian Aboriginal Children'.
1:356. HARRIS, M. J., DUFFY, B. J. and BEVERIDGE, J.: 'Studies on the Small Bowel of a Group of N.S.W. Aboriginal Children'.
2:995. LICKISS, J. NORELLE: 'Health Problems of Sydney Aboriginal Children'.
2:1001. WISE, P. H., EDWARDS, F. M., THOMAS, D. W., ELLIOTT, R. B., HATCHER, L. and CRAIG, R.: 'Hyperglycaemia in the Urbanized Aboriginal'.
2:1007. EDWARDS, L. D.: 'Malnutrition and Disease in Pre-School Aboriginal Children in the Walgett Area of N.S.W.'.
The Australian Journal of Experimental Biology and Medical Science
1966, Vol. XLIV:709. ELLIOTT, R. B. and MAXWELL, G. M.: 'Predominance of Lactose of Small Molecular Size in Duodenal and Jejunal Mucosa of Australian Aboriginal Children'.
Australian Paediatric Journal
1969, 5:71. JOSE, D. G., SELF, M. H. R., STALLMAN, N. D.: 'A Survey of Children and Adolescents on Queensland Aboriginal Settlements'.
5:109. ELLIOTT, R. B., MAXWELL, G. M., KNEEBONE, G. M. and KIRKE, D. K.: 'Lactose Digestion and Breast Feeding: A Nutritional Survey in Australian Aboriginal Infants'.
Queensland Institute of Medical Research
1968, 23rd Annual Report of the Council.
The American Journal of Clinical Nutrition
1969, 22:716. MAXWELL, G. M. and ELLIOTT, R. B.: 'Nutritional State of Australian Aboriginal Children'.

15 BROOM, LEONARD, 'Educational Status of Aborigines', *The Australian and New Zealand Journal of Sociology*, 1971, 7, 1 (in press).

16 Radio 3AR, 1 February, 1971, 'Australian Aboriginal Culture Today'.

17 BOOTH, LAWRENCE H. J., 1970: *Origin*, Vol. 3, No. 4, p. 8.

18 As reported by Mr. A. Grey, Department of Adult Education, University of Sydney. It is significant that at a Commonwealth sponsored and Abschol-run seminar called 'Aborigines and Pre-Schools' held at U.N.S.W. in February 1971, a number of Aboriginal participants recommended to governments that Aboriginal languages such as Pitjantjara be taught to both white and Aboriginal school children, since it had as much of a place in Australian education as Indonesian and the like.

19 McAVOY, MRS. THELMA, as reported in *The Australian*, 3 February, 1971.

20 TAFT, R., 1970: 'Attitudes of Western Australians Towards Aborigines', in *Aborigines in Australian Society*, A.N.U. Press, Canberra.

21 WESTERN, J. S., 1969: 'The Australian Aborigine: What White Australians Know and Think About Him—A Preliminary Survey', *Race*, X, 4:411-434.

22 LIPPMANN, LORNA, *op. cit.*, pp. 58-80.

23 BANTON, M. P., 1959: *White and Coloured*, Jonathan Cape, London, p. 37.

24 LIPPMANN, LORNA, *op. cit.*, p. 63.

25 *Ibid*, pp. 61-63.

26 WILLIAMS, R., JNR., 1964: *Strangers Next Door*, Prentice-Hall, Englewood Cliffs, New Jersey, p. 200.

27 HANNAM, CHARLES L., 'Prejudice and the Teaching of History', *The New Era*, Vol. 51, No. 6, p. 157.

28 (a) Numerous statements of solidarity with other black groups made after their return by the five Aboriginal representatives to the Black People's conference in Atlanta, Georgia, September, 1970.
(b) Resolution passed by Aborigines Advancement Council, Western Australia, December, 1970 deploring anti-Semitism in the Soviet Union.
(c) Statement of protest by Aboriginal Sports Foundation at the proposed participation of an Aboriginal player in a South African all-white tennis tournament, January, 1971.
(d) Newspaper article by an officer of the Aborigines Advancement League, Victoria in January, 1971, also protesting against this apparent support of an apartheid regime.

3

PREJUDICE TOWARDS ABORIGINES IN
AUSTRALIAN LITERATURE

E. T. Brash

With the publication of *Coonardoo* (1929), *Capricornia* (1937), *The Time-less Land* (1944), *To the Islands* (1958), *Yandy* (1959), and other novels that deal with Aboriginal themes, it might be reasonably claimed that Australian writers have started to function as voices of protest against the prejudices and injustices that have been displayed by white immigrant Australians towards the black tribes they displaced. Any such claim should not be made with too great a sense of satisfaction however, for during the period of early European expansion and settlement in Australia, also the period of the worst excesses of inhumanity and violence against Aboriginal man, there was no such protest. Australian writers in respect to this aspect of our society, failed to operate as voices of vision in their own time or to display the awareness and sensitivity inherent in the definition of a creative artist.

The appearance, during the last forty years, of novels that, for the first time, present Aborigines as major characters in a sympathetic manner, is as much indicative of a belated softening of social prejudices towards Aborigines as it is of greater awareness among Australian writers. Geoffrey Dutton[1] implies this when he states that Aboriginal themes have become the 'easiest and safest topics for literary indignation.' 'Easy' here suggests that the writer who wishes to feature Aborigines as victims of white injustice has an abundance of readily available historical material to draw on. 'Safe' suggests that the writer who uses such material can trumpet his version of our national crimes without fear of hostile social or literary reaction. There is little danger of the writer's being 'tarred and feathered'.

It is possible to go further and argue that literary 'finger-pointing' and 'breast-beating' have become acceptable methods of purging the national conscience, or at least that of the Australian reading public, of any feeling of guilt felt about the two hundred or so years of contact and conflict that have proved to be almost genocidal for the Aboriginal people. Works that vividly depict the inhumanity of our forebears or contemporaries enable both writer and reader to 'pass by on the other side of the road', suitably removed from any suggestion that they themselves could be in any way involved or blamed. In Donald Stuart's *Yandy*, the station manager nicknamed 'Chicken-burster' who satisfies his lust on unwilling and immature lubras, and Elkery, the insensitive, harsh (almost sadistic) superintendent of the government Aboriginal settlement in Gavin Casey's *Snowball* seem to be deliberately 'blackened' to fill 'scapegoat' roles. It is interesting to note that both novels mentioned here, in addition to featuring white characters who embody 'total

badness' in their dealings with Aborigines, also feature white characters who
come close to being totally 'good' in such dealings ('good', as seen by the
white writer). Greg Stapleton in *Snowball* and Don McLeod in *Yandy* seem
to derive at least part of their nature from their creator's desire to make some
kind of atonement for the 'bad' whites in the novel—or at least to make a
balance. Don McLeod in particular is far too obviously groomed for the role
of redeemer.

> 'He is all you have been told, old friend. He is a proper man, with a
> good yoonbah, a good style. For years he has been learning the things
> that trouble our people, and his heart is with us. Make no error, he
> will not lead the People half-way and then turn aside. He is not like
> other white fellers; his mind is made up that our people must have a
> real place in the land, a chance to learn good things and be their own
> masters. I tell you, my friend, what this man will start will go on
> when you and I are finished, and children not yet here will not see the
> end of it.'[2]

It would be interesting to know how Aboriginal readers respond to this
exception to the white rule; whether he is acceptable or whether he is
rejected as too much an embodiment of white liberal sentiment. Still,
irrespective of reaction among Aborigines, this type of novel containing these
types of characters will continue to appear because they have much more to
do with the catharsis of the white soul than the satisfaction of the black
reader.

The writer who portrays the prejudices of others is, in so doing, exercising his own judgement and feelings, and thereby often reveals a good deal
about himself. Mary Durack furnishes a good example of such a revelation in
her book *Kings in Grass Castles*.

> 'My father's attitude to the native question was somewhere between
> that of grandfather and those of his associates who thought that any
> sort of consideration for the blacks was sentimental and ridiculous.
> I find it easier to imagine grandfather, with his quick Irish temper,
> taking a stockwhip to a native than I can my father who was not
> impulsive or quickly roused to anger, and I can imagine neither of
> them shooting a man in cold blood or using a gun except where
> necessary. Both disliked anything in the nature of blood sports and in
> later years when Member for the Kimberley District, my father,
> appalled by the wanton destruction of bird life he loved brought in a
> bill for its protection north of the 20th parallel. None the less he
> would have been embarrassed in these early years to have been
> thought unrealistic about the blacks . . .'[3]

In this frank representation of the prejudices of her immediate forbears,
Miss Durack's father's attitudes are placed alongside her grandfather's and
those of their associates. There is no overt indication of either rejection or
acceptance, for these attitudes are discussed calmly and dispassionately.
Indeed the calmness of her presentation makes it appear natural, within the
context of an early Australian settler community, that there be no 'consideration' for blacks and that whippings and shootings ('where necessary') should
be used to control them. Miss Durack's honesty and frankness are praise-
worthy. We may assume, however, that if she is careful enough in her family
chronicle to distinguish her father's attitudes 'to the native question' from her
grandfather's, she would also wish to distinguish her own attitudes from
either of theirs. Other of her novels,[4] and her encouragement and assistance

of the part-Aboriginal writer Colin Johnson, would seem to establish her as a writer not at all prejudiced against Aborigines and yet one wonders what corridor of her mind enabled her, within one paragraph, to quickly move from a discussion of the treatment of Aborigines to a comparison with 'bloodsports' and a reference to the preservation of Australian bird life.

Perhaps this could have been dismissed as an embarrassing structural flaw but for other disturbing instances when Miss Durack's own voice intrudes cynically into the narrative. She appears to be having more difficulty than she is prepared to admit in separating her own attitudes from those of the two preceeding generations of her family. For example, in describing the hanging of some Aborigines in the presence of their fellow tribesman, she is confident enough to interpret for us what the spectators thought and felt about the events they were witnessing, even though she herself was not present.

> 'To satisfy the outcry of the inhabitants after the death of Barnett and others, sentence of death was passed on several natives sent to Freemantle for trial. These were returned to Hall's Creek so that justice could be carried out on the spot and as many of their countrymen as possible gathered in to witness the execution and take heed therefrom. But after all the moral was lost on the blacks. Some laughed and applauded believing the hanging to have been staged for their entertainment . . .'[5]

Two of the comments here—the 'moral was lost on the blacks' and their 'believing' that the execution had been 'staged' for their entertainment—can represent no more than her uninformed surmisings or her uncritical acceptance of hearsay, passed on with an added touch of cynicism.

It may appear unfair on Miss Durack that her work be picked over to reveal such flaws and lapses, but the point is general, not personal. The white Australian writer is heir to a literary heritage that came to easy terms with the unlovely facts of our treatment of Aborigines by ignoring, condoning or supporting them. The writers of this century who seem to want to face up to the injustices and inhumanities meted out by our society have had to first struggle to free themselves and their own feelings from what has been generally said and published. It is understandable then that, in the portrayal of Aborigines, these writers have had difficulty in positioning themselves as artists in relation to their created characters. It is understandable too, that such writers display unevenness in tone and feeling, and that their works are seriously flawed by lapses into cynicism or sentimentality.

The active part played by Australian writers in the demeaning of the Aborigine and in the justification of prejudices against him is not generally realized or admitted. The revelation of the presence of strong racial prejudices in the works of Henry Lawson[6] has taken many Australians by surprise. The Lawson image, popularized by biographers, critics and schoolteachers since his death, has been shorn of a plume that waved jauntily in the cap of Australian 'mateship' that he wore so proudly. The shorn feather is the fierce dislike of non-white ethnic groups which was an essential feature of the spirit of the outback. Lawson himself made no attempt to hide his dislike and it is indicative of the decreasing acceptance of such hostility that it has been deliberately glossed over. If, in his works, Aborigines receive less vituperative and cynical comment than the Chinese, it is because, in their depleted and weakened numbers, they were seen as less of a danger than the irrepressible 'Celestials' whose hordes threatened, in Lawson's mind, to

descend upon Australia from the north. There is more of ridicule than
vitriol in his attitude to Aborigines, though his manner is uneven. In *The
Drover's Wife*,[7] rather than destroy the picture of the heroine's patience and
long sufferance in the face of loneliness and hardship, Lawson himself steps
in on her behalf to cynically denounce the Aboriginal 'King' who, employed
to chop wood, builds the wood pile hollow. On the other hand, Aborigines
can receive favourable comment from him, but only when they measure up
on his scale of 'white' values. In *The Black Tracker*, the Aboriginal who
deliberately 'loses' the trial to protect a friend is praised thus:—

> 'But ah! there beat a white man's heart
> Beneath his old, black wrinkled hide.'[8]

Of course there are writers whose prejudice is far more openly hostile
and not tempered by such sentimentality. Alexander McDonald's book, *In
the Land of Pearl and Gold* (1904) purports to be a factual account of his
experiences as a prospector in early Australia and New Guinea. He and his
companions are plagued by Chinese and Aborigines until they solve the
problem by attacking the Aboriginal camp under cover of darkness, after
having first laid a false trial to the Chinese camp. They are then able to relax
in glee as their enemies beat each other up. McDonald has enjoyed indulging
in a variation of that brand of humour, identified by O'Dowd, which draws
mirth from seeing a Chinaman knocked down in the street and kicked by
some champion of Australian manhood.

A particularly strong example of open hostility towards Aborigines in
Australian fiction can be found in Brian Penton's novel *Land-Takers*. His
sub-title, 'The Story of an Epoch' implies that the book has historical
accuracy. It was first published in 1935, and is thus separated by time from
the events and the social atmosphere it claims to represent.

Great pains are taken to make the Aborigines in his story appear totally
treacherous, savage and degraded. Penton provides his own note of intrusive
bitterness when, in describing the effect of the arrival of the Aborigines, he
claims that all the cattle 'evacuated the locality' adding, 'even the stupid
sheep hated the smell of the blacks,' and, as if justifying the sheep's attitude,
comments on the Aborigines' appearance—'not like men—somehow sub-
human . . . those faces could have belonged to the old age of the world but
never its dawn'.[9]

Penton obviously thought it necessary to give as powerful a picture as
possible of the degraded nature of the Aborigines in order to justify the
bloody massacre that is to follow, when the white heroes totally annihilate a
tribe. In painting the massacre, Penton's description matches the spirit of the
indiscriminate killing.

> 'Cabell watched the blood trickle down the face of the black he had
> shot. A rush of fierce satisfaction seemed to strip the tired skin from
> his body . . . he gave a wild halloo. "Give it to them boys!" he shouted
> and emptied his pistol through the flimsy gunyah . . . Cranky Tom
> needed no encouragement . . . as far as Sambo was concerned it was
> part of a day's work . . .
> 'Three times they stopped firing and waited for signs of life in the
> camp . . . a flight of spears betokened it. But fewer and fewer spears
> came over and the fourth time they let up there was none. They
> waited for five minutes and gave the camp a last volley, then came
> out from the bush.

'Their shots had ripped the bark gunyah to pieces. Some had fallen over, revealing huddled bodies inside. Here and there one groaned. It was left to Tom to finish these off . . .'[10]

The readiness of some Australian writers to feature Aborigines without obtaining adequate information about them is surely a form of prejudice. Too often the writer is content to deal in second-hand anthropological or historical data of dubious value, and too often his portrayal does not get past his own fascination with the exotic and with the display of superficial cultural trappings. Ion Idriess (*Drums of Mer, Wild White Man of Badu*) extracts maximum romantic adventure from the well-worn anthropological report that primitive people welcomed the first white men as the returning spirits of their own ancestors. Too often the writer is not interested in portraying Aborigines as individuals in their own rights. Rather his interest in them is only that they can provide easily malleable proof of the superior resourcefulness and sagacity of the white man as he moves among the black. Australia has its own Rider Haggard novels in books like *The Wild White Man of Badu* (1950) and there are echoes of Daniel Defoe in Jack McLaren's *My Crowded Solitude* (1926)—the title is a misnomer, for his hero (McLaren himself) has plenty of companions, but they cannot be taken as real company for they are Aborigines.

The popular demand for romantic variations on the theme of the isolated white man among the blacks is illustrated by Charles Barrett's book, *White Blackfellows* (1948), which contains fourteen stories each featuring a different white, or group of whites, isolated among savages. The stories range from that of William Buckley, which is based on documented, historical fact, to the improbable tale of Louis Trégance who is saved at the last moment from being roasted and devoured by New Guinea cannibals when he responds to the heathen high 'priest's' masonic handshake! Not only is he released on the strength of this handshake but immediately hailed as the sun god, 'Otaroo'!

Barrett, who has gone to a good deal of trouble to collect these stories, offers his own explanation for their popularity. Such stories were, he said, intended originally for the poorly educated people of Britain who were 'sufficiently intelligent to be curious about wild countries and primitive races.' Such readers also liked 'useful knowledge . . . but would only take it with sugar: strange, romantic, adventures, cannibals and dusky kings'.[11] The collection and publishing of these stories in Australia in 1948 would indicate that the curiosity of Australians for the strange, the primitive and the romantic has not yet been satisfied.

Such curiosity threatens the development of serious literature on Aboriginal themes, and also the development of indigenous Aboriginal literature in English. The same was true for Africa where Wole Soyinka, a leading Nigerian writer, complained that the European taste for the exotic—grass huts and bare bosoms, cannibals and witch doctors distracted writers from what should be their prime concern, the close portrayal of human experience.

Prejudice may be evidenced when a writer completely ignores the existence of a group while dealing with matters which concern that group. It is difficult to argue that a writer should have included reference to Aborigines in her novel when in fact she didn't, but when Dymphna Cusack writes one of the few Australian novels that deals with inter-racial attitudes, and makes no mention at all of Aborigines one wonders how they were screened from her artistic view. In *The Sun in Exile* (1955), the heroine, a young, white

Australian girl, travelling to London by sea, falls in love with a black Nigerian student who joins the ship in the Caribbean. As far as Jamaica the passengers had been all white, but visits to non-white ports of call, and the taking on of a number of coloured passengers at Trinidad leads to a great deal of comment about 'blacks' by whites. It is interesting to note that, in the course of the novel, references are made to Africans, American Negroes, Indians, Polynesians and New Guineans but not one reference is made to an Aborigine. The Australian girl eventually marries her black boyfriend in London and becomes involved with him in the campaign for a better deal for the black man in the Commonwealth. The Australian Aborigine is again left out of the picture.

When the white Australian writer does attempt to closely and accurately portray Aborigines, he is undertaking a difficult task. It is difficult enough for a writer to achieve an adequate representation of human experience within the context of his own culture. Always, in so doing, there is the danger that his vision will fail him, or his creative powers will be unequal to the task. It is far more difficult when he has to strain his vision across the wide cultural gulf that separate even modern urban Aborigines from their white counterparts.

The unfortunate fact is that most writers attempting Aboriginal portrayal have approached their task glibly without even making the effort to obtain a close personal view of those they describe. It is not surprising then, that Australian writers rarely reveal any clear insight into Aboriginal culture. Perhaps Daisy Bates[12] is an exception, and her own life illustrates the tremendous outlay of time and effort required if one is to bridge cultural gulfs. In contrast to Daisy Bates, Eleanor Dark[13] attempts the portrayal of an Aboriginal character of major proportions after having admitted to a sense of her own abysmal ignorance. The only sources she acknowledges are European 'authorities' on Aborigines. To cover the gaps in her understanding she produces a kind of ethnographic patchwork in which data about a number of tribes is attributed to the Port Jackson tribe. Bennilong himself is partly drawn from history (as seen by whites), but the rest of him is 'purely imaginary'. When Miss Dark interprets what Bennilong thinks and feels, the reader must recognise that this is more accurately an expression of Miss Dark's own mind than that of the original Bennilong, or any Aboriginal like him. This is quite apparent when Bennilong observes similarity between the white man's God and Bai-ame, the 'Good Spirit'.

In spite of the difficulties of cross-cultural literary portrayal, it should have been possible for Australian writers to depict Aboriginal characters in more depth and with more sensitivity than has hitherto been the case. Too often a novel gives early promise that is not fulfilled, for the Aboriginal characters do not rise above the level of the 'stock' figure, the ethnic 'type', or the caricature. This is the case with *Snowball* in which the old, ex-tracker hero could be taken as the original Australian Uncle Tom. He patiently waits at the back door of the pub, courteously asks a white to buy him his beer, accepts it gratefully and goes home to his shanty to drink. His gratitude over the benevolence of his white friends is never in danger of being displaced by his consciousness of the raw deal white society has played him. Gavin Casey's attempt to feature Aborigines in an urban setting, rather than the inevitable outback is welcomed, but his characterization lets him down badly.

Randolph Stow's novel *To the Islands* is also let down by his failure to imbue his Aboriginal characters with sustained vitality. Justin is a version of the faithful 'Man Friday' who stays with the wandering white hero till the bitter end. The greatest disappointment however is Rex who, at the outset of the novel, returns unannounced to the mission station where he had been brought up and from which he had been banished for his misdeeds. His return throws him into conflict with the sixty-seven-year-old white mission superintendent, Heriot, who had originally banished him. Rex's manner is defiant towards Heriot and gives promise of drama to follow.

'Across the face of Rex, as he turned away, and across the faces of the men, a slow grin flickered. Twenty years ago, or even fifteen, this threat from Brother Heriot might have been dangerous; but the old man was weak now and had changed, or perhaps all white men had changed, at all events the whip was gone . . .'[14]

This defiance flares briefly into violence and then fizzles into contrition and repentence. In the final stages Rex 'gently and humbly' accepts the present of a rifle from the dying Heriot.

Rex as a fully-achieved character, playing a more positive role (even though it may have ended tragically for him), could have been a far more convincing character and perhaps the first Aboriginal literary hero of major proportions.

Nawnim in Xavier Herbert's *Capricornia* may already hold claim to that title even though in birth, education and social position he is not fully Aboriginal. His importance as a character in the novel relates more to his efforts as a half-caste to gain a place in a white dominated society than to his place in Aboriginal society. He does on occasions establish links with Aborigines and samples Aboriginal life but understandably his experiences here are handled with less confidence and energy than the 'white' areas.

Katherine Susannah Pritchard in *Coonardoo* can claim to have created an Aboriginal heroine with warmth and depth. The unevenness of her portrayal results from the great difficulty of representing a character who is, at the one time, an uneducated Aboriginal 'child' of the bush and the intelligent mainstay of the cattle station and its white owners.

Alf Dubbo, the visionary artist in Patrick White's *Riders in the Chariot* (1961) represents an interesting development in Aboriginal characterization. White concentrates on exploring and illustrating the awareness of a man who is first and foremost an artist and secondly an Aborigine. No time is wasted in establishing Alf's tribal identity, as the main attention is given to those influences, including white foster parents, that moulded his artist's sensibility.

If the white Australian writer is to achieve greater success in his efforts to represent Aborigines and Aboriginal life, in both traditional and modern context, he is going to have to make a greater effort at cross-cultural projection. The rarity of success by any artist dealing with any culture other than his own underlines the difficulties involved in this. In spite of his best intentions and efforts, the artist's vision may remain limited and distorted by his own cultural orientation.

It is worth bearing in mind, however, that the difficulties of cross-cultural literary portrayal differ only in degree and not in kind from those of all literary portrayal. An artist cannot hope to attain a close sensitive view of any person or group except as he forgets his own being (including his prejudices) and attempts to actually become the character he is creating, be that character white or black.

The most dangerous prejudice of all for writers is when they reject the principles that should be operative in all art and adopt a set of 'special rules' for dealing with different ethnic groups. Nor should a socially depressed group be offered 'special consideration' in literature for, ultimately, literary paternalism and condescension are more destructive to the human spirit than the display of open hostility.

There is cause for some optimism about the place of Aborigines in Australian literature. Fortunately, most of the overt displays of prejudice against them have ceased, and many of the more insidious forms should appear less frequently as writers are prepared to attempt Aboriginal themes with sensitivity and enterprise. There is the possibility that some forms will persist and others will appear. One such possibility is that writers will attempt to confine Aboriginal themes in literature to rural and tribal settings at a time when Aboriginal man's greatest struggle is to be accepted as a culturally distinct group within all areas of Australian society. Writers will also, no doubt, repeatedly give in to the popular demand for the romantic and exotic, and Aboriginal custom and history will be worked and reworked to provide the necessary ingredients.

The greatest cause for hope however, is that Australians will increasingly be able to look to Aborigines themselves to represent their own feelings, reactions and aspirations in literature. Kath Walker and Colin Johnson are early contributors to a potentially rich area of Australian literature.

REFERENCES

1 DUTTON, GEOFFREY. *The Literature of Australia*. Penguin, 1964, p. 436.

2 STUART, DONALD. *Yandy*. Georgian House, Melbourne, 1959, p. 47.

3 DURACK, MARY. *Kings in Grass Castles*. Corgi Books, 1967, p. 305.

4 ——, *Keep Him My Country*. Angus & Robertson, Sydney, 1966.
The Courteous Savage. Nelson, Edinburgh, 1964.

5 ——, *Kings in Grass Castles*. p. 320.

6 PEARSON, W. H. *Henry Lawson Among the Maoris*. A.N.U. Press, Canberra, 1968.

7 LAWSON, HENRY. *The Bush Undertaker and Other Stories*. Angus & Robertson, Sydney, 1970.

8 Quoted by W. H. Pearson, *op. cit.*, p. 8.

9 PENTON, BRIAN. *Landtakers*. Cassell, London, 1935, p. 132.

10 *Ibid.*, p. 166.

11 BARRETT, CHARLES. *White Blackfellows*. Hallcroft, Melbourne, 1948, p. 225.

12 BATES, DAISY. *The Passing of the Aborigines*. Murray, London, 1938.

13 DARK, ELEANOR. *The Timeless Land*. Collins, London, 1944.

14 STOW, RANDOLPH. *To the Islands*. McDonald, London, 1958, p. 61.

4

RACIAL PREJUDICE AND ABORIGINAL ADJUSTMENT: THE SOCIAL PSYCHIATRIC VIEW

J. Cawte

' "A BLACK CAMP" IN NEW SOUTH WALES, AFTER THE ANNUAL GIFT OF BLANKETS FROM THE GOVERNOR.

'The Blacks of Australia are, with the exception of the Bosjemen, the lowest and most irreclaimable of the native tribes with which we are acquainted. After strenuous efforts, commencing sixty-four years since, they are now exactly what they were when first discovered. They speak a little English, some have even been taught to read and write well; but, although occasional instances of affection and fidelity are found among them, just as we meet with tame foxes and pheasants, they are as a race truly irreclaimable.

'The illustration upon the preceding page represents the Camp of a party of New South Wales Blacks after they have received the annual gift of blankets which it is usual to present to them on her Majesty's birthday. The tent-shaped erection is a gunyah, the nearest approach to a dwelling at which the Blacks of this region have arrived. It is formed of a few branches of wood, covered with sheets of the bark of the gum tree, which they strip off with remarkable ingenuity. The men are armed with spears, or the boomerang—that curious weapon which thrown at an enemy or game flies in an excentric direction, returning if required after striking to the feet of the thrower. This was long considered to be peculiar to Australia, until the discoveries at Nirevah proved that it was known to Nimrod and the Assyrians.

'The club, in native language a nullah-nullah, is equally employed in smashing out the brains of a fallen enemy and correcting a lazy or refractory wife. Bows and arrows are unknown to them.

'Those tribes which are not in receipt of blankets from the Government, still continue to manufacture very warm and beautiful cloaks of oppossum skin, which they wear with the hair side inwards, the other side ornamented with geometrical patterns drawn with wonderful accuracy. The opossum is to the Black what the raindeer is to the Laplander: the flesh is their food, the sinews make thread, and the skins are used not only for cloaks but for buckets or water-bags used in crossing deserts.

'The Correspondent who has favoured us with the preceding Sketch appends the following well-timed reflections: "The mysterious and wonderful arrangements of Divine Providence are brought forcibly to our minds on viewing the modes of life of this peculiar people, existing without a wish beyond hunting the forests, and living precariously on food which they obtain by climbing the immense gum-trees, wholly ignorant that at their roots the most precious metal has been concealed for thousands of years; generation after generation of Aborigines has passed away, unconscious of the riches concealed beneath the surface of their native hunting-grounds, perchance sufficient to have made them the most powerful race under the sun." '

From *The Illustrated London News*, April 24, 1852, p. 314.

Two thoughts (at least) may strike the reader of this newspaper item of colonial times. Bosjesmen—how extraordinarily low and irreclaimable these tribesmen must have been, to have surpassed Aborigines. And how tenacious racial prejudice appears when mid-nineteenth century attitudes are compared with those of present-day Australia. The reader is apt to conclude that racial prejudice, like adultery, is an aspect of human adjustment, and that there is no evidence that it can be eliminated. On the other hand, there is evidence that, when it is allowed to flourish, or perhaps become exploited for political or conquest purposes, there is a danger of a runaway spiral, of dire consequence for the victims and for the whole social system. Most readers of this book will assume that if the hazards of racial prejudice, especially its extreme forms, are self-evident, social violence is never far away.

The psychiatrist can offer no unitary explanation of racial prejudice. However, he can point out that those who feel that discriminatory attitudes have their origin in social and economic forces, or those who are optimistic that such attitudes will eventually yield to educative efforts, will be disillusioned. We do not fully understand ourselves. Unconscious forces easily outwit good intentions. A well-known illustration comes from the U.S.A. In a case-report titled 'Integration, the Supreme Obscenity,' Daniel B. Schuster M.D.[1] examines the double standard in the sexual attitudes of the white man in Southern U.S.A. Racial integration (black and white) in the South may imply incest, in which the black man represents the brutal, sexually attacking father and the white woman the pure, undefiled mother. The one who is 'different' can epitomize the desired but forbidden object, and evoke a variety of irrational and destructive behaviours.

This American instance is mentioned not to suggest that it is also characteristic of Australia, but to illustrate how prejudice is determined by individual factors operating outside of conscious awareness, as well as by social, economic and political factors. Prejudice is thus regulated by a network of forces. Two observations from everyday life in Australia should dispel the notion, at the outset, that prejudice towards Aborigines is a behavioral entity, subject to a unitary or linear cause, and amenable to a specific remedy.

The first observation is that prejudice is a highly variable feature of white-black relations in Australia. In country towns, for example, discriminatory attitudes tend to be less strongly held by transient residents (school teachers, bank officers, highway workers etc.) than by permanent residents. In mining towns such as Mount Isa, the miners often disprove prejudice by their altruism and perhaps by their reaction formations. They tend to kill

Aboriginal newcomers from the Missions with kindness and with alcohol, until they lose their jobs.

The second observation is that prejudice is not necessarily related to colour. Some of the severest prejudice against Aborigines can come from other Aborigines—witness the Lardil-Kaiadilt tensions of the 1950s and 60s in the Wellesley Islands of the Gulf of Carpentaria.[2] Even in the cities, prejudice does not invariably originate from the European side. Some Aborigines, anxious and confused, find it hard to distinguish who are their friends, and by the sweeping exercise of a self-fulfilling prophecy— concerning whites in general and the police in particular—generate enemies. Thus, a young self-styled 'Coori' in a Sydney meeting attacked and palpably wounded a dignified barrister noted for his efforts in court on behalf of Aborigines, with the justification that 'he needed to be educated what it's really like to be a Coori'.

Apart from these necessary intimations about the complexity of the psychological origins of prejudice, it is not my allotted task to expound its psychology. Instead, I am under a broad editorial instruction to make some observations on Aboriginal psychological responses to alien contact, and on the assumption that adaptational problems exist, to outline the social and psychiatric approach that may ameliorate some of these problems. One of the problems indeed concerns the means of influencing European-Aboriginal prejudice, to which I shall allude later in this chapter. Since there is no space to review the literature on Aboriginal stresses and symptoms, I shall restrict references for the most part to the field work from the Schools of Psychiatry in the University of New South Wales and Melbourne University. Valuable clinical work is going on in many centres, though it is predominantly concerned with physical health rather than psychological adjustment.

European Australians are trying to adjust to the idea that Aboriginal Australians are not a dying race after all—the latest vagary of an unpredictable people that has always baffled Europeans. Aboriginal character is particularly elusive, unless one has the opportunity and capacity of an A. P. Elkin,[3] a T. G. H. Strehlow[4] or an R. M. Berndt[5] to spend long periods in intimate association. Most European Australians fall back on stereotypes of Aborigines: shy and retiring; spontaneous and carefree; irritable and quarrelsome; lacking in foresight and stamina. Few Europeans have ever perceived the range of Aboriginal psychological adjustments to alien contact, including its pathological manifestations. In recent years, the School of Psychiatry of the University of New South Wales has sent teams of workers into the field using epidemiological and psychiatric techniques. Studies have been conducted into the extent of Aboriginal discomfort, drawing attention to the signs, symptoms and behavioral expressions of Aboriginal anxiety. Before describing these studies, however, it will be desirable to review briefly significant features of the setting in which anxiety occurs in this instance. It should also be pointed out that any theory of adaptation that emphasizes anxiety as a central concept around which all behavioral phenomena may be ordered, should be treated with caution. However, in this case, the opposite mistake is more likely: Western observers tend to be unaware that indigenous peoples are anxious because the manifestations differ from Western ones. The evidence to be reviewed suggests that Aboriginal anxiety is overlooked because it is expressed differently and experienced at a more disintegrating intensity.

The Aborigines' position in anthropological literature and the world's image generally is that of 'primitive' or 'stone age' man who has been un-successful in identifying with modern Western society. In a country which modern technology has transformed into a land of affluence and opportunity, they are at the bottom of the socio-economic scale. Poorly represented in trade, industry, commerce and the professions, they live in inferior and often squalid conditions. It cannot be said that they are 'on the march' in the manner of, say, New Guineans. The gathering perturbation of European Australians tends to polarize them into two quasi-political movements. The more radical movement attributes Aboriginal difficulties to oppression by European colonists—by plunder, murder and denial of human rights. The more conservative movement attributes difficulties to Aboriginal 'primitive-ness', to biological and social shortcomings and to the cultural gulf between Aborigines and Europeans. Both views are simplifications and carry the over-tones of racial conflict. Both views ignore questions raised by ecological. sociological and psychodynamic studies. For reformers, the diversity and complexity of these problems seem to throw a kind of pall over straight-forward remedial social action.

Demographic upheavals have some relevance to Aboriginal anxiety. Aborigines have been subject to severe population fluctuations. Around 300,000 are thought to have been in Australia when European colonization began in 1788, though how this estimate is formed is obscure. The response to European contact was not to decline but to plummet towards extinction. All were soon dead in Tasmania. Elsewhere in Australia the effect of intro-duced pathogens, bullets, poison, and subnutrition consequent upon dis-possession of lands and disruption of social organization was such that, before World War II, they were considered a dying race. The main task for Australians was to 'smooth the dying pillow'. But advances in public health measures—chief amongst several influences—reversed the decline, until today a phase of rapid population growth amounts to a population bulge in some places and an explosion in others. Censuses lead to an estimate of 120,000 Aborigines, one third full-blood, one third mixed-blood, one third of recognisable Aboriginal origins and social orientation, though not so identi-fied in the censuses. This represents only one per cent of the total Australian population, but a natural increase rate several times higher. Today's Aboriginal birthrate is about forty per 1,000 per year, becoming as high as fifty in some full-blood groups—almost as high a birthrate as ever reported for human society. In the Bourke community being studied from our School, it is substantially higher still. Bourke Aborigines could undoubtedly claim the world record for the rate of human increase—if anybody coveted this kind of record.

This resurrection itself vitally affects adaptation. In the centre and north of the subcontinent, the subordinate and disadvantaged Aboriginal popula-tion is not a minority one. These are the regions of the minerals industries that are pouring new wealth into Australia's economy, but offering little work for the indigenous populations. Though the Aborigines' poverty is not increasing, they are not sharing equally in the economic growth, so that the relative inequality may be increasing. These demographic and economic changes have further overthrown the family as a social system responsible for the training and emotional security of children, and as a social system articulating with society at large.

Aboriginal communities congregate at four points of culture contact, conveniently termed bush, outback, fringe and city.[6] Bush Aborigines live in detribalizing, multitribal clusters at Christian missions and government settlements in the north and centre; a few of them live at more remote outstations and still fewer remain semi-nomadic at least for part of the year. Outback Aborigines live in a relationship with the cattle industry as stockmen or housegirls. Fringe Aborigines, of mixed descent, live in shanty settlements on the outskirts of country towns, a few 'passing' into the town to assimilate with the Europeans. City Aborigines usually congregate in a few streets of the older slum suburbs of the capitals, having come from the country to look for work.

Although these different assemblages identify themselves as Aboriginal, it follows that there is not one Aboriginal social problem but many, not one Aboriginal social character but many, not one pathology but many. They share some themes such as cultural exclusion,[7] but the universality of such themes amongst Aborigines has been exaggerated by the stereotypers. A typically stereotyped trait is 'walkabout'—a pidgin term to describe the movements of a foraging horde around the countryside. Bush and outback Aborigines still 'walkabout' but for vacations and to visit relatives. In fringe-dwelling Aborigines, 'walkabout' reflects the changing location of the labour market for seasonal and unskilled workers. In some individuals it represents the vagabondage of the socially isolated man, reared in poverty, relieving tension by alcoholism and petty crime. Despite all these themes, the portmanteau word 'walkabout' survives in many an employer's mind as a characteristic of all manner of Aborigines and, to boot, one that diminishes their industrial capacity.

We may first direct our attention to 'bush' Aborigines. Since it is reasonable to suppose that adaptive difficulties existed before European colonization, it is unwarranted to relate all their difficulties to the alien contact. The role of the natural environment, especially the 'fluctuating abundance' should not be neglected. Comparative studies that match one Aboriginal group with another reveal how human adjustment is influenced by ecology.[8] An unsatisfactory human ecology is capable of producing social fragmentation that begets mental disturbance, that in turn begets more social fragmentation, in a downward spiral of malfunctioning. The overlooked question concerns the extent to which the adaptation of Aboriginal groups was always affected by the fluctuating abundance that is so conspicuous a feature of the ecology of Australia.

This group of Aborigines is deeply concerned with, and regulated by, sorcery. A series of complaints of sorcery that we studied clinically in their social contexts reveals that the effective agent is usually the victim, not the sorcerer. About a third of victims prove to be suffering from a physical disease such as tuberculosis, which they and their confrères interpret as sorcery. In another third, the victims are suffering from psychiatric conditions, their complaints of sorcery again serving as the culturally-regulated rationalization. In most of the other cases, there is an interpersonal conflict in which the accusation of sorcery has been levelled by the victim against an antagonist in order to manipulate the climate of opinion of the group—a kind of 'games people play'. In very few cases is there a transitive sorcerer—victim sequence of the 'classical' kind described by Aborigines, and recorded by those who accept what they say. This situation might be understood as an example of cognitive dissonance—tales of sorcery are oft repeated in order to reinforce their credibility. Clinical study of complaints of sorcery also reveals that they become more prevalent in situations of alien contact—rather than less prevalent as might have been expected. For example, they are often more common in 'outback' Aborigines, chiefly multi-tribal aggregations, than in more cohesive 'bush' communities. This suggests that social fragmentation affects the complaints of sorcery.

As a castaway clings to his upturned boat rather than swim for the distant shore, 'bush' Aborigines cling to folkways that give rise to grave social strains today. One such retention of Aboriginal customary law is polygyny in Arnhem Land. Baby girls are bestowed to a 'promise man' of the right marriage subsection. The system gives older men several wives of varied ages, but leaves wifeless perhaps half of the young men. Two factors, amongst others, made the system workable in former times: a surplus of women associated with high mortality in men, and ritual sexual sharing as in the Kunapipi ceremony. Male mortality and the Kunapipi have largely succumbed to European law and order, so that polygyny survives in what is now a functionally unbalanced state. The resulting conflict between peers, between families and especially between the older Aboriginal generation and the younger is well depicted in Kinship and Conflict.[9] Splits and coalitions associated with retention of now inappropriate cultural norms are the more troublesome to these Aborigines in that they offset their chances of local political union to achieve common purposes.

'Fringe' Aborigines are noted for their strong identity as Aborigines—even if they are half European—and for their cohesiveness as an outgroup to European society. This cohesiveness is further strengthened by the existence of the caste-barrier and by the strong Aboriginal pressures towards maintaining group obligations and loyalties.[10] However valuable this cohesiveness may be, it should not be assumed that Aboriginal families are necessarily integrated or that they provide a supportive system for the raising of children in today's world. The Aboriginal family as a childbearing system has undergone drastic alterations,[11] and the impact of these changes on character formation in children has been insufficiently studied.

A methodological innovation that sheds light on the relationship between the family, childbearing, and character, is the three-generation descent group study. In a study in Central Australia, we recorded psychiatric disorders in about thirty people in three generations of one descent group of the Walbiri. In this lineage, the older generation contained a concentration of aggressive personalities and paranoid states. The middle generation showed organic disorders of a kind that would have proved fatal in traditional life. The younger generation, with limited exposure to risk as yet, reveals a tendency towards schizophrenic disorders. This study suggests that an evolution in personality and personality disorders is taking place.[12]

This is not the place to discuss the psychiatric theory that it takes three generations to make a case of schizophrenia, but it should be pointed out that this Walbiri lineage, after about twenty years of culture contact, parallels in miniature the adaptational history of Aborigines towards the European colonists. The latter history may also be divided into three phases, with reactions resembling those in the Walbiri genealogy. In the initial phase, reaction was assertive with brief opposition. In the second, physical deterioration was the keynote, produced by introduced pathogens, sub-nutrition and disruption of effective cooperation between kin. In the third phase, with further fragmentation of family relationships, the characteristic features were withdrawal and failure to become involved in European society. It is fair to state that a fourth phase, now beginning, involves efforts by European Australians to 'rehabilitate' the Aboriginal family into a Western form through welfare pressures, medical care, education and socio-economic betterment. So far these efforts have had only limited success.

The unprecedentedly high fertility and survival rate recently bestowed by medicine and welfare, though splendid in some ways, has introduced a pathos to the situation that we noted on a recent medico-sociological expedition to Arnhem Land (1968). Thirty women of childbearing age were interviewed in one village, one at a time, using the vernacular language and under reasonable rapport—unusual conditions for such an enquiry. Sixteen were not aware that European women used techniques of postponing pregnancy. Fourteen said they knew this, but several had only learned it from the expedition members during this visit. Asked if they would like to use the European techniques, twenty-six said yes and four said no. Of the twenty-six who said yes, many were desperately eager to have some form of family planning and asked further questions. Some of the women interviewed were trying to stop having babies by sexual abstinence, others by magical methods, both traditional and idiosyncratic. These methods given an indication of cultural beliefs likely to affect clinical practice involved in the introduction of planned parenthood: 'Spread the milk of the narrawu tree on your menstrual rag . . . put your menstrual rag in a crab-hole . . . stop eating fish and honey . . . eat hot stones with your meat . . . cut up your placenta and throw it in the salt water . . . heat the wax from the *mayping* tree and sit on it during menstruation . . . to get rid of the baby tie cords tightly around your belly and hammer it hard . . .'

Because good rapport is usually lacking, Europeans who contact Aborigines fail to perceive the extent of their problems and fail to appreciate that Aborigines, in general, do not regard themselves as fit and healthy. They often communicate their complaints in a tersely 'coded' fashion that invites underdiagnosis. Our study in northern Queensland that went to the very considerable trouble of administering (in the vernacular) a modified Cornell Medical Inventory Health Questionnaire to a tribally oriented population produced striking results. Ninety-one per cent of the adult population was tested. There were five high peaks of complaints, concerned respectively with musculoskeletal pains, respiratory troubles, insomnia, lassitude, and anger. Musculoskeletal complaints were no surprise: the Aborigines' physique is better evolved for long distance walking than for lifting heavy objects. Respiratory complaints were predictable from the atmospheric conditions of dust and smoke, and the extreme diurnal temperature variations. The insomnia—surprising to observers who see Aborigines sleep during the day—reflects a crowded and disturbed sleeping environment and, in many cases, poor health, anxiety and depression. Lassitude came as no surprise, since it was known that this population is subject to hookworm infestation and to dietary uncertainty. Suppressed anger was understandable in a people little experienced in high density group living. What was perhaps surprising is the remarkable consistency of this complaint pattern in all the groups, though the highest levels of complaints were found in the older age groups, the women, and the more socially disadvantaged people.

In outback and fringe Aborigines, a set of symptoms not adequately recorded by questionnaire methods, and not complained of by the subjects themselves, is the tendency to alcoholism and gambling. These anxiety-reducing devices give rise to further difficulties that contribute to the downward spiral of malfunctioning. Where alcohol is not available in more protected Aboriginal communities, we find petrol sniffing is resorted to by bands of stimulus-hungry youths. Patterns of drinking have been described amongst fringe Aborigines.[13] Although alcoholism is found in many Aboriginal people, it is open to question whether it is more prevalent than in European Australians. What is clear is that Aborigines are less protected against its severe effects by their economy, by their social network and by the availability of medical services. In the crowded environment of slum, fringe or settlement, even a small number of alcoholics has a more disintegrative effect on the community in general.

Indeed, of all the changes enforced upon Aborigines by the alien contact, perhaps none is more disruptive than high density camp life, especially in people that normally spent only a small part of the year congregated together. Many of the traits commonly attributed to Aborigines may in fact be artefacts of camp life. Camps erupt in periodic brawls that often become riots involving most of the community, until the police intervene to carry off combatants to the lock-up. That these riots are not merely due to drunkenness is obvious, because they occur also on 'dry' missions and settlements. There they are put down to disputes over women. Whatever their origins, the riots are as disastrous for harmony in the camp as they are for the blackfellow's social image before the whitefellow. They feed white prejudice.

A few of these riots have been observed and recorded by us. Characteristically the spark that ignites the riot is a child. A child beats another, the defeated child's mother protests to the victor's and receives a blow with the fist, the husband retaliates with a stick, the relations and in-laws join in. Coalitions crystallize around old grievances. Soon there is a mélée of fifty people. Equally characteristically, between riots, the ethos of the community is one of tolerance and—especially—of evasion of confrontation. The popular Aboriginal 'ideal man' is often restrained, generous, a peacemaker who never confronts another with his grievances until these become serious. Thus he becomes the victim of the carping wife, the dependent relation, the forgetful borrower and the stealthy manipulator. Europeans see Aborigines as indecisive and lacking initiative. Observation of riots suggests that this is related to evasion of confrontation and to the necessity to consult group opinion rather than take an individual stand and so run the risk of group conflict. It is an ethos that puts Aborigines at a disadvantage with Europeans, who expect communication of a more direct kind, with irritability expressed but controlled.

The other important affliction of the European contact upon Aborigines today is impoverishment, associated with poor education and employability. The late Oscar Lewis' inferences on poverty as a culture which perpetuates certain character traits have an obvious attractiveness for some observers of Aborigines. Reared in poverty, it is comprehensible that their limited concept-formation and present-time orientation to life might prohibit mastery of the world of regular work, technology, education and affluence. A warning is in order. The 'culture of poverty' theory is, itself, in danger of becoming a rationalization that can inhibit social action directed against poverty. It is possible to apply the personality theory of poverty more strongly than Lewis himself intended. Middle-class observers who have not lived among extreme poverty may fail to appreciate the power of unsatisfiable want on those who do. Poverty is a yoke that the most capable man may not throw off. After repeated attempts at betterment, frustrated by debts, family expenses and uncertain employment, even the well-organized personality gives up. Those of us who have had the privilege of working among different sections of Aborigines remember best those sterling characters of whom this is a sadly true comment.

The Social Psychiatric Unit

In what follows, I outline a plan adapted to the needs of outback Australia, setting aside for the moment a consideration of urban problems, which are great enough, but in which I have limited professional experience. Firstly, in order to develop services adapted to the psychological needs of these Australian communities, health departments should contemplate a ring of psychiatric ecologists or field units around the margins of the outback. A psychiatric ecologist is one who gains a practical knowledge of the human hazards of his spatial zone. He provides some individual treatment, but his major role is to carry out mental health consultation with the helping professions such as schoolteachers, doctors, nurses, welfare officers, clergy, police and magistrates in order to enable them, within their limitations and according to their opportunities, to act to advantage in mental health. There are, as yet, no social psychiatrists trained to meet this dual responsibility in Australia, where the profession is young and the public demand is not explicit.

The needs of a scattered community cannot be met by the present practice of stationing a psychiatrist to receive referrals in the nearest base or city hospital. This 'expert' is not likely to come to grips with social disturbances some hundreds of miles away, when only the 'patient' is removed to his care. He is not part of the community, does not directly contribute to it, may not identify with it nor understand it, and may well be ignored by it.

A region that contains a population of 15,000 or more approximates to the social geographer's concept of a self-sustaining community: one that polarizes around a center capable of providing reasonable services for education, health and recreation, thus giving opportunities for reasonable social adjustment to the normal range of personality types. A ring of such communities runs around Australia through Mount Isa, Charleville, Longreach, Bourke, Broken Hill, Mildura, Port Augusta, Kalgoorlie, Port Hedland, Derby, Darwin and possibly Alice Springs. Psychiatry is part of the technology of establishing such communities, but only if it is ecologically sensitive, organized in social units. Our School's unit in Bourke, New South Wales, is a prototype.

The term 'human ecology' as used in connection with the adaptation of people to particular spatial environments contains a hint of euphemism. It evades the term 'psychiatry'. This is justified at the present time because 'psychiatry' is defensively perceived by some people as relating only to the asylum and its accompaniments in that epoch. The human ecology team, or social psychiatric unit, that we advocate consists of a general psychiatrist, a child psychiatrist and an anthropologist or social psychologist with clinical experience, applying their knowledge to the problems of health. Let us suppose, for purposes of illustration, that regular visits to the Mornington Island community in Queensland form part of the schedule of such a unit. The problems to which it would have to direct its attention may be illustrated from an actual visit by our team. (If I dwell on settlement Aborigines rather than on the other groups, it may be because I am convinced of their peculiar importance to the future of the country. In these regions, settlements have overnight turned into Aboriginal towns.)

Psychiatric First-Aid

Psychiatric first-aid at an Aboriginal settlement can suppress symptoms of disturbance, regardless of their origin. Some symptoms are self-evident to the layman, as in over-excited, restless, interfering behaviour; or in depressed, withdrawn, uncontributing behaviour; or in deluded, suspicious, unreasonable behavior. Frequently, however, psychiatric symptoms are camouflaged by a variety of disturbances of conduct, or by complaints of physical ill-health. A society fragmented by rapid social change may expect a higher incidence of symptoms, both overt and concealed. These disturbances can produce, in a feedback manner, further disruptive effects on family or village life. The Kaiadilt on Mornington Island illustrate how social fragmentation begets mental disturbance, and how mental disturbance begets further social fragmentation on a runaway spiral of malfunctioning. Yet many of these symptoms benefit from medication. The recently introduced tranquillizer and antidepressant preparations surpass in efficacy anything previously available. We have seen them decelerate these runaways. Their efficacy, like that of the surgeon's knife, spells danger; it should hardly be necessary to say they cannot be prescribed casually, without adequate knowledge of the individual, of the family and social group. Because of the scattered nature of the outback, it is obvious that these preparations must sometimes be placed in the hands of those who are not strictly qualified to use them, and who therefore need regular supervision of a psychiatric field unit in their use.

Mental Health Consultation

The Mission on Mornington Island has trained individuals in the supervision of village sanitation and similar matters. To what extent might councillors, village police or others of status be active in mental hygiene as well? We noticed the various opportunities during our sojourn on Mornington. The undercurrent of sorcery (puripuri) and spirit intrusion (malgri) provides one opportunity for mental health consultation. We found that a strong belief in these supernatural events correlates with neurotic symptoms. (Aborigines are not the only ones with a literal belief in these complaints. At one Mission, a European counteracts Aboriginal magic by constraining victims to hold the New Testament—logical behavior if sorcery is thought of as supernatural. Readers of accounts of sorcery in popular literature might have gained a similar misunderstanding of its nature.)

In every complaint of sorcery, there is an opportunity to discover the victim's grievance or sickness. Some Aborigines need only minimal prompting and encouragement to perceive that human problems underlie the supernatural complaint. If this opportunity is taken over a period of time, by those Aborigines and Europeans capable of doing so, it is probable that many sick people will get diagnosis, and that adherence to sorcery will weaken. Banishment tactics merely reinforce it, driving it underground where it flourishes and exerts a more disruptive influence on the society.

Council meetings designed to foster political awareness and experience provide another good opportunity. At the Council meetings on the Island, we saw *ad hoc* mental health consultation on community problems, though it was not, of course, identified in these terms. An example was the subordinate position of the Kaiadilt, who emigrated from Bentinck Island to Mornington Island, and who are socially disadvantaged and often discriminated against. They are described by the dominant Lardil with the familiar epithets heard in European society about its ethnic minorities. Most Lardil do not see this problem primarily as one of assimilation of Kaiadilt to Lardil. But after a characteristic 'race riot' a far-sighted Lardil spokesman, Prince Escott, proposed that everybody stop talking about 'Bentinck people' and use, instead, the term 'New Mornington Islanders'. Council discussed how to deal with racism on the Island. It seemed that the isolated enclave of the Kaiadilt at the edge of the main village perpetuated scapegoating and discrimination. A rearrangement of housing might offer a partial solution without further disorganizing the Kaiadilt. The existing gain from group cohesiveness amongst the Kaiadilt was minimal anyway. It was worth a judicious trial. Such pragmatic considerations form the agenda of mental health consultation which could be promoted by a field unit.

We usually have the co-operation of the Europeans connected with the community. The European nursing sister stationed at the Mission contributed her experience of local adjustment problems that greatly assisted our clinical examination. She expressed gratification at her improvement in insight and management as the result of her participation in the survey. The Aerial Medical Officer for the region, stationed at Mount Isa Base Hospital about 300 miles to the south, was in radio contact. This permitted discussion of disorders amenable to measures of the type called psychiatric first-aid. As an instance of collaboration between field team and Aerial Medical Service, an item of correspondence will serve.

'The Aerial Medical Officer,
Mount Isa Base Hospital,
'Dear Dr.:

'We are chiefly concerned to find out something about the psychological adjustment and to correlate this with cultural and economic circumstances. We are carrying out examining, questionnaires and inventories, and will let you have a copy of our findings. A few people were seen this week suffering from disturbances of a kind likely to be helped by pharmacological measures. Following the radio conversation with you we prescribed in some of these cases.

T.C.: Paranoid schizophrenia with nocturnal disturbances occasioned by fears and hallucinations. He benefits from Trifluoperazine 2 mgm. nocte.

Q.M.: Depressive state with hypochondriacal and suicidal preoccupations. Seems to be benefiting from Amitriptyline 50 mgm. t.d.s. If he still cannot be involved in some constructive activity (the Superintendent will make a special effort) we can arrange a period in Charters Towers for protection and rehabilitation-training.

I.O.: Epilepsy, observed in a grand mal seizure by one of us. Given Phenytoin 30 mgm. b.d.

N.H.: Transitory delusional state following first visit to mainland last year, said there to be schizophrenic. No evidence of schizophrenia in her present adjustment. Chlorpromazine reduced from 400 to 100 mgm. daily and could be suspended if she remains well on your next visit.

E.C.: Episodes of limb paralysis, undoubtedly conversion hysteria. The conflict centers around domesticity, childbearing and the present unwanted pregnancy. She could have oral con-

traceptive under Sister's supervision before her husband's
next annual visit.

U.B.: Eleven year old boy, regular bedwetter, likely to benefit from
Imipramine 25 mgm. nocte, could be raised to 50 mgm. if
necessary.

M.U.: Four year old child, diagnosed epileptic, given Phenytoin
30 mgm. b.d.

'There are also several periodically disturbed women whose
fertility has outrun their mothering and general coping capacity. In
the city we would normally prescribe oral contraceptive tablets, if
they requested. We discussed the situation with Sister and the Superintendent, and with their approval sent samples from drug houses,
about 24 months supply in all. These women include S.M. and F.C.
Regular supervision of tablet taking is of course the problem. You
might consider other family planning methods.

'Yours sincerely,

(Signed).'

Important as the relay of information between clinicians is, it is even
more important to impart orientation, guidance and instruction to the staff
of the Mission, including the schoolteachers. It is the staff who remain in
daily contact with the people and who have the best opportunity of acting to
their psychiatric advantage. This is the service of mental health consultation
that a visiting field unit might be expected to offer: not so much direct
advice, as ensuring that all available alternatives are carefully considered.

Anti-Institutionalism

An aspect of Island society highlighted by the Council meetings is its
institutionalism, using the term in its medical connotation. The community is
institutionalized after the manner of mental hospitals, prisoner-of-war camps
and sanatoria for chronic illnesses such as tuberculosis and leprosy. Effects
on the personalities of 'inmates' include apathy, loss of initiative and regres-
sion from attempts at self-sufficiency. Rowley[14] suggests that concentration of
Aborigines under authoritarian control in Missions, Government stations and
settlements serves the purposes of getting unwanted minorities out of the
way, affording them protection from immoral influences outside and
influencing their attitudes and conduct within. He considers that the institution system possesses great inertia, because managers of such institutions,
forced to look to head office for advancement and promotion, follow the
objectives of frugality, avoidance of 'trouble' and optimistic reports, rather
than of the initiative and independence of the inmates.

Psychiatry is slowly and, on the whole, successfully engaged in overcoming its own institutionalization in the asylums of a previous era, sometimes abolishing these establishments and, where this is not yet economically
possible, employing social techniques inside and outside. These techniques
include group development through meetings and activities, with augmented
contact with the community at large. The experience gained in this movement could speed the process for others. On the Island, for example, it is
important to determine whether the pattern that we noted of avoidance of
confrontation and periodical riots is an Aboriginal characteristic, or the
expected result of nomadic factions learning to live in a permanent camp, or
an artefact of institutionalism.

Mother and Child

Fundamental to the development of character are the early transactions between mother and child. The relationship between mother and child on the Island is affectionate and indulgent, but in the conditions prevailing, insufficiently organized around the child's informal instruction. It affords poor socialization and preparation for school and industrial life. Pre-school training is essential if the child is to gain more from this initial period. The young mother and her infant form a diad that should have the opportunity of being involved in drawing, reading, writing and spoken English. Infants, in this way, would receive better reinforcement than at home, with less regressive pull by the family away from westernization. Conduct of the kindergarten should be the task of young Aboriginal women trained in the work. This training should be carried out in groups, because our experience shows that Island girls sent away singly for training are threatened by the cultural shock and nostalgia, and some have been subject to psychiatric breakdown. Dr. Barry Nurcombe's pre-school in the Bourke project seems an excellent model, aspects of which should be widely copied.[15]

Aboriginal wives and mothers face many difficulties in their status climb relative to husbands, and in their occupational change, but none more threatening than their recently acquired overfertility. As pointed out, where we have succeeded, in the medical setting, in breaking the barrier to communication, we find that these wives resent their fertility and would prefer to control it. The impression apparently gained by Europeans that settlement women enjoy having another baby every year, is a defensive fable. Contraceptive assistance should be available for Aboriginal women on request, as it is for their Western sisters, bearing in mind that oral hormones require daily regularity and that the intra-uterine device is a more practicable method.

The interest of the child psychiatrist is not confined to the pre-school years. He can help protect the teacher's sensitivity to individual differences. One of the teacher's tasks is to detect the innovator or emulator, the somewhat rare Aboriginal personality type that can accept change. Our tests show that this trait exists in varying degrees; once the flame is found it should be fanned. Two contrasting techniques of teaching involve respectively the criticism of errors and the reinforcement of successes. Our strong impression is that Aboriginal children tolerate the former technique poorly. Yet it is the very method one frequently hears in Aboriginal classrooms. The angry criticism and sarcasm of a teacher is probably less a technique to achieve compliance and increased effort, than his response to overwhelming burdens imposed by his task. It seems to me that Aboriginal classes should be only half the size of European, not twice as large as is often the case in my experience. Teachers then might be able to concentrate better on teacher support/approve behavior than on desist/disapprove behavior. In such an atmosphere of award, student attentiveness should increase.

Training Transcultural Workers

Application of mental health principles is limited in this difficult situation by the availability of trained workers. Psychiatry has been effectively represented in most Australian Universities only in the past decade or less. It takes at least ten years to train a matriculated student to be a psychiatrist—more for a child psychiatrist or a social psychiatrist. It is not surprising if transcultural psychiatry is as yet poorly represented, because it involves further anthropological experience and regional exposure.

Those who work in this field have an obligation to ensure that their knowledge and experience is transmitted in University teaching. I have often stated a view that transcultural psychiatry should be regarded as part of the technology of social change at the interface of the culture contact in this part of the world. The dominant European society needs education and information just as much as the subordinate minority. This teaching should be a responsibility of a modern University, and of other centres for the training of potential field workers such as Teachers' Colleges, Police Colleges and Technological (trade-training) Institutes. At the present time, many University curricula represent almost any exotic area of study in preference to this one.

Public Information and Misinformation

Better information is needed on the present extent and influence of racial prejudice in Australia. Some prejudicial ideas are being offset by a growing spirit of liberalism and interest in alternative hypotheses. A few may fade with better public education. One would expect, for example, that the 'dying race' concept of Aborigines, acceptable before World War II, cannot survive many more years in the face of published population statistics, or the evidence of tourists' own eyes in central and northern communities where the rate of growth is so fast. The 'quite happy' misconception of Aborigines is a defensive denial of problems by Europeans, perhaps in part fostered by the Aborigines' capacity for spontaneous gaiety and their apparent unconcern with middle-class values; it can scarcely withstand information of the sort now available. The 'send them back to the bush' idea should die, if only because there is no bush left to which to send them. The truth is that there is no return to an aboriginal culture possible for Aborigines, and if health and growth is the aim, there can be no standing still in the present marginal society. The 'lazy, unreliable, gone walkabout off the job' idea associates the undeniable industrial inefficiency with nomadism, in which hard work is intermittent between periods of idleness. The better substantiated hypothesis is that industrial inefficiency is associated with poor education and the values imparted by the culture of poverty, and that these personality traits have much to do with training and environmental opportunity, so limited for Aborigines.

Racial prejudice is infinitely resourceful. The 'biologically inferior' conviction interprets the 'childlike mind' and social evidence of inferiority, as arising from biological endowment rather than from social circumstances. The fact is that there has been very little scientific study of racial differences in performance or in potential. Even the term 'primitive' conveys to ethnocentric people the idea that Aborigines represent in an evolutionary sense some lower species of hominoid. The more reasonable hypothesis is that the Australian Aborigine is modern man, whose technological retardation is accounted for by millennia of isolation from the remainder of mankind, and by the poor natural opportunities for the development of agriculture offered by this continent. The 'biological equality' hypothesis is admittedly more acceptable to those who have had the opportunity to live with tribally-oriented people and to admire the complexity of their environmental knowledge and their systems of art, religion and kinship. Man for man, such Aborigines often have a better knowledge and involvement in the arts than the Europeans having the chance to observe them.

Mental Health Implications of 'Assimilation'

Whenever and however 'the Aboriginal problem' is aired, a comment on the official Australian policy of 'assimilation' is inevitable. Is the 'assimilation' programme a syndrome of racism? The official policy towards Aborigines, stated in 1951 and fairly widely accepted by the community, has an object described as assimilation and is intended to ensure that

> 'all Aborigines and part-Aborigines are expected eventually to attain the same manner of living as other Australians and to live as members of a single Australian Community, enjoying the same rights and privileges, accepting the same responsibilities, observing the same customs, influenced by the same beliefs, hopes and loyalties as other Australians.'

At the time this policy was enunciated, it was considered the most desirable of the various alternatives, including integration and segregation, since more than two-thirds of the Aborigines were 'either detribalized or well on the way to losing their tribal life'. Whatever its demerits, it is an unequivocal rejection of apartheid by the Australian law. Objections to the policy were voiced in Aboriginal and other quarters, so that, in 1965, the statement of the policy was significantly altered to include the possibility of free choice by Aborigines in the matter:—

> 'The policy of assimilation seeks that all persons of Aboriginal descent will choose to attain a similar manner and standard of living to that of other Australians and live as members of a single Australian community'.

These policy statements were adopted by a Conference of Commonwealth and State Ministers concerned with Aboriginal welfare and incorporated into the aims of the various regional administrations.

The protagonists of the policy of 'integration'—including many Aborigines—sought support for the concept that Aborigines should retain their identity by continuing to live in Aboriginal groupings but seeking to raise progressively their economic and educational status to that of European-Australian society. The debate between the supporters of 'assimilation' and 'integration' became heavily charged with theoretical and semantic difficulties and tends to obscure that what is really taking place in much of Australia is a third alternative, one that very few people officially favour—segregation. Instead of assimilation or integration we are witnessing the perpetuation of a disadvantaged, culturally deprived, subordinate minority without the skills or opportunity for satisfactory employment or social betterment.

The policies of assimilation or integration could be considered satisfactory from the point of view of the mental health of Aborigines—if either were attainable. The same cannot be said for the actuality, segregation, fraught with the dangers of social tension. Australian society might apply the warning of Harvard's James B. Conant[16] concerning the under-employment of early school leavers and their subsequent life in the slums: 'I am convinced we are allowing social dynamite to accumulate in our cities'. If segregation is taking place, it is because economic and social reality is frustrating the intentions of the official policy of assimilation. Economic and social reality determine that the Aborigine does not, in fact, possess freedom of choice to assimilate into European society. This has led to earnest criticism of the official policy:—

'if we couch our policy in wide and glowing terms but at the same
time refuse to extend to the Aboriginal people the means by which
they may accomplish the same objectives as other Australians, then
the policy may be rightly written off as a sham.'[17]

The point of remedial application is sometimes placed at the population
level, sometimes at the level of national policy. Rowley[18] sees it as a fundamental gap in the background, purpose and intention of our native policy
which, if not closed, will continue to frustrate all those engaged in native
welfare programmes. Schapper[19] sees the centralization of Aboriginal welfare
duties within a single government department as a terrible mistake which
will delay advancement and the narrowing of the socio-economic gap. Such
centralization conveniently removes onus and initiative from powerful
government departments such as Health, Education, Labor and Social
Services.

After Medicine, the Law

The reader is justified in feeling that the more powerful social institutions in the European-Australian order have scarcely begun to think about
the culture contact. Social psychiatry has a contribution, but as with the
other welfare institutions, effort will be ephemeral unless backed by the law
of the land. Since loss of property rights and economic, educational and
social disadvantage have arisen from inadequate legal safeguards for the
native occupants of Australia in the early phases of colonization, it seems
now that nothing but radical and imaginative legislation can redress the
situation. Tasks of this magnitude in health, education and economic opportunity require the active and informed support of the country as a whole; in
Western society this is only likely to be expressed through legal enactment,
and not through charitable intention.

The medical profession has been little interested in the social adaptation
of Aborigines, and, possibly for this reason, feels free to point the finger at
another professional group that has been just as undistinguished. With some
notable exceptions, the legal profession—especially those lawyers who are
also legislators or influence legislators—have not espoused the cause of this
disadvantaged minority. Mr. D. A. Dunstan, a lawyer who has been Premier
of the State of South Australia, caused to be enacted legislation likely to
improve Aboriginal land title and employment in that State. In this way, an
attempt was made to retrieve the original intentions of the South Australian
Company to find a political expression of J. S. Mill's moral philosophy. While
each State and Territory of Australia has its own policy, work is done piecemeal through a variety of organizations—political, social welfare, trade
union, church and cultural. The Federal Council for the Advancement of
Aborigines represents a majority of these organizations, but not necessarily
Aboriginal opinion. Aboriginal opinion is not necessarily developed or cohesive. The influence of the Government Office of Aboriginal Affairs, created
after the 1966 Referendum on Aborigines, is awaited rather wistfully by
many. These who apply successfully for the funds which it controls are
grateful for its patronage. Whatever the organization, it is emphasized that
further legislation is needed now to promote the systematic advantage of
Aborigines—in health, education and economy.

One arrangement encouraging to individual Aborigines is a legal aid
service, conducted by lawyers along the lines of the California Rural Legal
Assistance Agency (C.R.L.A.). A beginning has been made with the legal

aid service in Redfern, Sydney, instigated by Professor J. H. Wotten, Dean of the Faculty of Law in the University of New South Wales. An ombudsman to study the growing complaints against officialdom would also serve a useful purpose. The active interest of the legal profession in these areas would materially assist Aborigines and the small army of European workers trying to pave the way for them. But these techniques, in some ways, try to repair a machine that has become obsolete, although the encouragement they offer to Aborigines cannot be underestimated.

Marginal Estate Legislation

If a social psychiatrist were asked to advise guidelines for legal enactments, he would begin by trying to define the problem in an operational manner. Let us say that the basic problem is the emergence of numerically strong ethnic communities that are socially and culturally disadvantaged. Many of the settlements, missions, and reserves that are turning overnight into 'towns' already contain more than a thousand souls. City enclaves are also growing. The reciprocal problem is that legislation based on the assimilation principle, though an advance on what went before, is not adapted to this changing situation, and may now lead to a piecemeal 'patching-up' application and a false sense of public security. Many people now think that Conant's 'social dynamite' is accumulating in these communities. Unless the Australian public can be educated to accept a more systematic and more costly policy, it will have to stand by and watch the rise of large poverty-stricken communities (large, thanks to public health) in regions of low economic opportunity. In these communities, thousands upon thousands of children are growing up excluded from European culture, deprived of Aboriginal culture, educationally disadvantaged, with low industrial potential.[20] If opportunities do not improve these children will have no alternative but to become second class citizens, the forefathers of an apartheid that nobody wants and everybody fears.

In order to combat these trends, 'marginal estate' type of legislation is advocated for these communities, supplying teeth to existing provisions. Described succinctly, marginal estate laws are designed to promote successful adaptation in a defined region. They observe certain principles:—

(i) *Structure and Intent.* Under such an Act, a State or Territory of the Commonwealth could declare a district or community a marginal estate if it fails to attain certain economic criteria. The criteria are not to be defined ethnically. During a period of declaration (to be reconsidered at intervals of five years) the State Government, enabled by supporting Federal grants, would require its departments to spend higher than their normal budget in these areas. This would permit heightened activity by Education, Health and Mental Health, Housing, Child Welfare, Labour and Industry, Decentralization and the other Departments concerned. A rough analogy may be found in 'Drought Relief' provisions. The increased expenditure is not channeled through Aboriginal Welfare, in order to avert the familiar danger of paternalistic control; but Aboriginal Welfare, working with representatives of the community has the vital liaison and advisory function.

(ii) *The Principle of Self-Regard.* If mental health is defined in terms of personal comfort and social efficiency, it is axiomatic that enough self-regard must be built into the personality and then sustained by the environment. Self-regard is normally learned during early socialization of the child from introjection of positive parental attitudes, but however well or ill this

process goes, it may be threatened by too much adversity in maturity. Many
Aborigines detect elements adverse to their self-regard in the assimilation
policy itself. They want better conditions and opportunities, but are hurt by
the emphasis on community absorption or dispersal. They want the chance to
participate in any local planning that affects them, so that it is important that
marginal estate legislation should offer it them. Such legislation should
should emphasize consultation between the community and the administering officials and organizations.

(iii) *The Principle of Reward.* The direction taken by the expenditure
is extremely important for personality development. Money has to be spent
not merely on the provision of services, but on their efficient delivery,
especially in the case of education and health. Money going to individuals in
the form of pensions should be kept to a minimum, in favour of rewards for
performance. The principle of immediate reward, or operant conditioning, is
one of the most potent means of changing disorganized behavior. Where
this principle is neglected, intractable neurotic and personality disorders
result. Where it is systematically applied, even conditions such as stuttering
may respond dramatically to the situation of immediate reward. The
individual becomes the operant of his own conditioning.

(iv) *The Principle of Health.* Enough has been said here of the limited
appreciation, by both Europeans and Aborigines, of the low levels of fitness
in Aboriginal communities. Many studies have demonstrated the prevalence
of enervating if not disabling morbidity. Our own studies have demonstrated
a generally parallel course of symptoms of personal discomfort and social
inefficiency. Australia has good health services, but in these communities
various barriers oppose their delivery. The training of peer-related health
aides, such as we are trying to accomplish at Bourke (I do not mean
'hygiene assistants') may bypass some barriers. The field psychiatric unit,
previously described, is another component of improved health care delivery
that Australia has scarcely begun to think about. Since education is an
essential aspect of psychological fitness for modern society, education and
training in all age groups must be greatly advanced. The language-stimulus
technique developed at our School's pre-school in Bourke, conducted as a
research project by Dr. Barry Nurcombe, has demonstrated such gains that
there seems little reason for not adopting such techniques more generally.[21]
Little reason, that is, except the availability of money and organization of the
kind envisaged in marginal estate legislation, or its equivalent.

(v) *The Principle of Community Development.* As already noted,
many communities are so beset by factions and coalitions that there is little
likelihood of cohesive social action. It is hard to find a hundred Aborigines to
agree on anything. This is probably an inevitable phase of emergence from
the chaos of extremely rapid social change and disintegration. Despite this, it
is our experience that the catalytic effect of a skilled social change agent in
a community produces worthwhile achievements, which add greatly to community development and to *amour propre.* Obvious and easy projects should
be undertaken first, to lessen the discouragement of failure. Examples are the
small trade store on the reserve selling non-perishable goods at wholesale
prices, or the reserve-operated mini-bus that competes with the prestigious
but disastrously costly town taxi-service. Enterprises of this kind keep the
money (often from child endowment cheques) circulating longer in the
community, instead of disappearing smartly into European pockets. The
principle of the social change agent has received only elementary scrutiny in

Australia. It seems an important principle of marginal estate legislation, which operates a planned economy for the region, with a five year plan within a twenty year plan for that community.

Where community development is manifestly impossible because of lack of local resources, resettlement must be considered. It should usually be family resettlement of a whole primary group, rather than individual emigration to places of better employment. This requires high levels of organization and support over a period of years, if it is not to fail. The New South Wales Department of Decentralization, for example, if it were to promote such movements, might have to be restructured into a Department of Regional Development, as in Canada.

❆   ❆   ❆   ❆

In this paper there has been space only for the barest possible outline of these proposals. Marginal estate legislation, wherever proposed, will elicit some indignant responses.

Does not this legislation discriminate in favour of Aborigines? Of course; this is essential if discrimination against them is eventually to be neutralized or modified. If Australia were to undertake a systematic and expensive programme for Aboriginal advancement, will there not be racial conflict in the future? Of course; racial conflict is part of human nature, so long as people think in terms of 'we' and 'they'. White and black Australians can only do all that is possible to diminish the present inequality of opportunity, and afterwards live with the conflict.

The world is full of crusaders. The practical contributions to social reform usually have to await the study of the problem in breadth and depth. It is my view that social psychiatry can make a contribution to the definition of the problem. Its role has been described in more forceful terms by Margetts[22] in Canada.

'Apart from the interest and study value offered by clinical psychiatry in faraway lands, the tabulation of our psychological knowledge about all people has two practical aims. The first is the *promotion* of improved methods of case-finding and clinical care around the world. The second is an emphasis on how to stay healthy, and even alive. Unchecked individual and secondary mass psychopathology could destroy the human race.'

ACKNOWLEDGEMENT

Some of the material quoted in this chapter is reprinted by permission from Cawte, John (1971) *Cruel, Poor and Brutal Nations,* University of Hawaii Press; and from Cawte, J. E. (1969) 'Psychological Adjustment to Cultural Change', in *Studies of Anxiety,* Ed. by A. Stoller and B. Davies, *Australian and New Zealand Journal of Psychiatry,* Vol. 3, No. 3a.

REFERENCES

1 SCHUSTER, D. B. (1969), Integration, the Supreme Obscenity: a Case Report. Paper at Fall Meeting, The American Psychoanalytic Association, New York City, abstracted in *Psychiatric Spectator,* V. III, No. 3.

2 CAWTE, JOHN (1971), *Cruel, Poor, and Brutal Nations.* University of Hawaii Press.

3 ELKIN, A. P. (1954). *The Australian Aborigine; How to understand them.* Third Edition. Angus and Robertson, Sydney.

62   The Parameters of Conflict

4 STREHLOW, T. G. H. (1947). *Aranda Traditions.* Cheshire, Melbourne.

5 BERNDT, R. M. (1951). *The influence of European culture on Australian Aborigines.* Oceanie V xxi, 3.

6 STANNER, W. E. H. 1968.

7 BRODY, E. B. (1966). *Cultural Excursion, Character and Illness.* Amer. J. Psychiat., 122, 152.

8 CAWTE, op. cit.

9 HIATT, L. (1965). *Kinship and Conflict. A study of an Aboriginal Community in Northern Arnhem Land.* Australian National University, Canberra.

10 FINK, RUTH A. (1957). *The Caste-Barrier. An obstacle to the assimilation of part-Aborigines in northwest New South Wales.* Oceania, V. 28, No. 2, 100-110.

11 BECKETT, J. (1965). *Kinship, Mobility and Community among Part Aborigines in Rural Australia.* Int. J. Comparative Sociol. V. 6, No. 1 1-23.

12 CAWTE and KIDSON (1965). *Ethnopsychiatry in Central Australia II. The Evolution of Illness in a Walbini Lineage.* Brit. J. Psychiat. 111, 1079.

13 BECKETT, J. (1964). *Aborigines, Alcohol and Assimilation.* In Aborigines Now, ed. Marie Reay, Angus and Robertson, Sydney.

14 ROWLEY, C. D. (1966). Some questions of causation in relation to Aboriginal affairs. In *Aborigines in the Economy,* ed. by I. G. Sharp and C. M. Tatz. Brisbane, Jacaranda Press.

15 MOFFITT, P. and NURCOMBE, B. (1971). Intervention in Cultural Deprivation: The Comparative Success of Pre-school Techniques for Rural Aborigines and Europeans. *Australian Psychologist,* March.

16 CONANT, J. B. (1964). *Slums and suburbs.* New York, New American Library.

17 STEVENS, F. S. (1966). The role of coloured labour in North Australia. In *Aborigines in the Economy,* ed. by I. G. Sharp and C. M. Tatz, Brisbane, Jacaranda Press.

18 ROWLEY, C. D. (1962). *Aborigines and other Australians.* Oceania 32, 247-266.

19 SCHAPPER, H. P. (1968). *Administration and welfare as threats to Aboriginal Assimilation.* Austral. J. Social Issues, V. 3: 4, 3-8.

20 'Children of Arnhem Land' (1968, University of New South Wales School of Psychiatry, by John Cawte and Douglass Baglin, 22 mins. colour, sound) is a documentary depicting this situation for one such community, adopted as a training film by the N.S.W. Department of Welfare.

21 NURCOMBE, B. and MOFFITT, P. (1970). Cultural Deprivation and Language Defect, *Australian Psychologist.* Vol. 5, No. 3, p. 249.

22 MARGETTS, E. L. (1965). *Transcultural Psychiatry.* Editorial in Canadian Psychiatric Association Journal. V. 10, No. 2.

SYSTEMS OF PREJUDICE

5

ABORIGINES AND THE POLITICAL SYSTEM

P. Tobin

'Australia has been won by a hundred years of bloodshed'
—*an old Queensland squatter*[1]

AN OVERT SYSTEM

1 A Colonial System

For the Black man in Australia, there is a system—the White System, an indifferentiated white totality wherein he has no place and whereby he is suppressed. The over-riding reality is his blackness or, at the very least, his non-whiteness. In such colonial situations, it must be understood that 'what parcels out the world is to begin with the fact of belonging to or not belonging to a given race, a given species'.[2] Does Australian experience reveal the 'predication of decisions and policies on considerations of race for the purpose of subordinating a racial group and maintaining control over that group?'[3] Has such policy been expressed at institutional and individual levels of activity? It is the attempt to consider the Aboriginal perspective, rather than the assumptions of the White Australia world view, that is crucial to any assessment of the relationship between Aborigines and White Australia.

The institutionalization, restraint and imprisonment of Aborigines on reserves and mission stations effected a straight-jacketing of Aboriginal resistance to the enforced terms of white settlement, shackling them from the time of Cook's illegal proclamation of sovereignty[4] onwards. To formalize the situation, the Protection and Welfare Acts of the various states were passed, instituting systems of control by white managers, welfare officers, missionaries and police. In these circumstances, resistance 'could be expressed only through non-co-operation with authority, affront to middle class mores, withdrawal, or small scale acts of defiance (usually in country towns or Aboriginal institutions)'.[5]

Similar patterns of tribal administration appeared in Africa, India, the United States and Canada, where other indigenous peoples were restricted, geographically, to segregated reserved areas by English-speaking conquerors.[6] This sub-system of British colonialism riding the imperative to 'Take up the White Man's burden/... To serve your captive's need/... Your new caught, sullen peoples/half-devil and half-child'[7] was to aim at the destruction of indigenous culture and social organization and to break down communal land holding systems. Its inability to accommodate demands for indigenous communalism and the threat to it of such demands is still current in the Gurindji and Yirrkala land rights struggles and Aboriginal land rights generally, in Bougainville, and in the reluctance of the Commonwealth to give capital grants to co-operative ventures. Submission to these demands

65

would threaten notions of Crown sovereignty of land, and theories of private
ownership and capitalist economic relations, so that only individual ownership can be tolerated. Mr. Justice Blackburn, in the recent Northern Territory
Supreme Court case of Milirrpum and Others v. Nabalco Pty. Limited and
the Commonwealth of Australia, summed up the situation succinctly:—

> 'a principle which was a philosophical justification for the coloniza-
> tion for the territory of less civilized peoples: that the whole earth
> was open to the industry and enterprise of the human race, which had
> a duty and the right to develop the earth's resources. The more
> advanced peoples were therefore justified in dispossessing, if neces-
> sary, the less advanced'.[8]

Likewise, the dominance of white ideas had to be established and, to this
end, it was found that tribal religions were too 'barbarous' to be allowed to
flourish regardless of their sophistication or humanitarian idealism.

Accordingly, Aboriginal people were to be presented with a social over-
view in which their place was defined for them by their conquerors.[9] The
totality of the white presence and experience seemed unshakeable, and its
hegemony over ideas was to preclude the development of a pan-Aboriginal
consciousness which could explain their subject position. It may be that, only
out of their struggle for justice, will the Aboriginal people re-define themselves in their own terms and develop the revolutionary consciousness necessary to counter the white world view and establish their own social dynamic.
Symptomatic of this Eurocentrism, has been the currency of such concepts as
'intelligent parasitism' to describe the life style thrust upon a decimated
people,[10] and earlier notions, both popular and academic, that Aborigines
represented the lowest living form of human life.

'Divide and rule' was another British colonial device availed of in
Australia. In some cases, the remnants of mutually hostile or foreign tribes
were placed together on the same reserve or mission to counteract each other
and to divert attention away from the administration. Another variant of this
technique appeared in the form of the Black or Native Police first formed in
New South Wales in 1842, and still in force today on reserves in Queensland.
One instance of its practice was the formation in 1848 of a New South Wales
Native Police Force raised for the Middle District, and to be under white
officers. The Commandant, Captain Frederick Walker, recruited in the south,
from four different tribes, each speaking a different language, and employed
them in the north against tribes which were quite foreign to them.[11] Governor
Sir George Gipps viewed the formation of the Native Police with the hope
that subjection to military discipline would prove advantageous to the civilization of the race.[12]

2 New South Wales

From August, 1824, to December, 1824, martial law was proclaimed by
Governor Brisbane west of Mount York, over conflict between 'natives and
settlers'. By 1881, New South Wales had appointed a Protector and, in 1883,
a Board for the Protection of Aborigines. After the passing away of the
policies of extinction, 'smoothing the dying pillow', an authoritarian paternalism prevailed under the New South Wales Aborigines' Protection Act,
1909-63. The Protection Board later changed its name to the Aborigines
Welfare Board in 1943, signifying a change in policy, and was abolished in
June, 1969, being replaced by the Provisions of the Aborigines Act, 1969.
Under the old Act (1909-36) s. 4 (1), the Commissioner of Police was

Chairman of the Protection Board. The police officers in country towns were responsible to the Protection Board for the good behaviour of the Aborigines in the reserves. Under s. 8, police, as 'officers under the Board', were given the right to enter a reserve while s. 19 classified police specifically as agents of the Board with the right of inspection. They were thus able to enter people's homes at will (as persons acting under the Board's direction) and intimidate the Aboriginal inhabitants (as police officers). Despite various amendments the statutory position remained similar until 1969. Writing of this state of affairs in 1955, with respect to the settlement nine miles out from Brewarrina, North-West New South Wales, it was noted that the 'officers entered and inspected Aborigines' houses unannounced and uninvited, interfered in domestic quarrels and suppressed behaviour not in keeping with European standards. The people sometimes referred to the old Protection Board as the 'Persecution Board'.[13] Reserve managers and police worked in close liaison, leaving little recourse to outside agencies for any Aborigine bold enough to question either administration or law.

Reaction to official policy resulted in the formation of various Aboriginal rights organizations made up of both Aborigines and whites. The names of these organizations were to reflect the changing fashion and emphasis in Aboriginal affairs, ranging from the official policies of protection, preservation and welfare to the later partisan policies of advancement and Aboriginal rights (to be followed through, perhaps in the 1970s, by Aboriginal liberation). In 1911, the white academic Association for the Preservation of Native Races was formed, and, in 1927, Ted Maynard's Australian Aborigines Protection Association appeared which, in particular, concerned itself with the abolition of the Aboriginal child apprenticeship system in which children were subject to sweatshop conditions of child labour. The Australian Aborigines League was formed in Melbourne in 1932, and, in 1937, one of its Aboriginal members, William Cooper, organized a petition for an Aboriginal representative in Parliament, and, in 1938, a 'Day of Mourning' was held. Sydney saw the formation, in 1937, of the Aborigines Progressive Association which was to involve Aboriginal leaders like Bill Ferguson, Pearl Gibbs, Bert Groves and others[14] who were to become the earliest of the Aboriginal representatives on the reconstituted Welfare Board. This upsurge in Aboriginal consciousness was deadened, some Aborigines say, by the intervention of World War II. Reports of meetings of up to ninety Aborigines at La Perouse Reserve, Sydney, with representatives from all over New South Wales gathering under the old fig tree, are available. Petitions, deputations and detailed submissions to the State Parliaments were made. A Committee for Aboriginal Citizenship Rights was formed in New South Wales in 1938, but disbanded in 1943 when its organizers felt that, with the new Welfare Board, its job had been done. Smaller, scattered church and welfare organizations existed but few ventured into the realms of Aboriginal rights and self-determination. The Aboriginal Fellowship, organized in Sydney in 1956, was to merge with other groups in 1958 to form the first national Aboriginal rights organization, the Federal Council for the Advancement of Aborigines and Torres Strait Islanders (F.C.A.A.T.S.I.). This Council was chiefly responsible for the successful Federal referendum held in 1967, which gave Aborigines full citizenship rights. Since then, the National Tribal Council has been formed in several states and, as an all Aboriginal body, had the potential, notably in Queensland, to form the militant and dynamic wing of the Aboriginal movement.

3 Queensland—A Contemporary Colonial Model

In Queensland, the pattern has been similar. Reserves holding over 1,000 people are common. The now infamous Aborigines and Torres Strait Islanders Affairs Act (1965) enacted a virtual policy of apartheid, dividing people into assisted or non-assisted categories as rough indications of those who lived on or off reserves.[15] Assisted Aborigines continue to have the full weight of the Act, Regulations and By-laws upon them, a trinity which renders their life entirely dependent upon the Director of the Queensland Department of Native Affairs and his reserve managers. Native Police, under Regulations 67-9, enforce policy and petty regulations, often as muscle men, being allowed a few personally extracted gratuities. Many people on reserves are thus frightened into silence. Reserve councils are supposedly vested with some autonomy and initiative in decision making, but save for a few individual councillors, are usually under the direct control of the manager.[16] By-laws are to be made by such councils from time to time as they see fit (s. 46 [1] A.T.S.I.A. Act) though subject to ratification from the Director (s. 46 [8]). In practice, a roneoed departmental set of by-laws is circularized to the reserves with blank spaces on the front, left for the name of the individual reserve and relevant dates of acceptance and ratification.

Apart from pre-existing restrictions on an assisted Aborigine's rights of assembly, movement, free speech, wages, working conditions and standing at law, the by-laws under s. 46 (1) give the reserve council the functions of local government on the reserve. Such by-laws include—Chapter 3, s. 4: formal requirements for reporting to work; Chapter 1 (a): no person shall consume intoxicating liquor or (h) gossip causing domestic trouble or annoyance; Chapter 6, s. 4: no person shall urinate or defecate except in toilets provided, nor s. 5, expectorate on the footpath or any building; Chapter 23, s. 1: there shall be no public functions unless prior approval is obtained from the Council after prior consultation with the Manager; Chapter 24, s. 1: no person shall practice or pretend to practice sorcery including bone-pointing and pourri-pourri—such offender may be removed from the reserve/community. The continued existence of such provisions after several generations of reserve life indicates the self-perpetuating, self-fulfilling and self-prophesying nature of the entire system—all to the eternal detriment of the Aboriginal 'inmates'.

4 'The Australian Blackfeller'—The Concomitant of Colonialism

All men are men. The Black man is the creation of the White man. Black powerlessness was a White creation which attempted to ascribe to Aborigines, an image moulded out of their institutionalization and emasculation. This image, particularly in country areas, plays a dominant role for whites in the justification of the maintenance of the Aborigines' repressed conditions of life. Stereotyped as inferior, shiftless, dirty and lazy,[17] he is the brother of the phenomenon noted by Satre[18]—'the native', that would-be domesticated species neither man nor animal,

> 'Beaten, under-nourished, ill, terrified—but only up to a certain point —he has, whether he is black, yellow or white, always the same traits of character; he is a sly-boots, lazy-bones and a thief, who lives off nothing and understands only violence'.

Numerically and materially worse off than his colonial brothers, and lacking any immediate economic value, the Aborigine was to have no value of his own.[19] This phenomenon is cited by Stanner[20] 'what we think of as mildness or passivity is neither of those things. What we are looking at is one of the most familiar syndromes in the world. It is a product mainly of four things—homelessness, powerlessness, poverty and confusion—all self-acknowledged and accumulated over several generations'.

Something similar is true of the Indian position in the United States, where the administrative structure generated considerable psychological stress among the tribal population.

'Frequently the stress became intolerable and tribesmen responded with behavioural patterns of apathy, hatred, hostility and at times destructive action similar to what one finds in subordinated ethnic groups the world over. Indians oftentimes directed such emotions and actions at other members of the subordinated group, and seldom could individual tribesmen take integrated, efficient action toward overcoming the sources of their stress.'[21]

Today, Aborigines are calling for an end to black powerlessness and are seeking self-determination in their own affairs or at least the power and organization to act as a common interest pressure group.[22]

A COVERT SYSTEM

The Continuance of the System Amongst Fringe Dwelling People

Aboriginal repression can only be countered by Aboriginal self-assertion. Legislation and welfarism are only marginal solutions, directed from above at a grass roots problem which is not administrative but social. In New South Wales today, legislation giving State control over Aborigines has been repealed, yet Aboriginal powerlessness, poverty and repression remain, and Aborigines continue to be kept in their place. In the past, 'police surveillance of the continuing responsibilities of government came to be the normal medium for contact between the various departments and Aborigines'.[23] The central role played historically by police in Aboriginal affairs does not appear to have much altered.

1 Social Control, Resistance and the Law

We now attempt to apply this perspective to the particularised and non-institutional situation of fringe dwelling Aborigines.[24] Walgett is a country town in North Western New South Wales with a total population of 2,000 people, of which some 800 are of Aboriginal descent. As of 1969, no Aborigines were allowed as members of the Walgett Returned Services Club, nor into the lounge bars of its two hotels, which were impliedly reserved for 'cockeys', i.e. graziers. No Aborigines were members of the Tennis Club, the Bowls Club, the Golf Club or the Pony Club. In 1970, the local Methodist minister, Rod Jepsen, was forced to leave the town because of his church being black-balled by its white members. He had joined an Aboriginal sit-in in one of the segregated pubs. The twelve shire-councillors were all graziers. They brought the money into the town, and it was to them that the town owed its continued existence. However, the area economically continued to decline. The Walgett Police Inspector claimed, in 1969, that over the previous twelve months, of a total of 1,400 arrests for the town, 1,000 were of Aborigines; thus they constituted over 70 per cent of those arrested, though only 40 per cent of the town's population.

Aboriginal 'crime' consists largely of Petty Sessions offences against good order; namely drunkenness, disorderly conduct, offensive behaviour, indecent language, vagrancy, begging alms, petty theft, etc. Many offences involve alcohol. Thus, in small country towns, a stereotype of Aboriginal crime develops to rationalize the tension between the theory of equal rights for Aborigines and the practice of Aboriginal subjection, viz.:—

—there is something inherent in the Aboriginal makeup—he is not a fighter.

—there is something inherent in the Aboriginal constitution that he cannot take liquor.

—most Aborigines are resigned to their fate in court and want to get out as quickly and easily as possible with 'time to pay' their fines.

(a)   Regulars and Resistance

'If you were kicked in the teeth every time you stood up for something, what would you do?' For the fringe dwelling Aborigine, to apply reason to his every day life can only convince him of its irrationality. Hopelessness and the logic of grog make natural companions. Drinking has become a form of social defiance among an otherwise defenceless minority,[25] directed against white authority and the conflicting nature of the demands made upon it by white society. Dougie Young sings 'The people in town just run us down. They say we live on wine and beer, but if they'd stop and think if the boys didn't drink, there'd be no fun around here'.[26]

You get a more genuine response to a man's life and problems on pay day when he gets drunk than at most other times. He will probably be more aggressive, more talkative and less inhibited by either individual whites or by whites in authority positions. He knows the Aboriginal people have been duped, he just doesn't know what to do about it. Rowley has suggested a further reason for the serious affects of alcohol on Aboriginal life in the vulnerability to, and nature of, leadership in Aboriginal society, particularly the effects of alcohol on the elders of the tribe in whom authority was vested, and on the women.[27]

Between the resistance and the drink fall the 'regulars', who may or may not be regular offenders. They are, however, known to the police for whatever reason, and are systematically arrested and fined. There were between forty and sixty in Walgett and they were usually arrested during the weekend period for offences involving alcohol. Often, the men had been working outside town during the week and had come in for a drink on the weekend. Police waited for them with a paddy wagon parked outside the hotels, sometimes coming inside to make arrests.

There seems to be an important overlap between regulars and 'stirrers', i.e. those men most active in asserting their own rights and the rights of their people. White authority figures designate such activity as 'cheekiness', and the so-called troublemakers are correspondingly dealt with.[28]

'Few Australians realize the number of men who were probably potential leaders but who, being seen as trouble-makers, were quietly whisked away to places where they had no influence.'[29]

Palm Island, in 1957, provided a good illustration of this pattern when the four men who led an island-wide strike against the manager were removed from the island and their families. The people there had held the island for three days until armed police from Townsville seized the ringleaders from their homes early one morning and led them off the island in handcuffs. Stevens[30] reports a 1953 case of unrest on a mission station which the missionary attributed to the 'pink ideas' of some of the young bloods. The trouble nearly developed into a serious riot and the Director of Native Affairs was called in, resulting in the removal of some of the young 'hot-heads' under close government guard. Another similar case, in 1966, involved people from Edward River Mission.[31] A slightly different case, but equally as instructive, arose out of a series of incidents at Murin Bridge Settlement, New South Wales, in which two Aborigines individually, on different occasions, tried to organize protests against certain forms of official action. Though supported by their people, when the spokesmen confronted the staff no one else came forward to voice disapproval.[32]

A 'Jacky Jacky' is the converse of the cheeky character. The Australian equivalent of the Uncle Tom of American black power parlance, Jacky Jacky was the faithful Aboriginal guide to the explorer Kennedy, who aided his wounded master against 'hostile blacks'. The pattern of individual black trackers, Native Police and today, those who accommodate the administration and white authority too readily, is seen by some Aborigines in terms of collaboration with the invaders.

(b) Police

Police are particularly active in areas where Aborigines are present. Walgett, in 1969, was an inspectorate with some thirteen police, though four were stock inspectors. Police discretion in arrest situations involving Aborigines is particularly wide and, whereas an arrest may normally be made in one out of five arrest situations, the proportion of arrests here may be much higher. The class and social bias of the law, together with the nature and function of its enforcement, results in the high proportion of arrests— who are the vagrants, who are most likely to get drunk, and who are most likely to be in a street or public place while drunk? Indeed, the inapplicability and ineffectuality of legal sanctions against Aborigines convicted of offences arising through the consumption of liquor has been noted by many commentators.[33]

'It's pretty bad up there', you may hear Aboriginal people say, which means conditions and, in particular, the relationship between Aborigines and police, are at a low ebb. Police brutality is a constant accusation in Aboriginal Australia. Many Aboriginal men we talked to in Walgett claimed that, at some stage or other, they had been 'done over', and we were to witness a number of incidents ourselves. One case was that of an old man sitting on a bus seat on a Sunday afternoon, being seized for no apparent reason by a patrolling constable, thrust towards the back of a paddy wagon, stumbling, then being pulled prostrate along the road towards the nearby police station. Another case involved an Aboriginal stockman, who, while attempting to enter the segregated lounge bar area, after having been drinking in the public bar of a local hotel, was severely beaten by the publican, who then had the man arrested for drunkenness. The man, profusely bleeding from nose, eyes and mouth, and virtually unconscious, was left in gaol for nine hours without medical attention despite efforts to bail him out. Subsequently, he spent three or four days in hospital and the Council for Civil Liberties, Sydney, took up the case. No charges of assault were proffered by the police against the white assailant whose public bravado and disdain for both Aborigines and the law indicate the callous attitudes of certain types of outback whites and officials. They recall the sentiments voiced by the accused in the Myall Creek massacre, 1838, that 'it was hard that white men should be put to death for killing blacks', or expressed from the bench more recently by Mr. Justice Wells of the Northern Territory Supreme Court, who, in a 1934 judgment, stated that 'retributive justice was all that the savage mind could understand'.[35] Similar strains run through the fate of the 1929 report of the massacre of thirty-one Aborigines, which was ordered to lie on the table by the Commonwealth Parliament and was subsequently never printed. Police officers were implicated in the murders.[36] Aborigines might well look at the law which sanctioned the theft of their land, their physical annihilation and their continued subjection, and query its bona fides.

(c) The Legal Process

The legal process, that conglomeration of White power and State power exercised in conjunction with the local social structure of country towns, and the police, present to anyone outside the system, uneducated and powerless, an incomprehensible and insuperable barrier. In country towns, a key function of the law is to keep the peace, to keep Aborigines in their place, often as a useful pool of casual labour.[37] Walgett Aborigines were convinced that they were discriminated against by the police simply because they were Aborigines. 'The law in this town is like a wrestling match—it's all pre-arranged', said one man. In general, Aborigines are presumed guilty unless they can prove themselves innocent, 'for if it's not one Aborigine then it's another'. Further, they feel that the white man gets a better go from the police than they do and is less likely to be picked up for committing the same kind of offence.[38] Police activity is increased in areas of Aboriginal settlement. Frequent themes in the accusations against the police were that 'we are treated worse than animals' and 'we are not recognized as human beings'. 'Why,' they ask, 'is the white man always down on us?' Police were seen as 'suppression agents' and 'bullies'. Aborigines usually are not aware of, and have never been taught, their legal and civil rights as citizens despite the application of the legal maxim that ignorance of the law is no defence. Aborigines tend to say what they feel is expected of them by white authority figures, who, at all times and in all places, are pre-eminent. Most people fail to distinguish between charge and conviction, arrest and trial and so on. Most men want to get everything over as quickly as possible, hoping for bail and a fine with time to pay. The whole cycle is regarded as one of the unavoidable trials of a black man's life. He has no guarantees of his rights, criminal or civil, and, in Walgett, we could not find one Aborigine who had brought a civil action.

Legal and procedural technicalities are easily harnessed to confuse an Aboriginal accused. In court he is unlikely to, or fearful of, indicating any irregularities in the arrest, charges, treatment or conduct of the case. He is probably not aware that he doesn't have to answer questions or make a written statement when charged in the police station. Leading questions and statements asked by the interrogating policeman can be designed to produce evidence to prove or dismiss any charge. Evidence so obtained may be used in court. He has been through it all before, the court appearance is an elaborate game. There is no purpose to it, thus there is little motivation to fight the case on the terms offered by the white court system. Another conviction won't make much difference and there is little social stigma attached to petty convictions. As with the Aboriginal accused, so too with the Aboriginal witnesses. They fear police victimization, fear losing their jobs by taking off time to go to court, particularly if it is in another town. Once in the witness box, our adversary system of law, in the guise of a police prosecutor, will begin to confuse and contradict the hesitant witness, who may end up saying what he thinks the court wants him to say. Hence the frequent difference in the official accounts given to the police, lawyers and courts and the unofficial accounts given to family and friends. All this, though, only assuming a witness gets into court and has not been bought off by a flagon of port. Appeals against sentences and convictions are not common, but when undertaken, they have usually been engineered by sympathetic whites. The idiosyncrasies of white juries in small country towns are well known, but what the pattern is with respect to Aboriginal convictions, especially in cases involving conflict with whites, has yet to be determined.

When bail is granted and paid, this may well become the fine as there may be no re-appearance for trial and no attempt may be made by the police to enforce appearance. If the accused is remanded in custody for a more serious offence, or where bail cannot be met, other problems arise. While in custody and probably without legal representation, his chances of organizing a defence are slim, if indeed he bothers at all. Allegations of men being left in gaol for long periods before they come to trial are recurrent. Petty Sessions cases involving Aborigines are not usually defended and it is only in the case of more serious charges that he will have access to the Public Defender. Occasionally, a well meaning local lawyer may defend, without charge, or the Council for Civil Liberties may appear, but such a situation is neither comprehensive nor very effective in tackling the root of the problem. As most Aborigines have previous convictions, a pattern is discernable in small country towns in which circumstantial evidence in association with a community assessment of the man's character is sufficient to convict. Laxness in the conduct of cases is also evident.[39]

Local legal men tend to have no over-view of the problem, their position being that, as the Aboriginal question is a socio-economic problem, the law is in no way to blame for it and, in fact, stands outside it. When local lawyers are retained to appear for Aboriginal litigants, problems arise in country towns since business comes from the local whites, not blacks, and what little Aboriginal work there may be is largely non-remunerative. Should a case of black versus white arise in a country town, then, given the social status and vested interests of a lawyer, he is reluctant to become too involved (though this conflicts with his legal ethics). Thus we have the emergence of the celebrated institution, the 'plead guilty' lawyer—such practitioners being referred to as 'Guilty Smith' etc. Lawyers admit advising an Aboriginal accused to plead guilty as being the simplest and best way out for all. Reputedly, to plead guilty means a lighter fine or sentence. Most Aborigines plead guilty for this reason, through hearsay and because of a wish to cause as little trouble as possible, either for themselves or others. For people to plead not guilty involves a much lengthier and more intricate hearing which would clog up the courts. Accordingly, police encourage people to plead guilty by threatening to level other charges as well. One of the lawyers interviewed in the Walgett study claimed to have overheard a police officer instructing an Aborigine to plead guilty outside the court. At first, when questioned, the officer denied this, though when pressed he alleged it was policy from 'higher up'.

The general rationale for such processing of petty offences committed by Aborigines is that they are usually guilty, and if it's not them then it's one of their mates. The Clerk of Petty Sessions at Walgett was convinced that, in at least 95 per cent of cases, Aborigines were guilty. A Kempsey magistrate and most of the justices of the peace and lawyers spoken to felt the same way. Magistrates, particularly circuit magistrates, often have a heavy case load and, in some instances, may themselves prefer a plea of guilty in order to speedily expedite matters currently before them. This attitude is even easier to hold if the person concerned has little or no social, economic or political influence in the town. In these circumstances, a miscarriage of justice, no matter how brazen, is bound to be overlooked, and repercussions in the rare event of such cases coming to light are slight.[40] As is generally the case with an accused in a Police Court (Court of Petty Sessions), magistrates tend to take the police word over and above that of the Aborigine. Traditionally, magistrates, clerks of petty sessions and other court officers all come up through the Department of Justice and identify closely with the police, who together with them make up the Police Court system. Thus the cycle is complete.

2 Conclusion

At best, the law as an instrument of social control is in a logical and practical dilemma when dealing with Aborigines. It cannot hope to deal with the problems confronting the Aboriginal people but, historically and by default, finds itself in this position. Thus, in effect, it becomes an instrument of social control, of maintaining good order for a European society, and the large proportion of Aborigines up for drunkenness and offences against good order indicates the many who have tried to re-assert themselves against the all pervasive white totality which confronts them. Because of their deprivation and exploitation, this re-assertion may take forms which are socially unacceptable to the wider community. Aboriginal imprisonment rates are very high[41] and it is interesting to note that already, in prisons like Long Bay in Sydney and Stuarts Creek in Townsville, a 'soul brother' spirit among black prisoners is emerging.

At worst, the law is simply the formalization of the historical status quo in country towns, and its practice forms a system of control replacing the earlier more explicit forms of colonial practice.

REFERENCES

1 Quoted by E. B. Kennedy in *The Black Police of Queensland*, London, John Murray, 1902, p. 34.

2 FANON, FRANZ *Wretched of the Earth*, Penguin, 1967, pp. 31-2. He adds that 'This is why Marxist analysis should always be slightly stretched every time we have to do with the colonial problem'.

3 The definition of racism given by Stokely Carmichael and Charles V. Hamilton in *Black Power*, Pelican, 1969, p. 19.

4 STANNER, PROF. W. E. H. *After the Dreaming*, Boyer Lectures, 1968, A.B.C. Publications, p. 60.

5 ROWLEY, C. D. *The Destruction of Aboriginal Society*, A.N.U. Press, 1970, p. 2.

6 DOBYNS, HENRY F. 'Therapeutic Experience of Responsible Democracy' in *The American Indian Today* (ed.) Stuart Levine and Nancy O. Lurine, Pelican, Baltimore, Maryland, 1970, p. 268.

7 From Rudyard Kipling's poem *White Man's Burden*.

8 *Sydney Morning Herald,* Wednesday, 28th April, 1971, p. 6.

9 *Antonio Gramsci* by Alastair Davidson, *Australian Left Review,* 1968, p. 35. See also Fanon *supra* and at p. 190 where he states that 'in the colonial situation dynamism is replaced fairly quickly by a substantification of the attitudes of the colonizing power'. Many Third World theorists see subject colonial peoples and colonial powers in terms of the relationship between social classes. Thus, with respect to Aboriginal consciousness and the application of the class conflict analogy to the colonial world, we may try to understand the Aborigines' position using Gramsci's analysis that 'while a social class usually has a common world view, it was sporadic in its manifestation and because of social and intellectual subordination the class borrowed the world view of the dominant class, although it was frequently in conflict with its own inarticulate world view'.

10 See attack on Prof. A. P. Elkin's concept of the process of 'intelligent parasitism' in Frank Stevens' *Aboriginal Labour in the Cattle Industry at the Northern Territory,* A.N.U. Press, 1971 (In Press).

11 KING, P. 'Problems of Police Administration in N.S.W. (1825-51)', *R.A.H.S. Journal of Proceedings,* Vol. 44, 1958, Part 2, p. 59.

12 BARKER, S. K. 'Governorship of Sir George Gipps', *R.A.H.S. Journal of Proceedings,* Vol. 16, 1930, Part 4, p. 254.

13 HIATT, L. *Aborigines in Australian Society,* 1st Edition, A. F. Davies and S. Encel (eds.), 1965, Cheshires, Melbourne, quoting from Ruth A. Fink, 'Social Stratification: A Sequel to the Assimilation Process in a Part Aboriginal Community'.

14 See generally Jack Horner's forthcoming biography on Bill Ferguson, an Aboriginal leader, his life and times.

15 See Uri Windt 'Brown is Bonza', U.N.S.W. Abschol, 1969—Analysis of the Queensland Act (mimeo).

16 See the work of C. Tatz and F. Stevens, especially Tatz 'Natural Justice and the Rule of Law', *Australian Quarterly* No. 3, 1963.

17 WESTERN, J. S. 'The Australian Aboriginal, What White Australians Know and Think About Him—A Preliminary Survey' in *Race,* Vol. 10, No. 4, April 1969, p. 411.

18 SATRE, J. P. in his introduction to Fanon, *supra* p. 14.

19 ROWLEY, *supra,* p. 17.

20 STANNER, *supra,* pp. 44-6.

21 DOBYNS, *supra,* p. 271.

22 Aborigines Advancement League, Victoria, Annual General Meeting, 30 August 1969, 'Statement on Black Power'.

23 STEVENS, F. *Aborigines* in *Australian Society,* 2nd Edition, p. 374, referring to J. H. Bell 'Official Policies Towards the Aborigines in N.S.W.' *Mankind,* Vol. 5, No. 8.

24 Much of what is said here is taken from the writer's survey undertaken in *Fringe Dwelling Rural Aborigines and the Law in N.S.W.* Abschol, Sydney, 1969 (mimeo).

25 BECKETT, J., in 'The Land Where the Crow Flies Backwards', *Quadrant,* July, 1965, p. 38.

26 'The Land Where the Crow Flies Backwards', Dougie Young sings from the Aborigine Camp, recorded in the field by J. Beckett, Wattle Records.

27 ROWLEY, *supra,* pp. 30-1.

28 Noted also by Stevens, 'High Noon at Normanton', *Smoke Signals,* October 1969, p. 10.

29 STANNER, *supra,* pp. 45-6.

30 'Protection or Persecution', *Dissent,* Winter, 1969, No. 24, p. 29.

31 *Ibid.*

32 HIATT, *supra,* p. 285, quoting from Beckett, pp. 99-100, A.N.U. Thesis, 1958.

33 See the statements of the late Mr. Justice Kriewaldt, Chief Justice of the Supreme Court of the Northern Territory, 1951-60 in 'The Application of Criminal Law to the Aborigines of the Northern Territory', 1960, 5 *W.A. Uni. L.R.I.*

34 For North Australia see F. Stevens 'Protection or Persecution' in *Dissent,* Winter, 1969, pp. 27-8.

35 Quoted from A. P. Elkin—'Australian Aborigines and White Relations—A Personal Record' in *Royal Australian Historical Society, Journal of Proceedings,* Vol. 48, Part 3, pp. 218-9.

36 ROWLEY, *supra,* p. 288.

37 See P. Hasluck, *Black Australians, A Survey of Native Policy in Western Australia 1829-1897,* 1942, p. 196.

38 See Lance Forsyth's 'Australia's Deep North', *Australian,* 4 July, 1966.

39 For example, *The Stuart Case,* K. S. Inglis, M.U.P. Melbourne, 1961. And 'The Nancy Young Case', John Carrick and Geoff Robertson, *Blackacre 1970,* Journal of the Sydney University Law Society.

40 *Ibid.* Professional and criminal negligence actions are not available to Aborigines. Legal authorities, in practice, are reluctant to institute such proceedings.

41 For example see the figures for Western Australia in 'Imprisonment of Aborigines and Part-Aborigines in Western Australia', M. V. Robinson in *Thinking about Australian Aboriginal Welfare,* Department Anthropology, Uni. W.A. (ed.) R. M. Berndt, 1969, p. 17.

6

LEGAL STATUS OF ABORIGINAL PEOPLE: SLAVES OR CITIZENS

J. Little

The substance of this chapter was part of the address the writer proposed to deliver as one of the three counsel for the Aboriginal plaintiffs in the Yirrkala land rights case. Most of the rest of the address was directed to showing, by an investigation of the legal history of New Zealand Maori land rights, that those land rights were a product not of New Zealand legislation but of a principle of English colonial common law applicable also to Australia. When the writer rose to speak, the court was informed that the other members of the plaintiffs' legal team—senior counsel, a second junior counsel and solicitor—objected to him being heard. After brief argument the court refused to hear him.

* * * *

In the early days of British colonialism on this continent, what, in the eyes of English law, was the status of Aboriginal people?

Were they conquered subjects at the mercy of the Crown? Slaves? Wards of state? Aliens, and if so, friendly or hostile? Legal non-entities? Persons unworthy of legal protection and liable to be shot on sight because of their alleged propensity to eating human flesh? Or were they simply British subjects with all the civil rights of British subjects?

Generally speaking, at common law only British subjects of full status were accorded land rights that were protected from arbitrary exercise of the Crown prerogative.

To try to determine the status of Aboriginal people according to English law, I propose to follow three legal-historical trails. First, the development of the constitutional status of the Australian colonies; secondly, the treatment accorded Aboriginal people by English law; and finally, the rise and decline of slavery.

The first trail begins long before the Aboriginal people of Australia were disturbed by the British.

I shall join it in 1609, when Lord Coke gave judgment in *Calvin's case*. He said, in the course of it —

> 'But a perpetual enemy (though there be no wars by fire and sword between them) cannot maintain any action, or get anything within this realm. All infidels are in law . . . , perpetual enemies (for the law presumes not that they will be converted, that being . . . . a remote possibility) for between them, as with the devils, whose subjects they be, and the Christian, there is perpetual hostility, and can be no peace . . . if a Christian King should conquer a kingdom of an infidel,

and bring them under his subjection, there *ipso facto* the laws of the
infidel are abrogated, for that they be not only against Christianity,
but against the laws of God and nature, contained in the decalogue'.[1]

A conquered Christian kingdom was dealt with less severely. Its laws
stood till altered by the conquering English king, who could govern conquered territories in virtue of his prerogative, unhampered by Parliament.[2]

British occupation of North America began at about the same time as
Calvin's case, and for some time thereafter English courts seem, a little
uneasily, to have regarded the transatlantic colonies as conquered from
infidel nations.[3]

As a matter of national or municipal law, as opposed to international
law, Indian land claims were therefore ignored.

In 1774, as the American War of Independence loomed, the thrice
argued and tensely followed case, *Campbell v. Hall*,[4] was decided. At issue
was the constitutional status of the British Caribbean Islands, Grenada. In
the course of argument, one counsel said of Lord Coke in *Calvin's case*—

'He takes a difference between the conquest of a Christian kingdom
and the kingdom of an infidel: this has been long enough justly
exploded, . . .'

to which Lord Mansfield retorted —

'Don't quote the distinction, for the honour of my Lord Coke.'[5]

Later, in his judgment, he said —

'. . . laws of a conquered country continue until they are altered by
the conqueror. The justice and antiquity of this maxim is incontrovertible; and the absurd exception as to pagans, in *Calvin's case*,
shews the universality of the maxim. The exception could not exist
before the Christian era, and in all probability arose from the mad
enthusiasm of the Croisades.'[6]

Did *Campbell v. Hall* leave New South Wales, annexed about fourteen
years later, in 1788, a conquered colony?

The answer is that it did not, and the reason, perhaps, is that during this
fourteen years Britain suffered the shock of the American War of Independence. One of its lessons for the British was that colonists had to be treated
with more respect.

As soon as New South Wales had a respectable number of free settlers,
it was accorded the constitutional status of an uninhabited colony acquired
by settlement. That was a category known in theory by lawyers,[7] national
and international, but seldom encountered in practice, at least not by English
lawyers. Its peculiar feature was that it left British settlers with the customary rights and liberties of British subjects, in particular, protection from
arbitrary exercise of the King's prerogative, by which, in conquered colonies,
the King could govern and, in particular, confiscate land at will without
compensation.

Even Sir James Stephen, the so-called 'Over-Secretary' of the Colonial
Office, as early as 1822,[8] placed New South Wales in this category, and he,
as much as any man, strove to protect Aboriginal people, in particular their
land rights. Both he and his father were associated with the Clapham Sect, of
which I shall say more later.

In many cases decided by the New South Wales Supreme Court after
its establishment in 1823,[9] New South Wales' place in this category was
never doubted, and on the 1st May, 1849, in a special report in which Sir
James Stephen had a hand, on a proposed bill for the separation of Port

Phillip from New South Wales and the extension of representative institutions to Van Diemen's Land and South Australia, the Privy Council had no hesitation in including Australia in the category of 'colonies acquired . . . by the occupation of vacant territories'.[10]

If the law considered that, before British occupation, Australia was unoccupied, how did that leave the Aboriginal people? Had they the same rights as British colonists, or were they legal non-entities?

Though constitutional lawyers deliberating on their lofty pedestals managed to overlook or ignore Aboriginal people just as some international lawyers today do not recognize the People's Republic of China, Aboriginal people were not considered legal non-entities for the obvious reason that lawyers with their feet on the ground of Australia kept running into them.

So walk with me, please, down the second trail, which winds a good deal, to discover the treatment accorded Aboriginal people by English law.

In the first twenty or thirty years of British occupation, the rule of law barely existed in New South Wales because so many of the British occupiers were convicts or soldiers. As a result, the legal position of Aboriginal people received the same scant attention as most other legal matters.

Captain of Marines, David Collins, was the first British law officer in Australia, though he was not a lawyer. He was the first Judge Advocate and a close friend and sometime secretary to Governor Phillip. Fortunately he has left a reliable account of New South Wales' first fourteen years.

Early in his book entitled *An Account of the English Colony in New South Wales*[11] he wrote —

> 'It being observed with concern, that the natives were becoming every day more troublesome and hostile, several people having been wounded, and others, who were necessarily employed in the woods, driven in and much alarmed by them, the governor determined on endeavouring to seize and bring into the settlement, one or two of those people, whose language it was absolutely necessary to acquire, that they might be taught to distinguish friends from enemies.'

What, you may ask, was the legal status of the Aboriginal people if they could be seized at will by the King's representative—wards, perhaps?

Proclamations stressed equality of treatment for colonists and Aboriginal people breaching public order. And Captain Collins records that a few convicts were whipped for attacking Aboriginal people, though not that any of the latter were subjected to British legal process.

But they were subject to their own legal process, with the full blessing of the colonists, as Captain Collins relates —

> 'The natives who lived about Sydney appeared to place the utmost confidence in us choosing a clear spot between the town and the brickfield for the performance of any of their rites and ceremonies; and for three evenings the town had been amused with one of their spectacles, which might properly have been denominated a tragedy, for it was attended with a great effusion of blood. It appeared from the best account we could procure, that one or more murders having been committed in the night, the assassins, who were immediately known, were compelled, according to the custom of the country, to meet the relations of the deceased, who were to avenge their deaths by throwing spears, and drawing blood for blood.'[12]

On the 4th May, 1816, Governor Macquarie issued a proclamation prohibiting the blood process of the Aboriginal people 'as a barbarous custom

repugnant to the British Laws, and strongly militating against the Civilization of the Natives which is an Object of the highest Importance to effect, if
possible'. As was customary in British official documents until the late 1830s,
'natives' were distinguished from 'British subjects'.[13]

The proclamation also stated that 'such of the Natives as may wish to
be considered under the Protection of the British Government, and disposed
to conduct themselves in a peaceful, inoffensive and honest Manner, shall be
furnished with Passports or Certificates to that Effect'.[14] And a despatch of
additional instructions dated the 14th July, 1825, by Earl Bathurst, then
Colonial Secretary, to Governor Darling directed the Governor, when necessary, to repel 'Aggressions' (by Aboriginal people) 'in the same manner, as if
they proceeded from Subjects of any accredited State'.[15]

Does this imply that Aboriginal people were aliens?

In the second decade of the nineteenth century, one or two Aboriginal
people may have been convicted and punished with execution or exile on
charges of murder or rape, but these cases, if they occurred, were apparently
later forgotten by the Sydney law authorities, because the New South Wales
Supreme Court, established in 1823, declined to hear charges against
Aboriginal people in its early years.

Chief Justice Dowling of that court, when called upon to advise
Governor Gipps in 1842 about a prosecution of an Aboriginal man at Port
Phillip, said —

> 'It is true that, soon after my arrival in the Colony in 1828, I found
> an opinion prevailing that the Supreme Court could not take cogni-
> zance of offences committed against Aborigines, and, in one or two
> instances, the Court, from the difficulty of administering Justice
> between them according to the Rules of English Law, forbore trying
> these individual cases. The question of jurisdiction was not however
> argued at the Bar, and from the great infrequency of such cases, the
> course taken was silently adopted from conformity, rather with the
> impression prevailing, than as the result of deliberate Judgment. In
> the Month of April, 1836, however, the question was solemnly raised
> before the Supreme Court in the Case of an Aboriginal named *Jack
> Congo Murral,* arraigned for the Murder of another Aboriginal named
> *Jubinguy.* The Court having assigned Counsel and Attorney for the
> defence, a Plea to the Jurisdiction was put on the Record, to the effect
> that the Prisoner'

was under Aboriginal, not British law.

> 'The Attorney General demurred to this Plea, which brought the
> question of Law fully before the Court, and it was solemnly argued
> by Counsel before Sir Francis Forbes, then Chief Justice, and the
> Puisne Judges Dowling and Burton. The Court took time to advise on
> the Case; and, on a subsequent day, the united opinion of the Judges
> was publicly delivered in full Court by Mr. Justice Burton, by which
> the Plea to the Jurisdiction was overruled, obliging the Prisoner to
> plead to the charge.'[16]

According to another report, Jack Congo Murral's counsel also argued —

> '. . . the natives are not protected by those [i.e. British] laws, they are
> not admitted as witnesses in Courts of Justice, they cannot claim any
> civil rights, they cannot obtain recovery of, or compensation for, those

lands which have been torn from them, and which they have probably held for centuries. They are not therefore bound by laws which
afford them no protection.'[17]

Aboriginal people were not admitted as witnesses because of a Christian
chauvinist prejudice that persists to this day. It was stated as early as the
8th July, 1805, by Judge Advocate Atkins in his 'Opinion on the Treatment
of Natives'. He said —

'. . . the evidence of Persons not bound by any moral or religious Tye
can never be considered or construed as legal evidence.'[18]

On the 16th August, 1824, Attorney General Bannister, writing to
Under-Secretary Horton of the Colonial Office, said —

'They have not that sense of religion, which authorises the taking of
an oath by any form. The consequence is a very frequent denial of
Justice to them.'[19]

He recommended legislation to render their testimony admissible by
providing a sanction other than the oath.[20]

Fifteen years later, in 1839, a local Act[21] was passed, but it was
promptly disallowed by the Colonial Secretary on the legal advice of the
Attorney General and Solicitor General. They said, in their opinion dated the
27th July, 1840 —

'To admit in a Criminal case the evidence of a witness acknowledged
to be ignorant of the existence of a God or future state would be
contrary to the principles of British jurisprudence.'[22]

But, they added —

'We should have supposed that the Aboriginal Natives might have
been sufficiently instructed before being produced as witnesses to
render their evidence admissible according to the established rules of
Law, which do not define the distinctness of Religious ideas or to
what degree the belief in a future state is to be fixed to qualify a
witness to take an Oath.'[23]

This reasonable suggestion was apparently not implemented back in New
South Wales because, in 1843, the colonial authorities obtained the passage
of an Imperial Act[24] authorizing colonial legislatures to pass acts making the
testimony of Aboriginal people admissible. Not till 1876 did the New South
Wales legislature pass such an act.[25]

The reluctance of the Crown law authorities to prosecute Aboriginal
people evoked a reaction from some colonists. That is clear from the trial on
the 18th May, 1827, of Lieutenant Lowe for the murder of an Aboriginal
man while the man was being held in custody. The two giants of the Sydney
bar appeared for the Lieutenant to object to the jurisdiction of the Court.
Mr. Wentworth argued —

'. . . why were so many [Aboriginal people], who have of late been
apprehended for the murder of British subjects, turned loose from the
gaols? They were rightfully turned out, because they could not legally
be tried. If they could be legally tried for offences committed against
us, they could also be tried for acts committed among themselves, but
it is well known to be a matter of everyday occurrence among them to
commit the greatest enormities, and yet the civil Magistrate takes no

manner of notice, because he has no legal authority to do so .... Punishment and protection are co-extensive; and it therefore follows from the inability of the Court to punish the Natives for aggressions against the whites, that it has no jurisdiction to punish the latter for aggression against them .... It is difficult to find out what character to give the aborigines of this country.'[26]

Dr. Wardell argued that an Aboriginal man was neither an alien, friend or enemy, nor a subject of England. He could not be tried in a British court. Assuming, as alleged, the Aboriginal man for whose death Lieutenant Lowe was standing trial had killed a colonist, Dr. Wardell said —

'... nothing could be fairer with regard to any people living in a state of nature, than to punish them in the very way in which they themselves would punish others.'

Taking the other assumption—that the deceased had committed no offence—he argued —

'Now, if we look at what they are, anthropophagi, eaters of human flesh, how did writers view them? Lord Bacon said that they were to be looked on as a people prescribed by all law ... Lord Bacon is followed up by the commentator, Mr. Barbeyac, who contends that even had the natives committed no offence, but possessed that propensity to eating human flesh, they would justly be proscribed, that an exterminating war carried on against them would be justifiable, and destroying one of them would be no more than destroying that which was offensive to heaven.'[27]

Chief Justice Forbes rejected these submissions and the trial proceeded.

In the 1830s, colonialism advanced deep into the hinterland and relations between the colonists and the Aboriginal people worsened. Aboriginal people were prosecuted to placate the cry that, if colonists were to be tried for offences against Aboriginal people, then the converse should follow. In about 1835, eight Aboriginal people were sentenced to death by the Supreme Court for offences allegedly committed on colonists in the district of Brisbane Water, though the sentence was commuted to confinement on Goat Island, where they were employed in cutting stone.[28] The Supreme Court's reversal of itself in *Jack Congo Murral's case* was, no doubt, a response to the clamours of some colonists. In 1838, there was uproar when seven white men were convicted, sentenced to death and executed for the massacre of the Aboriginal community at Myall Creek.

The tension of the 1830s produced one positive result. It forced the Colonial Office to rule authoritatively on the status of Aboriginal people. The Colonial Secretary, Lord Glenelg, was spurred into action by a report by Major Mitchell of a conflict with Aboriginal people in which the Major's party shot some Aboriginal people.

In his despatch to Governor Bourke dated the 26th July, 1837, Lord Glenelg said —

'Your Commission as Governor of N.S. Wales asserts H.M.s Sovereignty over every part of the Continent of New Holland which is not embraced in the Colonies of Western or Southern Australia. Hence I conceive it follows that all the natives inhabiting those Territories may be considered as Subjects of the Queen, and as within H.M.'s allegiance. To regard them as Aliens with whom a War can exist, and against whom H.M.'s Troops may exercise belligerent rights, is to deny that protection to which they derive the highest possible claim from the Sovereignty which has been assumed over the whole of their Ancient Possessions . . . If the rights of the Aboriginals as British Subjects be fully acknowledged, it will follow that, when any of them comes to his death by the hands of the Queen's Officers, or of persons acting under their Command, an Inquest should be held to ascertain the cause which led to the Death of the deceased.'[29]

Did it not also follow that, if their rights as British subjects were to be fully acknowledged, their 'Ancient Possessions' would also have to be respected?

To discover how Lord Glenelg was able to conclude so casually that Aboriginal people were British subjects and to appreciate the full significance of this conclusion, I ask you to march with me down the last trail—the rise and decline of slavery.

Traditional English slavery, villeinage, was almost extinct by the end of the sixteenth century, but by the same time, and earlier on the Continent, another form—based on ethnic difference—arose. By the eighteenth century, England was the greatest slave trader, if not the greatest slave owner, in the world.[30]

But, in the late eighteenth and early nineteenth centuries, the impulses that produced the French Revolution were moving the low church evangelicals who became known as the Clapham Sect, and their allies to their campaigns to abolish, first slavery in England, then the slave trade and finally slavery throughout the British Empire.[31]

Their first success came in 1772 when Lord Mansfield, after delaying judgment with the expressed hope that Parliament would resolve the issue for him, ordered the slave, Somersett, to be freed, despite Lord Mansfield's concern that, as a result, about fourteen or fifteen thousand slaves would have to be released in England, involving a loss to their proprietors of £700,000. The strong public opinion in favour of Somersett seems to be reflected in Lord Mansfield's judgment. He said —

'The state of slavery is of such a nature, that it is incapable of being introduced on any reasons, moral or political; but only by positive law, which preserves its force long after the reasons, occasion, and the time itself from whence it was created, is erased from memory: it's so odious, that nothing can be suffered to support it, but positive law. Whatever inconveniences, therefore, may follow from a decision, I cannot say this case is allowed or approved by the law of England; and therefore the black must be discharged.'[32]

This decision did not apply to the colonies.

The next victory of the Clapham Sect was the outlawing of the slave trade, but their crowning success came with the passage of the Abolition of Slavery Act of 1833.[33] It was one of the few Acts passed after the American War of Independence that the British Parliament applied throughout the British Empire.

Its key section, twelve, provided —

'. . . that from . . . the . . . First Day of August One thousand eight hundred and thirty four Slavery shall be and is hereby utterly and for ever abolished and declared unlawful throughout the British Colonies, Plantations, and Possessions Abroad.'

What, you may ask, did this do for the Aboriginal people, because from their inception the Australian colonies had not tolerated slavery?[34]

The answer depends on what slavery was. The Abolition of Slavery Act of 1833 did not define slavery. One has to turn to American legal literature for a definition. The American legal encyclopaedia, the Corpus Juris Secundum, contains the following statements —

> 'A slave has been defined as a person who is totally subject to the will of another; a person who is the chattel or property of another and is wholly subject to his will. Slavery is defined as the state of entire subjection of one person to the will of another; a condition of enforced compulsory service of one to another.
> 'The law of African slavery in the U.S. was a system of customary law.
> 'In the slave states color indicating African descent gave rise to a presumption that the person was a slave.
> 'Generally, a slave had no civil, social, or political rights or capacity, except those conferred on him by statute.
> 'As a general rule a slave could not acquire or hold title to property or an interest therein.'

The most instructive decision is probably that of the United States Supreme Court in *Dred Scot v. Sandford*,[35] decided in 1857.

The issue was whether persons 'whose ancestors were negroes of the African race, and imported to this country [the United States], and sold and held as slaves' were, when emancipated or born of parents who had become free before their birth, citizens of a State within the meaning of the United States Constitution and therefore entitled to seek the assistance of Federal courts. A majority of the Court held they were not.

> 'On the contrary', they said, 'they were at that time [i.e. of the Declaration of Independence and when the Constitution of the United States was framed and drafted] considered as a subordinate and inferior class of beings, who had been subjected by the dominant race, and, whether emancipated or not, yet remained subject to their authority, and had no rights or privileges but such as those who held the power and the Government might choose to grant them.[36] ...
> 'They had for more than a century before been regarded as beings of an inferior order, and altogether unfit to associate with the white race, either in social or political relations; and so far inferior, that they had no rights which the white man was bound to respect; and that the negro might justly and lawfully be reduced to slavery for his benefit. He was bought and sold, and treated as an ordinary article of merchandise and traffic, whenever a profit could be made by it. This opinion was at that time fixed and universal in the civilised portion of the white race. It was regarded as an axiom in morals as well as in politics, which no one thought of disputing, or supposed to be open to dispute; and men in every trade and position in society daily and habitually acted upon it in their private pursuits, as well as in matters of public concern, without doubting for a moment the correctness of this opinion.
> 'And in no nation was this opinion more firmly fixed or more uniformly acted upon than by the English Government and English people. They not only seized them on the coast of Africa, and sold them or held them in slavery for their own use; but they took them

as ordinary articles of merchandise to every country where they could make a profit on them, and were far more extensively engaged in this commerce than any other nation in the world.'[37]

It seems fairly clear from this judgment that the United States slave power considered slavery as practised by the British to be more than a relationship of an owner to an owned. Chattel status and enforced compulsory service were, to slavery, merely an outward form to a central core or essence, which was the customary or tacitly approved denial to black people of the common law or basic rights and privileges accorded to whites. With African people in the Caribbean islands, the denial did appear in the guise of chattel status and enforced compulsory service. With Aboriginal people in Australia, it appeared primarily as land plunder, with enforced compulsory service a secondary aspect.

From the 1st August, 1834, onward, the British banished from their jurisprudence not merely any particular outward form of slavery but also, I suggest, its central core or essence.

The British House of Commons and the King and his advisors apparently thought so, because on the 2nd July, 1834, the House resolved[38] to present an Address to the King praying that the natives of the British Empire be secured 'in the due observance of justice and the protection of their civil rights' and that the King direct his colonial governors and officers accordingly; the King acceded to the request and the Colonial Secretary accordingly sent a circular despatch to colonial officials around the Empire directing their attention to the principles contained in the Address.[39] The despatch was dated the 1st August, 1834, the day of the abolition of slavery.

This was the background to Lord Glenelg's untroubled conclusion in 1837 that Aboriginal people were British subjects with all the rights of British subjects.

It was the background that led to the establishment of South Australia in 1836[40] and New Zealand in 1840[41] on the express basis that Aboriginal people of those colonies were British subjects to whom land rights were accorded. South Australia was the only Australian colony settled from England after the 1st August, 1834.

Because they were particularly reactionary, the colonialists controlling the Australian colonies, even after 1834, did not respect the civil rights of Aboriginal people, in particular their property rights, though almost from the beginning of their occupation of Australia, they knew that Aboriginal people held estates in land. For example, Captain Collins said, in his Account—

'But, strange as it may appear, they have also their real estates. Ben-nil-long, both before he went to England and since his return, often assured me that the island Me-mel (called by us Goat Island), close by Sydney Cove was his own property; that it was his father's, and that he should give it to By-gone, his particular friend and companion. To this little spot he appeared much attached; and we have often seen him and his wife Ba-rang-a-roo feasting and enjoying themselves on it. He told us of other people who possessed this kind of hereditary property, which they retained undisturbed.'[42]

One therefore reaches the conclusion that the refusal of the colonialists to respect Aboriginal land rights after 1834 was a refusal to acknowledge the abolition of slavery by law. The colonialists illegally and perversely clung to the principle of slavery stated in *Dred Scot's case.* To them, black people were 'an inferior class of beings' who 'had no rights or privileges but such as those who held the power and the Government might choose to give them'. In short, they were slaves, not citizens.

REFERENCES

1 7 Co. Rep. 1a, pp. 17a and 17b; 77 E.R. 377, pp. 397 and 398.

2 *Ibid.*, p. 176; p. 398.

3 BLACKSTONE, *Commentaries* I. pp. 106-108.

4 LOFFT, 655; 98 E.R. 848.

5 *Ibid.*, p. 716; p. 882.

6 *Ibid.*, p. 741; pp. 895 and 896.

7 BLACKSTONE, *Commentaries* I. p. 107.

8 H.R.A. (IV), vol. 1, pp. 412-415.

9 For example, *Macdonald v. Levy* (1833), I Legge 39, pp. 45 and 51; *R. v. Maloney* (1836), I Legge 74, p. 77.

10 P.P. (House of Commons), 1849, vol. 35, p. 34 of Papers relative to the Proposed Alterations in the Constitution of the Australian Colonies, Presented to both Houses of Parliament by Command, May 25, 1849.

11 1971 Australian Facsimile Edition No. 76 of the 1798 London edition reproduced by the Libraries Board of South Australia, p. 49.

12 *Ibid.*, p. 328.

13 H.R.A. (I), vol. 9, p. 143.

14 *Ibid.*

15 H.R.A. (I), vol. 12, p. 21.

16 H.R.A. (I), vol. 21, pp. 656 and 657.

17 *R. v. Jack Congo Murral* (1836) I Legge 72.

18 H.R.A. (I), vol. 5, p. 502.

19 H.R.A. (IV), vol. 1, p. 554.

20 *Ibid.*, p. 555.

21 Aboriginals Competent Witnesses Act, 3 Vict. No. 16.

22 H.R.A. (I), vol. 20, p. 756.

23 *Ibid.*

24 6 & 7 Vict. c. 22.

25 Evidence Further Amendment Act, 40 Vict. No. 8, s. 3.

26 *Sydney Gazette,* 23 May 1827.

27 *Ibid.*, 21 May 1827.

28 H.R.A. (I), vol. 17, p. 718—Bourke to Secretary of State, 1 May 1835.

29 H.R.A. (I), vol. 19, p. 48.

30 See generally, Edward Fiddes, 'Lord Mansfield and the Somersett Case', 50 L.Q.R. 499.

31 See generally, E. M. Howse, *Saints in Politics: the Clapham-Sect and the Growth of Freedom;* Paul Knaplund, *James Stephen and the British Colonial System, 1813-1847.*

32 *Somerset v. Stewart,* Lofft 1, p. 19; 98 E.R. 499, p. 510.

33 3 & 4 W. 4. c. 73.

34 H.R.A. (I), vol. 1, p. xix, Phillip to Home Department, about 1786, 'there can be no slavery in a free land, and consequently no slaves'.

35 19 Howard 393.

36 *Ibid.*, pp. 404 and 405.

37 *Ibid.*, pp. 407 and 408.

38 Commons Journals 1834, vol. 89, p. 449.

39 H.R.A. (I), vol. 17, pp. 491 and 492—Spring Rice to Bourke.

40 See Letters Patent made 19 February 1836, erecting the province of South Australia (set out in *South Australia v. Victoria* (1914) 18 C.L.R. 115, pp. 119 and 120); proclamation given 28 December 1836 by Governor Hindmarsh published in the *South Australian Gazette and Colonial Register*, vol. 1, No. 2, of 3 June 1837; 'Written communications relating to the Contents of the Instrument intended to establish the Province of South Australia and the Protection of the Aboriginal Inhabitants thereof, passing between the Colonisation Commissioners for South Australia, the Colonial Office and the Law Officers of the Crown, prior to 19 February 1836' (Microfilm C O 13/3, 4 and 5/).

41 See Charter given 16 November 1840, for erecting the Colony of New Zealand etc. published in P.P. (House of Commons) 1841, vol. 17, p. 32 of Copies of Extracts of Correspondence relative to New Zealand, Ordered by the House of Commons to be printed, 11 May 1841; Sir William Martin, *England and the New Zealanders. Part 1, Remarks upon a Despatch from the Rt. Hon. Earl Grey to Gov. Grey dated 23 December 1846.*

42 *Op. cit.*, 599.

7

ABORIGINES AND THE ADMINISTRATION OF CRIMINAL LAW

Elizabeth M. Eggleston

In the past, Aborigines throughout Australia have been subjected to laws which discriminate against them. Over recent years, this legislation has progressively been repealed, so that the number of discriminatory provisions now remaining is far smaller than at earlier periods of Australian history.

It is clear that, even if all discriminatory legislation were to vanish overnight, that would not be the end of discrimination against Aborigines. Legislation is only the most obvious form of discrimination. It spells out and authorises forms of discrimination which otherwise might have existed without legal sanction. The repeal of legislation removes the legal authority for certain practices; it does not automatically guarantee that those practices will cease. It also leaves untouched other practices which were never the subject of legislation.

In a United Nations Study of Equality in the Administration of Justice, the Special Rapporteur stated: 'It seems that most discrimination in the administration of justice on grounds of race or colour is now *de facto* discrimination'.[1] That view was based on information about more than eighty countries, including Australia. A study of the administration of criminal law in Victoria, South Australia and Western Australia[2] supports the conclusion that *de facto* discrimination is most significant in relation to Aborigines in those three states.

Legislation which, on its face, discriminates against Aborigines in relation to the administration of criminal justice is rare in those states. But instances of *de facto* discrimination occurring at various stages of the criminal justice process were found. It is proposed to examine some of these instances briefly before proceeding to a consideration of how discriminatory practices may be overcome.

The initiation of criminal prosecutions rests, in most cases, in the hands of the police. Thus, police action usually represents the first stage in the process of setting the machinery of the criminal law in motion. The police are under a duty to act without favour or affection, malice or illwill. But policemen are not immune from racist attitudes which afflict other sections of the community.

In practice, the police have considerable discretion in the institution of prosecutions. Faced with the problem of allocating scarce manpower resources, police authorities can choose to enforce certain laws and ignore others. The exercise of this discretion may produce a situation in which one racial group suffers more than its fair share of prosecutions. For years the South Australian police were tolerant of the illegal sale and supply of liquor by sporting and other clubs.[3] It is unlikely that many Aborigines benefited from this police blind eye which contrasts strongly with the spotlight which some policemen shine on Aborigines suspected of offences against discriminatory laws. In the far north of Western Australia, it is still an offence for Aborigines to 'receive' liquor. One over-zealous policeman followed a white man and two Aborigines into the bush to observe them drinking, even though he was not on duty at the time. He charged the white man with supplying liquor and the Aborigines with receiving liquor. Since restrictions on Aboriginal drinking have been abolished in other parts of the state and it is clear that this law will soon be totally obsolete, the police might well have considered that this was one law which need not be enforced vigorously. Instead, their enthusiasm for its enforcement does not appear to have waned, either because it is comparatively easy to find Aborigines offending (since all that is required for conviction is to prove possession of liquor; no degree of drunkenness is necessary) or because policemen genuinely believe that it is dangerous to allow Aborigines even to hold a bottle of alcohol.

There is a common white stereotype of the drunken Aborigine. No real evidence exists that excessive drinking is more prevalent among Aborigines than in the general Australian population.[4] It may appear more common because Aboriginal drinking is more visible. Aboriginal homes frequently lack privacy, and Aborigines, particularly those living on reserves, are often subject to close scrutiny by police and welfare officers.

Even within an overall policy of enforcement of a particular law, the police may exercise discretion in relation to charging in individual cases. There is clearly a general policy that laws against drunkenness will be enforced, but some individuals found drunk in the street are sent home rather than arrested. In one Western Australian town, the local police adopted an invariable practice of arresting drunk Aborigines and not letting them go home to the reserve. This policy was reflected in the extremely high rate of charges against Aborigines in this town.

The police can be criticised for exercising their discretion in a way which effectively discriminates against Aborigines, in that white lawbreaking is more often overlooked. But the police can reply, with some justification, that in these cases the Aborigines have committed offences, and the fact that whites have committed other offences should be treated as irrelevant to the question of the propriety of police action.

It is impossible to justify other cases in which Aborigines were framed by police. One Aborigine was arrested for drunkenness because he had been 'cheeky' to police the night before. Fortunately he was able to see a doctor who took a blood sample. Since this showed no alcohol he was acquitted. The idea that a 'cheeky' Aborigine should be taught a lesson carries a flavour of nineteenth century colonial thinking, but unfortunately it is not yet dead in this country.

In some cases, police use improper methods to obtain confessions from Aborigines. No evidence is available as to whether this occurs more often with Aboriginal suspects than with whites. The High Court of Australia has recognised[5] that uneducated, poor defendants need more protection than others do when confronted with police interrogations. Most Aborigines clearly fall within the vulnerable class, being poorly educated and lacking financial resources.

After arrest, most defendants have a right to be released on bail. In the first place, police fix the amount of bail. Statistics derived from a sample of

4,000 cases heard in ten Western Australian country towns in 1965 show that the percentage of Aborigines released on bail was smaller than the percentage of whites who regained liberty before trial.[6] This discrepancy was mainly due to the poverty of the Aborigines, who were unable to raise the amount of bail money required. But, in some towns, the local police had a definite policy of not releasing Aborigines on bail. The same policy was found to operate in certain South Australian towns. A blanket policy of not releasing Aborigines on bail is clearly contrary to law, since each case should be examined on its merits. Far from regarding the accused person's race as the one determining factor, the police should consider only whether the individual defendant will later appear for the court hearing if he is released on bail.

The next stage of the criminal justice process is the trial itself. When being tried on a criminal charge, it is usually an advantage to be represented by a lawyer. Aborigines find it difficult to arrange private legal representation, mainly because they cannot afford legal fees. Legal aid schemes provide some representation for Aborigines, but existing schemes are limited in the services they offer. In the majority of cases tried in the courts, Aboriginal defendants are unrepresented. The same is true of white defendants, but many of them are better able to represent themselves, being better educated and more articulate.

Many Aborigines experience difficulty with the English language, even if it is the only language they speak. For tribal Aborigines, it is a foreign language and they require interpreters as well as lawyers in court.

It has been claimed that Aborigines are in a better position than whites of the same socio-economic status as far as representation is concerned, because they have welfare officers to represent them. To the extent that welfare officers do appear in court and do succeed in representing the interests of Aboriginal defendants in the same way that a lawyer might do, this is a fair claim. Not surprisingly, it is only the exceptional individual welfare officer who is capable of such advocacy. Welfare officers are not legally trained and they have varying views of their functions in court; some do not accept or even understand the duty of an advocate to his client.

More serious is the fact that, in many cases, they are subject to the conflicting claims of the welfare of their Aboriginal clients and the interests of the department which employs them. A South Australian case illustrates the injustice which can be inflicted on an Aboriginal defendant in such circumstances. Four Aboriginal boys pleaded guilty in the Juvenile Court to charges of store-breaking. The store was on an Aboriginal reserve and the property allegedly stolen was government property. The magistrate committed them to a reformatory, largely on the basis of an unsworn statement made by an officer of the Department of Aboriginal Affairs. In this statement, the officer seemed to be concerned more with producing a favourable image of the department's administration of the reserve and with persuading the magistrate that the boys should be severely punished for the offence against government property than with ensuring that justice was done. A reformatory sentence was more severe than might have been imposed if the defendants had been represented by an independent lawyer, able to put their side of the story and to bring out evidence in mitigation of the offence. A lawyer might even have advised them to plead 'not guilty' and they might not have been convicted.

After the defendant has been convicted, the court has the task of sentencing him. The court usually has a discretion as to what sentence is imposed and often is able to choose between gaol and a fine. In Western Australia, proportionately more Aborigines than whites are sentenced to imprisonment. The imbalance is so great that, in 1965, Aborigines made up almost a quarter of the prison population, although they were only responsible for 11 per cent of total convictions.[7]

The Aboriginal prison population represents the terminal stage in the criminal justice process and should be a challenge to the conscience of every Australian. If we allow the system to continue operating as it does at present, we are condoning criminal law administration which produces a racially discriminatory effect. It is clear, even from this brief examination, that discrimination occurs at various stages of the process from the initiation of prosecutions to final incarceration in prison.

What is not so clear is the extent to which this discrimination results from racial prejudice on the part of law enforcement and judicial officers. There are certain ambiguities in the situation which suggest that it would be misleading, because too simple, to say that so many Aborigines are in prison because police, justices of the peace, magistrates and judges dislike blacks. No doubt the prejudices of some individuals play a part, but it is probable that the disabilities of Aborigines before the law are shared to some extent by other groups of comparable low socio-economic status. It was suggested earlier that poverty was the factor chiefly responsible for the failure of Aborigines to raise bail. Poverty also restricts access to legal representation and in other ways affects defendants adversely.

The phrase 'comparable low socio-economic status' perhaps contains the crux of the problem. In fact, few whites are as poverty-stricken as most Aborigines. Moreover, Aborigines are further outside the cultural mainstream and have difficulty understanding the white legal system. The further question then arises: why are Aborigines at the bottom of the heap in affluent Australia accompanied by so few whites in comparable material circumstances? For an answer, it is necessary to look at the history of white-Aboriginal relations in this country. It is a history in which the outstanding features are that the Aborigines were dispossessed of their land and thus of their economic resources and that this was frequently done by violent means. Having been deprived of resources, the Aborigines became and have largely remained paupers on the fringes of white society.

This general history is not unique to Australia, though naturally it differs in detail from the history of other countries in which invading whites confronted indigenous peoples. In the United Nations study mentioned earlier, the situation of racial groups who are also poor is adverted to: 'Where a certain ethnic group in a country is economically underprivileged what is said in [this study] under the heading of "Property" applies to that group, and its members are placed in a position of double disadvantage'.[8]

These considerations suggest that an improvement of the Aboriginal position before the law requires a two-pronged attack. On the one hand, reforms are needed in the administration of the law and attention should be directed to changing legal institutions and the way they operate in practice. At the same time a broader approach is needed, one which attempts to remove Aboriginal poverty and to provide resources so that Aborigines are able to meet other members of the community on more equal terms.

Dealing with the narrower approach first, some attempts have already been made to provide special protection for Aborigines who become involved with the law. One example is the special legislation in Western Australia relating to Aboriginal confessions. Section 31 of the Native Welfare Act provides: 'No admission of guilt or confession before trial shall be sought or obtained from any native charged or suspected of any offence punishable by death or imprisonment in the first instance, and if any such admission or confession is obtained it shall not be admissible or received in evidence'. This now applies only in the north and east of the state.

Does this section amount to discriminatory legislation which should be swept away? In the United Nations study, reference is made to the separate systems of courts which function in some countries to hear cases involving specific ethnic groups. 'Some of these court structures may be discriminatory in effect; others may be concessions to traditional tribal patterns or types of temporary legitimate protection of minorities'.[9]

A similar comment may be applied to a legislative provision like section 31 of the Native Welfare Act. Such legislation may be justified as 'temporary legitimate protection' of a minority group, most of whose members suffer the disadvantage of inadequate education and poverty and, therefore, need greater protection than other members of the community. But then it may be asked: 'How is it possible to distinguish legislation for which such a justification can be found from legislation which is "discriminatory in effect"?' This problem is not easy of solution but it is suggested that one test of whether legislation is discriminatory or preferential is whether members of the group affected have expressed resentment of it or, on the contrary, have requested its enactment.

No separate system of courts for Aborigines now exists in Victoria, South Australia or Western Australia. Western Australian law at one period provided for special Courts of Native Affairs which were authorized to consider tribal custom. The relevant legislation was operative between 1936 and 1954.[10] More recently, tribal law has been unofficially recognised in various ways in South Australia and Western Australia.

The Courts of Native Affairs in Western Australia were constituted by a special magistrate and a protector nominated by the Commissioner of Native Affairs. The legislation provided that tribal custom could be taken into account in mitigation of sentence, but not as a complete defence to a charge. It also enabled the court to 'call to its assistance a headman of the tribe to which the accused person' belonged, but it was not clear in what capacity the head man was to act, whether as an assessor, a witness for the defence or an expert witness.

Despite repeal of the Native Courts legislation in 1954, the ordinary courts in Western Australia are still able to consider tribal custom as a factor in mitigation of sentence. Courts have considerable discretion in relation to the matters they take into account in fixing sentence. If a defendant leads evidence showing that he acted in accordance with Aboriginal custom, the court is certainly acting within its powers if it uses that evidence to justify a lenient sentence. This is also true in the other states.

As recently as 1964, six Aborigines charged with conspiracy to murder another Aborigine claimed that the killing was dictated by tribal custom. They pleaded guilty in the Supreme Court of South Australia and led evidence that the deceased had been guilty of a serious tribal crime. He had stolen important corroboree stones and sold them to a white man. In killing him, they were administering tribal justice. The judge made allowance for these matters in determining sentence, saying that 'if they were white men convicted of a similar crime they could expect sentences many times as severe as those I am about to impose.' The four older men were sentenced to two years' imprisonment and the two younger men to one year.

The question of recognition of tribal custom arises in relation to the very small number of nomadic Aborigines with little contact with whites and the larger group of 'traditionally oriented' Aborigines, defined by Berndt as 'those people whose life is still meaningful in traditional Aboriginal terms.'[11] It can hardly be relevant for the large group of detribalised Aborigines, even though many of them have not fully accepted the wider Australian culture.

The desirability of establishing separate courts, or modifying the procedure of existing courts, is a wider question which could affect all Aborigines, whether they have lost their tribal heritage or not. Some magistrates hearing Aboriginal cases have already carried out the experiment of holding the court on an Aboriginal reserve and relaxing the rules of evidence so that any Aborigine who wants to speak on the matter before the court is permitted to do so.

In my view, any attempt to hand over more responsibility to Aborigines in relation to the whole legal process is to be encouraged. Aboriginal defendants are more likely to feel that they have been accorded justice after trial by their peers than when they have been judged by members of the alien white society. To ensure trial by peers, it would be necessary to provide courts, staffed by Aborigines, who are genuinely representative of the Aboriginal community, not of a white administration. If this is considered impracticable or inadvisable, an alternative would be mixed tribunals of white judges or magistrates sitting with Aboriginal assessors. In this way, Aborigines would be able to express their views and become involved in the legal system in a role other than that of passive defendant.

Aborigines could also seize the initiative by taking active steps to employ lawyers in both criminal and civil cases. Individuals may not be in a position to do this, but Aboriginal organisations will see this increasingly as one of their functions. Specialist bodies like the New South Wales Aboriginal Legal Service have a vital role to play in supplying services requested by Aborigines. American Indian tribes which have retained lawyers on a permanent basis can testify to the value of the practice.[12] Not only does it often result in favourable dispositions in legal cases, but it also involves Indians in the affairs of the wider community on a more equal basis than hitherto.

Finally, as suggested earlier, it is doubtful whether Aborigines will ever be truly equal before the law until their social and economic status has been raised to a level comparable with that of the rest of the community. The problem of discrimination in the administration of the criminal law will not be solved by reforms directed solely at the legal system. Measures required to improve the standard of living of the Aboriginal community include health, housing, education and employment programmes. But these programmes will fail to achieve their purpose unless accompanied by a sympathetic understanding of Aboriginal attitudes and cultural differences.

REFERENCES

1 *Study of Equality in the Administration of Justice*, Report submitted by the Special Rapporteur, Mr. Mohammed Ahmed Abu Rannat, United Nations Economic and Social Council, E/CN.4/Sub.2/296 (10 June 1969), p. 39.

2 EGGLESTON, E. M., 1970: Aborigines and the Administration of Justice, unpublished Ph.D. thesis, Monash University. Individual cases cited in the remainder of this paper for which no source is given are taken from fieldwork notes for this thesis.

3 Report of the Royal Commission into the law relating to the sale, supply and consumption of intoxicating liquors and other matters (including matters dealt with by the Licensing Act, 1932-1966) (Govt. Printer, Adelaide, 1966), p. 7.

4 The view of Dr. J. G. Rankin (formerly) Senior Physician, Alcoholism Clinic, St. Vincent's Hospital, Melbourne, appears to be that excessive drinking among Aborigines may be no more prevalent than among white groups of comparable socio-economic status, such as Skid Row men. (Report in *Australian*, 3 February 1970, p. 4).

5 *R. v. Lee* (1950) 82 C.L.R. 133.

6 EGGLESTON, *op. cit.*, p. 83. Only 14.3 per cent of Aborigines were released on bail; 33.6 per cent of whites were granted bail by the police. The cases in the sample cover all types of criminal offence, including drunkenness and traffic offences.

7 EGGLESTON, *op. cit.*, p. 15-16. South Australian prisons also have a large Aboriginal population. No statistics are available for Victoria.

8 Study of Equality in the Administration of Justice, p. 40.

9 *Ibid.*, p. 42.

10 Aborigines Act Amendment Act, 1936 (W.A.). Repealed by Native Welfare Act, 1954 (W.A.).

11 BERNDT, R. M., in Stanner, W. E. H., and Sheils, H. (eds.), 1963: *Australian Aboriginal Studies* (O.U.P., Melbourne), p. 386-7.

12 DOBYNS, H. F., in Levine, S., and Lurie, N. O. (eds.), 1970: *The American Indian Today* (Penguin), p. 268-291.

POLITICS OF PREJUDICE

8

ABORIGINES: LAW AND POLITICAL DEVELOPMENT

C. M. Tatz

> When I hear a man talk of unalterable law, the effect it
> produces upon me is to convince me that he is an unalterable
> fool.—*Sidney Smith*

Charles Rowley once said that Aborigines are far more in need of lawyers
than welfare officers.[1] To students I assert that while recourse to law and
legalisms may be a dead letter for American Negroes and Africans in South
Africa, it is an important first beginning for the indigenous people of
Canada, New Zealand and Australia.

A most neglected area in analyses of the political development of new
states is the role of law in such development. But in the advancement and
development of indigenous minorities within states, study of the role of
legal institutions by administrators and academics has not even begun. In
Australia we have a scattered series of researches into Aboriginal relationships with the criminal law,[2] among the best of which is 'The Trials of
Nancy Young' which appeared in *The Australian Quarterly* in June, 1970.
The fact is that we have a high degree of Aboriginal involvement in criminal
proceedings. But neither academically nor in administrative practice do we
have much concern with Aboriginal participation in civil law processes, with
law as an agent of social change, with law as a source of initiative attitudes,
ideas and norms which may have a modernizing and innovative impact on
white-Aboriginal relationships.

*   *   *   *

Ralph Braibanti[3] has defined political development as essentially a
series of ultimate progressions—with periodic regressions and even oscilla-
tions—from ascription to personal achievement, from ambiguity to certainty
in the use of public power, from alienation and withdrawal to enlightening
participation in collective social life, from coarseness and coercion to refinement and sensitivity in public action, from contraction to expansion of free
choice. Charles Hamilton,[4] the Negro leader and scholar, has defined the
Black Power aspect of political development as a systematic attempt to make
legitimate participants, not simply recipients, out of black people.

There is no doubt that law has often been, and will continue to be, an
impediment to these progressions. South Africa is a classic case of the use of
law as an instrument to effect radical social change of a negative kind. There
law has institutionalized many levels of non-white achievement. Law has
disfranchised an enfranchised people, thus changing legitimate participants
in the political system to recipients of whatever government deems is in their
best interests. Law is attempting, uniquely, to re-tribalize a largely detribalized people. Coarseness and coercion have become part of the 'South

African way of life'. There law has perverted and subverted law. Fundamental assumptions about innocence until guilt is proven, about rights of appeal, about judicial pronouncements on validity of laws, have been abrogated. One can be imprisoned without trial, be 'deemed' guilty by an official, be deported from one's own country; one can find oneself in court attempting to prove to the satisfaction of the State that one did not commit a crime; one can find oneself guilty of sabotage and treason, where today those indictments have a unique South African meaning. Alexander Pope's phrase about 'breaking butterflies on a wheel' is well illustrated in South Africa—where law and legal institutions are used as a bludgeon with which to 'pacify' a population and to maintain a minority's ideology.

But however imperfect legal institutions may of their nature be, one cannot conceive of political development outside the ambit of law.

The first attribute of political development is agreement on a fundamental polity of the state, typically embodied in a constitution. The relevance of law here is obvious. A second attribute is the establishment of a set of formalized institutions, and here administrative law is crucial. A third attribute of political development is the capability of maintaining national integration through orderly and just accommodation of cultural, religious and similar divisive forces. In reality legal means are heavily relied upon to achieve this integration, mainly through what Arens and Lasswell[5] call sanction law.

The fourth attribute is that a state in transition must have the capacity to blend elements of popular feeling—in markedly disparate stages of development—into an aggregate, an aggregate which must be normatively consistent with the basic polity of the state. Legal research here is vital: because while the polity often derives from western sources, the popular will often derives from indigenous sources, and western constitutional norms are often divorced—even in language—from the mainstream of the indigenous social order. Our ethnocentrism demands that Papua-New Guineans, tribal Aborigines, Maoris and others should—by some kind of osmosis—imitate and emulate not only our western polity but also our western political institutions. I believe that legal research, in full consultation with tribal Aborigines, will have to find a reconstructed indigenous tradition: one in which strands of thought equivalent to our assumptions have been identified and woven into a cohesive new doctrine. Only then will many sections of the indigenous communities really begin to participate meaningfully in political life.

Finally, the fifth attribute of political development is the involvement of the entire population in political life—power-sharing, power diffusion, politicization, mobilization, or the 'participation explosion'. This characteristic has always been given the most attention. But no concern has been shown for the quality of such participation, that is, for such factors as literacy, responsibility, understanding of issues, to the quality of civic culture generally. The emphasis has been on the acceleration of involvement—involvement almost indiscriminate and for its own sake. Accelerated power-sharing causes stress and crisis, because new states often do not have the institutional structures necessary to convert demands into action.

Law and legal institutions are relevant to this demand-conversion crisis and regrettably no systematic studies have been made of these adjustment mechanisms. One such adjustment is the concept of ambiguity. Ambiguity is a powerful force. It can be used as a control device and is commonly used by most administrations as a means of power: uncertainty, unease, ambivalence, diffusion of responsibility. A mature political system must be characterized by focused accountability, clarity of policy, courageous acceptance of decision-making by officials, and a high degree of rationality and insight. The effects of ambiguity may appear as a syndrome: frustration, alienation, withdrawal from political life, violence. The amount of alienation resulting from ambiguity needs to be measured: the role of ambiguity both as a regulator and as an agitator of crisis has not been studied. It is in areas such as these that legal sociology could well begin as a discipline in Australia.

       *   *   *   *

Without straining credulity, I believe that several of the aspects and themes mentioned above are highly relevant to indigenous minorities *within* politically developed states. As aspects, they do not necessarily form a coherent, logically sustained doctrine, nor can they: many of them are isolates, and I will treat them as such.

From Ascription to Personal Achievement

By ascription I mean the act of assigning, imputing or attributing a characteristic or status to a person. In Australia we have at least thirty current statutes which ascribe certain characteristics to a considerable proportion of the Aboriginal race, mainly the 'tribal' Aborigines in Queensland, Western Australia, the Northern Territory and South Australia. These attributes are usually negative: such as inability to manage their own affairs and property, unworthiness for inclusion in industrial awards, inability to handle liquor, inability in relation to certain rules of evidence in courts, inability to govern their own communities and so on. The ascriptions are blanket ones, applying to these particular racial groups as a whole—from which the individual has to seek 'exemption'.

A great advance in Australia was the coming into operation of the *Welfare Ordinance* in the Northern Territory in 1957. Reference was made to declaring an individual a ward by virtue of *his* individual manner of living, *his* ability to manage his own affairs, *his* personal associations, and *his* standard of social habit and behaviour. In theory, this was the first Aboriginal act to specify application on an individual basis. But such legislative advance was crippled by the administrative decision to declare as wards all full-blood Aborigines who could be 'censused' at the time. Even now— after the repeal of that Ordinance and the theoretical abolition of the wardship concept—there is no legal exemption in certain contexts: for example, Aborigines on settlements and missions cannot be paid other than 'Aboriginal' rates of pay—unless appointed to staff positions.

From the overall ascriptions flow a number of consequent subscriptions. In most cases Aborigines on settlements and missions are paid lower than the normal award rates. In many instances it is considered that Aborigines are unable to 'handle' social service payments, especially child endowment, and 'services' are ostensibly supplied in lieu. For the same reasons many aged and invalid pensioners are either fed or rationed to varying levels and are given a 'pocket money' component of their benefit by the local authority. Especially in Queensland, those Aborigines under the control of special legislation (the so-called 'assisted Aborigines') are provided with a curator to manage their property and financial affairs. Theoretically in that state, a child born to assisted parents is born free. However, the statute allows the Director of Aboriginal Affairs to declare as assisted any such child under the age of seventeen. In practice he does so: and all ascriptions of the parents are visited unto their new-born children. I once pointed out that the Emperor Justinian would have demurred at this situation. He humanized Roman Law by declaring that children born to slaves should not necessarily or logically suffer the incapacities inherent in their parents' condition.

My contention is this: while the acts of legislatures may not appreciably alter the personal prejudices of an adult public, legislative actions can probably alter overt patterns of interaction between groups—both negatively and positively. Put another way, governmental action need not await a change of public mind and attitude. I am decrying the cliche which says that advancement of the Aborigines depends on a change in public attitudes: I am saying that much of the public attitude stems from the fashion and trend set by legislation.

For example, so long as legislation ascribes Aboriginal wage worth as somewhere below the basic wage—let alone the award wage—why should employers of Aborigines rate them and pay them any differently? One cannot but see as hypocrisy the Commonwealth's intervention in the *Cattle Station (Northern Territory) Award Case* in 1965-66.[6] With the North Australian Workers' Union, the Commonwealth sought to have Aborigines included in the award, thus seeking 'industrial justice' for Aborigines on cattle stations. Yet at the time two-thirds of the Territory Aborigines were directly and indirectly under the control of the Commonwealth—and that population was being paid no more, and often less, than Aborigines on cattle stations. There has to be some logical sympathy for the cattlemen's cry: 'why should we pay more when the Welfare Branch rates them at some $5 a week plus rations?'

It has been misinterpreted or phoney biology translated into inadequate law, rather than miscegenation, that has helped create persons of peculiar 'non-category' in some instances—the twilight zone 'part-Aborigines'. The ascription is clear, as in Queensland: if one has, legislatively, certain 'drops of the blood', or a 'strain of the blood', then one may find oneself legislated in or out of the particular and special administrative system that applies to Aborigines. As in South Africa, the consequences of race classification are vital for the classified person: place of domicile, a host of civil rights, legal status, income horizon and so on are affected. And in some states of Australia, there are many legal, social and economic consequences for those legislatively classified as quadroons, octoroons, half-castes, and full-bloods. Quite arbitrarily and unscientifically, each group has ascribed to it a separate set of characteristics based on some spectrum of an artificial 'civilization' scale related to these precious haematological drops.

Governments are able to set the tone and pace for the public—and most certainly for Aborigines—by repealing ascriptive legislation and replacing it with simple, enabling legislation; that is, acts which allow for the creation of special departments[7] which can seek funds for the social, economic and political advancement of persons of Aboriginal descent, or who choose to identify themselves as Aborigines, or who are identified as such by other Aborigines. (In the end, I believe that self-identification is the only sane and moral approach to the question of identification and classification. It is an approach that the Federal Government could well seek to persuade the States to adopt.) Such legislation can act as a catalyst of social change: it can have a powerful innovative impact on pervading white attitudes.

*   *   *   *

From Ambiguity to Certainty

Earlier it was said that ambiguity is a powerful force, often used by administrations as a means of creating uncertainty, ambivalence and diffusion of responsibility. Of this latter, Australian Aboriginal administrations are a classic case. There are seven major governmental administrative units for Aborigines, apart from a plethora of mission and pastoral property administrations: Victoria, New South Wales, Queensland, Western Australia, South Australia, the Northern Territory (Commonwealth) and the Office of Aboriginal Affairs, Prime Minister's Department. There are six basic sets of legislation,[8] many different definitions of Aborigines, and conditions for those defined as Aborigines vary greatly from place to place. Although the 1967 referendum gave the Commonwealth concurrent power with the States to legislate for State Aborigines, the *status quo ante* has persisted. The population involved is estimated at 130,000 people. Without doubt, Aborigines are per capita the most over-administered minority anywhere in the world.

The ambivalence and diffusion of responsibility—indeed the conflict of responsibility—is nowhere better illustrated than in the Commonwealth's jurisdiction. At present there is before the Supreme Court of the Northern Territory a case brought by the Aborigines of Yirrkala against the Commonwealth Government and Nabalco Pty. Ltd., an aluminium company, for recognition of their title to the Gove Peninsula land area, and for compensation for lands excised or exploited by the aluminium company. The Department of the Interior, headed by the Minister, Mr. Peter Nixon, controls the Northern Territory Administration, a subdivision of which is the Welfare Branch. The Office of Aboriginal Affairs is part of the Prime Minister's Department. The Minister of Aboriginal Affairs, Mr. W. C. Wentworth, is also Minister of Social Services, and in this latter capacity only has full control of the staff of this Department. In theory he has ministerial responsibility for Aboriginal Affairs—but no related department under his control which is really specific to his office or to actual administration of Aborigines. Apart from that ambiguity—and there are similar ones relating to Aboriginal education—we are currently witnessing the spectacle before the Court of one Commonwealth arm, Interior and the Welfare Branch, opposing the Aboriginal case tooth and nail; and another arm, the Office of Aboriginal Affairs, supporting in principle the Aboriginal case. The outward appearance is one of the Department responsible for Aboriginal advancement (Interior and the Welfare Branch) supporting the rights of a mining company against the people whose rights they are statutorily obliged to advance. We are also witnessing the unique spectacle in Federal bureaucratic life of two arms of government in major conflict, both using common Treasury funds and owing a common allegiance to the Crown: one arm for Aborigines, the other 'agin' them. And in case the ambiguities were not cloudy enough, the Minister of the Interior announced in Parliament—the day the Land Rights Case resumed in the Canberra Supreme Court—that 'recognition of land rights would not help the Aboriginal people of the Northern Territory'.[9]

There is current speculation that the Commonwealth 'cannot afford to lose this case', that is, the Department of Interior view is said to be *the* Commonwealth view. There is obvious speculation that if Interior loses, it will appeal. There is rumour that should it lose on appeal, the Commonwealth will legislate to 'rectify the situation', that is, put Aboriginal claims to land beyond any doubt—and beyond any reach. In the same breath, so to speak, Mr. Gorton told Parliament last October[10] that 'in recent years most

discriminatory legislation against Aborigines has been abolished: we intend
to see that this process is completed in the life of the next Parliament upon
both State and Federal levels'.

Queensland represents another highwater mark in ambiguity. When the
Aboriginal legislation was amended in 1965, the then Minister (the late
Premier, Mr. J. Pizzey) indicated to the public that the guiding light for the
new legislation has been Article 1 of the U.N. Declaration of Human
Rights.[11] He then proceeded to produce a carbon copy of the repressive 1939
legislation, which in turn was based in large measure on the 1897 legislation.
To the new Act, he added such innovations as detention in dormitories for
periods of up to six months for such 'crimes' as (a) committing an offence
against 'discipline or good order'; (b) without lawful permission leaving,
escaping or attempting to *escape* from the reserves; (c) committing 'any
immoral act or immoral conduct'; (d) being 'idle, careless or negligent at
work' or without just excuse, refusing to work or wilfully mismanaging work.

The ambiguities resulting may not be consciously Machiavellian, but
they inevitably create a great deal of unease and uncertainty in Aboriginal
minds. More than unease and uncertainty, the ambiguities and contradictions
create hostility and bitterness—or frustration, alienation, withdrawal and
eventually, violence. It should come as no great surprise when the 'docile
ones' suddenly begin to throw an assortment of home-made incendiary objects
into the mechanisms of the mining industry. When that happens
there will doubtless be another ambiguity rung in—Red agitation or Black
Power agitation. Not only is this ubiquitous tactic out-dated and old-
fashioned in Aboriginal affairs, it has also proven over the years to be
irrational and unfounded.

There are a number of options that the Federal Government can
exercise in the next three years. My own view is that given the tremendous
enlightenment and radical-thinking of the Office of Aboriginal Affairs, the
government should place its bets on that particular organization—now part
of the Department of the Environment, Aborigines and the Arts—and should
back it with the legislative power to create clear-cut policies, rationalized
programmes and focused accountability. The record indicates that the
Department of the Interior section controlling the Northern Territory
Administration has been a serious impediment to Aboriginal socio-economic
and politico-legal development in the Territory—it should certainly not be
allowed jurisdiction over the rest of Australia's Aborigines.

✿   ✿   ✿   ✿

From Alienation to Enlightening Participation

Charles Rowley has also rightly said that Aborigines are the most totally
conquered of all indigenous minority groups. They have no claims to make
on their conquerers, no treaties to guarantee rights and obligations, no
hitting power or sanctions behind their demands. There is only our moral
obligation, a now highly developed sense of the need to atone for the past
and to keep pace with a general world ethos of non-discrimination.

The level of alienation, frustration and bitterness among Aborigines has
been described elsewhere.[12] The question to be asked is whether there has
been or is now any sense at all among Aborigines of Aboriginal participation
in decisions affecting them. Put another way, has our national polity made
any provision for the accommodation of Aboriginal views?

Aboriginal participation is essentially regulated by law. All Aborigines

have a State franchise—in Queensland as recently as 1965—and they have
had a Federal franchise, on a voluntary registration basis, since 1961. Apart
from this mildly meaningless sense of participation, several administrations
have made more positive attempts to provide for Aboriginal decision-making.

In Queensland there is a system of Aboriginal Councils, the detailed
provisions of which make it plain that officials have overriding veto power.
These Councils consist of two elected and two nominated Aborigines, any
one of whom may be removed by the Director of Aboriginal Affairs, and each
of these Councils is responsible to the Reserve Managers. Elsewhere in
northern Australia there are a series of local mission and settlement councils
and social clubs—none of which can be described as having any significant
or useful autonomy. Their level of decision-making is restricted to the harm-
less, the petty and the trivial.

In Victoria and New South Wales, Aborigines Welfare Boards were
until 1968 the statutory bodies charged with Aboriginal administration. In
New South Wales, in a Board of eleven, there were two elected Aborigines.
In Victoria, in a Board of eleven, there were two nominated Aborigines.
Today both states have established new administrative systems, as a result of
which there are Advisory Councils consisting entirely of Aborigines in New
South Wales, and eight Aborigines out of thirteen members in Victoria.
Aboriginal reaction to these Advisory Councils is quite clear: since officials
pointedly refer to their *advisory* role, Aborigines see them as 'toy telephones',
instruments into which they can speak—but at the other end of which there
is no one to listen.

Consultation is the new catch-cry on the lips of most administrators.
Consistent with this, several attempts have been made to have discussions
with Aboriginal leadership and to select Aboriginal leaders as liaison officers.
The participation-consultation mechanisms that exist, however, are based
very much on western notions of representativeness and representation structures. Our notion of committees, councils, chairmen, treasurers, secretaries,
agendas and rules of procedure have been foisted upon Aborigines—as if
they were the only valid forms or vehicles for decision-making and spokes-
manship. One of the reasons for the failure of these mechanisms to 'produce'
is that they are intrinsically alien to the cultural configurations of the
indigenous societies. With the vast anthropological research material available, it seems a not too difficult exercise to interpret the indigenous system of
decision-making and to create structures that have strands of indigenous
thought and practice substitutive for our equivalent cultural assumptions.
Another reason for failure of these councils as participation-consultation
mechanisms is that the western constructs made available to Aborigines are
not the constructs of administration that are used in the mainstream of white
society today: they tend to be the council-type systems of the early colonial
eras. What some Aborigines want is what the student movement wants: not
an elitist hierarchy based on distant and indirect representation, but valid
participatory democracy. They also fully perceive tokenism for what it is.

In short, legislation can simply lay down that appropriate mechanisms
will be created for the participation-consultation process. It can and should
eliminate the present prescriptions of councils, which lay down elaborate
details as to powers, hierarchy, methods of election and nomination, voting
procedures and the like. Such a change in legislation assumes, of course, that
the veto powers of officials are recognized as inconsistent with power-
diffusion and participation, and accordingly eliminated. It also assumes that

what governments envisage by and through consultation is their willingness
to give credence to what Aborigines say is in their best interests—and to act
in accordance with that credence.

○   ○   ○   ○

From Coercion to Sensitivity

In Queensland Aboriginal legislation there is undoubted coercion: a
strong penal flavour in the legislation and regulations, together with a
possibly stronger penal flavour in actual administration of the law.[13] Both in
law and in practice there is still a great deal in Aboriginal affairs of what
Rowley calls the gun and the whip, or the threat of the gun and the whip.

Referring to the style of administration, there are a number of ways in
which what I call sensitivity can be achieved. I will discuss only two in this
context, namely, Aboriginal participation in civil law processes and the
possible use by Aborigines of certain artificial legal structures.

I know of only three major cases in which infractions of Aboriginal
rights have been pursued in civil courts, that is, pursued by Aborigines or
on their behalf: the Cattle Station (Northern Territory) Award Case in
1965-66, the case of Frank Gananggu and Elsie Darrbuma,[14] and the present
Yirrkala Land Rights Case. These cases represent what I call open, publicly
adjudicated refinement, refinement in contrast to the closed, private, often
clandestine coercive system of control that is still very much in operation in
parts of Australia.

In 1963 I described the 'kangaroo courts' operating on Queensland settlements (see
Reference 12)—courts which not only failed to observe the rules of natural justice
but which also imprisoned Aborigines for 'offences' which could not warrant that
term in the wider Australian society. While there has been some change in the
composition of these 'courts', their authoritarian and vindictive flavour remains
today. Earlier this year an Australian senator enquired into the jailing of an
Aborigine on a Queensland settlement for a period of 70 days. The Department
of Aboriginal Affairs justified the sentences on the ground that the visiting magistrate had clearly concurred in the sentences by signing the settlement court record
book. The accused received 14 days' imprisonment for two counts of behaving in
a disorderly manner; 14 days for drinking liquor on a reserve; 14 days for behaving
in a riotous, violent and disorderly manner; 7 days each for two separate counts of
using obscene language, and 14 days for the following:

> 'Chapter 4 (1)(e) By-laws:
> That on the 1st May, 1970, at X —— in the Magistrates Court District
> of Y —— in the State of Queensland you did make use of insulting words
> to wit "Z —— you bloody big poofter" so near to a public place namely
> X —— Watch-House, X ——.'

All sentences were cumulative. It should be noted that all seven charges arose
from one episode on one day, and the language charges all related to the same
man, a member of the so-called Aboriginal police force. The Department's final
'justification' for these sentences was that the accused had been on 22 charges
since 1963: which is not difficult if you can chalk them up seven at a time,
roughly one for each expletive vented against the management.

One signal failure of administrations has been in not pursuing civil
claims on behalf of the Aborigines whom they 'represent'. The record shows
that throughout Australia no more than a handful of cases have been taken
up by administrations on behalf of aggrieved Aborigines. It is beyond plausi-
bility that in all these years civil damage has been suffered by only some two
dozen Aborigines. In the period I examined in the Northern Territory,[15] 1953
to 1963, the Welfare Branch did not bring a single prosecution against a

cattleman for his failure to abide by a bookful of regulations affecting his conduct towards Aborigines.

The Cattle Station Case was taken up by the North Australian Workers' Union. The Land Rights Case is being partially financed and strongly pressed by a group of Methodist ministers and laymen. (It is probable that the Federal Government will assume most of the costs of this case: which is yet another ambiguity for the Aborigines to mull over.) Frank Gananggu and Elsie Darrbuma were an Oenpelli Mission couple who were removed to East Arm Leprosarium. Their children were removed from them—as was the custom—by the nursing nuns and fostered out to couples at Bathurst Island. On discharge from the leprosarium—a relatively new process—they sought the return of their children. This was denied. A Darwin lawyer, Mr. R. Ward, took their case and sued in the Supreme Court for the return of the children to their natural parents. The Court ruled against the Oenpelli couple. Thereupon a small, private Melbourne group, of which I was a member, obtained the free services of a Melbourne QC to launch an appeal to the High Court. That Court refused leave to appeal from the Supreme Court decision. The battle was lost but I believe a principle won, namely, that mission and government authorities will of necessity think twice before they remove and foster children in this customarily arbitrary manner in the future.

The Cattle Station Case was a victory for Aborigines, albeit with a three-year waiting period before the decision became operative. The Gananggu case was lost and it appears likely that in the end, the land rights case will be lost—*politically*—by the Aborigines. Nevertheless, the presentation of grievances before independent tribunals, the attendant publicity, the relative equality between plaintiff and defendant as achieved by batteries of contesting lawyers is a definite advance on the one-sided combats that take place in most Aboriginal contexts. The difficulty here will be to convince Aborigines that even though white man's justice in the courts goes against them, there is still some value in prosecuting their grievances in the civil courts. The time has also surely come for administrators to assist Aborigines in prosecuting claims and assure Aborigines of access to, and participation in, this fundamental legal process in a democratic society.

A second important step lies in the legal incorporation of various Aboriginal communities. At present, with perhaps three exceptions,[16] most Aboriginal communities—whether tribal or fringe-dwelling—stand 'naked' before administrative organization, whether governmental, mission or pastoralist. The individual Aborigine has none of the security that normally comes from organization membership, especially in his dealings with criminal and civil law processes. He has no recourse to the financial, or, in the end, moral support of fellow *organization* members. This is truer of the socially disorganized fringe-dwelling, part-Aboriginal communities than of the more cohesive full-blood tribal communities. The time has come to incorporate Aboriginal rights under some legal umbrella and provide the people, as Rowley suggests, with more lawyers and fewer welfare officers. Perhaps legal incorporation—along the lines of the successful Maori Incorporations recognized by the *Maori Social and Economic Advancement Act*—will give the Aborigines greater confidence and, through the respective mouthpieces of welfare officer and lawyer, greater articulacy. In the end, I suggest that white administrators will give greater credence to the 'incorporated' viewpoints of Aborigines than has ever been given to the claims or complaints of the

'naked' individual. Certainly this is the case in Canada. The inherent respect
for Indians shown by officials is acknowledged by the latter to be due to the
presence alongside Indians of lawyers. Said Thucydides: 'You know as well
as we do that right, as the world goes, is only in question for equals in power;
the strong do what they can, and the weak suffer what they must'. Perhaps,
but my suggestion may produce a totally different psychological basis: not
the organization man versus the naked indigene, but the corporation lawyer
versus the departmental lawyer. These may not be fighting at the same
weight but the imbalance is not as it is now in Australia—a heavyweight
thumping or 'counselling' a bantam.

Legal incorporation does not have to wait for community education and
sophistication. Tuition before rights—the Australian philosophy of
gradualism—can in fact be greatly accelerated by incorporated bodies
demanding or seeking the legal recognition of rights immediately.

Another legal construct used in New Zealand could well be considered
for Australia. It is one which has the merit of having been built on the
foundations of a traditional Maori system. The *Maori Welfare Act* of 1962
provides for the establishment of Maori Committees, one of whose many
functions is the imposition of penalties, not exceeding ten pounds, for various
offences. They include riotous behaviour, drunkenness, disorderly behaviour
in hotels and at Maori gatherings and driving under the influence. The
accused may elect to be charged before an ordinary court under the
Summary Proceedings Act or by the Maori Committee. He cannot be
charged in both places, and if he chooses the latter, he must be given 'a
reasonable opportunity of being heard in his own defence'.

I have attended several of these Maori Committee meetings acting as a
court. The rules of evidence would upset the legal purist, but a genuine
community justice is done and seen and felt by all to be done. Here Maoris
are adjudicating on Maoris before open mixed audiences. There is a shame
factor involved in an accused confessing before his elders. Many cases are
civil, involving the Committee acting in a social welfare role. By this system
ordinary courts are not over-burdened, and contact with police (the arresters
are Maori wardens or police who hand the accused to the wardens), remand
prisons and courts is obviated. To me, this is a grand example of sensitivity
and refinement: it is the antithesis of a private and special code of settlement
'law', which law, as in Queensland, has often been specifically excluded from
review or challenge in the ordinary courts.

❖   ❖   ❖   ❖

From Contraction to Expansion of Choice

Australian governments indicated in 1965 that henceforth Aborigines
would have a choice in matters affecting them. By this was meant that no
longer would Aborigines have to attain the same manner of living as other
Australians, and share the same hopes, customs, loyalties, habits and beliefs.
Presumably the choice implied is between total assimilation and the preservation of a particular Aboriginal life-style. To support the latter, governments
indicated their intended encouragement of Aboriginal culture, and subsequent official statements have suggested that a serious aim is the restoration
of Aboriginal pride, dignity and self-reliance.[17]

Such choices are non-choices unless accompanied by legislative and
administrative changes to remove the present obstacles to choice. The

majority of Aborigines live their lives within the restrictions and constraint
of special legislation: of statutes which all too often express values opposite
to those expressed as policy aspirations. The great majority of Aborigines
live their lives within the confines and fences of settlements, missions and
pastoral properties—in what Erving Goffman calls 'total institutions'.[18] He
says:—

> 'A total institution may be defined as a place of residence and work
> where a large number of like-situated individuals, cut off from the
> wider society for an appreciable period of time, together lead an
> enclosed, formally administered round of life. Prisons serve as a clear
> example, providing we appreciate that what is prison-like about
> prisons is found in institutions whose members have broken no laws.'

These institutions arose in an era when the political philosophy was
protection-segregation, when special 'inviolable' reserves could protect
Aborigines, in their thought-to-be diminishing days, from a variety of white
predators.

I began by saying that the role of law was a much neglected area in the
process of political development. I am not saying that law, legal institutions
and legal structures are together the magical cure-all for the ills that beset
Aboriginal affairs in Australia. What must be stressed is that law and
legalisms are important first beginnings for Aborigines. And the best beginning, in my view, is new law, refined and sensitive law, that will dismantle
the existing barriers of Aboriginal development. Said S. I. Hayakawa:—[19]

> 'But the extensional facts are that "federal power" or "states' rights"
> may *both* be used *either for* or against the liberties of the individual.
> Federal power can tyrannize, but it can also protect individuals
> against the tyrannies of states, or states against the tyrannies of great
> national corporations or combines. States can also tyrannize or protect
> against tyranny. Most of the uproar about "federal power" and
> "states' rights" has *no meaning* apart from specific proposals as to
> *what powers* (state and federal) are to be exercised in *what ways* for
> *what purposes.'*

The locus of power in this country should be federal, unambiguous,
single and publicly accountable; to revoke the multitude of constricting and
constraining state legislation; power to alter the legal minority of an ethnic
minority; power to foster the political growth of a race whose society has
been successfully destroyed by law and its administration. While there is still
a chance to stave off the final stage of the ambiguity syndrome, violence, it
seems unalterably foolish not to do so.

ACKNOWLEDGEMENT

This paper was first published in *The Australian Quarterly*, Volume 42, No. 4,
December 1970, and is reproduced here with the kind permission of the
Quarterly editor.

REFERENCES

1 In *Aborigines in the Economy*, eds. I. G. Sharp and C. M. Tatz, Jacaranda,
  1966, p. 343.

2 Apart from six or seven articles—written between 1935 and 1969—the first
  major analysis of the application of criminal law to Aborigines is the doctoral
  research of Miss Elizabeth Eggleston at Monash University. This work
  examines—in relation to Victoria, South Australia and Western Australia—

such aspects as the nature of court hearings, arrest procedures, bail facilities, legal aid facilities, criminal offences specific to Aborigines, comparative sentencing and the nature of the indigenous legal system.

3 In this section I have drawn on the work of Professor Ralph Braibanti, chairman of the Center for Commonwealth Studies, Duke University: see his chapter 'The Role of Law in Political Development', in *International and Comparative Law of the Commonwealth*, ed. R. R. Wilson, Duke University Press, 1968.

4 HAMILTON, CHARLES V. 'Black Power and What It Means', in *The 1969 World Book Year Book*, Field Enterprises Educational Corporation, Chicago, p. 271.

5 ARENS, RICHARD, and LASSWELL, HAROLD D. *In Defence of Public Order: The Emerging Field of Sanction Law*, New York, 1961.

6 Conciliation and Arbitration Act 1904-1964: C. No. 83 of 1965: *In the Matter of Cattle Station Industry (Northern Territory) Award*, 1951.

7 I do not subscribe to some current thinking that Aboriginal administrations should be abolished and Aborigines 'thrown onto community resources'— because such resources have a bad habit of putting Aborigines at the bottom end of their service queues.

8 The most important of these are: *The Aborigines and Torres Strait Islanders Affairs Act* 1965, *Aborigines and Torres Strait Islanders Affairs Act Regulations* 1966, Queensland; *Aboriginal Affairs Act* 1962-1967, *Prohibition of Discrimination Act* 1966, *Aboriginal Lands Trust Act* 1966, South Australia; *Native Welfare Act* 1963, *Natives (Citizenship Rights) Act Amendment Act* 1964, Western Australia; *Aboriginal Affairs (Amendment) Act* 1968, Victoria; *Social Welfare Ordinance* 1964, *Wards' Employment Ordinance* 1957-1964, *Crown Lands Ordinance* 1964, Northern Territory; *Aboriginal Affairs Act* 1969, New South Wales; *Aboriginal Enterprises (Assistance) Act* 1968, Commonwealth of Australia.

9 *The Age*, Melbourne, 4 September 1970.

10 Quoted from 'Kunmanggur', No. 3, December 1969, Office of Aboriginal Affairs, Canberra. See also Governor-General's Speech, 'Senate Hansard', 3 March 1970, at p. 13.

11 'Introduction by Hon. J. A. Pizzey, M.L.A., of a Bill to Promote the Well-Being of Aborigines and Torres Strait Islanders, 1965', a reprint of the Minister's first and second reading speeches to the Legislative Assembly, Government Printer, Brisbane, pp. 20. At p. 14 he said: 'Article (1) of that declaration has particular reference to our thinking on this Bill and, to my mind, has guided its preparation. That Article reads as follows:—"All human beings are born free and equal in dignity and rights. They are endowed with reason and conscience and should act towards one another in a spirit of brotherhood".'

12 See my article 'Queensland's Aborigines: Natural Justice and the Rule of Law', *The Australian Quarterly*, Vol. XXXVI, No. 4, December 1964; my 'Some Aboriginal Thoughts', *Dissent*, Spring, 1965, No. 15; see also 'Survey of Race Relations in Selected Country Towns', Lorna Lippman, Monash University, roneoed, 1970; see also editions of *Koorier*, newsletter of the National Tribal Council, published in roneoed form by Bruce McGuinness, Director, Aborigines' Advancement League, Melbourne.

13 See my 'Aborigines: Equality or Inequality?' in *The Australian Quarterly*, Vol. XXXVIII, No. 1, March 1966. For an analysis of some specific Queensland attitudes, see Frank Stevens, 'Weipa: The Politics of Pauperization', *The Australian Quarterly*, Vol. 41, No. 3, September 1969. See also his chapter, 'Aborigines', in *Australian Society*, eds. A. F. Davies and S. Encel, 2nd ed., Cheshires, 1970.

14 See *The Age,* Melbourne, 12 March 1966.

15 'Aboriginal Administration in the Northern Territory of Australia', Ph.D. thesis, Australian National University, 1964.

16 Don McLeod's Nomads Ltd. group at Pilbara; the Cummeragunja reserve community in New South Wales, and the Mugarinya group in Western Australia.

17 GORTON, JOHN GREY: 'Our basic aim is to give our Aborigines the opportunity to be self-supporting, and to end the mentality of the hand-out. We want them to choose for themselves their own future, and to regain their initiative and independence,' *op. cit.*, 'Kunmanggur', p. 1 (see note 10).

18 GOFFMAN, ERVING, 'Asylums', Penguin, 1961, p. 11.

19 From 'The World of Law', ed. Ephraim London, Simon and Schuster, New York, Vol. I, 'The Law in Literature', p. xiv.

9

PARLIAMENTARY ATTITUDES TO ABORIGINAL AFFAIRS

F. S. Stevens

Robert Park, in his essay 'The Problem of Cultural Differences', noted the permanency of community attitudes which, although formulated in one life-time, linger on to condition the minds and actions of people many genera-tions removed from the original point of contact or experience.[1] Dewey, in the same light, believed that 'without this communication of ideals, hopes, expectations, standards, opinions from those members of society who are passing out of the group life to those who are coming into it, social life could not survive'.[2]

Accordingly, there is a time gap between the basic reasons for the creation of community attitudes and their final departure from the value systems of those who live in the society concerned, but who may never have experienced the causes of the particular process of opinion formulation. In Australia, official policies towards the original inhabitants of the continent have been patently slow to adjust to the rapid developments of social conscience and science, both here and overseas. And yet, the people who are involved in the administration of Government programmes for Aborigines, believing themselves to be persons of good intent, rarely stop to consider the value systems on which current legislation and administrative techniques are based. For whilst, on the one hand, a community might spend considerable sums of money in endeavouring to make an economic impact on a problem with which all are concerned, it is of little avail unless the changes in the social structure are both mental as well as material. It is here, in the philo-sophical basis of the so called Australian 'Assimilation' programme for Aborigines, that one may look for the true chances of success of the pro-grammes of assistance which have been extended over the past decade, and ask whether they are founded on genuine goodwill.

There is little doubt, for example, that the Australian attitudes to Aborigines in the nineteenth century were founded on both opportunism and ignorance. It is a question of some moment, just how far these two con-siderations condition peoples minds in 1970. The record of the 1880s, when Australia's racial policies were formulated, at least, is perfectly clear:—

> 'Those who, during the last few months, have been bringing more prominently under public notice the sad case of the country's Aborigines [had been] acting the part of Job's comforters, for they [were] directing attention to an evil which [was] utterly irremediable and amenable only to palliative treatment. The Aborigine [was] a doomed man . . . . He [was] a spineless creature with all the savagery taken out of him (impossible to correct and doomed to perfidy)

Christianity . . . never [having been] intended for the black-fellows. Its higher ideals they are incapable of understanding.'[3]

By the turn of the century, the concept of the dying race came into common use and belief, one author even considering that they had already perished.[4] But, in the process of dying, they seemed to have the ability to cause degeneration in those who came into contact with them as well:—

'The blackfellow is not the noble savage he is depicted; that if he lacks one thing more than the other it is virtue; their songs, rites and ceremonies are utterly revolting and fiendish, but if you add a few white vices, and then ask the question as to the possibility of chastity among the women, the idea at once becomes preposterous. No less preposterous, therefore, is the idea of black women being outraged unless it is by stopping their supply of tobacco. As to the numerous murders being attributable to white men violating the moral laws of the tribe, I have already shown it to be impossible when such laws do not exist.'[5]

The literature of later years presented a different tone, as writers started to question the basis of the generally held assumptions regarding Aborigines and the policies which had conditioned their relationships with the European community. Daisy Bates took up the challenge in the twenties with the question 'Our Aborigines: Can they be preserved'.[6] In the thirties, apart from the increasing production of anthropologists, one witnesses the enquiring tone of literary output on the subject—'Turn to the Right: A Maligned Race' (1933),[7] 'A Despised Race: the Vanishing Aborigines of Australia' (1936).[8] Gradually, the old ideas concerning Aborigines were challenged as writers and social workers came closer to the problems involved in the adjustment of both communities to one another.

A change in public opinion was clearly distinguishable by the time the Second World War was declared: 'What is Their Destiny?',[9] 'The Future of the Australian Aborigines',[10] 'Some Australians Take Stock',[11] and 'Anthropology and the Dying Australian Aborigines',[12] are titles typical of the questioning attitude of the many writers who became not only interested in the subject but considerably active and vocal. The contributions of the anthropologists to the subject of Aboriginal and European adjustment were vast, both in quantity and perspicuity. Elkin's classic work, *The Australian Aborigines*, published in 1938, undoubtedly elevated the tone of general debate.[13] Other anthropologists, in particular many who had trained under Elkin in Sydney, refused to be restrained by old prejudices.

It was not, however, all change, as the old prejudices mingled with the new. The Melbourne *Argus* in 1938, seemed to set the tone:—

'From a practical point of view (intermarriage with Aborigines) would only [be considered by] the dregs of the white race . . . and the inevitable result would be undesirable on grounds other than colour . . . Aborigines [are] a backward and low race. Unfortunately for the self esteem of many worthy survivors of a dying people, it is the simple self evident truth . . . . The Aborigines . . . cannot be treated as a modern, civilised race. They are properly regarded as a dying relic of a dead past, and as such should be treated with the broadest tolerance and humanity.'[14]

By the post-war years, the literature on the subject of Aborigines had developed a new dimension. No longer were writers looking at a 'Dying Race', as they came to realise that the problem, far from shrinking was becoming greater, at least in numbers. 'Aborigines Increasing: Not a Dying Race',[15] 'Is White Australia Doomed',[16] 'No Dying Race',[17] 'The Sustaining Ideals of Australian Aboriginal Societies'[18] was the new tenor.

The change in mind of the chroniclers of the age was also reflected in those responsible for the vast mat of legislation which had been woven to contain the clash between the two races during more than a century of contact; a conflict which had been founded on the readily accepted premise of the inferiority of the Aboriginal race and its inevitable extermination.

The legislators mirrored the changing value systems of the community, but vacillated between the old and the new as such matters as retaining political office conditioned their planning. In the deliberations of the politicians over demands for alteration to the many Aboriginal Acts and Ordinances throughout the country, one is able to obtain a clear picture of the values which were held by the community and which affected human relationships in everyday life. Indeed, as the legislative system was designed to take care of their total needs on the bumpy road to the cemetery,[19] it is not possible to consider the framework of native ordinances except within the confines of parliamentary attitudes thereto. It was in the debates of the legislatures that the flesh was put on the skeleton so that administrators could accomplish what they thought the elected representatives considered needed to be done. In this community of attitudes, one may look for the real causes of the failure of Australia's assimilation programme. It is significant in this respect that, some three decades after the conceptualisation of policy in these terms, less than 1 per cent of the indigenous population might be considered to be enjoying the equality and status of ordinary citizens of the Commonwealth.

Federal Parliament

The values of the Parliamentarians and the public generally, in the 1930s, were conceived on the basis of very little contact with the native races. By this time, only an impoverished, diseased and ill-nourished remnant of the original inhabitants remained in the settled areas. Government policy and economic necessity restrained the remaining survivors in the far corners of the continent where their main experiences of European society were gained through contact with pastoral or mission entrepreneurs.

In these circumstances, the average citizen's concept of Aboriginal society and the mutual response of the two races fell far behind the considerations of academic theorists. But the political leaders of the thirties were not all without foresight, although, at times, a stand in favour of the increased appropriation of government resources to assisting the dispossessed race might have reacted unfavourably to their political interests.

One of the errant Members of what were normally more conservative programmes, was the Honourable J. McEwen,[20] then Minister for the Interior, who, in accepting the reports of a number of enquiries by prominent anthropologists into the position of Aborigines in the Northern Territory, set the tone for a period of readjustment in Aboriginal policies throughout the country. Following these studies and a Board of Enquiry into the administration of Aboriginal welfare in 1935,[21] the Northern Territory Administration was encouraged to report that it 'held the conviction of the ultimate possibility of adapting the Aboriginal to the conditions of western civilisation . . .'[22]

The new temper of national thinking on the subject of indigenes was also marked by the first conference of Commonwealth and State Aboriginal authorities in Canberra, in 1936. The meeting concluded: 'That (it believed) that the destiny of the natives of aboriginal origin, but not of the full blood, lies in his ultimate absorption by the people of Commonwealth, and it therefore recommended that all efforts be directed to that end.'[23]

Elkin summed-up the 1930s in the following way:

'The decade 1930-39 was characterised in Aboriginal affairs by an advance from a negative protectionist policy and outlook, to a conviction and demand that a positive forward looking policy should be framed and put into operation, and that steps should be taken to have a unified system (or at least closely collaborating systems) of aboriginal administration for the continent.'[24]

Indeed, by 1938, he was encouraged to write:—

'Interest in the Australian Aborigines as human personalities has increased during the past few years, and nowadays there is a growing desire not only to treat them justly, but also to help them rise culturally . . . if only we knew how. We realise that we have done them much wrong and injury during the past one hundred and fifty years, through ignorance and even more through callousness and indifference. Our great need, therefore, is to understand them and the cultural problems which confront both them and ourselves. Given a right understanding, governments, administrative officers and missionaries would be qualified to formulate policies and methods designed to assist the Aborigines in the task of adjusting themselves to the great changes which have come upon them. Australia should still be theirs as it is ours. Their very presence in the country imposes on us a dual mandate to seek their good as well as our own the unwritten but human terms of which we should endeavour to fulfill.'[25]

The new emphasis in policy was endorsed at a political level by the formulation of the Commonwealth Government's policy on Aborigines in 1939. McEwen, who issued the statement, considered that, in the past, 'Aboriginal policy appeared to have been one of merely dealing with the physical needs of the natives as the needs became apparent' and that, in the future, the Government should establish some firm guide as to its intention so that certain objectives might be established and achieved. A desirable end in this regard, he believed, was for 'these native Australian people (to be raised in) their status so as to entitle them by rights, and by qualification to the ordinary rights of citizenship, and (to) enable them and help them share with us the opportunities that are available in their own native land.'[26]

The intervention of the war prevented the Federal Government from applying the major review of administrative procedures and policies needed to achieve this purpose. However, the general elevation of rates of pay and conditions extended by the Armed Forces to Aborigines in Northern Australia,[27] and the response of the Federal Government in the immediate post-war years, indicated that the new Administration shared the views of the then Deputy Leader of the Opposition, if not in detail, at least in broad principle.

The urban Australian, being placed in a new relationship with Aborigines by virtue of the war, undoubtedly faced a period of reappraisal as one airman readily comprehended:—

'At our cattle station in the north of Australia, we have the good fortune to be near a tribe of blacks. Down South one hears of the decadence and lack of intelligence of the Australian Aboriginal, but I can assure you that such a conception is entirely false. I've never seen more virile, energetic and well built specimens than the young men of the tribe. These natives are very friendly and willing workers.'[28]

The next major review of national policy in relation to the native people was not undertaken until 1948, when there was a conference of officials responsible for Aboriginal Affairs in Canberra. The defeat of the Labor Party at the 1949 elections prevented the immediate implementation of policy then being agreed upon, but, at the same time, it provided the opportunity for the new Government to consider the outlines laid down by the Minister for the Interior in 1939, now Deputy Prime Minister, and to pass judgement accordingly.

In 1950, Mr. Paul Hasluck, then a private Member in the House of Representatives, began a campaign which he claimed was aimed at arousing 'the Australian nation to some sense of its responsibility for its shortcomings' in the treatment of Aboriginal residents.[29] On becoming Minister for Territories in 1951, he summoned a conference of Federal and State Ministers concerned with Aboriginal policy with a view to adopting a set of objectives towards which each Department would work. He considered it 'desirable that there should be uniformity throughout Australia in the enjoyment of privileges of citizenship.'[30] The conference adopted a policy of 'assimilation'.[31] Assimilation was later defined as having the object of ensuring that:—

> '... all Aborigines and part-Aborigines [attained] the same manner of living as other Australians and live as members of a single Australian community enjoying the same rights and privileges, accepting the same responsibilities, observing the same outcome and influenced by the same beliefs, hopes and loyalties as other Australians.'[32]

Although the concept of 'assimilation' in broadest terms was accepted in so far as it conceded the elevation of Aboriginal living standards and opportunity levels, many groups interested in Aboriginal welfare raised objection to it. They believed that the need for Aborigines to embrace the total system of values laid down by the European Christian section of the Australian community was impertinent, and that self-determination should be conceded to the Aboriginal groups within the community. In this sense, they argued, Aborigines should be considered and treated no differently from the numerous other racial minorities which had been established in the country.[33]

Following pressure from voluntary groups interested in native welfare, the Conference of Ministers responsible for Aboriginal Affairs, in 1965, changed the policy objective slightly, but significantly, to read: 'The policy of assimilation seeks that all persons of Aboriginal descent *will choose* to attain a similar manner and standard of living of other Australians and live as members of a single Australian community.'[34] The definition was further refined at the same time by the addition of another sentence: 'Any special measures taken are regarded as temporary measures, not based on race, but intended to meet their need for special care and assistance to make the transition from one stage to another in such a way as will be favourable to their social, economic and political advancement.'

During this period, the interests of the protagonists for the Aboriginal cause, although enjoying wide public support did not always find their views acceptable to the parliamentary representatives who held both the responsibility for legislation and the financial ability by which the native community could be elevated within the broader framework of Australian society.[35]

In three decades the philosophy underlying native policy in Australia had been completely reversed . . . moving firstly from segregation to assimilation and then, almost as a gesture to the uncertainty of mind, granting the possibility of equal but separate development. Finally, as the additional sentence added in 1965 shows, the official statements on policy were adapted to explain why none of the objectives had been achieved.

To the details of these considerations, we must now turn.

The Northern Territory

The political history of the Northern Territory during the period under review was conditioned by a legislative process promoted through, firstly, a government-nominated advisory council, and secondly, a partly elected council, with semi-parliamentary authority.

At no time have legislative decisions of the Northern Territory been made through a parliamentary system responsible to the electors living within its boundaries. Developing from a series of Federal resident representatives, who knew little local restraint, through to a system of qualified parliamentary procedures, in which, at all times, the nominees of the Commonwealth Government were assured of a majority, the legislative mechanism of the Territory might be considered more the responsibility of the wider community of voters of the Commonwealth of Australia than that of the residents of the Northern Territory itself. Consequently, control of policy was retained by the elected representatives of the Australian people in Canberra,[36] and up to 1964, at least, the Department of Territories in the National Capital continued to 'approve, reject, vary (and) comment' on legislative proposals.[37]

It is important to consider the development of native policy in the Northern Territory before the possibility of public review in a semi-elected House, in order to achieve an understanding of the structural arrangements which were made for the Aboriginal community, at that time a majority of the population. The isolation of the Northern Territory together with vast uninhabited areas which were expensive to administer, meant that official edicts had to be popularly accepted if any respect for the law was to be maintained. Consequently, if only in a rough way, an element of 'responsible government' was achieved. The actions of administrators in the field of Aboriginal affairs, as well as in the wider canvas of domestic politics were not without the possibility of censure, both from the immediate actions of the local population, by the acceptance or rejection of their decrees, and through the more constitutional recourse of parliamentary lobbying within the Commonwealth chambers.[38]

Following the Commonwealth's assumption of its responsibilities in the Northern Territory in 1911, the Government's main activity was aimed at determining the nature and the magnitude of the problem it had inherited in relation to the indigent population. Aboriginal numbers, for what an estimate was worth, stood at 22,000[39] at the time of the beginning of Federal power. There were only 3,310 persons of European descent in the area.[40] By 1936, the number of full bloods had declined to 16,846 with additionally, some 884 persons of part Aboriginal extraction.[41] The European population was still only 5,305;[42] 3,433 Aborigines were considered to be in regular employment.[43]

The Commonwealth initially approached the Administration of Aborigines through the appointment of a Special Commissioner, a well known anthropologist, Professor Baldwin Spencer.[44] Spencer's work was contained mainly in the form of a report to the Federal Government.[45] On his withdrawal from the Territory, the Administration of the Office of the Chief Protector fell foul of the scandals that originated out of the Administrator's hands.[46] Native children were left to starve in the ensuing confusion and all were refused public schooling up to the Second World War.[47]

Several significant official investigations were made, however, into the conditions and requirements of Aboriginal policy in the Northern Territory prior to the Second World War. These were conducted by Bleakely,[48] in 1929, and Thomson, in 1936.[49] A Board of Enquiry was also established in 1935 to investigate allegations of maltreatment of Aborigines in Central Australia.[50] Thomson's report was of more far reaching importance than that of his predecessor, as the basis of his recommendations created the principles for the geographical organisation of Aboriginal people up to the time of writing. Thomson proposed that:—

> (i) the remnant of the native tribes in Federal Territory not yet disorganised or detribalised by prolonged contact with alien culture be absolutely segregated, and that it be the policy of the Government to preserve intact their social organisation, their social and political institutions, and their culture in its entirety;
>
> (ii) the native reserve, Arnhemland, be created an inviolable reserve for the native inhabitants, and that steps be taken at once to establish and maintain the absolute integrity of this reserve;
>
> (iii) similar steps be taken to render inviolable any other reserves in which the native population remain undetribalised.

He then called for reorganisation of the public service, increased penalties for offenders against Government policy, revision of the administration of justice in relation to Aborigines, the establishment of a Department of Native Affairs under a trained Director and the beginning of Commonwealth pressure on the States to produce a uniform policy in relation to indigenes.[50a]

Although Thomson was able to witness the establishment of a separate department of Native Affairs in the Northern Territory immediately prior to the Second World War, consideration of many of the other aspects of his policy recommendations was delayed until the return of peace. In the meantime, the administration of Commonwealth responsibilities in relation to Aborigines in the Territory drifted along in extremely impoverished circumstances. Even by 1939, the Federal Government were spending less than £1 per head on the welfare of the people that they had taken over as part of the political consideration of federation.[51] As can be imagined in the circumstances, the staff and administration which was provided for the vast areas involved was completely inadequate and, as at least one observer has commented, the Government regulations in relation to Aborigines were 'observed more in the breach than in fact.'[52]

If Thomson's concern was primarily with the protection of the Aboriginal social, cultural and political organisation 'until and unless a sound working policy and one in the best interests of the Aboriginals is established'[53] the interest of other officers of the Administration appeared to be directed towards the growth of the half-caste problem.

The Chief Protector, cum Medical Officer-in-Chief, did not achieve the legal powers necessary for the performance of his task until 1927.[54] At that time, and until 1938, Dr. C. E. Cook held the joint title and office. On the non-medical side of his responsibilities, Dr. Cook 'feared the emergence of a coloured group outnumbering the whites, which, if living in depressed conditions, would be "revolutionary in outlook" and which would present an "incalculable future menace to purity of race in Tropical Australia"'. Cook proposed encouragement of marriage between half-caste girls and Europeans and believed that eventual success in eliminating the 'colour problem' altogether would only come through prohibiting miscegenation.[55] The first Director of Native Affairs, E. W. P. Chinnery, did not agree with the Cook proposals for intermarriage between half-castes and whites, and decided upon a policy of strict segregation of the half-caste population to help them 'to build up and develop a community life and social organisation of their own'.[56] He was appalled by the 'familiarities between certain whites and Aboriginals around Darwin [which] have no parallel in the world [and feared] for the future of the white race'.[57]

Although the amount of funds made available to the Department of Native Affairs were substantially increased immediately after War,[58] the next major review of Aboriginal policies in the Northern Territory was not made until the elevation to office of the Liberal-Country Party Coalition Government in 1949. In the interim, however, the Labor Party Administration had announced its intention of conducting a wide review of social and economic affairs in Northern Australia, with the establishment of the North Australia Commission. The work of this body was abandoned on the defeat of its sponsors in office.[59]

By 1950, the numbers of elected members in the Northern Territory Legislative Council was increased and a system of Parliamentary Hansard reporting was instituted. From that date, historians are in a better position to document the reasons for the implementation of policy than in the past.

The legislative introduction of what might be considered as Hasluck's 'new programme' for the assimilation of Aborigines came in 1953. Aborigines in the Northern Territory had been controlled under the Aboriginals Ordinance of 1918. The definition of an Aborigine, under that Act, included some half-castes as well as full blood persons. The half-castes, whose affairs could be controlled by the Director of Native Affairs, included those living with an Aboriginal spouse, those who habitually lived or associated with full bloods, those under twenty-one, females not married to a European and those over twenty-one who, in the opinion of the Director, were incapable of managing their own affairs.[60] As the 'half-castes [had] become so much an integral part of the Northern Territory and [were] so much economically bound up with the every-day work of the Territory', the Government considered they 'should receive some amelioration of what could be a protective law but if vigorously carried out could be restrictive and repressive.'[61] Accordingly, the Welfare Ordinance of 1953 removed control over half-castes and persons of lesser blood.

The new policy in relation to full bloods was also set out in the Ordinance which, although the Government had a majority of Members in the Legislative Council, met with a stormy passage through the House. The application of the Ordinance, it was claimed, was to be based on need, not race. Only by declaration of the Director of Welfare was a person to become subject to the conditions of the Act. Consequently, all natives in the Territory were to be exempted from the Aborigines Ordinance and were only to come under the ambit of the new legislation when, and if, considered to be in need of care. The grounds for declaration were to be those persons who, in the opinion of the Administrator, by reason of their:

  (i)   manner of living
  (ii) inability, without assistance, to adequately manage their affairs
  (iii) standard of social habit and behaviour, and
  (iv) personal associations

required the assistance of the Government agency established for the purpose.[62]

The method of declaration provoked much resistance in the House,[63] one Member declaring that it was 'an attempt to . . . repeal Magna Carta.'[64] So incensed were Members about this aspect of the Ordinance that one of the Government appointees announced that:—

> 'Like the Acting Crown Law Officer, I am a Government Nominated Member, but if, by voting for such a Bill, I continued my career in the Public Service, I would prefer to vote against it and resign tomorrow, so strongly do I feel on this matter'.[65]

Members were concerned, not so much about the total control over a person's being and property that was ascribed to the Administrator, but by the arbitrary and somewhat shallow standards by which he would be allowed to judge persons in need of his assistance.[65a] The resistance of the Members in the House was successful, at least in one respect. The Government delayed the introduction of the Bill until the next session and then added additional criteria, as to who might be declared, in the following form:—

> 'A person shall not be declared a ward (if he) is
>
> (a) A person who, under Part V of the Northern Territory Electoral Regulations—
>
>   (i)   is entitled to vote at an election of a Member of the House of Representatives for the Northern Territory;
>   (ii) would, but for his being under twenty-one years of age, be entitled to enrolment . . . .
>   (iii) would, but for his not having resided in Australia for six months continuously, be entitled to enrolment . . . to vote at such an election.
>
> (b) A person who holds a certificate of exemption issued and in force, under Section Four of the Immigration Act 1901-1949.'[66]

As Part V of the Electoral Regulations of the Northern Territory excluded 'Aboriginal natives of Australia' from voting, only full-blood Aborigines could be declared Wards.[67]

The Government's limitation of the restrictions inherent in the Ordinance to Aborigines, by a rather circuitous route, was not without reason, as its promoter explained:—

> 'In modern times, it is desirable . . . to avoid discrimination by legislation against any particular group of people and to avoid *even appearance of discrimination*. If this is accepted, then Members will readily accept also the need for avoiding the use of the word "Aborigine", that acceptance of course, brings about certain drafting difficulties, indeed, very considerable drafting difficulties' . . . .[68]

Not that justice should be done . . . but that it should appear to be done!

That members had no objection to the arbitrary application of powers to Aborigines, to which they themselves took the strongest exception, might be gauged from the fact that the altered version of the Ordinance differing substantially only on the one point, was welcomed by the main opponents of the earlier legislation.[69]

Under the Aboriginals Ordinance, the Chief Protector was the guardian of the person and property of the ward, his wife and children, and had power to 'protect [him] against immorality, injustice, imposition and fraud'.[70] Under the new Ordinance, the negative aspects of protection were replaced by more positive concepts of advancement. The Director of Welfare was to:—

    (i)   promote their social, economic and political advancement . . . .

    (ii) arrange . . . [for their] education . . . .

    (iii) promote their physical wellbeing, . . . inculcate proper habits of hygiene and sanitation and to improve their standards of nutrition and housing . . . .

    (iv) detect, prevent and cure disease . . . .

    (v) . . . arrange for the vocational training and obtain suitable employment for them . . . .

    (vi) provide such relief and assistance as is necessary . . . .

    (vii) exercise a general supervision and care over matters affecting their welfare.[71]

He was also charged with authority to run institutions and reserves.[72]

The Welfare Ordinance required the Director to maintain a Register of Wards[73] without which, of course, the Ordinance would have been meaningless. Much of the energy of the Branch was put into compiling this document. The first issue of the Register of Wards, known in the Territory as the 'Doomsday Book' or 'Stud Book'[74] was issued in May 1957, but contained many inaccuracies.[75] Indeed, as later experience has shown, the problems involved in accurately describing a person's racial origin in a primarily illiterate, and sometimes polygamous, environment placed severe doubts on the publication as a legal document.[76] It contained some 15,700 names.[77]

In an endeavour to correct the false entries and omissions, the Director of Welfare submitted another list of some three thousand names to the Administrator for prescription in 1962. The Administrator stated that he would refuse to declare persons over sixty-five or under fifteen as Wards of State, and questioned the basis on which the list before him had been compiled. As he was not assured that there had been any personal investigation of the individuals' respective abilities as laid down by the Welfare Ordinance, he refused to declare the list of people before him to be Wards, reasoning that it would be an invidious decision to place such severe restriction on personal liberty without some knowledge of the alleged impediments of the persons concerned.[78]

Although few full blood Aborigines were omitted from the Register of Wards, other than the three thousand the Administrator refused to include, one native did challenge his declaration through the Court.[79] The Welfare Branch pursued the issue to an unsuccessful conclusion, the judge releasing the individual from the conditions of the Ordinance with the statement:—

    'It must be most humiliating for a man able to care for himself to be told where he can and cannot go or do'.[80]

Consequently, some ten years after the legislation to establish the Register of Wards, the document remained a static instrument, with no additional persons being added to it and with a significant number of people, over whom the Ordinance was intended to operate, being born and growing up outside the conditions of the Ordinance.[81] The inability of the Welfare

Branch to control Aborigines through the means of the Register of Wards
virtually struck a death blow to the system which had been planned. This,
together with the reluctance of the Branch to prosecute anybody for viola-
tions of the regulations made under the Ordinance and the Wards Employment Ordinance, with the exception of liquor offences, and the fact that
attempts to adjust the system brought forth a plethora of legislation, circumscribed its effectiveness in many ways. In eleven years, up to 1964, the
Ordinances and Regulations relating to Aborigines were changed some
seventeen times.[82]

In these circumstances, few people, other than those in the Welfare
Branch, knew what their liabilities, rights or duties were and few cared. As
Tatz has pointed out, the administration of the system continued without any
appreciable change from the time when the policy was designed for
segregation.[83]

The elected Members in the House continued to object to the operation
and administration of the Welfare Ordinance, reserving their severest criticism for the method by which the original Register of Wards was established
and the procedure by which other persons might be included therein. Others
questioned the establishment and expansion of settlements and the general
allocation of funds to the Welfare Branch and the results being achieved.[84]

In 1962, the Welfare Ordinance was considerably altered to allow wards
to marry without permission of the Director.[85] It also became necessary for
the Director to make an application to the Court for an order to control the
property of individual wards.[86] However, the major restraints on personal
freedom remained. But the political pendulum had now swung in a different
direction. The Commonwealth Government decided to grant voting rights to
Aborigines, and accordingly brought down enabling Legislation in the
Federal House.[87] The Northern Territory followed suit in the same year.[88]
This, of course, annulled the basis of the old system and other methods had
to be found.

In introducing the new legislation, the Director of Welfare declared that
'greater progress probably than was made in the preceding 70 years' had
been achieved since 1953. 'Aborigines have advanced to a stage where they
find the present restrictions . . . increasingly irksome', it was believed,[89] and
therefore they should be removed. Not only was attention to be given to the
Welfare Ordinance, but discrimination against Aborigines in general law was
also to be removed.[90] Although there was general accord in the Council as to
the principles involved in the Bills, some Members again displayed concern
both as to the administration of the Welfare Branch and the adequacy of
finance which was being provided for the new programme.[91]

Removal of the basis of restraint, in 1964, was mainly related to the
political and social relationships of Aborigines and did not mean that the
Government, at that stage, was prepared to introduce full equality. The
Director announced that, as 'consideration [had not been given] to the form
of the new Legislation [which] . . . might cover employment conditions of
Aborigines and persons in occupations and industries not at present covered
by awards', it was proposed to continue the provisions of the Wards Employment Ordinance.[92] This meant that the method of prescription which had
been presented in the form of the Register of Wards, although never effective
and never really implemented, was to continue to affect the employment
relationships of Aborigines.

Despite the hesitant and fractional basis on which the Government was prepared to grant equality of citizenship to the nation's first inhabitants, the matter was, to some extent, taken out of their hands by the trade union movement. In 1965, the North Australian Workers Union applied to the Commonwealth Conciliation and Arbitration Commission to vary the Cattle Station Industry (Northern Territory) Award.[93] The object of the move was to embrace Aborigines in the coverage of the award and to grant to them conditions of employment and wages at least equal to the minimum remuneration enjoyed by European workers. The Union itself, however, has had a poor history in the assertion of Aboriginal rights. Although it won the case, the conditions of Aborigines on Northern Territory cattle stations still fail to reflect the general affluence of Australian society. In recognition of this fact, the Commonwealth Government has recently established a committee of enquiry to investigate the reasons for failure in this area.[94]

Queensland

If the parliamentary considerations of native policy in the Northern Territory were tempestuous during the past thirty years, the legislation environment in Queensland is notable for the accord which was experienced in policy determination and the static nature of the law affecting Aborigines. The debates of the 1930s, of the Queensland House, are of greater importance in considering present administration of Aboriginal affairs in that State, as the Legislature was not to be given the opportunity of appraising the value of its policy, with the exception of the excising vast areas from native reserves for mining purposes, until 1964. Consequently, the only guidelines which were laid down for Administrators were established in an era when the rights of racial and political minorities were not as energetically pursued as today.

There were, of course, differing opinions on the details of policy, and variations in attitudes of political partisans, but overall, on the few occasions that the Queensland Legislature was given the opportunity to discuss Aboriginal affairs, there was mutual self esteem in what had been accomplished. The importance of the political environment and the absence of effective opposition to the implementation of native policy was heightened by the fact that one party, the Australian Labor Party, remained in Government benches for a virtually uninterrupted period of thirty-five years. Whilst the Commonwealth in the Northern Territory and the other States were going through a period of critical self analysis in relation to their policy towards indigenes, Queensland basked in the belief that their natives had been 'given more than fair consideration.'[95]

The unity of purpose of the political parties within the Queensland Parliament, in relation to native affairs, demands further analysis when it is realised that the philosophical basis of legislation during the period under consideration shifted from that of segregation of the native people, to a newfound liberalism which aspired to absorb the Aboriginal people into the wider European community through a policy of assimilation. At almost all stages of policy determination, both governing and opposition parties displayed a degree of unparliamentary accord with the decisions being made.

With the exception of the release of a large number of part-Aboriginal persons from the conditions of the legislation, the basis of the present Act, introduced in 1939, was simply a 'consolidation of all the legislation affecting Aborigines in Queensland'[96] the purpose of which was for 'the Chief Protector . . . to exercise more control over (Aborigines) in the future than in the past.'⁹⁷ 'Practically every provision contained in the principle Act (1895) and the amending Acts [had] been inserted in [the] Bill.'⁹⁸

The tenet of the legislation was both protectionist and segregationist. The protectionist philosophy of the legislators was derived from the widely held, but increasingly unacceptable, premise that the Aboriginal race was doomed to extinction. The segregationist philosophy had a less rational base. 'The Full Bloods are going out of existence. They are doomed no matter what we do,'⁹⁹ the House was told. But the Minister for Health and Home Affairs provided more compassionate tones on introducing the Bill: 'The Aborigines of this country have received a very bad deal indeed from the white people who took their territory. The conscience of Australians generally has been sufficiently aroused to make them want now to do what they can for the remnant of the race.'¹⁰⁰ Demonstrating the practical terms in which the States' native policy was cast he continued:—

> 'One of the wrong views on the Aboriginal question was that if he was thrown a bone occasionally he could go and look for the rest of his food. That view has been altered. It is now realised that the Aborigine can only work if he is well fed. Consequently, the chief task of the missions is to provide that food. If he gets that food then he works as well as anybody else.'¹⁰¹

He then went on to demonstrate the effect of good feeding with a boxing anecdote. Rejecting suggestions of Aboriginal cowardice he claimed:

> 'They had the physical capacity to endure not only pain but also the energy of fighting. We found that by putting them on good solid food . . . we could put in the ring men who could give many of the local boys some hurry-up.'¹⁰²

To this, the Leader of the Opposition added an almost Roman theme: 'Built up with good food they become excellent soldiers.'¹⁰³

The Minister encouraged the House to believe that a pragmatic attitude to Aboriginal problems should have preference over a more sophisticated approach, claiming that:—

> 'In recent years Aborigines have become fashionable. All sorts of people have sprung up with ideas as to what should be done with them. A new race of anthropologists has come upon us demanding appointment in the Department controlling Aborigines. By taking a short crammed course in Anthropology in the wild outback of Sydney, they say that they became the only people who are qualified to handle native affairs and that the people in the department here who have been associated with the natives over a long period of years should make room for these experts. A little common sense is the thing that is required in the treatment of Aborigines.'¹⁰⁴

And Members concurred:—

> 'Of course it is necessary to be firm to be kind to Aborigines. I found that in teaching [Aborigines] in an industrial training school that behind this veil of harshness and apparent severity, the Aborigine was made aware that something kindly and to his benefit was intended. So that if the local Protectors appear to be harsh they are really only carrying out the work delegated to them.'¹⁰⁵

Only one of their number, however, appeared to be concerned about 'the harsh treatment meted out to Aborigines in some instances by the police' as he related a story of the illegal banishment of an Aboriginal youth from a Southern town. His evidence was met with silence by the House and without

comment by the Minister.[106] The Minister's only thoughts on the unique legal
processes of discipline employed by his department and the police being
that: 'Palm Island is a different settlement altogether. The natives who are
difficult to deal with are sent to Palm Island. It is not a very fertile spot but,
bit by bit, they are getting the land under crop.'[107]

As justification of the extraordinary system they had built up, many
Members emphasised an alleged lack of intelligence in Aborigines. The
Minister felt that the Thursday Islanders had 'proved capable of doing a
great deal for themselves and did not need the strict control that was exercised over the mainland Aborigines.'[108] The Leader of the Opposition agreed
that 'as one guided by reports of the Department the intelligence of the
Island Aborigine is much higher than that of the mainland native.'[109]

But the main question which caught the attention of the Members was
the problem of miscegenation which would arise if too much tolerance was
granted to the 'coloured people'. In particular the 'concern [was for] the half
caste'.[110]

'By this Bill [the Government] prepared to eliminate the half caste
from control unless a court places him under the control of the Chief
Protector of Aborigines. After taking over the whole of the half castes
in the country some years ago for the purposes of investigation we
have found ... that it has been possible to exempt from control
almost the whole of them.'[111]

And that such freedom was to continue provided they *behaved themselves*.[112]

Mr. Nicklin, Leader of the Opposition and later Premier, was particularly worried about the problem of half castes and suggested it could be overcome in two ways:—

'Gather together the whole of the remnants of the Aborigines in
Queensland and place them in reserves so that they will be removed
from contact with irresponsible whites [and] the half caste problem
will be overcome to a great extent.'[113]

For those 'unfortunates' already with us he suggested

'That it might be of great help in eliminating almost entirely the half
caste problem of this State if we adopted the principle that is operating in the Dutch East Indies. There is no social crime to marry with
the natives ... the further intermarriage of the Dutch with the quadroons has been the effect of gradually eliminating the half caste.'[114]

But the Leader of Opposition's thoughts on breeding out the half
caste fell, to some extent, on deaf ears, as Members believed that 'there
would be a very strong conventional feeling against any such alliance in this
country.'[115] Others took the objection even further:—

'I understand that, under this Bill, if a half caste so desires, he may
live with full blood Aborigines. If he adopts this attitude, of course,
he will not in any way hinder the progress of the white race.

'On the other hand we may be giving the half caste too much liberty
by this Bill. We can be too generous as well as too strict. It may not
be wise to give the half caste the same privilege as the white man.
One of the speakers told us that the blackfellow ... I think he meant
the blackgin ... was very lovable. We must be careful to see that the
half caste is not given the same liberties that are enjoyed by the
whiteman. We do not want any further mixing of the population. We
want to keep the white race white .... The half caste is a danger to

the population. He has already got his leg in (laughter) and we want to see that the position does not get any worse.

'We do not want to see any more half blood people born into this world.'[116]

Another Member, agreeing with these sentiments, felt that 'it made [him] sad to see children who are, almost, but not quite, white', and that mothers with half caste children would be persuaded to 'lease their children to others to be educated and to go out and work amongst the white population. Then these girls would probably marry and no one would be any wiser about their parentage.'[117] Indeed, he informed the House that, so desperate was the problem, that 'Lady Goodwin visited one of the mission stations and was shocked to see white children in the class of black and half caste children who sang for her.'[118]

Developing the theme of segregation, one Member expanded the Nicklin suggestions by requesting that the whole of the Aboriginal population of the state be removed to Cape York Peninsula so that 'the Aboriginal race [could be] preserved in its purity.'[119]

'The reserves should be situated in country that is not of very great value to the white population, because then the whites would not be very much inclined to go there. The Oaklands mission station [was] situated in [his] own electorate but it was too close to white settlement. The result is that it is hard to keep the blacks entirely separated.'[120]

But the Minister objected to these suggestions:—

'In keeping with the attitudes of the whites towards the Aborigines there has always been an urge to take the best land away from them. I have had to resist agitations for the removal of the Aboriginal settlement at Baramah Creek, simply because it was excellent farm land. It was the attitude in the past that they should be given land that was not useful to whites.'[121]

Concluding the debate, one Member of the Opposition considerably strengthened support for the Government by warmly reflecting that:—

'The opportunities for the two races to intermingle are not so great now and as time goes on there shall be a very great decline in the number of half castes. That is all for the good of this country. I think, therefore, that in our system of controlling the remnant of the Aborigines, we have something of which we can be proud.'[122]

Following the 1939 debates, laying down policy which was to remain effective for the following quarter of a century, the House was given few opportunities to express its feelings on the questions of native affairs. Indeed, Members appeared little interested in the topic as they continued to bask in the warmth of a job they considered well done. It was not until the mining potential of native reserves was discovered in the second half of the 1950s, that the House and the Minister in charge of Native Affairs sought to bring the objectives of policy under review. Indeed, as evidence of the acceptance of the good work being accomplished by the Department of Native Affairs, Members asked, on average, less than one question per year on Aboriginal affairs between 1939 and 1956. Approximately two-thirds of these enquiries concerned defaults in relation to cash being handled by departmental officers. The ratio of Members' time devoted to the less fortunate members of the community, however, showed a sharp increase following the tabling of the Comalco Bill, covering special mining leases in the Cape York native reserves. As though part of the new-found interest in the conditions and opportunities of the indigenes, Members' enquiries about their welfare increased to an average of six per annum between 1957 and 1962, to twenty questions in 1966.

Judging from the limited Parliamentary debates, but also from questions and asides, Members' attitudes appeared to change little during the post-war years. The only possible exception to this was a decline in the public sponsorship of segregation. There was, however, a realisation that the Aboriginal problem was becoming larger within the State and that the provision which had been made for the native population had not been adequate nor in the most desirable form. Far from the problem resolving itself by the disappearance of the race, or their elevation into the ranks of the European community, as was the desire of most theorists, their numbers multiplied. Embracing some twenty thousand persons at the turn of the century, their ranks remained steady up to the end of the 1930s.[123] However, from the Second World War to the present, the number of people of acknowledged Aboriginal descent within the State doubled. Of these, the Department remained directly responsible for some twenty-eight thousand.[124]

Many of the attitudes of the parliamentarians which were, no doubt, broadly reflected in the community outside and expressed prior to the Second World War, lingered on. That an appreciation of the complexity of the problem continued to escape the Minister might be gleaned from his appraisal of the needs of Aboriginal education in 1946:—

'We have a splendid education system for the benefit of the natives. There are classified teachers in charge of schools but it is also the practice to select the brightest boys and girls and appoint them, with remuneration, to handle some of the lower grades and thus ease the burden of teaching on the teachers in the higher grades.'[125]

The Department's educational activity, he felt, was encouraging the natives to take an entirely different attitude to life. To assist in this respect, the Boy Scout movement was introduced to Government settlements, with patent advantages:—

'Some boys instead of walking with a slouching Aboriginal gait, now walk in an upright and manly way, as the result of the training they got from their scoutmasters'.[126]

But there were still reservations about the ability of Aborigines to respond to corrective treatment:—

'I do not think that the Aborigines will ever have the mentality to reach the same standard as we whites have achieved. We have evidence that over the years there has been a gradual decline and that eventually the race will disappear. The best we can do is preserve the race as long as possible and we do this in our settlements. Medical men are in constant attendance to protect their health. That is the best we can do. Money is not what these people want. All they want is comfort in life. After all the settlement is not an employment agency: it is an attempt to do something in a humane way to preserve the race.'[127]

Following a descriptive interlude in which one Government Member referred to indigenes as 'niggers', 'bucks', and 'blackgins', without interjection or protest, he remonstrated:—

'I hope that the Aboriginal race is never exterminated but I cannot agree to allow natives to intermingle freely and unfettered with the

white community. We know that a gigantic problem faces America
with the Negros today. Fortunately, for this country, the number of
our natives are small and we shall be able to cope with them.'[128]

Members were, however, beginning to question the methods of operation of settlements:—

'Any police inspector or officer of the D.N.A. will bear me out when
I say that the natives fear going to settlements. They fear going to
settlements just as much as a young white man fears going to prison.
The only way certain school teachers in the back country can make
Aboriginal children do certain things is to threaten to send them to a
settlement.'[129]

But there still remained the 'common sense' approach to native
discipline similar to that considered by the Minister in 1939.

'After all the native is a very hard subject to handle; you cannot
handle him quietly. I have seen the treatment that policeman have
given them, not because they desired to be cruel but because they
wished to demonstrate that they, the policemen, were their masters.
If they had not done that, then the native would have assumed an air
of equality or superiority; he would have cast off his inferiority
complex.'[130]

The major activity surrounding Aboriginal affairs in the Queensland
Parliament during the 1950s and the first three years of the 1960s concerned
the granting of mining leases over Aboriginal Reserves on Cape York
Peninsula, and the methods of compensation involved. Many requests were
also made for the investigation of allegations of brutal treatment of
Aborigines. It was also claimed, on frequent occasions, that Aborigines
experienced difficulties in the withdrawing of their money from the
Aboriginal Trust Funds. All of these, with one exception,[131] were denied by
the Minister. Aboriginal policy took a decidedly different turn, not unexpec-
tedly, in 1957.

Although the Ministers concerned, or their representatives, attended the
post-war national conferences on Aboriginal affairs, at which the guidelines
of the assimilation programme were laid down, the House was not informed
of the change of policy from that of segregation, nor was any opportunity
extended to appraise the value of the 'new' programme until the debates on
the Comalco Bill in that year. It was then that the Minister for Health and
Home Affairs announced the new objectives:—

'The Government's Aboriginal Welfare Policy is based on the belief
that the coloured people of this State should be prepared to take their
place as honoured equal members of the community enjoying all the
rights and privileges and at the same time accepting the responsibility
of citizens. [Also] that no one should retard their advancement in
culture, knowledge and modern skills .... Inherent in this policy is
the aim and desire that our Aboriginal people should become
economic self-sufficient units of the community at the earliest possible
time.'[132]

Though little positive advance had been made in the material conditions
of Aborigines, he was even prepared to reverse the recommendations made
by Mr. Nicklin, his Premier, whilst Leader of the Opposition. 'Both from a
humanitarian as well as a national point of view, it is essential that our native
people be not kept for ever segregated as interesting museum pieces.'[133]
Through the discovery of vast mineral resources on the native reserves, the

'national point of view' and 'Aboriginal advancement' now happily coincided. But the Department of Native Affairs added words of caution to the parliamentary deliberations and reasserted traditional policy:—

'Nothing which has been adduced in discussion, correspondence or debate can justify any major alteration of Queensland Government policy with respect to its Aboriginal and half blood peoples. The basic features of that policy are exemplified by "The Aboriginals Preservation and Protection", the statute under which Native Affairs administration operates.'[134]

Another nine years were to elapse before the House was able to give attention to the new demands brought about by the change in policy by attempting to redraft the Act to suit the new purpose.

The old beliefs in the biological misfortunes of the Aborigines seemed to linger on, as

'it was considered that the mere enactment of legislation giving full citizenship to all Aborigines would serve no purpose other than virtually condemning the majority of . . . . Aborigines to a state of degradation contrary to all tenets of humanity.'[135]

The question of the readiness of Aborigines for, or the desirability of granting them, citizenship died hard. Following the extension of voting rights to Aborigines by the Commonwealth in 1962, the Minister for Education, being responsible for Aboriginal affairs, established a committee to investigate the possibility of extending citizenship rights to Aborigines.[136] In 1966, the Chairman of this Committee stated that he was 'still not convinced that he had done the right thing in making the recommendations to the House to give them (the Aborigines) the right to vote.'[137] Possibly this was a direct reflection of the continued reminder to the House that Aborigines were a 'comparatively inferior race'.[138]

In 1965, a new Act covering Aborigines was tabled in the House. Without significantly altering their status in the community, the Minister proudly announced:—

'From this Bill (Aborigines) will as a birthright, enjoy Australian citizenship status and will throughout their lives . . . benefit from all the rights and privileges of being citizens of Queensland, yet, additionally, they will have special benefits available if they so require'.[139]

Indeed, the very introduction of the Bill by the Minister was a contradiction in terms. He announced the transfer of local responsibility for the administration of Aboriginal affairs from police officers to clerk of the Magistrate's Court,[140] but failed to inform the House that in many areas where Aborigines were affected by the day to day administration of the Department, the local police officer is also the clerk of the Magistrate's Court.[141] However, he concluded that no longer would the police officer be the 'Great White Father'.[142]

His suggestion that 'it is far better to talk of the communities (in relations to settlements) rather than institutions'; but that complete autonomy for reserves was to be granted, 'but not yet';[143] that 'management of the property of an assisted person, execution of instruments, administration of estates, registration of creditors' rights [and] disposal of unclaimed moneys' would be still subject to certain 'arbitrary powers of the director'; that the right of the director to 'transfer *an assisted* person from a district to a reserve'[144] would be retained, seemed to deny his summum bonum.

Objection to the Act was strong:—

'For many years the administration has smugly considered that its
policy has been in the best interests of the Aboriginal population . . .
[and that] at the same time a paradox was created which instilled into
the minds of these people an inferiority complex . . . [and that they
rejected] the contention that they have not sufficient intelligence to be
trained to a standard sufficient to permit their ready assimilation . . . .
The main barrier confronting them is the atmosphere and environment generally in the white community. . . 150 years of settlement
and 100 years of government [suggest that] our opinions and methods
of administration have destroyed their will to be citizens.'[145]
But the Opposition was reminded, however, of the '40 years of Labor rule
[in which] Labor Members did not wake up to all the indignities and suffer-
ings of humanity, responsibility for which they are now trying to throw on
[the] Government's shoulders'.[146]

'The Minister said that the Bill was a step forward' but the Opposition
considered 'it a shuffle forward. It could be called "Bill of changed terms" '.[147]

'Of the twenty three terms mentioned, seventeen are changed names
. . . . Changed names and changed terms mean nothing to the
Aboriginal people. What is important to them is something that they
know is permanent, something tangible, something that they have
never had before . . . complete acceptance by people of this State.
They have never had it.'[148]

But undoubtedly a change of some kind had been made, and to arrest
the backward swing of the pendulum, the Minister announced that the
Government had finally decided to establish a Chair of Anthropology at the
University of Queensland and 'avail itself of the knowledge and information
provided from this valuable source'.[149] Alas, even Queensland had become
captive of the 'new race of anthropologists' from 'the wild outback of
Sydney'!

Regardless of the excellent work which has been carried out by the
Department of Anthropology at the University of Queensland, the State
Government still seems to have been a reluctant captive. Or possibly their
gaolers have been too kind! As is pointed out elsewhere in this collection of
essays, the fundamental basis of Queensland administration remains unchanged from the 1965 legislation, which in turn was based on the 1939 Act,
conditioned as it was by the ordinances of 1895.[150] A truly Victorian
situation!

Western Australia

The responsibility of the Parliament of Western Australia for Aborigines
resident within its borders may be traced back to the Constitution granted by
the Imperial Government in 1885; by Section 70, the new legislature was
required to establish a Department of Native Affairs which was to be responsible for medical services, education and the general welfare of the native
people.[151] The Constitution granted to the State made provision for the
expenditure of £5,000 per annum on natives, to be increased to one per cent
of the revenue of the State once it exceeded £500,000 per annum. Realising
that this could mean the devotion of considerable sums to native affairs, the
Colonial Government rescinded the section of the Constitution in 1897, at
the protest of the British Government.[152] Although the new State authorised
the conduct of Royal Commissions in 1905 and in 1936 to investigate the
execution of their trust,[153] Aboriginal welfare programmes in the Western

State were always inhibited by the most adverse population and land area ratio of all of the Australian States.

In 1908, there were, reputedly, 27,000 Aboriginal natives resident in the largest administrative area of the Commonwealth compared with 282,114 resident Europeans.[154] By 1936, there were approximately 24,000 full bloods and 4,000 lesser castes compared with 438,852 Europeans living within the State.[155]

This unfavourable balance undoubtedly placed greater strain on the Western State Budget than, for example, the Aboriginal population of Queensland and accounted, in some ways, for the more detailed consideration of Aboriginal policy in the Legislature. Expenditure from consolidated revenue, however, on Aboriginal welfare prior to the Second World War amounted to slightly more than one shilling per head of population or 18 shillings per resident Aborigine.[156]

The principal Acts relating to the control of the Aboriginal population in the period under consideration were passed in 1936. The redrafting of the legislation was a direct result of the Royal Commission into Aboriginal affairs in 1935.[157] This move was considered as a method of upgrading the act of 1905 so that it 'applied [to and] suited present day circumstances' as well as overcoming the 'great difficulties . . . found in administering the affairs of the Aborigines Department which was framed to suit the circumstances of other days.'[158] The Minister announced that, in general terms, the Bill was designed 'to give those who [were] deserving, a better chance to rise socially, and to give them some opportunity to rise from the position of being always in native camps.'[159] The temper of the debates in 1936, together with the consideration of policy which surrounded the amendments submitted to the House in 1938 and the ensuing Regulations under the Act in 1939, presents the reader with a fairly clear insight into both the thoughts of the governing Australian Labor Party and the mind of the Opposition.

The Australian Labor Party retained control of the Government Benches in the Legislative Assembly for approximately half of the period under consideration. However, because of the franchise structure of the Upper House, they were never able to ensure the response of that body to proposed legislation. Consequently, numerous acts were frustrated by resistance in Legislative Council. A varying combination of Liberal-Country Party coalitions retained control of legislative power during the balance of the period, and, invariably, were able to rely on the support of the Legislative Council.

The conduct of parliamentary debates in the Western State contained little of the disparaging racial content that was evident in Queensland. Even in the 1930s, Members rarely used derogatory terms in reference to their charges.[160] Any affront to the dignity of the native people seemed to be readily resisted in the debates in both Houses. In this respect, for example, objection was taken by Members, to suggestions that sexually wayward native women might be sterilised.[161] Restricted breeding, of course, was an important consideration in the Queensland House.[162]

The debate surrounding the 'modernising' of the Native Welfare Act, in 1936, did not attract partisan resistance as most Members considered that the reforms were overdue and, as the changes related mainly to the more formal aspects of procedure and law, they gave little opportunity for spirited opposition.[163] However, the mood of the House was one in which most Members considered that insufficient had been done for the original residents of the State. There was, in some ways, a self-effacing spirit in the Members' comments, which whilst recognising guilt, did not go to the great depths of redemption that seemed to possess the Queensland Legislature ...

'We are very arrogant and this legislation should remind us that our arrogance ought not to be on so high a plane as it is. We owe it to the native people of this country to see that at least our habitation of the country is not to their detriment .... I believe that fair and reasonable treatment is meted out by most people in the State to the natives [and] that no Act of Parliament could make the whole community perfect.'[164]

'We turn up our noses at their colour today after having taken possession of the territory that once belonged to them, and just because their colour is different from ours we say we will have nothing to do with them.'[165]

Again, in the West Australian House, there were no moves for the segregation of Aborigines which appealed so strongly to the Queensland parliamentarians. Evidence of segregation was even deplored. One Member, quoting examples of social segregation at race meetings, objected to the citizens' attitudes: 'We cannot expect [the Aborigines] to grow up into decent citizens under such conditions', he concluded.[166] Even the establishment of separate living areas for Aborigines was resisted: 'A while ago there was a movement on foot to place natives on reserves. To attempt to do so would be distinctly unwise.'[167]

Those who sponsored such moves, however, did not fear miscegenation, but more the damage which was being done to native communities by association with certain categories of Europeans 'who introduce all kinds of vices and trouble.'[168] Indeed, one Member added,

'The only trouble [he] ever experienced was due to the other class of travelling labour sometimes engaged on stations; these men created trouble by interfering with native women and taking liquor into the native camps .... The life led by some of the natives was superior ... in some respects to that lived by certain white people.'[169]

Sexual licence in relation to the Aboriginal race, except from the aspect of exploitation involved, was not particularly frowned upon. One Member claimed that cohabitation was vital to the economic prosperity of industry in the State and that to impose a heavy penalty would have deleterious effects on the European workforce ....

'I am concerned about the development of the backcountry. If we impose a penalty of six months or three months (for cohabitation) convicted persons will be taken from their work on the stations and we shall be striking at the station owners, as it will be impossible to replace imprisoned employees.'[170]

Another defended bi-racial sexual activities with a more colourful appeal:—

'I have heard of a boundary rider going to a windmill with a 20,000 gallon tank seeing there a sylph-like figure arising from the water with no clothes on and receiving an invitation to join her in the tank. It is only natural in such circumstances a young man would get into trouble.'[171]

A more persuasive biblical reference closed the debate on promiscuity without, however, removing the prison term involved. 'Let him that is without sin cast the first stone ... and there was not a stone thrown'[172] ... and nobody in the House uttered a word!

Members were also particularly concerned about the total impact of legal restraint on Aborigines: 'This regulation reeks of bureaucratic control, swivel chair control and places these people on an unfair footing from the very beginning'.[173] 'Are they held in duress . . . are these natives convicts',[174] Members demanded to know.

Others resisted the very tenor of the Bill:—

> 'The Bill should have been presented to us with a reverse policy contained in it. Where a person can claim to have received a fair education and to be living a decent life, he should not be interfered with any more than coloured importations . . . . I disapprove of any law which would interfere with the domestic comfort of these families . . . . These unfortunate people should not be persecuted simply because of the mishap of their birth.'[175]

Objection to the restrictive sections of the Act did not all come from the Labor side of the House. In particular, the Opposition led a strong attack on the tabling of Regulations under the Act in 1939. Initially they objected to sixty-five regulations and were successful in having many removed or redrafted.[176]

The Legislative Council pursued a slightly different course from that of the Assembly on the question of miscegenation, and it is possible that this fundamental variation in approach might have accounted for the resistance to change which was generated in the Lower Chamber at a later date when the Liberal/Country Party coalition governments gained power. On the important question of racial tolerance, one Upper House Member offered the suggestion that 'the long distance view is to breed these people [half castes] right out; but as long as the half caste can mate with the full blacks, the process is being reversed',[177] and called for a complete prohibition on full blood Aborigines marrying half caste persons.

Similar to the Queensland attitudes, there was even a demand in the Upper House for the removal of half caste children from their parents so that their assimilation into the white community might be expedited.[178] But the proponents of this course were not without compassion as they recommended that the State should actively pursue the question of maintenance suits against the wayward fathers of half caste children.[179]

There appeared to be broad concurrence amongst Members of the Western parliament as to the principles involved in the Bill. Dissent was over detail. Only on one occasion was the inherent ability of natives questioned, when a Member referred to what he thought was common knowledge that the mentality of Aborigines was equal to that of a child of twelve or fourteen years of age.[180] Others, however, were not so sure that this was correct; 'many of these people have just as much intelligence as the average whiteman', was their reply.[181] And then again,

> 'You know, sir, from your long experience . . . that there are many full bloods who are well educated and can speak English and understand it just as well as many of us. And they have the ambition to do something for themselves. But they are all coerced by this measure [the Regulations] and the parent Act. What is the use of encouraging individuals to be self reliant and then forbidding it by legislation.'[182]

The innate ability of Aborigines was but rarely challenged in the West. 'I have been frequently surprised at the wonderful work produced by

Aboriginal and half caste children. They are capable of turning out work which is the equivalent of similar work produced by white children in any part of the metropolitan area.'[183]

The spirit of the pre-war consideration of native affairs in Western Australia was summed up by three Members responding in general terms:—

> 'Speaking generally to the Bill, we should do everything possible to make happy the lot of the Aborigines we still have in our midst'.
>
> '. . . the wellbeing of the native races is too important for the question of finance to stand in the way.'[184]
>
> 'Much of our trouble today arises from the fact that Governments in the past have not seen fit or were not able to provide money to do what the Department considered necessary!'[185]

With the advent of hostilities, the legislature witnessed a decline in the time Members devoted to endeavouring to improve the conditions of the native inhabitants. The House, however, did find opportunity to debate a motion calling for a select committee to investigate the costs involved in a more complete programme of assistance for Aborigines, and for the transmission of a request phrased in the terms of the committee's finding to the Federal Government.[186] It also passed a motion extending citizenship rights to those natives who had served in the Armed Forces and made an effort toward endeavouring to expedite the admission of other natives to citizenship ranks.[187] In the Constitutional Referendum of 1944, seeking the extension of various rights to the Federal Government, the voters of Western Australia favoured granting additional power to the Commonwealth Parliament. One subject included in the grant was Aboriginal Affairs. Failing the successful outcome of the referendum, the State House passed an enabling act to achieve the same purpose. New South Wales and Queensland rejected the proposals outright.[188]

The legislature, did, however, pass a most contentious bill in 1941. This prohibited Aborigines living above the twentieth parallel moving to the South. The object of the Legislation was alleged to be designed to contain the disease of Leprosy.[819]

By the Native Administration Amendment Act 1947, however, restraint on the movement of Aboriginal residents within the State was greatly relaxed.[190] The prohibition on movement from the North remained.

The demands for improvement of the legislation relating to native residents brought a further request for a broad enquiry into the conditions of administration in the form of a limited 'Royal Commission'. This was granted in 1948, in the person of F. A. E. Bateman.[191] The report which was produced enabled the proponents of liberalisation to document many of the allegations they had been making in the House, and the proceedings were used as evidence in the debates which began to take a more partisan form.[192]

A positive change in the attitudes of the Government Members became apparent in 1950. The explanation by the Minister responsible for native affairs, of the reason for change, broadens one's understanding of the hesitancy with which some Members had previously approached the question of Aboriginal welfare. In introducing a Bill to liberalise the Native Administration Act, the Minister explained that the Government considered the suggestion necessary to:—

> 'enable the modernising and liberalising of this State's attitudes towards its natives [firstly] because public opinion . . . is swinging

rapidly toward the thought that in the past insufficient opportunity has been afforded the Australian native to show exactly what he can do in a useful way. The second reason is that anthropologists and other scientists have recently been busy with the task of assessing the relative mental potentials of several types of humans with special emphasis on colour. *They have reported that all races and colours attain the same level. I admit my surprise at that result. I certainly did not anticipate it, but there it is.* I mention this because it implies that given the opportunity adequately to train and occupy his mind, the Australian Aborigines and half castes as well, are capable of the same output of useful work and thought as the ordinary man in the street, and for that matter, as the ordinary Members of this House.'[193]

Although the particular Bill referred to by the Minister was not pursued, the House approved a private Member's Bill to reduce the time for objection to application for citizenship by Aborigines from two months to one month. It also ensured that children of natives achieving citizenship retained such rights, regardless of the fate of their parents' status.[194]

One of the problems which was beginning to assert itself in Western Australia at this time was the fact that the West Australian criteria for citizenship of Aborigines were not the same as those in the Northern Territory.

The problem was most acute in the North-West, where part-Aboriginal drovers and stockmen found that, on crossing the Western Australian border, they immediately lost any privileges they might have possessed in the Northern Territory and consequently had to adopt an entirely different mode of life.[195]

During these debates, considerable concern was expressed by various Members that the restraints which were placed upon native residents of West Australia were in conflict with the terms of international agreements, and could react to the embarrassment of the Commonwealth. This was a theme that was to consume the interest of a number of the more vocal Members for some considerable time during the 1950s.[196]

The proceedings in the House between 1950 and 1958, before the Australian Labor Party reverted to the Opposition benches, reflected an intense interest in the question of Aboriginal welfare. Almost annually, a Bill to relax the restraints placed on Aboriginal residents was submitted to Members. Except for certain minor alterations, the sponsors of the particular legislation were unsuccessful failing, mainly, to obtain a majority in the Upper House. As an almost direct product of this interest in the legal conditions of residence of the State's original inhabitants, there followed a multiplicity of questions concerning the operation of the various acts under which they lived. Enquiries of this nature rose from an average of four per annum in the immediate post-war years to over seventy-five in 1957.[197]

The period was also marked by a number of major and minor public outcries relating to the social and economic environment of the indigenes. Some of these were the result of reasonable complaints based on well-reported investigations, and others appeared to be the result of a rather irrational oversensitive public response to the circumstances of the State's dispossessed minority. Of the first type, possibly the 'Warburton Range Controversy' was the most important and of the second the 'Pindan Movement' the most notorious.[198]

But the exposure of the depressed circumstances of Aboriginal existence were not related solely to desert tribes or pastoral employers. Responsibility often came right home to the Government departments concerned:—

> 'The Mogumber native settlement is a festering sore and a reflection on every one of us. The settlement contains school children, medical cases, V.D. cases, indigent natives and blind and deaf natives. They are all herded together. I went to the school there and I believe that the average intelligence of the children is nearly as good as white children. Their work was outstanding. There were boys and girls of various ages together and the school teacher in talking about them and in impressing her worry about the conditions said: "In this class there are three pregnant girls and I expect there are some with venereal disease. There are compounds for both young men and girls but it can be seen that the heavy link mesh netting has been torn down so that there is no hope of keeping the sexes separated. The natives who go there to recuperate or who go there because of trouble with the police are able to roam from one end of the place to the other." '199

Further stimulus to the public debates was achieved through the appointment of an unconventional commissioner for Native Affairs, in 1948. S. E. Middleton, a remarkable man by any standards, was the first and only chief executive in Aboriginal affairs in Australia to have the benefit of formal anthropological training.200 To this, he added a background of experience in the New Guinea public service, from where he recruited some of his previous compatriots. It was not long before he publicly displayed his dissatisfaction with the conditions under which he was expected to work.201

One Member accused the Commissioner of being 'frankly propagandist' in his annual reports and took particular exception to his allegations that:—

> 'the conception (of the inferiority of Aborigines) had been handed down from generation to generation and this idea was given legal expression in the passing of legislation reflecting the attitude of mind held by legislators and electors of the day. Aborigines were classed as "natives" and this immediately connotated a state of "apartness". It approved of their pauperisation on the one hand and on the other directed a form of control which bordered on unwarranted interference with personal liberty unparalleled in the legislative treatment of any other people of the Commonwealth or Pacific territories.'202

Middleton's open criticism of the basis on which the State's native policy was founded, undoubtedly played an important part in provoking the Labor Administration into active pursuit of forwarding the Aboriginal cause in the House, as well as forcing the Liberal/Country Party opposition into analysing the reasons for their resistance of the claims that were being made on the Aboriginals' behalf. Indeed, some of the Opposition Members took exception to Middleton's 'unheard-of' partisanship and called for his censure, if not dismissal.203 But, by 1953, the Commissioner was becoming even more outspoken about the difficulties both he and his native charges were facing:—

> 'The future of these people lies in our hands. They must be given a point of commencement and that point is the immediate removal of this worthless legislation that bars their pathway to opportunity and

eventual assimilation. Without this basic requirement neither they nor we, who are their official sponsors can readily progress. The remedy and the means of effecting it lie in the hands of the electors of this State.'[204]

Middleton continued in his searching criticism:—

'It is a dismal admission for me to make, I know, but the one piece of legislation which most effectively deprives Aborigines from exercising their basic civic rights and imposes on them a heavy burden of administrative discrimination and restriction is that which purports to be the welfare measure enacted for their benefit . . . that is the Native Administration Act. Whatever the intention may have been when this Act was first passed in 1905 its effect on the Aborigines today, and particularly those of the South, is calamitous. Almost universally it is regarded as being an intolerable undemocratic restriction of the personal liberty of a section of our community. We, who are charged with the unpleasant duty of administering it, regard it as repugnant to basic humanitarian and welfare principles, practically devoid of any common ground with the people we are trying to help and creative of more misunderstanding, dissatisfaction and abuse than any other piece of similar legislation known to the free world today. Because these prohibitive and restrictive clauses are written into the Welfare Act, Aboriginal natives naturally enough blame and criticise officers of the Department for action taken under the provisions of the Act by the police and other authorities.'[205]

And, again, he turned his attention towards his European sponsors:—

'The great obstacle to [Aborigines] development, uplift and eventual assimilation is colour prejudice. This is something which is outlawed in other countries but which in Australia is entirely beyond the scope of administrative or Government control. It can be eliminated only by self-purging on the part of those who entertain it. Ignorance and prejudice have in the past nullified all efforts to improve the lot of the natives by providing better administration, education and training facilities in this State.'

What is more, he added 'Experience over the last five years has proved conclusively that where the recommendations of the Department conflict with the political self-interest, they are frequently shelved or put aside'.

Specifically, he described his officers' field experiences:—

'In this Territory [the Murchison] even those who claim to be pro-Aborigine submit that an Aborigine "must be kept in his place". Police officers contribute strongly to that policy in almost all instances . . . to fight against discrimination and prejudice in the Murchison is to fight the entire recognised social system of the white community.'

And, again, he attacked what he considered was the pragmatic basis of the continued degradation of his charges:—

'[The] inadequacies in living conditions coupled with the restrictive provisions of our existing legislation, which amongst other things makes it an offence for a native to do something which is no offence if done by a white man, only tend to create . . . an anti-social attitude the consequences of which succeeding generations will live to regret.'[206]

Middleton was not alone in his criticism of the provision that had been made for the native people. The Press and other Government departments added stimulus to the debates.[207] Although the evidence given by the police normally added fuel to the Opposition cause, the Reports of the Department of Health supported Middleton's scathing criticisms.[208] In its 1952 Report, it seemed to join direct forces with the Commissioner and also risk the displeasure of the Opposition:—

'Most of the males are employed by the white population on farms and in townships. They live in fairly close proximity to the whites but there the resemblance ends. Although those earning award rates of wages have to pay income tax and social service contributions and all draw child endowment for the children, not one has yet been provided with a house by the State Housing Commission although they contribute to the country's finances from whence the State Housing Commission draws its funds. Denied access to their former hunting grounds, which are now devoted to the whiteman's agricultural and pastoral pursuits, they are compelled to work for the whiteman for their livelihood and yet are denied a communal life with him. They are condemned to live in shacks and shelter on the fringe of townships and only too frequently the only place where there is water and material from which they can built their shelters is the town's sanitary site.

'Need one be surprised at the standard of hygiene and sanitary conscience of a community brought up in an area devoted to the disposition of whitemen's rubbish and excreta?

'There can be no doubt that the initial step to be taken in their habilitation is the provision of housing approximating in standard to that of the rest of the community and education of the young in the ability to live therein. It is impossible to teach any man to use a tool unless he is given the tool with which to practice. It is not possible to learn the art of living on a sanitary site.

'There can be no doubt that the majority of natives are at present incapable of using proper housing accommodation which is up to white standard. Nevertheless, unless efforts are made to educate them in its use, they will never learn.'[209]

In 1952, the House was encouraged to pass the Acts Amendment (Confession by Natives) Bill, as 'natives [were] likely to make a statement in the manner suggested by or in the way they think would be acceptable to authority' and, consequently, needed additional protection because of such peculiarity. But the sponsors were forced to withdraw the legislation.[210] Again, in 1952, the House rejected a measure designed to alter the definition of an Aboriginal to 'place all [persons] less than full Aboriginal blood on the same level'.[211]

However, the debate provided interesting insight into the hesitancy some Members had in admitting Aborigines into the full ranks of the community. In sponsoring the Act, Minister for the North-West claimed:—

'Intermarriage has set the Department a difficult task in trying to establish what proportion of blood a person may have for the purpose of determining on which side of line he will be classed. The Commissioner's Report at present on the table of the House indicates that his officers are dealing in fractions as small as 1/128ths to decide whether a person of mixed blood is eligible for social service benefits or citzenship rights.

'In the Commonwealth Social Services Act the line is drawn at half blood and although people are taxed at the same rate as every other taxpayer, a fraction as small as that which I have mentioned can disqualify them for old age, invalid and widows' pension. If they are exempt from the Natives Administration Act or have citizenship rights, they then qualify.'211

The Minister's reasoning was not strong enough for some Members, as one person on the Opposition benches recognised:—

'[Granting citizenship will] take away that care and protection which the native has and throw him to the whole wide world.'

Interjector: 'What do you mean the whole wide world?'

Speaker: 'It will leave him open to every possible and feasible method of exploitation.'

Interjector: 'Is he not able to cope with it?'

Speaker: 'Of course he is not and the Honourable Member knows it. Fancy a man who is 1/128th native being able to cope with whitemen's laws. It is just too silly.'212

In 1954, a Bill was submitted to the House to grant citizenship to all Aborigines who had served in the Armed Forces overseas for a period of more than six months. The measure was readily passed with little debate.213

In 1953 and 1954, the Labor Administration again tabled a Bill for the liberalisation of the Native Administration Act. On this occasion, the recommendations met with a better response, although at first it failed because of the inclusion of the right to drink for Aborigines. Although the Act which was passed achieved the admission to citizenship of half castes and lesser bloods, the alterations to the Act, with one exception, were rather circumscribed in their impact. Many of the changes related to public or social relationships between Aborigines and Europeans.214 For example, one section which was considered either out of date or impossible to administer was the prohibition on Aboriginal women being, after sunset, within two miles of a tidal creek in which pearling boats are moored. The artificial nature of the restraint became obvious when the Port of Fremantle was declared a creek for the purposes of the Act.215 Another section which was removed was that relating to special penalties for Aborigines who appeared in public insufficiently dressed. As one speaker pointed out, by current standards even the most scantily attired Aborigine possessed a greater sense of decorum than some of the residents of certain Perth seaside suburbs.216 The section removed also contained special reference to loitering by Aboriginals. This had been frequently used by the police to unduly harass native residents of country towns.217 Restraint in relation to reserves and areas prohibited to natives was also relaxed. Special courts and penalties relating to tribal practices were abandoned.

But the Minister still considered many sections of the Act 'reprehensible', as 'some people . . . retain the idea that the class of person termed "native" must be kept down, that an inferiority complex must be fostered among these people and that under no circumstances are they to be given anywhere near the equal rights and privileges accorded to the rest of the community.'

Of considerable importance in the increasing mobility of Aboriginal people within the State was the relaxation (but not abandonment) of the section which prohibited native persons resident north of the twentieth parallel from travelling South. For some years prior to the Bill, evidence had been presented to the House which demonstrated clearly that the laws, as

they were administered, had little to do with the original reason for the
imposition of the ban—the containment of leprosy.[218] Besides, the medical
fraternities attitude to the disease had changed considerably in the meantime
and its incidence had rapidly diminished.[219]

The general object of the Government in the suggested legislation was
to replace the previous basis of total restraint with that of one of selective
and declarative prohibition similar to what they considered, erroneously, was
the case in the Northern Territory.[220] The Minister believed, for example,
that there would be only about five hundred Aborigines[221] who would have
to be declared under the Act and that there would be no widespread
prescription.[222]

The Government again attempted to liberalise the Aboriginal Acts in
1956 and 1957, without success. In 1956, they tabled the Native Welfare Act
Amendment Bill, which was defeated,[223] and, in 1957, the Natives (Status as
Citizens) Bill, was presented. The latter was not proceeded with.[224]

The most searching attack on the principle of restraint by the State,
however, came in their attempt to repeal the Natives (Citizenship Rights)
Act in 1957. This particular piece of legislation had been established by the
Liberal Party Government in 1947 and had, as its basis, an alternative
method of declaration of persons fit for citizenship rights. Whereas, previously, the responsibility for removing the embargo on the individual had
been administered by a magistrate, the 1947 Act had placed the power in the
hands of a Board consisting of a magistrate, a member of the local Roads
Board and a prominent citizen.[225]

Although the Labor Government proposals to admit all natives to the
rank of citizen failed in 1957, they again attempted to liberalise the conditions affecting Aboriginal restraint in 1958, announcing that it was 'still
determined that discriminating laws should be removed and [it] will
continue with its efforts in this direction'.[226] They attempted to achieve these
ends on this occasion with what one would have thought the rather
innocuous removal of the clauses relating to proof of abandonment of tribal
and native association on the part of the applicant for citizenship, as well as
the necessity to prove freedom from leprosy, syphilis, granuloma and yaws.
The Opposition in the Legislative Council, however, considered that the proposal was still the 'same old politics and plonk' and again rejected the
measures.

In 1958, the Labor Government was defeated at the polls and a
Liberal/Country Party coalition Government took office. With the appointment of the new Government, questions of Native Affairs did not loom so
large in the legislative programme. However, Members from the floor of
the House kept up the barrage of questions.[227] In 1960, the Government
amended the Native Welfare Act with a Bill that exempted the quadroon
(one quarter part native) stating that it was never intended that they should
have been embraced by the Act. As well they clarified the power of the
Minister to acquire land for Aboriginal purposes.[228]

In 1962 and 1963, the Government, surprisingly, promoted a number of
Bills which had the effect of accomplishing most things for Aborigines which
they had so sternly fought whilst in Opposition, the Minister announcing:
'We must concede that the natives of our State have made remarkable progress. I think that we can say that quite sincerely. While they still need some
help, many of them have reached the stage where they are ready for
complete assimilation.'[229]

With this patent change in attitude 'bringing forth almost identical type legislation'[230] which had been resisted in opposition for over a decade, the Government set to and either withdrew or amended a number of Acts[231] affecting Aboriginal freedom.

The general effect of this series of legislation was to elevate all Aborigines to citizenship with the right to vote.[232] The legislation also abandoned the previous power of the Department of Native Welfare over the property and income of Aborigines, removed restraint on their freedom of movement and granted them liberty to make contracts of employment.[233] Restrictions on cohabitation, and the containment of certain natives north of the twentieth parallel were also abandoned,[234] and the Licensing Act was amended to extend the right to Aborigines to drink.[235]

The Labor Party, now on the Opposition benches, congratulated the Government on its change of heart.[236] The Leader of the Opposition, however, claimed that the change in circumstances had been accomplished by 'the prodding of the United Nations'.[237] Other Members called for the dissolution of the Department of Native Welfare entirely and for the establishment of 'a Department for those in need of assistance irrespective of colour and circumstances'.[238]

Conclusion

The foregoing survey covering the slow, hesitant and, in parts, fractional alteration in official attitudes to Aboriginal affairs over a period of some ninety years, clearly brings out the principles of social change referred to by Park and Dewey at the beginning of this essay. However, what is remarkable in this situation is that the resistance to change has taken place in a community which, in keeping with world standards, is both highly educated and liberal, in the broadest sense of that term. More importantly, recalcitrance on the part of legislators has taken place in the face of the general pattern of enlightenment on the question of race relations throughout the world and, indeed, even clear expressions of opposition from the electorate.

Commissioner Middleton of Western Australia pointed out some of the reasons for this when he reported that, when "recommendations of the Department conflict[ed] with ... political self-interest, they [were] shelved or put aside'. More recently, the normally conservative journal, *The Bulletin*, claimed that 'many Country Party supporters want to keep Aborigines in a state of subjugation because they fear the consequences of Aboriginal advancement, especially the need to provide land for them'.[239] Although these comments may seem trite to students of politics, it comes as somewhat a shock to the less initiated to realise that people responsible for national policy would be prepared to pursue their own ends over those of the most impoverished and under-privileged section of the Western world, and it would seem, from the history of the situation, even be prepared to fabricate the record to achieve their purpose. Considered in the light of the social, cultural and genetic background of Aborigines and their exclusion from the mainstream of Australian society, parliamentary attitudes to Aboriginal affairs can only be considered racist in the extreme. The fact that, in 1970, there remained some twenty-three Acts of Parliament discriminating against Aborigines in those States most concerned with their welfare is ample evidence of the continuing influence of prejudice.[240]

REFERENCES

1 PARK, ROBERT EZRA. *Race and Culture; Essays in the Sociology of Contemporary Man,* Free Press, Glencoe, 1950, p. 3.

2 DEWEY, JOHN. *Education and Democracy,* New York, 1916. pp. 1-11. Quoted in Park, *op. cit.,* pp. 3-4.

3 *The Bulletin,* 19 June 1880 and 17 December 1887.

4 See for example W. Dutton 'A Dying Race', *Lancet* CLXXV, 1908, p. 1046. Also E. Milne 'Our Australian Aborigines: A Doomed Race' in F. A. Fitzpatrick, *Peeps into the Past,* 1914. Also Rev. William H. Fitchett, 'The Tragedy of a Perished Race', *Life,* Melbourne, September 1908, pp. 272-276.

5 From a report by pastoralist Alfred Giles, 1899, whose views were alleged to be subscribed to by the Government Representative in the Northern Territory, the Hon. L. J. Parsons, Queensland Parliamentary Debates, 1 April 1965, p. 3165.

6 BATES, DAISY M., 1927.

7 MORELY, REV. W. *Aborigines Protector,* 1, 2 (June 1936), pp. 19-21.

8 GRIBBLE, REV. E. R., Sydney, 1933.

9 HANLON, E. M., 1938.

10 MONTIQUE, ASHLEY, 1938.

11 KEVIN, J. C. E., 1939.

12 STANNER, W. E. H. *Man,* 1938, 20.

13 *The Australian Aborigines: How to Understand Them,* Angus & Robertson, Sydney, 1938.

14 17 January 1938.

15 ELKIN, E. P. *Sydney Morning Herald,* June 26, 1952.

16 ELKIN, E. P. in *White Australia, Australia's Population Problem,* Angus & Robertson, Sydney, 1947.

17 DUGUID, C., Adelaide, 1963.

18 STREHLOW, R. G. H., Melbourne, 1956.

19 Q.P.D., 1939, p. 452. The legislation was designed 'to ease the bumps along the road to the cemetery'.

20 Now Sir John McEwen, retired, one time Prime Minister and Deputy Prime Minister of the Liberal-Country Party Coalition Government 1949-1970.

21 FOXCROFT, E. J. B. *Australian Native Policy,* Melbourne, M.U.P., 1941, p. 144.

22 Report of the Administration of the Northern Territory for the year 1937-38, p. 22.

23 Commonwealth Government Exhibit Book, Conciliation and Arbitration Commission, No. 830, 1965. Statement on Aboriginal Welfare and Employment Policy and Administration in the Northern Territory since 1918, p. 2.

24 ELKIN, E. P. *Citizenship for the Aborigines: A National Aboriginal Policy,* Angus & Robertson, Sydney, 1938.

25 *Ibid.,* introduction to *The Australian Aborigines,* Angus & Robertson, Sydney, 1938.

26 *Commonwealth Government's Policy with Respect to Aboriginals,* White Paper issued by the Hon. J. McEwen, Minister for the Interior, February 1939, pp. 1-3.

27 Applicable only to those directly engaged in the Armed Services. Aborigines seconded to the Army as labour assistants in the Northern Territory were

paid at the flat rate of 10d per day. (Report of the Administrator of the Northern Territory, 1946, Appendix 'C', p. 1.) The 1947-1948 vote for Aboriginal Affairs was £134,800—almost equal to the total revenue of the Territory in 1938-39. (Report of the Administrator of the Northern Territory, 1947-48, p. 21.)

28 *Sydney Morning Herald,* 11 December 1942. Quoted by E. G. Docker, *Simply Human Beings,* Jacaranda Press, Brisbane, 1964, p. 224.

29 *Native Welfare in Australia,* Speeches and Addresses by the Hon. Paul Hasluck, M.P., Minister for Territories, Perth, 1953.
Now Sir Paul Hasluck, Governor General of the Commonwealth of Austalia; also one time Minister for External Affairs in the Liberal-Country Party Coalition Government 1949-1970.

30 The Policy of Assimilation: Decisions of the Commonwealth and State Ministers at the Native Welfare Conference, Canberra, 1961, Department of Territories, Canberra.

31 DOCKER, E. G., *op. cit.,* pp. 207-235.

32 The Policy of Assimilation: Decisions of the Commonwealth and State Ministers at the Native Welfare Conference, Canberra, 1961, Department of Territories, Canberra, 1961, p. 1.

33 See for example D. Barwick, 'Economic Absorption without Assimilation: the Case of Some Melbourne Part-Aboriginal Families', *Oceania,* vol. 32, No. 1, 1962. Federal Council for Advancement of Aborigines and Torres Strait Islanders. Government Legislation and Aborigines, February 1964. R. E. Hausfield, 'An Integration Policy for Australian Aboriginal Groups', *Mankind,* vol. 6/2, 1963. T. E. H. Strehlow, 'Assimilation Problems: The Aboriginal Viewpoint', Adelaide, 1964. L. West, 'The Right to Choose', *Outlook,* vol. 6 (4), 1962.

34 Department of Territories, Canberra, Press Statement, 22 July 1965.

35 The Gallup Polls and public opinion surveys in post-war years in Australia always heavily favoured the Aboriginal cause. This appeared to be in direct contrast to the speed of legislative change in both the Commonwealth and most of the States. The 1967 Referendum finally presented the Governments with irrefutable evidence of the community's attitude on the subject. The question of public opinion polls on Aborigines is dealt with in some detail in Current Affairs Bulletin, Vol. 29, No. 9, 25 December 1961. *The Dark People.* See also *Courier Mail,* Brisbane, 1 February 1964.

36 See generally N. T. Abbott, *Australia's Frontier Province,* 1950. Also, Legislative Council of the Northern Territory, Select Committee on Political Rights, Darwin, 1963, and Northern Territory (Administration) Act, 1910-1962.

37 TATZ, C. M. 'Aboriginal Administration in the Northern Territory of Australia, Ph.D. Thesis, Australian National University, 1964, p. 273.

38 For an interesting example of how the authority of the Commonwealth might be challenged in the more practical level of the implementation of policy, see H. I. Jensen, 'The Darwin Revolution', *Labour History,* No. 11, 1966, pp. 3-13, where the Administrator of the Territory became the 'hostage of the irate residents and was shipped South'. This article also clearly documents the more seamy sides of early history and the beginnings of Aboriginal policy.

39 FOXCROFT, E. J. B. *Australian Native Policy,* Melbourne, 1944, p. 134.

40 Official Year Book of the Commonwealth of Australia, No. 5, 1912, p. 116.

41 *Ibid.,* 1937, p. 274.

42 *Ibid.,* p. 315.

43 *Ibid.,* p. 274.

44 Foxcroft, *op. cit.*, p. 135.

45 Baldwin Spencer, J. W.: Preliminary Report on the Aboriginals of the Northern Territory. (Report to the Northern Territory Administration, 1912), Melbourne, 1913.

46 Jensen, *op. cit.*, p. 5.

47 *Ibid.*

48 Bleakely, J. W., 'Report on Aborigines and Half Castes', Parliamentary Papers, XXI of 1929 (Vol. II, 1159). The Aboriginals and Half-Castes of Central Australia and Northern Australia. Parliament of the Commonwealth of Australia, Report, 1929, Sydney, 1930.

49 Thomson, D. G., 'Recommendation of Policy in Native Affairs', Canberra, 1937, Parliamentary Paper 56 of 1937-40, Vol. III, 805.

50 Report of the Administration of the Northern Territory, 1936, p. 15.

50a Thomson, *op. cit.*, p. 5.

51 See Foxcroft, *op. cit.*, p. 152. Expenditure from consolidated revenue on Aboriginal welfare in 1936 amounted to £6,921 or an average of approximately seven shillings and sixpence per resident Aborigine. (Year Book of the Commonwealth of Australia, No. 30, 1937, p. 242.) This was increased to approximately one pound per head in 1938. (Report of the Administrator of the Northern Territory, 1937-1938, p. 24.)

52 Kelly, J. H. *The Beef Cattle Industry of Northern Australia*, Bureau of Agricultural Economics, Canberra, 1952, pp. 172-3.

53 Long, J. P. M., 'The Administration and the Part Aboriginals of the Northern Territory', *Oceania*, Vol. 37, No. 3, pp. 184-201.

54 Cook, C., 'Medicine and the Australian Aboriginal: a century of contact in the Northern Territory', *The Medical Journal of Australia*, 1966, 1:559, April, p. 561.

55 Long, *op. cit.*

56 Docker, 513.

55 Long, *op. cit.*

58 For a general account of the experiences of Aborigines during the Second World War see F. R. Morris, 'The War Effort of Aborigines in the Northern Territory', *Australian Territories*, Vol. 5, No. 1, 1965, pp. 2-10.

59 Kelly, J. W. *Struggle for the North*, Sydney, 1966, pp. 153-157.

60 The Aboriginals Ordinance 1918-1953, s. 3.

61 Northern Territory Legislative Council Debates, 21 January 1953, p. 56.

62 Welfare Ordinance 1953, s. 14.

63 See N.T.L.C.D., 22 January 1953, pp. 80-96.

64 *Ibid.*, p. 96.

65 *Ibid.*, p. 91.

66 Welfare Ordinance 1953, s. 14 (2).

67 A full-blood Aborigine in this sense was ruled to be a person who contained a predominance of Aboriginal blood. There does not seem to have been a Court case on this subject and I am informed that all Government departments have operated on a ruling given by the Attorney-General's Department in relation to the Commonwealth Electoral Act in 1928. Discussion. Department of Territories, 28 April 1965.

68 N.T.L.C.D., 8 June 1953, p. 4.

69 N.T.L.C.D., 9 June 1953, pp. 30-31.

70 Aboriginals Ordinance 1918-53, s. 5 (f).

71 Welfare Ordinance 1953, s. 8 (a).

72 *Ibid.*, s. 8 (b) and (f)(iv).

73 Welfare Ordinance 1953, s. 16.

74 N.T.L.C.D., 16 May 1959, p. 888.

75 LANCASTER JONES, F. *A Demographic Survey of the Aboriginal Population of the Northern Territory*, Australian Institute of Aboriginal Studies, Canberra, 1963, p. 10.

76 *Ibid.*, pp. 8-12.

77 TATZ, *op. cit.*, p. 26.

78 Australia. Parliament, House of Representatives, 36:415-416. N.T.L.C.D. 15 August 1962, p. 3162.

79 Only about eighty full-bloods were intentionally omitted from the Register. F. Lancaster Jones, *op. cit.*, p. 12.

80 *Canberra Times*, 21 August 1962.

81 See *Australian*, 28 October 1967. 'Why Welfare is a Dirty Word to Aborigines'. See also N.T.L.C.D. 28 October 1959, p. 1017.

82 Welfare Ordinances, No. 16 of 1953, No. 6 of 1959, No. 2 of 1961, No. 12 of 1963, No. 21 of 1963, No. 18 of 1963, No. 46 of 1964; Wards Employment Ordinances, No. 24 of 1953, No. 9 of 1958, No. 6 of 1959, No. 2 of 1961, No. 2 of 1963, No. 18 of 1963, No. 46 of 1964; Regulations under the Wards Employment Ordinance, No. 9 of 1957, No. 4 of 1959, No. 17 of 1961.

83 TATZ, C. M. 'Aboriginal Administration in the Northern Territory of Australia', Ph.D. Thesis, A.N.U., 1964, p. 304.

84 For a summary of some of these major objections see the debates on the motion for an 'Enquiries into Principles and Operation of Welfare Ordinance N.T.L.C.D., 16 May 1959, pp. 871-893. The motion was defeated on Government appointees' votes.

85 Welfare Ordinance No. 12 of 1962, s. 15.

86 *Ibid.*, s. 13.

87 Commonwealth Electoral Act.

88 Northern Territory Electoral Regulations.

89 N.T.L.C.D., 19 February 1964, pp. 1515-1517.

90 The following Ordinances were to be amended: The Licensing Ordinance, The Police and Police Offences Ordinance, Interstate Aboriginals (Distribution of Estates) Ordinance, Dangerous Drugs Ordinance, Registration of Dogs Ordinance, Methylated Spirits Ordinance, Firearms Ordinance, Workers Compensation. Legislative Council of the Northern Territory: Report of the Select Committee on Social Welfare Legislation, 12 May 1964.

91 N.T.L.C.D., 18 May 1964, pp. 1889-1894.

92 N.T.L.C.D., 19 February 1964, p. 1513.

93 Commonwealth Conciliation and Arbitration Commission, No. 830 of 1965.

94 More detailed treatment of the background and development of labour policy and practice is covered in my publications *Equal Wages For Aborigines: The Background to Industrial Discrimination in the Northern Territory of Australia*, F.C.A.A.T.S.I., Sydney, 1968 and *Aboriginal Labour in the Pastoral Industry of the Northern Territory*, Canberra, 1971, in press.

95 A term used by the State Secretary, Australian Workers Union, in a letter on private file, dated 7 September 1967. This satisfaction was not limited to the Labor Party. Opposing the suggestion of a referendum designed to allow the Commonwealth Government to extend greater assistance to the States

in Aboriginal affairs the Leader of the Country Party Opposition (later Premier) Mr. Nicklin, reflected, in 1946, that 'the States have clearly shown that they can care for their Aborigines much better than the Commonwealth have demonstrated that it can care for the Aborigines who are its direct Aboriginal people.' (Queensland Parliamentary Debates, 1945/46, 19 March 1946, Vol. CLXXXVII, p. 2026.)

96 Queensland Parliamentary Debates, 1939, 20 September, Vol. CLXIX, p. 458.

97 *Ibid.,* 20 September, Vol. CLXXIX, p. 492.

98 *Ibid.,* p. 496.

99 This suggestion seemed to be readily subscribed to by other Members despite the fact that the Minister in charge of Native Affairs informed them that it was 'impossible to obtain an accurate census of Aboriginal population of the State'. (Q.P.D., 20 September 1939, Vol. CLXXIV, p. 484.)

100 *Ibid.,* Vol. CLXXIV, 19 September 1939, p. 452.

101 *Ibid.,* p. 454.

102 *Ibid.,* p. 454.

103 *Ibid.,* p. 455.

104 *Ibid.,* 20 September 1939, p. 485.

105 *Ibid.,* 19 September 1939, p. 456.

106 *Ibid.,* 20 September 1939, p. 491.

107 *Ibid.,* 20 September 1939, p. 487.

108 *Ibid.,* 19 September 1938, p. 452.

109 *Ibid.,* p. 455.

110 *Ibid.,* p. 458.

111 *Ibid.,* p. 452.

112 *Ibid.,* p. 456.

113 *Ibid.,* 29 September 1939, p. 488.

114 *Ibid.,* 19 September 1939, p. 456.

115 *Ibid.,* p. 458.

116 *Ibid.*

117 *Ibid.,* p. 459.

118 *Ibid.,* Vol. CLXXIV, 19 September 1939, p. 460. Lady Goodwin: Wife of Governor of Queensland, 1927-1932; Sir Thomas Herbert John Chapman Goodwin was born in Kandy, Ceylon, and had an extensive career as a British army officer in India and Europe. 'Sir John and Lady Goodwin were highly popular in Queensland. They were lovers of the open air, travelled widely in Queensland and took a keen interest in the social and economic life of the State'. Lack, *op. cit.,* pp. 607-8.

119 *Ibid.,* p. 461.

120 *Ibid.,* p. 462.

121 *Ibid.,* 29 September 1939, p. 485.

122 *Ibid.,* 20 September 1939, p. 497.

123 Year Book of the Commonwealth of Australia, No. 5, 1912, pp. 116, 120. *Ibid.,* No. 30, 1937, pp. 242, 312 and 374.

124 Annual Report of the Director of Native Affairs, 1965, p. 3.

125 Q.P.D. Vol. CLXXXVII, 19 March 1946, p. 2029. The monitorial system of teaching for European children was officially discarded in 1852 when Queensland territory was still part of New South Wales after William Wilkins of the

New South Wales Board of National Education had instituted a paid pupil-teacher system.—Report of Board of National Education, 1851, Fourth Report, Appendix I, Wilkins to Secretary, 30 June 1851, 3, and Fair Minute Book, Board of National Education, State Archives of New South Wales, 13 February 1952, 473.

126 *Ibid.*, p. 2028.

127 *Ibid.*, p. 2041, 20 March 1946, Vol. CLXXXVII.

128 *Ibid.*, p. 2037, 19 March 1946.

129 *Ibid.*, p. 2031.

130 *Ibid.*, p. 2038. The Chairman of Committees, left his chair to contribute this particular piece of information to the debate.

131 The exception related to the Administration of trust funds at Coen North, Qld. Q.P.D. 28 November 1957, Vol. 219, p. 1421. For example of denial that such was the practice see Q.P.D. Vol. 230, 20 September 1961, p. 426.

132 Queensland Parliamentary Debates, 28 November 1957, Vol. 219, p. 1432.

133 *Ibid.*, 25 September 1957, Vol. 218, p. 316.

134 Report of the Director of Native Affairs, Brisbane, 1959, p. 3.

135 Queensland Parliamentary Debates, 13 March, Vol. 220, p. 1848.

136 Although under the Chairmanship of a Member of the House this Committee was not a 'Parliamentary Committee'. Requests to view the proceedings have been rejected by the Minister concerned. Letter on private file, 7 September 1967.

137 Tape recording. In similar vein the Report of the Special Committee enquiring into Legislation for the Promotion of Aborigines etc. in 1964 contained a majority of recommendations for a special roll for Aboriginal voters. (Government Printer, Brisbane, 1964, p. 3).

138 Queensland Parliamentary Debates, 1 November 1962, Vol. 234, p. 1249.

139 Queensland Parliamentary Debates, 1 April 1965, Vol. 240, p. 3159.

140 *Ibid.*, p. 3155.

141 Q.P.D., Vol. 242, 7 December 1965, p. 2003.

142 *Ibid.*

143 *Ibid.*

144 *Ibid.*, p. 3157.

145 *Ibid.*, p. 3159.

146 *Ibid.*, p. 3191.

147 *Ibid.*, p. 3188.

148 *Ibid.*

149 Queensland Parliamentary Debates, 1 April 1965, Vol. 240, p. 3154.

150 An excellent collection of documents covering the intransigence of the Queensland Government and the Federal Government's attempt to ameliorate their policies has been made available in roneoed form by the State Co-ordinator 'Act Confrontation Campaign', 3 Kennedy Terrace, East Brisbane, Qld., 4169, dated 27 May 1971.

151 Constitution Act 1889, W.A.

152 FOXCROFT, *op. cit.*, p. 123.

153 Report of Royal Commissioner tabled 1936, W.A.P.D., 20 October 1936, p. 1204.

154 Year Book of the Commonwealth of Australia, No. 5, 1912, p. 116 and p. 120.

155 *Ibid.*, No. 30, pp. 241, 312 and 374, 1937.

156 Year Book of the Commonwealth of Australia No. 30, 1937, p. 242.

157 W.A.P.D., Vol. 97, 20 October 1936, p. 1204.

158 *Ibid.*, p. 1204.

159 *Ibid.*, p. 1206.

160 W.A.P.D., Vol. 132, 11 November 1952, p. 1960. It is possible that offensive commentary was edited from the Western Australian Hansards whereas they remained in the Queensland Hansards. However, this was denied.

161 W.A.P.D., Vol. 97, 13 October 1936.

162 See Q.P.D., 19 September 1939, p. 458.

163 W.A.P.D., Vol. 97, p. 1204, 20 October 1936. 'This measure is an amendment to the Aborigines Act of 1905—Great difficulty is found in administering the affairs of the Department under the existing legislation'.

164 W.A.P.D., Vol. 97, p. 2367, 3 December 1936 (Leader of the Opposition).

165 *Ibid.*, p. 2373.

166 *Ibid.*, p. 2392.

167 *Ibid.*, Vol. 98, p. 2384, 3 December 1936, and Vol. 97, p. 977, 6 October 1936, where objection even to placing them in camps was taken.

168 *Ibid.*, p. 2392.

169 *Ibid.*, Vol. 97, p. 2385, 3 December 1936.

170 *Ibid.*, 13 October 1936, p. 1069.

171 *Ibid.*, 29 September 1936, p. 823.

172 *Ibid.*, 14 October 1936, p. 1109.

173 *Ibid.*, Vol. 103, p. 705, 20 September 1939.

174 *Ibid.*

175 *Ibid.*, Vol. 98, p. 2390, 3 December 1936.

176 *Ibid.*, Vol. 104, p. 1497, 25 October 1939.

177 *Ibid.*, Vol. 97, p. 831, 29 September 1936.

178 *Ibid.*, 29 September 1936, also *ibid.*, p. 822; p. 830.

179 *Ibid.*, p. 833, also p. 718 above.

180 *Ibid.*, Vol. 98, 3 December 1936, p. 2388.

181 *Ibid.*, p. 2394.

182 *Ibid.*, p. 2390.

183 *Ibid.*, p. 986.

184 *Ibid.*, Vol. 98, p. 2392, 3 December 1936.

185 *Ibid.*, Vol. 97, p. 988, 6 October 1936.

186 *Ibid.*, Vol. 114, p. 1905, 22 November 1944.

187 *Ibid.*, Vol. 113, p. 825, 28 September 1944, Natives (Citizenship Rights) Bill.

188 *Ibid.*, 22 November 1944, p. 1908.

189 *Ibid.*, Vol. 107, p. 346, 26 August 1941.

190 *Ibid.*, Vol. 120, p. 1916, 13 November 1947.

191 Report on Survey of Native Affairs, Government Printer, Perth, 1948. For terms of reference see W.A.P.D., Vol. 119, 6 August 1947, p. 82.

192 See for example: W.A.P.D., Vol. 123, 6 July 1949, p. 356 *et seq.*, Vol. 124, 3 August 1949, p. 908 *et seq.*, Vol. 127, 29 November 1950, p. 2332, Vol. 136, 26 November 1953, p. 2108 and p. 2114.

193 W.A.P.D., 29 November, Vol. 127, p. 2331 (Emphasis mine).

194 *Ibid.*, p. 1317 *et seq.*, 18 October 1950. Natives (Citizens' Rights) Amendment Act.

195 W.A.P.D., 20 November 1957. Vol. 148, p. 3325. Where there was an exchange of letters between the Director of Native Affairs in the Northern Territory and the Commissioner of Welfare, W.A., regarding certain half castes of good repute travelling to Perth. See also Parliamentary Debates, W.A. 1958, Vol. 150, p. 1300, 8 October 1958. Although the same problem was also apparent in Queensland no reference was ever made to it in the Queensland House.

196 See, for example, W.A.P.D., 1950, Vol. 127, p. 1578. See also 1957, Vol. 138, p. 3678, 27 November 1957; 1958, Vol. 149, p. 668, 9 September 1968; 1958, Vol. 150, p. 1000, 23 September 1958; 1962, Vol. 162, p. 3266.

197 *Ibid.*, 1957, Vol. XLVII.

198 See Parliamentary Debates W.A., 1953, Vol. 136, p. 2107, 26 November 1953, where an Opposition Member accused the Government of 'playing into the hands of McLeod' (Leader of the Pindan Movement) by proposing to give half castes the right to vote.

199 W.A.P.D., Vol. 136, p. 2108, 26 November 1953. The conditions described were alleged to exist in 1947 and it was stated that the settlement had since been 'cleaned up'. The conditions referred to in the debate, however, are not dissimilar to those which were observed in many locations by the writer during field work in North Australia during 1965 and 1966.

200 See Annual Report of Commissioner of Native Affairs, W.A., June 1949, Perth (1951), p. 5.

201 W.A.P.D., Vol. 136, p. 2763, 16 December 1953.

202 Report of the Commissioner for Native Welfare quoted Parliamentary Debates W.A., 1953, Vol. 136, p. 2761, 16 December 1953.

203 See for example Parliamentary Debates W.A., 1953, Vol. 136, 26 November 1953, p. 2106. A Member of the Opposition objecting to the Commissioner's public statements 'I wonder where the public servants of this State are heading', 29 November 1957. See also Parliamentary Debates W.A., 1957, Vol. 148, p. 3973 29 November 1957, where a Parliamentary Select Committee was requested to reply to allegations made in the Commission's Annual Report. Also Vol. 148, 28 November 1957, p. 3781, 'I am sure no Member has been happy with him. His administration is all wrong because he was brought up in the wrong environment.' Also Parliamentary Debates W.A. 1957, 19 September 1957, Vol. 147, p. 1676 where disciplining of the Commissioner was called for.

204 Reported in the *Reliance Weekly*. Quoted Parliamentary Debates W.A. 1953, Vol. 136, 26 November 1953, p. 2106.

205 W.A.P.D., 16 December 1953, Vol. 136, p. 2767.

206 *Ibid.*

207 W.A.P.D., Vol. 134, p. 813. For discussions of the Report of Commissioner of Police see for example *West Australian*, 'Not Slaves nor Citizens', 11 October 1952, 5 November 1952, 26 January 1953.

208 See 1953 Parliamentary Debates. W.A., Vol. 134, 29 September 1953, p. 813.

209 Report of the Commissioner for Public Health, 1952, p. 13. Quoted in Parliamentary Debates W.A. 1952, 4 November, Vol. 132, pp. 1784-5.

210 W.A.P.D., Vol. 132, 29 October 1952, p. 1654.

211 W.A.P.D. 1952, 30 October, Vol. 132, p. 1724.

212 *Ibid.*, 4 November 1952, p. 1782.

213 Native Administration Amendment Act 1954, 7 December 1954. W.A.P.D. 1954, Vol. 14, pp. 3614-16.

214 The main difference between the 1953 Bill and the 1954 Bill was the retention of Par. 49 (Liquor) in the latter instrument. See W.A.P.D. 1954, Vol. 139, 16 September 1954, p. 1694.

215 *Ibid.*, Vol. 135, 10 November 1953, p. 1621.

216 *Ibid.*, Vol. 135, p. 1620.

217 *Ibid.*, p. 1621.

218 W.A.P.D., Vol. 178, 14 September 1950, p. 758.

219 *Ibid.*, Vol. 149, p. 2399, 11 November 1954; also Vol. 139, 5 October 1954, p. 1970.

220 *Ibid.*, Vol. 148, 20 November 1957, p. 3324.

221 *Ibid.*, 28 November 1957, p. 3801.

222 This, of course, was not the case in the Northern Territory where all full blood persons were in the process of being declared wards of the State. There were considerable misapprehensions about the Northern Territory system in the Western Parliament. See W.A.P.D., Vol. 148, 30 October 1957, p. 2691.

223 As part of this programme the Government also intended to amend those Acts which contained clauses discriminating against Aboriginal residents within the State. These Acts were: Constitution Act Amendment Act 1899-1955; Criminal Code; Dog Act; Electoral Act 1903-1948; Evidence Act 1906-1956; Fauna Protection Act 1950-54; Firearms and Guns Act 1931-56; Land Act 1933-1956; Licensing Act 1911-1956; Mining Act 1904-1955.

224 W.A.P.D., Vol. 148, 20 November 1957, p. 3324.

225 W.A.P.D., 1958, Vol. 150, p. 1673.

226 W.A.P.D., Vol. 151, 11 November 1958, p. 2083.

227 25 questions in 1959, 40 in 1960, 31 in 1961, 29 in 1962, 47 in 1963.

228 W.A.P.D., Vol. 155, 1 September 1960, p. 932.

229 W.A.P.D., Vol. 166, 27 November 1963, p. 3286.

230 *Ibid.*, p. 3262.

231 Native Welfare Act, Constitution Act, Electoral Act, Licensing Act.

232 W.A.P.D., 1962, Vol. 162, p. 1690-1961. An interesting aspect of the granting of the right to vote to Aborigines was that the measure was associated with the right of being counted in the Census; if Aborigines had been counted in the 1962 Census in Western Australia that State's representation in the Commonwealth House of Representatives would probably not have been reduced from 9 to 8. See Parliamentary Debates W.A., 1962, Vol. 162, p. 1678.

233 *Ibid.*, 1963, Vol. 166, p. 3052, *et seq.*

234 *Ibid.*, p. 3053.

235 *Ibid.*, p. 3270.

236 *Ibid.*, 1963, Vol. 155, p. 3262.

237 These demands first started to appear in 1959. See Parliamentary Debates W.A., 1959, Vol. 152, 24 July 1959, p. 389.

238 *Ibid.*, 1963, 3 December 1963, Vol. 166, p. 3472. This theory may not be without substance. Special reference to certain evidence relating to the influence of the International Labour Office on the scheduling of change in Australian Native affairs will be made later on.

239 *The Bulletin*, Sydney, 21 March 1971.

240 From a survey entitled 'Discriminatory Legislation Regarding Aborigines' issued at the meeting between the Commonwealth and State official concerned with Aboriginal affairs during the week 9-13 March 1970, Sydney, N.S.W.

10

BLACK POWER IN AUSTRALIA

Bruce McGuinness

White is Godly, so I've been told
Black depicts Vice and Sin,
Is this how they judge my goodness,
By the colour of my skin?

They call me Darkie, Nigger,
Blackie, Boong and Coon
And treat me like an animal,
But the tables may turn soon.

I'm speaking of Black Power,
It will make all Koories strong,
We'll make old whitey tremble
And realise his wrong.

So unite all dark skinned people,
Merge from the depths as one
And show the world that we can
Beat the white man with the gun.

Racial Discrimination

Racial discrimination began in Australia the day James Cook set foot on Kurnell. Since then, the Australian Aborigine has been subjected to 200 years of murder, rape and dispossession. Today the ultimate insult is heard in a typical pre-school yard limerick:—

Jacky Jacky him smoke baccy
Eat gwanna, snake and grub
He not given to White man's liven ,
Him belong in bloody scrub.

This brand of discrimination usually remains in European Australian minds, right through Australia's education system. At primary school, we have text books constantly referring to Aborigines as being dirty, Blacks, nomadic, etc. When Wentworth crossed the Blue Mountains, these same books state that they (the great White explorers) were accompanied by Blacks. It doesn't clarify the fact that the BLACKS showed them the way (surely if these White explorers were great, then the Aboriginal Guides must have been greater, for didn't they cross the mountains first?). Toward Secondary level, we find that the racist attitude of White Australians becomes somewhat subdued! Prejudices more veiled! Discrimination rather subtle! Nevertheless, the book-bias remains.

With the waning of the childhood years, these racist attitudes gain increased importance through the organisation of Australian society into various class groups.

In broad terms, the contact and comprehension level of European Australians might be classified in the following way:—

(i) *The Upper Class*—Hardly any, except perhaps introducing an Aboriginal sportsman at a formal dinner for some fund raising purpose;

(ii) *The Middle Class*—Some contact, but mainly by academics, anthropologists and fight managers, etc., but nowhere near enough contact to begin to know or understand Aborigines. Although, depending on what field they are in, the anthropologists and academics may form a close relationship with some aspects of Aboriginal life;

(iii) *The Working Class*—Much more contact is made at this level, mainly because it is the only level open to Aborigines. However, it doesn't necessarily follow that the understanding is any better. Usually the condition worsens, the working class Whites, of course, needing someone to stand on and deride, mostly because they have no wish to be low man on the totem.

Nevertheless, out of these groups, there emerges a sprinkling of people who are concerned enough to want to do something to remedy the situation. Mainly they are academics, students, trade unionists and politicians. Other types are most certainly involved, but the predescribed group make up the main body of Aboriginal sympathisers. Many have legitimate reasons for supporting the Aboriginal claims, others are just in it for what they can get out of it. Fortunately the latter are very few, and usually leave the field after a while. The ones that are left are genuinely anxious to assist Aborigines in the best possible way, the main difficulty, of course, being that they have little opportunity to consult at length with Aborigines. However, the more advanced groups go, sometimes, thousands of miles out of their way, to find out what Aborigines feel, and consider to be, the answer to the evermounting problems. These groups I feel for. I can relate to them without any difficulty.

There are, however, other Aboriginal orientated groups that do no talking with Aborigines whatsoever. They just assume that they know all. It is obvious, with each passing issue, that these individual groups do very little to further the aims of Aborigines. They do do a fair bit to further their own ideas of what the Aborigines want, but little for Aboriginal thinking or goals. In this group, one also witnesses a certain amount of individual racism, barely noticeable to the layman, but there nevertheless.

Government and Institutional Racism

These general community attitudes make it simple for institutional racism to thrive; e.g.:—

(i) The Federal Government doesn't exercise its legal right nor moral obligations to override State Governments on Aboriginal affairs as was given to it by the 1967 referendum;

(ii) Federal Government's refusal to recognise the fact that Aboriginal law needs to be respected;

(iii) The various State Governments' refusal to do much the same thing!

The Western Australian prisons are a good example of the legal apathy regarding Aborigines. Aborigines in that state constitute 2½ per cent of the State's population, yet the Aboriginal prison population is as high as 95 per cent in most areas.

The law and the penal system in Western Australia are openly discriminating against Aborigines. The following examples might prove the point:—

Statement by Aboriginal Girls from Kalgoorlie: 6 June 1969.

'We wish to make a complaint all together about the treatment of Aboriginal girls and women in Kalgoorlie. Our complaint is against the Native Welfare Department and the Police Department.

'When we go to the Native Welfare Department and ask Miss —— for a job she tells us to go away and come back tomorrow. "I am too busy to attend to you", she says. They are often too busy for us in the Office. They never appear for us in court though none of us in prison today is over 21 years, and some of us are juveniles. The police illtreat us very often and do not treat us like human beings. They punch us. They kick us in the guts. They push us to the ground and kick and tread on us. They hose us down and leave us wet and cold. They call us "black bitches", "black bastards", "chasers after white men", "black gins", ("black tunnel cunts"). We are being called names like these all the time which does not help our dignity. We have no future and no jobs. How can we live like other people if no one will help us.

—— who is deaf and should be in school was hit hard in the eye by a policeman. —— was stood up against a wall and punched by two policemen. —— has been punched by policemen. —— has had a policeman stand on her throat. —— was pushed to the ground and policemen kicked and trod on her.'

Statement by Aboriginal Woman at Yalgoo

'I was arrested on the 10.6.69 in Yalgoo. On this day I was in the house of my niece on the Native Reserve. My niece is ——. The door was bolted and I was in the kitchen cleaning up when the policeman came and kicked in the door. He walked in and arrested me. It was about 11 a.m. I was charged in the police station before the policeman and the JP ——. Mr. —— is 75 years old and should not be on the bench. There was only one JP present with the policeman. I did not go to court. I pleaded not guilty.'

Statement by Aboriginal Woman in Perth

'On Sunday 15 June 1969 I was sitting with —— on a lawn in a park near the river in East Perth. It was in the morning sometime and —— leg was aching. We had been on our way into East Perth and had only just sat down when a police car came up. We had not been drinking and had no drink and no bottles. Two policemen were in the car and they said, "You're sitting on private property". They then took us to the Police Station. As far as I could see, it was not private property but a park. There was not a sign up anywhere to say that someone owned it. The police said that it belonged to the water supply and because they told me it was private property I pleaded guilty to being unlawfully on premises. This is what they charged us with, and because they said it, I thought it must be true. Just the same, we were not doing any harm and would have moved off if they had told us to do so. It looked like a park and I appeal against the conviction and the sentence of three months.'

Institutional racism might be witnessed further in the off-handed way in which government officials responsible for Aboriginal affairs treat their charges. A recent example of this occurred over the claims of Aborigines to residence rights in the Sherbrooke Forest area of Victoria. This happened in the following way: The Victorian Ministry of Aboriginal Affairs recently attempted to silence the Aborigines Advancement League by using a request by that organization for financial assistance from the Government. The Director of Aboriginal Affairs, under instructions, told the AAL that, if it publicly denounced the Sherbrooke Forest Land Rights claim, finance would be forthcoming, if not, there would be no money made available to them.

There is certainly no doubt that the AAL was subjected to attempted political blackmail, a serious charge, but not unfounded, nor isolated. The Federal Government's reaction to this appeared in the following letter:—

'Dear Mr. McGuinness, This is to acknowledge your letters of 15 and 21 January. In view of our telephone conversation this morning, I am not going to comment on these letters. As I said to you, we will only wish to act in the *closest* collaboration with the Victorian authorities. I therefore urge you to continue negotiations with Mr. Worthy.

With Best wishes, (really)

Yours sincerely   Signed: (Barrie Dexter)
10.2.71   Director—   Council for Aboriginal Affairs.'

It is obvious from these examples that the standards which are applicable throughout European Australian society are not respected when it comes to Aboriginal affairs. Accordingly, it is up to Aboriginal Australians to determine their own priorities and the method in which they shall conduct their relationships with the rest of the community.

Black Power

'Black Power is the empowerment of Black people to be able to make decisions concerning their destiny and control the management of their own affairs.'

This is the accepted definition of Black Power overseas. It is neither violent nor non-violent. In some areas it is violent and in others, non-violent.

Here are two very quick illustrations: The late Dr. Martin Luther King was a Black Power advocate. He stressed quite emphatically that Black men should have power of government. The means to his end was 'Brother, we must turn the other cheek'. In more direct terms, he was a pacifist. He believed that no good could come of violence. His teachings are still practised widely in the U.S.A.

On the other hand, there are the Black Panthers. Their philosophy is 'Burn, baby, burn,' and to hell with 'Whitey'. They only have to look sideways at a white cop and violence erupts. Their very presence connotes violence, even when they do not want it. The lesson being, if you live by the sword, you must expect to die by the sword.

If these are the two extremes of Black Power, does either of them apply to the Australian Aborigines?

Black Power applies to all oppressed Black men. No one country has a monopoly on it. How it will be used in this country remains to be seen. Already we have two glaring examples of the Power of Black. The first was its introduction into Australia through the person of Dr. Roosevelt Brown. His presence alone aroused fear in both the White and Black community, whilst all he did was sit and talk with Aborigines. Because of this, people in Victoria branded him a 'stirrer', an 'agitator'. The Minister of Aboriginal Affairs, Mr. Meagher, heaved a sigh of relief on his departure: 'If we never see Mr. Brown again, it will be too soon.'

The results of Dr. Brown's visit are not yet fully realised, but the initial moves towards Black Power in Australia are being made by a few Aboriginal leaders. The rest of the Black population will be carried along by the impetus. The recent takeover of the Aborigines Advancement League in Victoria is evidence of this. Although it failed in the form in which it was presented, it made people, Black and White, sit up and reappraise the situation to the point where we now have twelve Black and four White people on the Management Committee. Previously, there were seven Aborigines and nine Europeans.

Black power is being felt, not only in Victoria, but also in other States. The Victorian Tribal Council has counterparts in New South Wales and Queensland. The Brisbane Council boasts an entirely Black organisation of forty-five members and, although Sydney is not as high in membership, it is entirely black. On top of this structure, we now have the National Tribal Council, not yet one year old, but already regarded as the most radical and powerful Aboriginal organisation in Australia. It has active members and affiliates in all States of the Commonwealth.

Radicalism is, of course, not limited to institutional affairs, but springs from the feeling of the people involved. As evidence of this, the Cunnamulla uprising is outstanding. Although the events which surrounded this outrage were sensationalised by the press, it clearly showed that Aboriginal people are able to meet violence with violence.

The walkout of the Gurindji people from the Wave Hill cattle station is another example of self assertion. They considered it better to camp at this particular spot, without any prospect of reasonable subsistence, than to work as cheap labour for Lord Vestey, the English cattle Baron. They have been at Wattie Creek for four years, and show no sign of wavering or giving in to their white overlords.

These are some examples of Black Power as it exists today, but what of the future?

Aborigines should take over full control of their own affairs, firstly within voluntary organisations, bypassing Government Departments such as State Ministries and the Federal Government. They will do it successfully because they will have the support of people from other minority groups.

They will receive further support from the Black Power Movement overseas and the White people who are supporting them now. These include tradesmen, doctors, barristers, scientists, anthropologists, truck drivers, church men, trades and labour councils and working journalists.

Black Power is inevitable, given the oppression that Aborigines have been under since the advent of 'Whitey'. They are tired of unfulfilled promises. They realise that they will never advance on promises. They want action. If the White powers won't oblige, then Black Power will.

It is absolutely essential to understand that Black Power is a cry of despair. The term 'Black Power' did not spring full-grown from the head of some obtuse philosopher. It is the cry of daily hurt and persistent pain. For centuries the Black man has been the unwitting dupe of White Power. Most Black men have lost faith in the White majority because White Power with total control has left them empty-handed. So, in reality, the call for Black Power is a reaction to the failure of White Power.

The similarities between oppressed coloured people in Australia and the United States clearly prove the point. Firstly, both come under the category —Black. Both have suffered oppression for two hundred years. Both know the full significance of squalor, hunger and degradation. They are both made to feel inferior from the very first days of comprehension. In schools at most levels, we are taught that white depicts goodness and black, evil. In Roget's Thesaurus there are some one hundred and twenty synonyms on blackness, of which sixty are offensive. Such words as blot, soot, grime, devil and foul. There are some one hundred and thirty-four synonyms for whiteness. All are favourable, expressed in such glowing terms as chastity, cleanliness and innocence. Just two or three more examples build up the picture: a white lie is better than a black lie; the most degrading member of a family is the black sheep; when a man is regarded in high esteem by his companions, he is referred to often as a White man, never Black.

With references like these, it is no wonder that Black men have been made to feel inferior to White men. But Black men will no longer stand for this. They want equal rights, equal opportunity. Most of all, they want to be heard. If Black Power is a means to this end, then it is justified.

There are, of course, other aspects to the Power of Black. Sex is one of these. When a White person observes a beautiful Black girl and a beautiful White girl walking side by side, it is the Black girl who draws the attention. Further to this, I know that the coloured girl will strike and arouse the White male more so than the White one. My past experience leads me to believe that Black men have the same attraction to White women. I have women go with me on dates because I am Aboriginal. They wanted to experiment with me. They wanted to have an affair with a coloured man. They wanted to know if sex was different with a Black man than with a White man.

They were not disappointed—and always came back. No brag, just fact!

Mine is not an isolated case. There are scores more. I know of numerous white men and women who have deserted their families, given up their homes and jobs to live with an Aboriginal as their husband or wife.

Another case in point is the mixed marriage, where nearly always it is White who pursues the Black to become his or her partner. Who can say what the attraction is? The only thing these people have in common is the colour of their skin which appears to act as a magnet to some individual Whites.

Not all Whites act in this way. There are plenty who wouldn't dare take a black person into their homes in daylight. But at night, into the bedroom, is a different story.

The gutter crawlers, who can be seen every night driving along the brothel areas of Melbourne, do not discriminate against Black women. At night who can tell the difference? It appears that, in this instance, discrimination is only practised from the trouser belt up!

My point here is that, if people can come together as equals on a four-poster, why not in hotel bars, trams, buses, picture theatres, swimming pools, hospitals, etc. Maybe it isn't racism as we see it. Maybe these would-be Sunday morning puritans fear their brothers' opinions. Perhaps they worry about what other people say. They might tolerate black people but never become socially involved with them. It is the old axiom—'I'm wrapped in Smokey Bear but I wouldn't let my daughter marry him!'

Perhaps one day all mankind will be equal—this I can believe.

But brothers—never!

ECONOMICS OF PREJUDICE

11

QUEENSLAND: AUSTRALIA'S DEEP SOUTH

A. & R. Doobov

ABORIGINES

The two indigenous peoples of Queensland, Aborigines and Torres Strait Islanders, number about 50,000 and 10,000 respectively.[1] The conflicts between Queensland Aborigines and the encroaching Europeans were similar to those in other parts of Australia. However, because of their isolation, more Aborigines in Queensland escaped the decimation experienced in other parts of the continent. In the second half of the nineteenth century, after it had become obvious that the rapacity of the white settlers was about to destroy the Aboriginal race, the Australian States initiated a policy of protection. In 1897, Queensland passed legislation which set up reserves onto which the Aborigines were herded. Later, when the need no longer was to protect but to restore lost pride, dignity, and self-reliance, other states abandoned this kind of protective but restrictive legislation. Queensland did not.

The Aborigines' and Torres Strait Islanders' Affairs Act of 1965 directly controls the activities of 20,500 'assisted' Aborigines (of whom 9,300 live on Government reserves or on missions) and 10,000 'assisted' Torres Strait Islanders. The other Aborigines, however, are still very much under its influence. This may be because they were brought up under this Act or its predecessors, or because they have relatives under its jurisdiction, or because they feel that the threat of their being declared 'assisted' if they commit any misdemeanour hangs over their heads.[2] In Cunnamulla, Aborigines told us about a non-assisted woman who had been gaoled for an offence which was totally obscure to them. They explained this, however, by assuming that the woman had first been declared assisted. This, for them, made arbitrary punishment something to be normally expected.

Because the effects of the Act dominate Aboriginal affairs in Queensland and because of the overwhelming psychological effects on Queensland Aborigines of seventy-five years of 'protection', this legislation will be examined in detail in this article. The basis of the Act will become obvious—complete control over the lives of the people under its jurisdiction.

Legislation[3]

The Aborigines' and Torres Strait Islanders' Affairs Act of 1965 cannot be considered in isolation. We must bear in mind the conditions and the attitudes of the people with whom it deals. They have been brought up under a system of absolute authority. Even the most trivial decisions were taken out of their hands. They have been forced to be idle and have seen their culture and way of life scorned and despised by the completely dominant white officials. The centre of their spiritual existence, their land, with its sacred sites and associations with the Dreamtime, has been stolen. Their customs and traditions have been discouraged, and in some cases forbidden, by such provisions as Reg. 21 of the 1939 Act, which requires permission to be given by an official for 'any native practices' and which stipulates that such practices must cease by midnight.

These Aborigines have grown up believing they have no rights at all and that they must always obey their white masters in every respect. Even if this is no longer legally so, this training ensures that they are unlikely to argue with the decisions of the manager of the reserve. Added to this is their experience of the fate of those who have argued with officialdom. In 1966, for example, three men from Edward River Mission were held on the Palm Island for periods in excess of twelve months, without trial, for demonstrating against the arbitrary search of their belongings by a European official.[4] It is also important to realise that the Aborigine on the reserve has very little formal education—until 1961, reserve schools taught only to Grade Four. Thus, even where the Act does give him some rights, e.g. the right to appeal, he is unlikely to know this and is probably unable to use it. The difficulty of access to the reserves for outsiders, maintained by the Department of Aboriginal and Island Affairs, ensures that he does not learn to exercise these rights.

Exemption and Declaration

The 1939 Act applied to all Aborigines living on reserves, as well as everyone with more than 50 per cent Aboriginal blood unless he had been exempted. These people and their children now come under the jurisdiction of the 1965 Act. Those not under the Act at present have usually at some stage received exemptions. They can now be declared assisted in three ways:—

   (i) They can apply and be accepted by the Director of Aboriginal and Island Affairs (Section 18).

  (ii) If the Director or any authorised officer finds a person 'has a strain of Aboriginal blood' and 'should in his best interest be declared' he may require him to appear in court and 'to answer the complaint and to be further dealt with according to law' (s. 20). The court may declare the Aborigine as needing assistance and put him under the Act.

 (iii) When an Aborigine or part-Aborigine comes before a court, the presiding officer may declare the Aborigine to need assistance and put him under the Act 'whether or not such person was convicted of the offence with which he was charged' (s. 21).

Exemption from the Act may be declared by the Director upon receipt of an application for exemption, or at his own discretion (s. 34).

Aborigines commonly refer to people not under the Act as being free. 'So my younger children,' an Aboriginal woman said to us when explaining how she had obtained her exemption, 'were born free'. This is not to say that all assisted Aborigines want to be exempted from the Act. As things stand, exemption means that the Aborigine must leave the reserve. Many Aborigines have lived there all their lives and still want to. Although they do not like the restrictions under which they live, they prefer them to being forced to leave their home. The restrictions, after all, have become part of their normal pattern of life.[5]

Freedom of Movement

Section 34 gives the Director power to move an assisted Aborigine not living on a reserve onto any reserve in Queensland, and, on the recommendation of an Aboriginal court, to transfer him from one reserve to another. In practice, such transfers are common, often without the recommendation of the court; and on at least one reserve, this occurs despite the active opposition of the Aboriginal council.

No person can live on or visit an Aboriginal reserve without the permission of the manager (Reg. 13). Residents thus live under the constant threat of expulsion—a threat not infrequently carried out. A resident of a reserve may not leave it, temporarily or permanently, without the permission of the manager (Reg. 70). Thus a non-resident Aborigine, born on a reserve and with parents still living there, can see them only with the permission of the manager.

Granting of this permission is by no means automatic. A typical example occurred at Palm Island last Christmas (1970) when, not only was a son refused permission to enter the settlement to see his mother, but the officials refused to tell the mother whether he had been given permission.

This denial of the liberty of movement causes more complaints from the Aborigines than any other provision of the Act.

Finance

Should it so decide, the Department can take complete control of the financial affairs of an assisted Aborigine, exercising all powers which he himself would otherwise have (s. 38). All his income is then paid into a trust fund account which is operated on by the Director or his delegate, who allocates to the Aborigine such funds as he (the Director) decides 'are required by the said assisted person or are necessary for payment of his just debts'. Abuses of this power are common. An Aborigine in North Queensland recently wanted to buy an electric guitar for $35. He had $400 in his account and had no dependants. He was refused permission. Another person with adequate funds was not allowed to buy a bicycle 'because then everyone would want one'.

The ability to take control of the finances of an assisted Aborigine can be a powerful method of punishment. In Normanton, as a result of their participation in a brawl in a hotel, two Aborigines were not allowed to withdraw money from their account. As their entire income was paid into this account, the families concerned were left to live as best they could from the charity of the rest of the community.

It is frequently not possible for an assisted Aborigine to obtain a record of his bank account. Requests for such a record are simply not answered or are answered with incomplete information. The secrecy with which these trust accounts are run and the enormous power of the trustees over their wards provide ideal conditions for the misappropriation of funds. Frank Stevens,[6] an accepted authority in this field, has listed several methods which he found were commonly used for this purpose and has given examples, which, if not unanswerable, have yet to be answered.

Employment

Assisted Aborigines may work on or off the reserve. Chapter 3, Section 1 of the prototype set of by-laws issued by the Department of Aboriginal and Island Affairs states 'All able-bodied persons above the age of 15 years resident within the community shall, unless otherwise determined by the manager, perform such work as is directed by the manager or person authorised by him'. Anyone working off the community may at any time be withdrawn from this employment by the Director (R. 72).

The wages of assisted Aborigines working off the reserve are set either by the appropriate industrial award or by the Department. Many cases of under-payment have been documented, mainly in North Queensland.[7] On the reserves, the wages are set by the Department and they vary from one reserve to another. The following figures are for Yarrabah, North Queensland, which has a cash economy. The Aborigines in question are responsible for purchasing all their needs from these wages.

	Aboriginal weekly wage	European weekly wage
Truck Driver	$20.00	$70.00
Tractor Driver	$12.00 - $18.00	$65.00
Labourer	$10.00 - $18.00	$60.00
Mechanic	$24.00	$75.00
Painter	$16.00	$65.00
Ganger	$20.00 - $25.00	$80.00
Carpenter (trained on reserve)	$20.00	$75.00
Police Constable	$12.00 - $18.00	$80.00
		(Equivalent occupation Editor's Note)

By comparison, no one who is not covered by the Aborigines' and Torres Strait Islanders' Affairs Act can be paid, legally, less than $46.40 per week. The average males wage, for all Queensland workers, is $78.50.

Health

Dr. Jose, in the 1970 annual report of the Queensland Institute of Medical Research, reported that of all Aboriginal children on reserves between the ages of six months and three years, 50 per cent suffered from growth retardation due to poor diet. He has also shown the infant mortality rate on twelve reserves and missions to be six times higher than the Queensland average[8]—in the one to four year old group it is thirteen times higher. The wages quoted above go a long way towards explaining these facts. In Australia, it is not possible to feed adequately a family on a weekly wage of $25—particularly when an average Aboriginal family has eight members.

Traditional Aboriginal diet was nutritionally sound. After their land was taken, the Aborigines were forced to live on what they could obtain from the whites. Tea and damper are now traditional 'Black fella's' food. Effective training in nutrition would sharply decrease infant mortality. Despite the enormous powers government officials have on reserves, and despite their willingness to use them for other purposes, it has never been considered necessary to provide this training.[9]

Other Restrictions and Powers

The lives of the assisted Aborigines are supervised in very considerable detail. Nothing is too trivial to be regulated. A man who enters or leaves a park other than through a gateway provided for this purpose infringes a by-law, as does the man who 'carries tales about any person so as to cause domestic trouble or annoyance to such person' (Ch. 4, S1, Ch. 17, S6). Nor is anything too private to be covered. A parent must bring up his children with love and care. If this love is considered insufficient, an offence has been committed. (Ch. 24, S3.)

The power of the Department to enforce obedience to all these restrictions is considerable. The manager may, at will, confine an assisted Aborigine to detention in a dormitory for up to six months. Further detention requires a report to the Director. If the Director and manager so wish, there is no limit to the period of detention (R. 70). Reg. 11 states that everyone on the reserve must obey all lawful instructions of officers of the reserve, while Reg. 10 states that all must 'conform to a reasonable standard of good conduct' on the reserve. In addition, anyone who 'does any act subversive of good order or discipline' commits an offence (R. 12). To complete this imposing list of powers, Reg. 17 enshrines the all-embracing offence of bringing onto the reserve 'anything which in the opinion of the manager' is likely 'to disturb the peace, harmony, order or discipline of such reserve'.

Aboriginal Councils

The apparent powers given to Aboriginal Councils seemed a liberal attempt to develop self-management on the reserves. Reg. 21 defines their role as that of 'local government of the reserve' and, as such, they are responsible for the 'good rule and government' of the reserve or community. The most pleasing aspect is the acknowledgement of cultural influences— such government is to be 'in accordance with Aboriginal customs and practices'. Furthermore, the Council is given the power and authority to make by-laws, such as 'regulating and controlling peace' (R. 22) and including setting maximum penalties which can be used in the Aboriginal Court (maximum of $40 and/or 14 days imprisonment). Other powers include passing by-laws to determine 'the direction, administration and control of the working and business of the local government of the reserve' (R. 22, 23) and it can also pass resolutions and levy fees, rents and dues (R. 20, 25). Despite the apparently wide powers assigned to it, the Council is continually subject to the Department. No by-law can have effect until approved by the Director (R. 28), and each order or resolution is subject to the will of the Manager, who may suspend it, 'either for an indefinite period or for such a period as he may specify'. (R. 31 (1).)

All communal income (rents, fines, dues) is paid into a Community Fund (R. 45). 'A disbursement shall not be made from a Community Fund unless the Manager approves' (R. 46). The Manager, accordingly, controls all the Council's finance and has another effective method of blocking any of its actions at will. No appeal mechanism exists. The Council consists of four assisted Aborigines, only two of whom are elected. The other two are appointed by the Director. It is noteworthy that, in the previous legislation, when the Council had less power, all its members were elected.

Any assisted Aborigine who has been convicted of an offence against the Act, regulations or by-laws in the previous two years is not eligible to stand for election (R. 33). The scope of the powers allotted to the Manager gives

him a considerable degree of control over such convictions and, thus, over
who is eligible to stand for election. The chairman of the Council is elected
by the Councillors. He may be, and commonly is, one of the appointed
members of the Council. The Director may remove any of the members of
the Council (R. 19).

Aboriginal Courts

The Act sets up an Aboriginal Court on each community. It consists of
Aboriginal Justices of the Peace or, if they are not available, members of the
Aboriginal Council, and deals with infringements of the by-laws or regula-
tions of the Act and with other minor offences (R. 48).

The members of the court receive no training in their duties. Usually
they do not fully comprehend the proceedings and are easily influenced by
anyone who does. This, together with their natural desire not to come into
conflict with the Manager, who has total control over the quality of their
lives, makes these quasi-judicial methods a sham.

Appeals

Appeals to a magistrate's court are available against most decisions that
the Act allows the Department to make on behalf of the assisted Aborigine.
However, an appeal must be made in writing. Considering the high rate of
illiteracy of Aboriginal adults (average education is about five years at
school), heavy dependence would need to be placed on white employees for
assistance in appeals against decisions of the Department which employs
them. An assisted Aborigine may not 'validly execute an instrument' without
the permission of the Department. Such an 'instrument' may be a solicitor's
agreement for the recovery of fees, so an Aborigine is unable to engage legal
assistance for any appeal he may instigate.

Appeals to a magistrate's court must be lodged with the clerk of the
court. Outside reserves, the clerk of the court is usually the district officer—
the man whose decision is being appealed against. This, again, is normally
sufficient to discourage any potential appellant. The fact that the appeal
mechanism is very rarely used is sufficient commentary on its effectiveness. It
seems that the basic reason for this is that since departmental officials wield
so much power, accepting their decisions is a small price to pay to avoid
antagonising them.

The Future

Prior to the introduction of the Aborigines' and Torres Strait Islanders'
Affairs Act of 1965, Aborigines and Aboriginal rights groups presented submissions to the special committee enquiring into legislation on Aboriginal
Affairs. They were assured by the government that the new Act would contain everything they wanted. They are still presenting submissions which in
turn continue to be ignored.[10]

During 1970 and 1971, a major co-ordinated campaign has been run
by these groups to persuade public opinion that the Act must be replaced by
a system that allows Aborigines and Torres Strait Islanders to determine for
themselves those policies which vitally affect their lives. In addition, the
Commonwealth Government, finding itself embarrassed overseas by blatant
racism at home, has pledged itself to remove all discriminatory clauses in the
Queensland legislation. As a result, it seems certain that changes will be

made to this law. The magnitude of those changes will reflect the struggle between the Aboriginal rights groups and an intransigent government.

One innovation has already been introduced. An advisory group has been set up, comprising the chairmen of the councils of all reserves and missions. Similar advisory groups in Western Australia and Victoria have not been very useful simply because they have no power. Nonetheless, by Queensland standards, a representative advisory group would be a significant forward step. It is unfortunate that it contains no representatives from the 11,200 assisted Aborigines living off the sixteen official reserves and missions. In addition, the restrictions under which the Councils operate and the fact that half their members are government appointees, cast grave doubts on the degree of representation the council chairman actually provide. It is difficult to find out whether a council chairman was elected or appointed to his council. Of the three people for whom we have this information, two were appointed.

In 1965, when the list of restrictions and powers was framed for the Aborigines and Torres Strait Islanders' Affairs Act, extra-ordinary powers were granted. It was made possible for the officials to exert complete control over their charges using only a fraction of these powers. This now gives the Government considerable room to manoeuvre. It can afford to make what would seem to be considerable concessions by removing many of the restrictions and powers, yet still retain a large measure of control. It is likely that they will do just this.[11]

If the Aborigines in Queensland are again to become a proud self-reliant people, the present legislation must be changed to allow them to determine their own future. The problems of the Aboriginal people of Queensland are complex and this step will not, on its own, solve them. But unless this step is taken, the problem cannot be solved.

TORRES STRAIT ISLANDERS

Historically, the Torres Strait Islanders have been fortunate. They lived a long way from the centres of European settlement and on land which the whites did not want. Therefore, they were to a large extent left alone. As a result, they still retain much of their own culture and their pride as an independent, self-reliant people.

The problems they face, while serious, are much less intractible than those of the Aborigines. Because these problems are the same throughout the Torres Strait Islands, this section of the article will deal with them specifically rather than make the generalisations necessary while dealing with the Aborigines.

Almost all of the Torres Strait Islanders are under the jurisdiction of the Aborigines' and Torres Strait Islanders' Affairs Act of 1965. The inhabited islands of the Torres Strait, with the exception of Thursday Island, are reserves under the control of the Department of Aboriginal and Island Affairs. Thursday Island is the business and administrative centre of the Torres Strait, and contains about half of the indigenous population of the area. The population of Thursday Island is 3,500, of whom at least 80 per cent are Islanders; the remainder are Aborigines, Europeans and Asians.

The other Islands are divided into three groups—Eastern, Western and Central. Two dialects are spoken, Eastern and Western. However, the most widely used language throughout the Torres Strait area is a type of Pidgin.

On these islands, the traditional system of land tenure by families is maintained, and is accepted by all the Islanders, although it is not legally recognised. The Island culture (mainly songs and dances), particularly among Western Islanders, is still strong. For example, at a birthday party we observed by chance, attended mainly by young people, only traditional Island songs and dances were performed.

Employment

Thursday Island has most of the available jobs. The pearling industry, once a large employer, particularly of people from the outer islands, is now being kept alive mainly by supplying shell for the pearl culture which itself is declining

There is an acute shortage of employment, especially on the outer islands. As a result, many of these islands are declining rapidly in population, and some are almost completely depopulated of able-bodied men.

Most Islanders on Thursday Island receive award wages, but some Department of Aboriginal and Island Affairs employees receive considerably less than award rates. A Department policeman on Thursday Island who works twelve-hour shifts (mainly at night) six days a week receives $20 a week. On the outer islands, the policemen are paid around $8 a week. The shortage of employment gives considerable power to any individual or group who controls a number of jobs. The Department of Aboriginal and Island Affairs does offer a fairly large amount of employment, both directly and indirectly, through the Island Industries Board which it, in practice, controls. The Department has a well-substantiated reputation for dismissing anybody who disagrees with it or its policies, and for terminating employment for purely arbitrary reasons. As one of our informants said: "Department and I.I.B. jobs no good. Too much in and out. They hire you today and if they're in a bad mood, they sack you tomorrow."

People living on islands other than Thursday Island are not eligible for unemployment benefits under the rules of the Department of Social Services because they live in areas where employment is not normally available. In addition, they have been officially informed that a man habitually employed at under-award wages is not eligible for unemployment benefits should he lose his job. This means that sometimes families find themselves with only child endowment to live on.

Education

All the islands have their own primary schools and Thursday Island also has a high school. Both the primary and high schools on Thursday Island are controlled by the Education Department, but the Island primary schools are controlled by the Department of Aboriginal and Island Affairs. These Island schools are mainly staffed by Island teachers, of whom the most recently appointed have completed three years secondary schooling and one year's training in Brisbane; most older teachers have no secondary education.

The Island teachers are paid $10 a week (they do not get free board). Those teachers with most initiative soon leave to take manual jobs at award wages. There are also five white teachers, seconded from the Department of Education, one at each of the larger Island primary schools. Most of the islands now have kindergartens, staffed by Island teachers with one year's training after three years at secondary school. Teaching is conducted in English in all schools, but, since English is not spoken in the homes, this causes difficulties. Most teachers on Thursday Island are young and in-experienced, and are there for a two year term only. Even for those who realise the problems and try to develop appropriate teaching techniques to cope with the situation, two years is not long enough for any real progress to be made. Research is needed to develop a curriculum suitable for these children, and teachers should be specially trained for this area. Children from the outer islands have to board in Thursday Island in order to attend high school. A small amount of accommodation, for boys only, is provided by the Department of Aboriginal and Island Affairs at the Torres Strait College. Other children must stay with relatives which, because of Thursday Island's housing shortage, usually means cramming into sub-standard and already over-crowded accommodation.

Housing

Most of the area of Thursday Island is unoccupied, unused land, held by the Commonwealth Government as a defence reserve. The total number of building blocks and sub-divisions used for residential purposes, including the section of the Department of Aboriginal and Island Affairs reserve used for housing, is 226. This means that an average of 15.5 persons are required to live on each block. Thus, there is an acute housing shortage, caused mainly by the shortage of land; and it is difficult to see an end to this prob-lem until the Commonwealth Government releases some of its land. Mean-while, landlords are able to charge exorbitant rents with impunity. For example, we found a thirty year old shack which was being rented for $10 a week. It was made of galvanised iron, fibro and pieces of packing cases, with holes in the roof and walls. The floor was concrete, on ground level. It was about 25 feet by 25 feet, with no interior partitions or electricity. The water supply was one tap outside. Sanitary provision was a simple earth closet. Accommodation of this type and at similar rents is common on Thursday Island. Sixteen people were living in this shack. A builder has estimated that such a building could be erected on Thursday Island for $982. Normal busi-ness practice expects a 13 per cent gross return on capital investment in real estate, out of which return the owner maintains the premises. Thus, a fair rent for this building, if new, would be $2.70 per week. Most Department of Aboriginal and Island Affairs employees live in Tamwoy Town, where houses are provided at $2 a week, not including garbage collection and water rates. These houses are approximately 24 feet by 24 feet unlined, unpainted fibro on concrete stumps. Electricity is not connected; they may have it installed at their own expense. The only water supply is a tap outside the back door. There is an earth closet and no bathroom. This is obviously substandard, but alternative accommodation, if it could be found at all, would be much worse. A Department employee who loses his job also loses his accommodation; on Thursday Island this is a disaster. A builder's estimate of the cost of erecting a new Tamwoy house is $1,435. Therefore, a reasonable rent for a new Tamwoy house plus land is $4 a week. Considering that the houses were built in 1958-59, $2 a week is not a subsidised rent.

The houses on the other islands are of two types. The older ones are similar to those at Tamwoy Town. The newer ones, which are being financed by the Commonwealth Government, are larger and of much better quality. However, they still do not have electricity, septic, sewerage or water inside the house. The housing situation on these islands is vastly better than on

Thursday Island, although there are contradictory reports on the adequacy of the housing programme.

Department of Aboriginal and Island Affairs

Every Islander we spoke to agreed on one point: their intense dislike of the Department of Aboriginal and Island Affairs and their desire to be freed from its control. Some people could not imagine life without the Department, but wanted someone to protect them from it. Most wanted to get rid of the Department. Those who had given the matter more thought realised that something would have to take its place, at least as an interim measure. They thought in terms of the Commonwealth Government or of some group they could set up themselves. This latter idea is probably influenced by the apparent success of the Moa Island Mining Co-operative.

Because families are split up between Thursday Island and the other islands, it is frequently necessary for them to travel from one to another. Apart from the occasional church boat or passing pearling lugger, the only means of transport available is the ships run by the Department. Permission must be obtained for making any journey and reasons given for making it. The Department can, and does, refuse permission at will. This need to obtain permission and the uncertainty of obtaining it, is probably the greatest single factor in causing the bitterness that is felt.

Anyone from the outer islands who wishes to go to Thursday Island to visit a doctor, must first convince a Department official he is sick enough. A woman we met had returned to Thursday Island with her son from a holiday in Cairns and now wished to go back to the island where they lived. She was refused permission without any reason being given, and she knew the boat was not full. She had no idea why she had been refused or whether she would be allowed on the next boat. Their decisions are as arbitrary as this. We also met an Island serviceman on his last leave before going to Vietnam. He was unable to marry his fiancee as he had planned because the Department refused him permission to travel on their boat. However, the intervention of a Parliamentarian, and through him, the Minister for the Army, was secured and eventually the situation was resolved.

The Island Industries Board runs shops on all of the Reserves and on Thursday Island. It also handles some produce of the marine industries, often buying it from the Islanders. Theoretically, it is a co-operative, with the Government appointing three directors and the other three being the group representatives. In practice, it is completely controlled by the Department, partly because of loopholes in its constitution. The Islanders' main grudge against the Island Industries Board is its refusal to give credit to Islanders. While white people can have credit simply by asking, virtually no Islanders, even I.I.B. employees of twenty years' standing, are allowed credit. This is all the more serious since the I.I.B. is the only place which supplies school books and uniforms. Other shops which do give credit are more expensive than the I.I.B. The I.I.B. is completely self-supporting and receives no subsidy from the Government.

Each Island reserve elects a council. Unlike those of Aboriginal reserves, these councils have no Department appointees, are freely elected, and seem genuinely to represent the people.

No Department officials actually reside on the outer islands. Each of the three island groups has one representative, in theory elected by the Councillors, but the Department seems to have fairly considerable control over who is elected to these positions. We found no-one who believed that these representatives actually represented the people.

Mining Co-operative

The Islanders have, in the past, mined small quantities of wolfram on Moa Island. They now wish to do this on a large scale using mechanised methods. They want to be in control of the mining themselves and retain ownership of the claims. The Department of Aboriginal and Island Affairs wanted a large company to mine the wolfram. The company would have owned the claims and paid royalties. However, the Islanders formed a co-operative, and with the aid of a $100,000 loan from the office of Aboriginal Affairs, submitted a successful tender. They feel that the Department will try to gain control of the co-operative.

The co-operative wants to use its profits to start up local industries such as fishing, fish processing and small scale agriculture. The co-operative also wants its own boats for transport. They feel that if they can provide transport and employment for all Islanders, then they will all be independent of the Department of Aboriginal and Island Affairs.

Conclusion

The solutions to the major problems of the Torres Strait Islanders are obvious—legislation that allows them to control their future, investment to set up local sea-based industries, the release of land for housing from the defence reserve on Thursday Island, a freely available inter-island transport system and the continuation of Federal Government housing finance. Of these several provisions, the key lies in one—effective legislation.

REFERENCES

1 This is based on the 3% per annum growth rate calculated by Lancaster Jones in *Australia's Aboriginal Population*, A.N.U. Press, Canberra, 1970, p. 34.

2 They are right—at least in theory (S. 21).

3 The Queensland Government has just foreshadowed changes to the present legislation. There is to be a review of Aboriginal representation on Reserve Councils. Aborigines will be granted freedom of movement off Reserves, and access to the Reserves will be controlled by the Councils. Freedom of choice will be given in the control of financial affairs, with provision for consultation with the administration or the Council. This information is based on news media reports of an agreement between the Queensland Premier and the Prime Minister of Australia. No more specific details are available. This emphasis on transferring powers to the Council is useless if the Councils remain as subject to Government control as at present, and much more information will be required to remove misgivings about the operation of 'financial consultation'. These proposed changes take no account of the 11,200 assisted Aborigines living off Reserves. Most importantly, however, there seems to be no attempt to change the basis of the legislation from control to self-determination.

4 See Frank Stevens 'Protection or Persecution?' *Dissent* No. 24 1969 p. 29.

5 The right of Aborigines to continue to live in the reserve areas as normal citizens of a democratic community is completely denied by present government policy. The Annual Report of the Director of Aboriginal and Island Affairs for 1969-70 states:

Reserves are deemed to be training and pre-employment establishments
. . . to provide all with full employment on Award rates . . . would
generally discourage and defeat the Department's policy for Aborigines
and Islanders to face the problems of living and working in the general
community of Queensland (p. 8).

6 STEVENS, FRANK 'Aboriginal Wages and the Trust System in Queensland'.
'Aboriginal Policy and the Dual Society in North Australia', paper presented
to the Conference on Aboriginal and Torres Strait Affairs, Cairns, September
1968. 'High Noon at Normanton', *Smoke Signals,* September 1969.

7 See reference 6 above.

8 JOSE, D., SELF, M. and STALLMAN, N. 'A Study of Children and Adolescents
on Queensland Aboriginal Settlements, 1967', *The Australian Paediatric
Journal,* V, June 1969, pp. 71-88.

9 Another government department, the Department of Health, is now taking
decisive steps to reduce the infant mortality rate amongst Aborigines.

10 For example, in 1964 the One People Australia League presented a submission
to the special committee saying in part:
'In preparing new legislation it is most desirable to prepare an *Entirely
New Act* designed to meet a new situation, rather than make any attempt
to amend the Act at present operating . . . Every effort must be made to
Remove all Restrictions from the Aborigines as a people.'
In 1970 a submission by Queensland and National Aboriginal Rights Groups
still found it necessary to say:
'The following proposal aims at replacing "The Aborigines' and Torres
Strait Islanders' Affairs Act of 1965" with legislation enabling these people
to have a more direct control over and responsibility for their own lives
. . . . The basic philosophy of this Act seems to be that the Aborigines it
covers must be closely controlled by the Department of Aboriginal and
Island Affairs.'

11 See reference 3 above.

12

THE QUEENSLAND ABORIGINAL WAGES SYSTEM

Barry E. Christophers, Joe McGinness

This article describes a system of law, the main accomplishment of which, has been to deprive a large group of Queensland Aborigines of dignity. It also attempts to highlight the campaign to afford the original inhabitants of the Northern state the right of access to and control of their own estate and affairs.

The practice referred to is the Aboriginal 'trust' fund administered by the government of Queensland. The methods of operation of the fund have been adequately described by Frank Stevens in an article entitled 'Lawful Injustice: The Trust Accounts System in Queensland'.[1] Possibly described, alternatively, as an 'Anatomy of Deceit', the essay spells out, in meticulous detail, the method through which many Queensland Aborigines are defrauded of their wages.

Briefly, the 'trust' fund system means that an assisted Aborigine in Queensland is not permitted the elementary freedom of managing his own property or income. As a basic principle of the system, an officer of the Department of Aboriginal and Island Affairs of Queensland may require the whole or part of the wages of an assisted Aborigine to be paid into a 'trust' fund. Pocket money is doled out from this fund only as a result of humble begging. Being agent for the government, the Commonwealth Savings Bank of Australia, another official institution, acts as banker to the Director of the Department for the purposes of the descriminatory system. The Aborigines on whose behalf the accounts are operated cannot require either the Department or the Bank to account to them directly.

Description by Queensland Government

The Aboriginal trust fund was once euphemistically described by the Queensland Government in the following terms:—

> 'These protected people have their wages and earning controlled to a limited degree. They receive their earnings, less a small percentage, banked to their credit in the Commonwealth Savings Bank—interest is earned on these deposits. The father or mother of a good family does the same as the Director of Native Affairs in protecting the earnings and spending of his wards.'[2]

Many people agree that it is an iniquitous system; but those with the power to end it, viz., the Queensland State Government and the Federal Government, have done nothing about it.

'Politics'

The Federal Government has stated that it will exercise its power to end this system, and other discriminatory legislation, in Queensland and

171

Western Australia by the end of this term of Parliament. Mr. Gorton, then
Prime Minister, was reported as saying:—

'The Commonwealth's main concern at this stage is with Queensland's
Aborigines' and Torres Strait Islanders' Affairs Act and Regulations.
These cover about 25,000 "assisted" Aborigines and islanders who live
on Government settlements and reserves. The Commonwealth, and
not the States, has the paramount responsibility for Aborigines as a
result of a decision made by Australian electors at a referendum
(May 1967). The Minister for Aboriginal Affairs has been working
closely with State Governments and leaving the administration of
policies to the States. But it still remains a Commonwealth duty and
responsibility to ensure that discriminatory racial laws do not persist
in Australia.'[3]

This attitude by the Federal Government was substantiated by a letter
from the Minister in charge of Aboriginal Affairs, Mr. W. C. Wentworth, to
the General Secretary of The Federal Council for the Advancement of
Aborigines and Torres Strait Islanders:[4]

'Dear Mrs. Bandler,

'I am writing on behalf of the Prime Minister, the Rt. Hon. J. G.
Gorton to thank you for your recent letter concerning assisted
Aborigines in Queensland.

'The Prime Minister has undertaken that the remaining discriminatory legislation affecting Aborigines will be removed within the life
of the present Federal parliament. The Aborigines and Torres Strait
Islanders Affairs Act in Queensland includes provisions, including
those relating to the control of property of "assisted" Aborigines and
Islanders (the "Trust Fund" System) which are discriminatory in
effect.

'Discussions were initiated some months ago between myself and
the Queensland Minister responsible for Aboriginal affairs about the
amendment of the Act and these discussions are proceeding at an
officer level. There is every indication that after the issues have been
discussed with representative Aboriginal and Islander people, amending legislation will be introduced in Queensland to remove all provisions which have a discriminatory effect. I have every confidence
that the time limit set by the Prime Minister will be satisfactorily met.

Yours sincerely,

(Signed)   W. C. WENTWORTH'

Since these two statements of policy there has been a change in leadership in the Federal Liberal Party. It is now doubtful that Mr. Gorton's and
Mr. Wentworth's promise will be honoured.

In the Commonwealth Parliament, the new Prime Minister, Mr.
McMahon, has provided grounds for misgiving in this respect.

'The second point related to the exploitation of Aboriginals if they
were given freedom over their own assets and funds. I had to agree
that in special cases there was a responsibility on the Aboriginal
councils, if they wanted to exercise that responsibility, to protect—not
to discriminate against—their own Aboriginal people. It was also
agreed that in cases of exploitation the administration itself should
have the right not so much to control but to protect. It is a measure
to protect the Aboriginal people themselves.'[5]

As, in the contemporary terminology of the Queensland Administration, all assisted Aborigines are 'exploited', this would be an adequate dragnet to continue to 'protect' them all. These Aborigines have been 'protected' for years by 'The Aboriginals Preservation and Protection Acts' (the word Protection was deleted in 1965). However, the discretionary legislation was camouflaged under the title of 'protection'. 'Protection' of Aborigines' assets and funds cannot be accomplished without control.

But, to achieve any sense of personal dignity, Aborigines must have unconditioned control over their own earnings—their wages paid in full direct to them—and with absolute freedom to dispose of this money as they wish. But their 'protectors' are concerned that economic freedom should lead to the further demands of personal and political freedom. People resent, of all things, protection, because it means restriction of their liberty lest they should make what their 'protectors' consider bad use of it.

Commonwealth Bank

The Commonwealth Savings Bank of Australia acts as banker to the Director for the fund.

Section 5 (1) of The Aborigines' and Torres Strait Islanders' regulations of 1966 states

'the Directors shall establish with the Commonwealth Savings Bank of Australia a trust fund or trust funds into which shall be paid all moneys, being the wages, property or savings of assisted persons. Interest at not less than the current rate fixed at any time by the Commonwealth Savings Bank shall be credited to the individual accounts in such trust fund or trust funds.'

The Commonwealth Banking Corporation took over the Queensland Government Savings Bank in 1920, and a partnership arrangement between the Queensland Government and the Commonwealth Savings Bank was agreed upon.

Unwittingly, the Commonwealth Banking Corporation became one of the links in the control of the economic affairs of the State's original inhabitants.

Early in 1969, a letter was sent by Federal Council for the Advancement of Aborigines and Torres Strait Islanders to the Managing Director of the Commonwealth Banking Corporation, Mr. B. B. Callaghan, asking that this Corporation disassociate itself from the trust fund system. In reply thereto, the following points were made:—[6]

'The Director of Native Affairs in Queensland conducts with the Commonwealth Savings Bank at Brisbane and Cairns branches, bulk accounts into which are paid personal funds of various aborigines and Torres Strait islanders. Within his own department, the Director maintains ledger accounts for each person concerned and the Director or his delegates authorise disposal of the funds. In other words, the Commonwealth Savings Bank merely maintains bulk accounts upon which the Director or his delegates drew cheques to provide funds for disbursement to individuals whose affairs are under the Department's control. So far as the Commonwealth Savings Bank is concerned, the position is that the Bank acts merely as banker to the Director of Native Affairs, in a normal customer-banker relationship, and has no control over the receipt by, or disbursement of funds to, the individuals under the control of the Department.'

The F.C.A.A.T.S.I. decided that the trust fund system did in fact violate the normal security of a Banker's trust and that it was wrong for the Commonwealth Banking Corporation to associate itself with this system. After considering the Bank's reply, the Council of F.C.A.A.T.S.I. passed the following resolution:—[7]

'Next year—1971—is the year set aside by the United Nations as the International Year for Action to Combat Racism and Racial Discrimination. As a gesture against racial discrimination, F.C.A.A.T.S.I. asks the Commonwealth Banking Corporation to refuse to handle this fund. F.C.A.A.T.S.I. feels that unless the Commonwealth Banking Corporation does dissociate itself from this form of discrimination it will be forced to transfer its business to another bank.

'The United Nations has set aside March 21st as a day in which there shall be protests against all forms of racial discrimination in the world. Unless the Commonwealth Banking Corporation acts by this date F.C.A.A.T.S.I. will transfer its account to another bank and it will ask its 68 affiliated organisations and all of its supporters to do likewise.'

One of the affiliates of F.C.A.A.T.S.I. (viz. the Council for Aboriginal Rights (Vic.)) agreed to implement this resolution. Implementation was initiated by the placing, in the national press, of the advertisement[8] which appears below.

Campaign form

Should a Queensland Aborigine still beg for his own wages?

NATIONAL CAMPAIGN

The abolition of the "Trust Fund" system in Queensland

An assisted Aborigine in Queensland is not granted the elementary freedom of managing his own wages.

A district officer of the Department of Aboriginal and Island Affairs of Queensland may require that whole or part of the wages of an assisted Aborigine be paid into a "trust fund". Pocket money is doled out from this fund only as a result of humble begging. The Commonwealth Savings Bank of Australia acts as banker to the Director for this fund.

Recently the Federal Council for the Advancement of Aborigines and Torres Strait Islanders decided that unless the Commonwealth Banking Corporation dissociates itself from the fund by March 21st, 1971, it will transfer its business to another bank.

I/We ....

Address ....

transact my/our banking business, with the .... branch of the Commonwealth Bank. I/We will transfer my/our business to another Bank unless the Commonwealth Bank dissociates itself from the "trust fund" system in Queensland by 21st March, 1971.

I/We ....

Address ....

do not Bank Commonwealth, but support your campaign.

Authorised by the Council for Aboriginal Rights (Vic.) on behalf of F.C.A.A.T.S.I.

After March 21st 1971 the campaign form was modified in the following manner. The paragraph commencing 'Recently the Federal Council' and ending 'transfer its business to another bank' was replaced with the words —
'In October, 1970, the Federal Council for the Advancement of Aborigines and Torres Strait Islanders decided that unless the Commonwealth Banking Corporation dissociated itself from this fund by March 21st, 1971, it would transfer its business to another bank. The Commonwealth Bank has not dissociated itself from this fund and the FCAA & TSI has transferred its business to another bank:'
Also the words 'unless . . . 1971' were deleted.

At the time of writing (late April 1971) about 120 people and organisations who bank Commonwealth have indicated in writing that they will transfer their business to another bank.

Protests

In addition to the foregoing aspect of the campaign, one of the authors (J. McGinness) has been engaged in field work among 'assisted Aborigines' who are forced to use this trust fund system. The following are some protests he has received from these people:—

> Pass Book No. at ——
> Mr. ——.
> C/- C.P.S.[9]
> —— N.Q.
> 18.12.70.

Dear Mr. McGinness,

My wife —— worked at X Station for over two years doing housework and never got any pay only tucker all the extra things she needed was paid for by me which was taken out of my pass book while I was away working at other places. I don't want the Aboriginal Affairs holding my wages in their bank as I don't have proper use of my wages and can't draw money I ask for at ——. Even at races time we can only draw certain amount and no more. Most times we draw we have to argue with the C.P.S. about the amount of money we want to draw.

I want to be able to bank my money in my own way at any bank and not have the Aboriginal affairs control my wages and money when we can't have free use. Hope you can help me about my wife's wages and this other matter. Thanks.

> Yours sincerely,

> ——

> D.N.A. A/C No. —— at ——
> C/- C.P.S.
> —— N.Q.
> 10.12.70.

Dear Mr. McGinness,

I would like you to help me get my clearance from the Aboriginal and Islanders department. I would like to manage my own affairs and free use of my wages and money and don't want it held in the trust fund by the department. Thank you for your help.

> Yours faithfully,

> ——

C/- Post Office,
—— N.Q.

Dear Mr. McGinness,
　I hear that your league is against the Queensland Aboriginal and
Islanders Affairs act and trying to change this law.
　I was under these laws before I came to work and live in ——.
Things were very hard in those days, specially money line, all our
wages used to be taken and put into the department trust fund and
it was hard for a man and him family to have proper use of his own
money. I fully agree with the League in how it is fighting for our
people to be free from all the Aboriginal and Island Affairs laws that
are now holding our people back.
　Good luck,

Yours sincerely,

—————

—— Station N.Q.
1.12.70.

Dear Mr. McGinness,
　Will you try and get me my freedom paper from the Department of
Aborigines and Island Affairs. I want to be free from the Act so I can
handle my own affairs, specially the money held in trust from my
wages. Thank you very much.

Yours sincerely,

—————

D.N.A. Pass book A/c ——

C/- C.P.S.
—— N.Q.

—— D.N.A. Pass book No. —— At ——
Dear Mr. McGinness,
　I want to get out from under the act so I can handle my own
money and affairs. All my money from wages is held by the
Aboriginal and Island affairs and I would like to have the right to
bank and use my money in the same banks as any other person. Will
you please help me.

Yours sincerely,

—————

Mr. ——
C/- C.P.S.
—— N.Q.
18.12.70.

Dear Mr. McGinness,
　I and my wife —— wish to have full control of all our wages and
money and not have it taken and put into the Aboriginal Affairs bank
where we can't get proper use like people who have money banked in
public banks.

In Normanton we are not allowed to draw what we want from our book when we go to the C.P.S. The little we do draw at odd times is not given to us without an argument. This is why we would like to have control of our wages and other money.

Yours sincerely,

—— A/c No. ——
D.N.A. Pass book No. —— at ——

—— A/c No. ——

Mr. ——
C/- C.P.S.,
Q'land.
18.12.1970.

Dear Mr. McGinness,

I and my wife —— both would like you to help us. We both want to have free use of all our wages and other money and the right to bank our money in any public bank and not in the Aboriginal Affairs bank where we don't have free use of our money.

Last year when I was working at (X) Station, I finished work about Christmas time besides all my wages being paid to the Aboriginal Affairs, a cheque which was to be my pocket money of $83.00 was sent to the C.P.S. ——. He made me change the cheque at the local store and pay $40.00 back into my bank as he seem to think that it was too much money for me to have at one time. I don't know if the money was put back into my bank, because when I asked to draw some money later I was knock back for the money I asked for. This is why we are not in favour of the way our money is held back from us by the D.N.A. bank.

Anyone who can read these gentle protests and remain unmoved surely, must have no soul.

Response and Criticisms

So far the response to the campaign has been poor. One reason for this is the campaign committee's lack of funds. Another reason is that Australians are reluctant to change their normal monetary arrangements—even though the change will cost only time. They may be free thinking on such questions as religion, sex and politics, but prudently conservative with the placement of their finances. A common attitude among unions, unionists and labour sympathisers is that the Commonwealth Bank is the 'people's bank'. It may or may not be the white people's bank, but at this instant in history, it is not the 'black' people's bank.

Another criticism of the campaign has been that, if the Commonwealth Bank decided not to handle this fund, a 'private enterprise' bank would take over.

The fact that the Commonwealth Bank is associated with the trust fund does not make the fund righteous. It is an evil system, no matter who handles it. For a private enterprise bank to take over, the Regulations under

'The Aborigines' and Torres Strait Islanders' Affairs Act of 1965' would have
to be amended. If this were forced on the Queensland Government, then
success would be near.

It is unlikely that, if an account was declared black by one bank,
another bank would accept it.

If a 'private enterprise' bank did accept this account, the public indignation would be sufficient to abolish the fund forthwith. One wonders if the
opposition to the campaign is merely an excuse to do nothing. The tren-
chancy with which racial discrimination is challenged should be unrelated to
the beliefs or status of those who practise it.

Another reason why the response to the campaign has been poor is that
the organisations and individuals working for Aboriginal advancement are
fragmented in their activities. Many affiliates of F.C.A.A.T.S.I. are working
on small State projects. Parochialism is rife within these groups and a mature
national outlook has yet to be achieved. In fact, the response to the campaign
by affiliates of F.C.A.A.T.S.I. and by individuals interested in the advancement and rights of Aborigines (with a few notable exceptions) has been
remarkably poor. Two notable exceptions so far have been the Armidale
branch of F.C.A.A.T.S.I. and the Newcastle Trades and Labour Council.

A national outlook is transiently achieved at the annual conference of
F.C.A.A.T.S.I. but this is ephemeral.

Racism still rife

One has to face the fact that racism is still rife in Australia. The mere
fact that such a campaign is necessary is sufficient evidence for this. Leading
the field by far in this regard, is the Queensland Government itself. The
reluctance of the Federal Government to intervene aggravates the stand of
the Queensland Government. The Commonwealth Banking Corporation,
hiding behind the facade of 'normal banking procedure', manifests passive
racism.

During the course of the campaign, racism has shown up in some
'unexpected' quarters. Campaign material was sent to many Unions throughout Australia. The following letter was received from a large Queensland
union in response to this mailing:—

'Your communication of the 16th ultimo addressed to our District
Secretary at —— has been forwarded to me for attention. All advices
should in the first place be forwarded to the Branch Secretary and
not to subordinate offices of this Branch.

'The question as to whether your National Campaign is a good one
or not is a moot point, and apart from the intention, the result being
attempted is not shared by all people who think in the best interests
of the Queensland Aborigine. It often happens that the people with
sometimes the best intentions do not represent the ultimate best
advantage.

'There is reference to an alleged letter supposed to be an interdepartmental communication (which raises the point, how was it
obtained, or was it only an observation and is that observation
correct). Further, were it so, the short blunt description of a person
who has not received an academic education, whilst it may be terse,
might be their way of coming to the point.

'The point referred to seems to indicate that the aborigine referred
to was not able to look after his own affairs and possibly had other

people, probably both white and aboriginal, who would take advantage of him the moment he received any money. There are many such cases where they have to be protected and we believe should be protected from themselves.

'In the matter of signing a petition to reject the Commonwealth Savings Bank as a banker, this is but begging the question and seems to be an abortive way of going about business. Suppose you did succeed and transferred to another bank. In that case, you would only be penalising one bank versus another bank and not getting to the alleged root of the trouble. To put it plainly, the Commonwealth Bank does not administer the Aborigines and Torres Islands Affairs Act. It seems to be a poorly thought out gimmick. Further, to write to this Union sectionally to take such action shows little knowledge of Union affairs.

The matter of where we bank is decided by a Branch Executive of a Union and confirmed and directed by the Executive Council of the Union. I attach, for your information, a cutting from the Courier Mail of even date with a statement from the President of the One People of Australia League, Mr. N. Bonner,[10] and it is quite evident that his views conflict with the views of your organisation, which supports the contention that I have tried to convey to you that "The great majority of the State's 27,000 'assisted aboriginals' wanted and needed the help and protection of the Aborigines' and Torres Strait Islanders' Affairs Act".

'I might add further, for your own information, that we as an organisation do something practical every day and every week of the year, in assisting not only in obtaining award conditions for all members (which includes Aborigines) but at the same time making representations and taking an active part in ensuring that they get paid award wages.'

The 'alleged letter supposed to be an interdepartmental communication" referred to us in our circular reads as follows:—

(of town X)

'Dear Sirs,

'—— (an assisted person) of X is travelling to both (town A) and (town B) and is expected back in (X) in approximately 6 weeks' time.

(He) is a waster and it would be appreciated if only small amounts were given for pocket money.

Yours faithfully,
District Officer
————,'

A/c as at 31/2/69—
$1981.72
These points need to be made —
(i) It was a Memorandum written by the District Officer in (X) to the District Officers in (Y) and (Z), and dated 16th April, 1969.
(ii) The original memorandum is extant and not 'alleged'. One of the authors has a photostat copy of this Memorandum.
(iii) It was obtained by the Aborigine in question who gave it voluntarily to an Executive Member of F.C.A.A.T.S.I.

Of course the existence of such a trust fund, where wages are not paid directly to the wage earner, is a terrible indictment of all Australian workers and their Unions. One would have thought that the violation of such a basic freedom of fellow workers would have caused Unions to act incisively to end this procedure years ago.

Unexpected opposition to the campaign came also from 'Christians'. The trust fund system, of course, operates on Church Missions and Government Settlements in Queensland. Those Churches involved are the Church of England, Presbyterian, Brethren, Roman Catholic and Lutheran. Some of these Churches are affiliated with the Australian Council of Churches, which, in turn, is affiliated with the World Council of Churches. Although the World Council of Churches made a grant to F.C.A.A.T.S.I. in 1970 (for a three year period) to help combat racism and racial discrimination in Australia, some of its affiliates are helping to incur expenses in this direction by participating in the trust fund scheme.

The following is a letter received from the Superintendent of a Church Mission in Queensland in reply to a request that he assist in abolishing the trust fund system on his Mission.

'Dear Sir,

'I refer to your enquiry concerning operation of the Dept. of Aboriginal and Island Affairs Trust Fund.

'We operate within this system, as there is no post office here we are unable to operate say a Commonwealth Savings Bank A/c system. Some of our people do open such accounts in various towns while out working, but it is impracticable to operate them from this distance.

'While appreciating your point of view, I feel sure that you do not fully understand the whole situation concerning employment, savings, etc., which in practice requires some such arrangement as the Trust Fund, at present, at least.

Yours faithfully,

Superintendent.'

'P.S. We do also have a local trust fund, and community fund operated on behalf of the Community and under the direction of the Aboriginal Councillors (Community Fund money). The local Trust Fund is voluntary and for the convenience of people who wish to deposit and save money. This accrues interest.'

And the following was received from a secretary of a Church Mission Board in reply to a letter soliciting aid in this campaign:—

'I have always felt that our Board can affect the situation best, not by frontal attack on the D.A.I.A. or the Queensland Government, which might or might not achieve the desired end, but would mean that doors of discussion and influence now open to us would inevitably be shut, but rather by exerting the pressure from case histories of where manifest injustice is done and by discussion to bring about needed reforms.

'We are fully in agreement with the ultimate abolition of the Trust Account system but are only too keenly aware by very bitter experience of the very vulnerable position vis-a-vis unscrupulous station managers that Aboriginal station hands hold and of course if the man concerned "hits the grog", we have the responsibility of looking after the wife and children for whom nothing is available from months of work of the "bread winner".

'I suppose it is inevitable that in any change some people will suffer but we cannot lightly take up such a campaign as you suggest because we are pretty heavily involved in the results of predatory white men, be they station owners or hotel keepers, or the people for whom we have responsibility.

'What I will do is to forward your letter and the campaign document to (X), our Mission for discussion with their Community Councils. If the Aborigines ask us to take up the campaign we would seriously consider doing so but until it failed we would do it along our own lines of communication.'

An Account Investigated[11]

One of the authors obtained a photocopy of a 'trust fund passbook' of an Aborigine who complained that he was being cheated by this system. An accountant[12] was asked to analyse this passbook. The following was his analysis of the account.

'Notes re Passbook No.

1. ADDITIONS
   A. Balance overstated April '68 by 40 cents.
   B. Balance understated 31/3/69 by $28.
   C. Balance overstated 30/6/69 by $10.
   B & C were adjusted by an entry in 11/12/69 where $18.00 was entered as a deposit. *A above has not been adjusted! The end balance of the book is out by 40 cents.*

2. DEPOSITS

	Wages		Sundry
Feb. '68 to 30th June, '68	$266.84	$7.17	Tax Refund
1st July, '68 to 30th June, '69	639.82	55.50	Tax Refund
1st July, '69 to Dec., '69	323.34	114.43	Estate M
		113.41	Tax Refund
	$1,230.00	$290.51	*Total* $1,520.51

TOTAL of deposits column of pass book $1,772.94

Less 1. Adjustment of error in additions entry Dec., '69	18.00		
2. Adjustment of entry supposed to be duplicated	114.43		
3. Adjustment of entry incorrectly debited —adv. E– R–	120.00	252.43	

Total Deposits per Summary Above $1,520.51

3. SALARY
   A. To be verified if possible.
   B. If he earned $24 per week then his gross earnings for '68/'69 would have been $1,248 and his employer should have

deducted $1.70 per week for income tax at single man rates, totalling $88.40 for the year.

His net earnings before any deductions for board or rations would have been:—

$1,248.00
—88.40
─────────
$1,159.60   The amount banked was $639.82

C. His tax refund (banked November, 1969) was $113.41. As shown above he would not have paid this much on a gross salary of $24.00 p.w.

4. *INTEREST*
There is no interest credited to the account between February, 1968 and December, 1969. Is this normal practice with these accounts and if so, why?

5. *OVERDRAWN BALANCES*
The account has been overdrawn on a number of occasions:—

Feb. '68
April '68
May '68/Sept. '68
Feb. '69
Nov. '69/Dec. '69

No savings bank will permit depositors to overdraw their accounts. Why has the account been overdrawn?

6. *SEQUENCE OF ENTRIES*
A. The first two entries in the pass book are dated 14/2/66 and 8/1/69. What happened in the 35 months covered by these consecutive entries?
B. Entries from February, 1968 to April, 1949 appear to have been made at the one time. All are initialled by one person.
C. The dates of the next entries revert to March, 1969, and run through to June, 1969. These entries are signed in two groups and have apparently been made at the one time.
The next sequence runs from July, 1969 to December, 1969.
E. The sequence then reverts to Nov., April, Oct., Nov., Dec., 1969.

7. *INHERITANCE*
It may be worthwhile checking with the probate office in Brisbane to check the amount left to Mr. .... by his relative.

8. *GROCERY ACCOUNTS PAID*
What authority did the Department have to pay these accounts?

9. It is possible that the ledger card kept by the Department may contain entries not shown in Mr. ....'s passbook. Even if it turns out that the ledger card correctly records the position, it still would not detract from the legitimacy of complaints about the passbook.
This Aborigine's pay since Jan. 1st, 1968 should have been approximately $46.00 per week less $2.50 for keep.'

Auditor-General's Report—Savings Bank Accounts

'Savings Bank accounts of assisted Aborigines and Torres Strait Islanders are maintained at Brisbane and Thursday Island. At 30th June, 1970, the Brisbane accounts aggregated $1,641,719 (1968-69, $1,612,623) and at 31st March, 1970, the Thursday Island Accounts totalled $412,433 (1968-69, $476,732) and were represented by the following investments:—

	Brisbane Accounts 30th June, 1970	Thursday Island Accounts 31st March, 1970
Loans to various Hospitals, Boards, &c.	$808,882	$45,219
Inscribed Stock	260,000	291,028
Commonwealth Savings Bank Accounts	548,257	75,986
Cash on Hand	24,850	200
	$1,641,719	$412,433

$624,243 was deposited in the Commonwealth Savings Bank Accounts. One would not like to think that it is this revenue that is in any way causing reluctance on the part of the bank to dissociate itself from this fund. If it is forced to do this by the sheer weight of protest then there will be no glory for it.'

STATISTICAL APPENDIX

THE HISTORICAL ORIGINS OF THE TRUST ACCOUNTS

Frances H. Lovejoy

The Aboriginals Protection and Restriction of the Sale of Opium Act, 1897, states,

'Every person desirous of employing an aboriginal or female half-caste under the provisions of this Act, shall forthwith, upon permission being granted by a Protector, enter into an agreement with such aboriginal or female half-caste, in the presence of any justice of the peace or member of the Police Force, for any period not exceeding twelve months. Every such agreement shall contain particulars of the parties thereto, the nature of the service to be rendered by such aboriginal or female half-caste, the period during which such employment is to continue, the wages or other remuneration to be paid or given by the employer for such service, the nature of the accommodation to be provided for such aboriginal or female half-caste, and the conditions on which the agreement may be determined by either party. Every such agreement shall be in duplicate and be attested by such justice or member of the Police Force, who shall forthwith forward one of the said agreements to the nearest Protector.'

Section 14 provides penalties for employment of an Aboriginal or a female half-caste without such written agreement, and Section 16 provides for supervision by a Protector or other authorised person of the conditions of employment. Sections 12 and 13 are broader, as they include male half-castes and relate to the continuation in satisfactory employment commenced before the act and the renewal of the annual employment permits. Under Section 31,

'The Governor in Council may from time to time, by Proclamation, make regulations for all or any of the matters following, that is to say,—

(1) Prescribing the mode of removing Aboriginals to a reserve, and from one reserve to another:

. . . .

. . .

(16) Providing for the due carrying out of the provisions of this Act;

(17) Providing for all other matters and things that may be necessary to give effect to this Act.'

Section 32 states,

'Such Regulations, not being contrary to the Provisions of this Act, shall have the force of law.'

Apparently the Bill for an Act is debated in Parliament, but Regulations are merely laid on the table without debate. It has sometimes been the practice to state general principles in the clauses of the Bill and to follow these with specific instructions in the Regulations.

In the 1899 *Regulations* relating to the 1897 *Act*, appears Regulation 8 relating to the 'form of agreement' under which an Aboriginal or a female half-caste could be employed. Part of the Memorandum of Agreement states,

'In consideration of which services the said employer agrees to pay the said employee (*or to a Protector or police officer at or other responsible person appointed by a Protector in this* behalf, as agent for the said employee) wages at the rate of payable ——, and to provide the said employee with the following accommodation . . .'.

Further on, Regulation 8 states,

'When a Protector or police officer, or other person appointed by a Protector in that behalf, receives any wages of an employee under such agreement he shall expend the same solely on behalf of the employee, and shall keep account of all moneys so expended by him. He shall when required, produce such account to any Protector or police officer.'

When the Act was amended in 1902, Section 12 was inserted providing in 12 (1) for a minimum wage for Aborigines and half-castes and 12 (2) which states,

'A Protector may direct employers or any employer to pay the wages of aboriginals or female half-castes to himself or some officer of police named by him, and any employer who fails to observe such direction shall be deemed to have not paid such wages. The Protector or officer of police who receives such wages shall expend the same solely on behalf of the aboriginal or female half-caste to whom they are due, and shall keep an account of such expenditure.'

Section 13 of this amended Act includes the property management provision, under which a Protector may,

'take possession of, retain, sell, or dispose of any property of an aboriginal . . . . Provided that the powers conferred by this Section shall not be exercised by the Protector without the consent of the aboriginal, except so far as may be necessary to provide for the due preservation of such property.'

Section 15 (4) of the Amendment Act of 1934 states,

'In Sections fifteen, sixteen and seventeen of[13] *"The Aboriginals Protection and Restriction of the Sale of Opium Act of 1897"* the word 'female' wherever it occurs in such sections as repealed.'

This finally extended the legal provisions to male half-castes regarding paying their wages to a Protector rather than to themselves.

In 1939, the Act was consolidated and amended by 'The Aboriginals' Preservation and Protection Act'. This changed the definition of 'aboriginal' to include those previously classed as 'half-caste'. Also a separate Act was passed for Islanders. Aborigines and Islanders were brought together again in the Act of 1965. Section 14 (6) states,

'A protector may direct employers or any employer to pay the whole or any portion of the wages of Aboriginals to himself or some other person on his behalf . . .'

This essentially retained the provisions of the 1934 Act.

The latest Act is *'The Aborigines' and Torres Strait Islanders' Affairs Act of 1965'*. This Act sees few changes in policy but many in jargon. The payment of wages to the Protector is now changed to management of property by the district officer under Sections 27, 28 and 29 and under Section 16, the Governor in Council has power to make Regulations on such matters as 16 (16),

'The establishment of such trust funds as may be necessary or desirable for the management and control of property of assisted Aborigines or assisted Islanders . . .'.

The Administration of the Wages Trusts Accounts

There are two categories of Aborigines in Queensland—those under the Act and those not. At present approximately one-half are under the Act. So far, the reader will have understood the general principles of the system.

The Aboriginal person may be employed, provided his wages are paid to the Protector, who is supposed to bank them on the Aborigine's behalf. Minor modifications allowed for the employer retaining a certain amount for keep, and some pocket money being paid direct to the Aborigine. What happens to the rest of the money in the trust accounts?

Under Regulation 12 of the 1904 Regulations,

'All wages or other moneys the property of aboriginals or half-castes received by a protector shall be deposited in the names of such aboriginals or half-castes, respectively, in the Government Savings Bank with himself as trustee. The protector may expend on behalf of any aboriginal or half-caste money held by the protector in trust for such aboriginal or half-caste, and the protector shall keep account of all moneys so expended by him. The protector shall, when required, produce such accounts to the Chief Protector or other officer authorised by him.'

This was amended in 1910 by the addition of the following sub-clause, 'Provided that the Chief Protector, with the consent of the Minister, may open a Trust Account with the Government Savings Bank, and shall place to the credit of such account any wages or other moneys, the property of aboriginals and half-castes, received by him, and shall keep, or cause to be kept, a proper record of the wages or other moneys so deposited, under the names of the aboriginals or half-castes in respect of whom such wages or other moneys have been deposited.'

This paved the way for the Chief Protector to operate an internal banking system; the Protectors did the day to day transactions with the Aborigines, and the Brisbane headquarters had the benefit of a large balance in a trust account, made up of the sum of the individual balances.

The author has not yet determined at precisely what date the Chief Protector realised that a considerable portion of this Trust Account could be invested for more than the savings bank rate of interest, and the difference between the income on the investment and the savings bank interest appropriated. That this practice has been going on for some time may be indicated by the fact that a question in the Queensland Parliament in 1935 revealed that £212,000 of the total balance of £254,410/2/4 was invested in Australian Consolidated Stock.

During the 1930s, instead of the Aborigines' obtaining relief from the same source as non-Aborigines, their savings bank interest was appropriated, and paid into a Standing Account for the relief of destitute Aborigines. The amounts of savings bank interest appropriated in 1933-34, 1934-35 and 1935-36 were respectively £8,364/14/1, £8,990/11/10 and £9,291/0/0.

The author has not yet determined for how long this appropriation of *all* interest continued. However, under the Regulations of 1945, Regulation 9,

'Money derived from the following sources shall be paid to the Aboriginal Welfare Fund to be established by the Treasurer for the general benefit of aboriginals —

(1) The difference between the amount of Savings Bank interest credited to the individual trust accounts of aboriginals and the total amount of interest credited to the total amount of all the trust accounts either from investments in bonds, inscribed stock, or otherwise.'

This tradition has been continued in Regulation 4 (1) of the Regulations of 1966.

This difference in interest can be quite considerable, as can be seen from the following amounts of interest paid into the Welfare Fund (converted to dollars).

	$
1963-64	30,434
1964-65	38,218
1965-66	2,994
1966-67	21,393
1967-68	18,505
1968-69	26,356
1969-70	20,986

The Welfare Fund obtains money, apart from the interest mentioned above, from reserve farm produce and livestock sales, rents of Department of Aboriginal and Island Affairs houses, sales in reserve retail stores, etc. It spends money on the stock for the retail stores, farm improvements, plant and stock, wages of Aborigines employed on reserves, training schemes for Aboriginal workers, and even in 1969-70, $56,000 on shares in Comalco Ltd. It may be noted the above information came from various issues of the *Queensland Auditor-General's* Report, as, unlike other states, Queensland does not have a financial appendix to its *Department of Aboriginal and Island Affairs Report.*

REFERENCES

1 *Aboriginal Quarterly,* Winter 1969.

2 Submission presented to the Select Committee appointed to examine the Aboriginals Preservation and Protection Act 1939-1946 by the Queensland Council for the Advancement of Aborigines and Torres Islanders p. 25. Quoting Queensland Department of Native Affairs Publication 'He has an arm—make his target possible'.

3 *The Age,* Melbourne, 20 July 1971.

4 Dated 10 February 1971.

5 *Commonwealth Parliamentary Debates.* 20 April 1971, p. 1663.

6 Commonwealth Banking Corporation, 1 April 1969.

7 Executive Meeting, 3-4 October 1970.

8 *The Australian,* 7 November 1970.

9 Clerk of Petty Sessions—The Clerk of the Court controls Aboriginal Trust Funds. In many Queensland country towns the Clerk of the Court is also the local Sargeant of Police.

10 Mr. Neville Bonner. A part-Aboriginal member of the Queensland Branch of the Liberal Party of Australia. Mr. Bonner was an unsuccessful candidate for election to the Senate of the Parliament of the Commonwealth of Australia in 1970, when he stood on a Liberal Party 'ticket'. Now member of the Senate of the Commonwealth of Australia following special nomination for a vacancy created by retirement.

11 It is the editor's opinion, following several years' field work in Queensland, that the discrepancies shown in this passbook are typical of many.

12 DREDGE, A. E., F.C.A.

13 It is a point of some interest, that, commensurate with the increased expenditure on Aboriginal affairs in Queensland over the years, the information provided for the public on the operation of the Department of Aboriginal and Island Affairs, through the Annual Report of the Director, has diminished in inverse proportion to the money available.

13

ABORIGINAL LAND RIGHTS

A. Barrie Pittock

Convention 107 of the International Labour Organisation, concerning the protection of indigenous and other tribal and semi-tribal populations in independent countries, states that

> 'The right of ownership, collective or individual, of the members of the populations concerned over the lands which these population traditionally occupy shall be recognised.' (Article 11)

In practice, such rights were not recognised in Australia until the passage of the Aboriginal Lands Trust Act of South Australia in 1966, and the Aboriginal Lands Act of 1970 in Victoria. Both these Acts provide for the recognition of Aboriginal title to only the small residual areas of 'Crown' land currently 'reserved' for the use of Aborigines in those two States. The respective State governments have interpreted these Acts, which directly affect only the small number of Aborigines resident on those 'reserves', as fulfilling the intentions of I.L.O. Convention 107.

The other State governments, and the Federal Government, have refused to recognise the principle of Aboriginal land rights, and the Federal Government has gone as far as to oppose the Yirrkala Aborigines in the Northern Territory Supreme Court in their claim for recognition of their title to the land at Gove Peninsula in Arnhem Land, even though the land involved was part of an Aboriginal Reserve until excised for mining purposes.

Curiously, however, 'special royalties are paid for the benefit of [Aborigines] if mining or forestry work is done on reserves or on land excised from reserves'[1] in the Northern Territory, which would seem to be some sort of de facto recognition of an Aboriginal economic interest or right in reserve land.

The question of recognising an Aboriginal right to land, or compensation for land, not presently reserved for Aborigines, but which was alienated from them at some time in the past, has not received serious attention from any Australian government. Indeed most white Australians, even if they concede the Aboriginal right to ownership of existing reserves, would tend to the view that past injustices are best forgotten. Unfortunately perhaps, the past cannot be forgotten, for it determines the present, and may well determine the future.

A deep sense of injustice, resentment, and bitterness pervades much of the rapidly growing Aboriginal and part-Aboriginal population. The historic process of dispossession has been the prime agent of Aboriginal pauperisation. Loss of the land has disinherited the Aboriginal people economically and spiritually, so that a spreading 'culture of poverty' amongst a growing coloured minority today threatens Australia with social and racial conflict.

The current situation calls for a reassessment of Australian history, particularly as it pertains to Aboriginal land rights. Hopefully, this may lead to a new willingness by white Australians to achieve racial justice in the present, and just compensation for past wrongs. Ideally this would lead, not only to the recognition of Aboriginal title to existing reserves, but also to restoration of Aboriginal ownership of other 'Crown' land, and to just compensation for land lost to the Aboriginal people.

In this chapter, we will look briefly at the history and significance of the land rights issue, so as to be able to put the current legal and political arguments into some sort of perspective.

Overseas Precedents

The right of subject people to their property, including traditionally occupied land, was first put forward by Francisco de Victoria, a Spanish professor of moral theology, in 1532, and again in 1542, by Bartholomew de las Casas, a Spanish priest who helped the Indian people of Mexico. Their views were incorporated into the Spanish 'Laws of the Indies' of June 11, 1594, which said,

> 'We command that the farms and lands which may be granted to Spaniards be so granted without prejudice to the Indians; and that such as may have been granted to their prejudice and injury be restored to whoever they of right shall belong.'[2]

In Canada, prior to the defeat of France in 1763, Britain, like France, had been inconsistent in its policy regarding Indian land rights. If anything, Indian land rights had been largely disregarded, but there was a growing awareness that the failure to render elementary justice was a potent cause of disorder and insecurity. The Crown had made numerous grants of land to settlers, usually leaving them to deal with the Indians as they would. This led to violent conflict with the Indians (as also happened in Australia with the Aborigines a century later), and the government was forced to act.

Thus, the Proclamation of the Crown, issued on October 7, 1763, declared that the Indians

> 'should not be molested or disturbed in the possession of such parts of dominions and territories as, not having been ceded to, or purchased by us, are reserved to them, or any of them, as their hunting grounds.'

It went on to prohibit royal governors and others in authority from making grants

> 'upon any lands whatever, which, not having been ceded to, or purchased by us, are reserved to the said Indians, or any of them.'

Further, persons who had actually taken up occupancy of land not ceded by the Indians were ordered, doubtless in vain, to remove themselves, and the Proclamation went on to make clear that land could only be purchased from the Indians by the Crown.

Thus were laid the foundations for the four great principles which were incorporated into Canada's treaty system: that the Indians possess occupancy rights to all land which they have not formally surrendered; that no land claimed by Indians may be granted to whites until formally surrendered; that the government assumes the responsibility of evicting all persons unlawfully occupying Indian lands; and that surrenders of Indian land may be made only to the Crown, and for a consideration.[3]

Indian treaties thus made in Canada are still in force, and their terms have been more or less carried out, although little was done until quite recently to set up schools and to assist the Indians to develop their land.

Following the American War of Independence, one of the first acts of the American Congress,before it had even adopted a Constitution, was to pass the Northwest Ordinance of 1787 which said concerning the Indians, that their 'lands and property shall never be taken from them without their consent'. To those familiar with TV Westerns, these may seem empty words; however, it is a fact that, by 1945, approximately 95 per cent of the public domain of the United States had been purchased from the Indians for a sum of about 800 million dollars.[4]

In 1946, the U.S. Congress set up the Indian Claims Commission to settle remaining claims by Indians against the U.S. arising 'from the taking by the U.S., whether as the result of a treaty of cession or otherwise, of lands owned or occupied by the claimant [tribe or group] without the payment for such lands of compensation agreed to by the claimant' and 'claims based upon fair and honourable dealings that are not recognised by any existing rule of law or equity.'[5]

In New Zealand, the Treaty of Waitangi, signed in 1840, established the rights of Maoris to 'the full, exclusive, and undisturbed possession of their Lands and Estates, Forests, Fisheries, and other properties . . . so long as it is their wish to retain the same in their possession', but, at the same time, it established that 'all rights and powers of sovereignty . . . were ceded to Her Majesty . . . absolutely and without reservation' and that Her Majesty had 'exclusive right of Pre-emption over such lands as the proprietors thereof may be disposed to alienate, at such prices as may be agreed upon.'

Thus it is, that the principles first enunciated in colonial Spain came to be adopted by Britain in her colonies, and became part of international law.

Two important principles are involved; firstly, that there is a fundamental difference between a change of sovereignty and a change of land ownership, and secondly, that the paramount title of the Crown to all the land in the kingdom is in fact less substantial than the right of use and occupancy of the subjects of the Crown.

The first point was well illustrated by the noted American authority on the legal rights of the Indians, Felix S. Cohen, when he wrote,

> 'It may help us to appreciate the distinction between a sale of land and the transfer of governmental power if we note that after paying Napoleon 15 million dollars for the cession of political authority over the Louisiana Territory [the U.S.] proceeded to pay the Indian tribes of the ceded territory more than twenty times this sum for such lands in their possession as they were willing to sell. And while Napoleon, when he took his 15 million dollars, was thoroughly and completely relieved of all connections with the territory, the Indian tribes were wise enough to reserve from their cession sufficient land to bring them a current income that exceeds each year the amount of [the U.S.'s] payment to Napoleon.'[6]

On the second point Cohen comments,

> 'It is true that . . . Indian possession was not considered a perfect title, and in the cases it is commonly said that legal title to such lands is in the United States, with a right of use and occupancy in the Indians. But these are subtleties of feudal legal theory which meant nothing to the Indians. Our courts have repeatedly said that the Indian right

of occupancy and use is as sacred as the fee title, and it is certainly more substantial than the naked legal title which legal theory locates in the [U.S.] Federal Government.'[7]

The Australian Contrast

How, then, do these principles and precedents apply in Australia? The traditionally accepted legal view is that expressed by Baalman:—

'By the year 1788, the paramount title of the King to the ownership of all land in the kingdom had become little more than a fiction so far as land in England was concerned. In that year, however, the fiction was transported into solid fact when Governor Phillip hoisted the British flag on the shore of New South Wales and took possession of the country in the name of the King. Although the small party of colonizers were probably quite unconscious of the fact, the royal overlordship of feudal doctrine had come out with the First Fleet.

'If any contemporary jurist had paused to concern himself about the prior title of the Aboriginal inhabitants of New South Wales, the concern must have been only momentary. Unlike the official attitude towards the Maoris of New Zealand some years later, when the British Government recognized native ownership of their own country, any rights possessed by the Aboriginals were simply repudiated. Nor was there any suggestion of paying or compensating them for their territory beyond a few paltry hand-outs of blankets and the like. John Batman, an enterprising settler in Van Diemen's Land, who became impatient at official ineptitude with regard to the colonization of the Port Phillip District, actually purchased from the Aboriginals a large tract of land in the vicinity of the present site of Melbourne. This early attempt at blackmarketing, however, was disallowed by the colonial government in an official proclamation which announced that any of His Majesty's subjects who claimed title to land by treaty or bargain with the natives would be regarded as trespassers on Crown land. The title to all "waste" land in the Colony was in the King as lord paramount, and could legally be disposed of only by His Majesty's Government.'[8]

Recognising the inconsistency between Australian policy in Papua-New Guinea as opposed to that towards the Aborigines in Australia, an official publication in 1960 stated of the position in the Territory of Papua and New Guinea:—

'*Respect for native land ownership was laid down as a basic principle of Australian administration in Papua over 80 years ago.* From the beginning in Papua, and in New Guinea since it was placed under mandate to Australia, following the First World War, successive Australian Governments have adhered strictly to that principle. Recognizing the fundamental importance of questions of land tenure to all aspects of policy in Papua and New Guinea, the Government has adopted as a long-term objective the introduction of secure, individual-registered titles for all native-owned land in the Territory. The Government's first step towards this objective was the setting up, in 1952, of a Native Lands Commission to try to establish a formal system of defining individual native ownerships of land in the Territory.'

It then went on to say:—

> 'At the time of first settlement in the Australian colonies all lands were
> deemed to be waste lands and the property of the Crown. In Papua
> and New Guinea, however, all land other than that previously
> alienated, was deemed to belong to the native people who occupied
> it.'[9]

What can account for this extraordinary piece of double-thinking?
Certainly the fault does not lie in the British Admiralty, whose rarely cited
secret instructions to Captain James Cook, dated the 30th day of July, 1768,
included the following:—

> '... You are likewise to observe the Genius, Temper, Disposition and
> Number of the Natives, if there be any, and endeavour by all proper
> means to cultivate a Friendship and Alliance with them, making them
> presents of such Trifles as they may Value, inviting them to Traffic,
> and Shewing them every kind of Civility and Regard; taking Care
> however not to suffer yourself to be surprized by them, but to be
> always upon your guard against any Accident.
>
> 'You are also *with the Consent of the Natives* to take possession of
> Convenient Situations in the Country in the Name of the King of
> Great Britain; or, if you find the country uninhabited take Possession
> for His Majesty by setting up Proper Marks and Inscriptions, as first
> discoverers and possessors.'[10]

Cook, and of course those who followed in 1788, were soon aware that
Australia had native inhabitants, and indeed Cook fired several musket
rounds at them as his landing party approached the shores of Botany Bay
that day in April 1770.

On 22nd August 1770, Cook formally took possession of the eastern
seaboard of Australia for King George III, the very same monarch who,
seven years earlier, had proclaimed the rights of the Indians of Canada to
the undisturbed possession of their lands.

It hardly seems fair to blame Cook personally for what followed: after
all, the meaning attached to 'possession by the Crown' was not for him to
interpret.

Many factors have been suggested as contributing to the disregard of
the Aborigines. The highly derogatory descriptions brought back to Europe
by the early Dutch explorers, and later by William Dampier, must have pre-
disposed the British to regard the Aborigines as the lowest form of humanity.
The lack of even a token practice of agriculture, such as was practised by the
Indian woodsmen of the east coast of North America, may well, to European
eyes, have signified a complete lack of attachment to the land, although this
impression must soon have been dispelled by closer observation. There was
certainly resistance by the Aborigines to the invaders, but perhaps the low
population density, difference in armaments, and lack of leadership rendered
this too ineffectual. Perhaps it was the lack of competition for the Aborigines'
allegiance by competing colonial powers, as had worked to the Indians'
advantage in North America, which rendered the Aborigines comparatively
powerless. Or perhaps it was merely that Australia was so distant in space
and time from the liberalising influences of metropolitan England that the
higher principles of colonial theory never came to be enforced in a frontier
situation ruled by 'practical' men. It could even be that the nature of the new

colony, which was set up as a convict settlement rather than as a trading post
or farming province, led to an initial failure to formulate a cohesive policy on
the 'native question'.

Whatever the reasons, Governor King's proclamation of 30 June 1802,
only fourteen years after the First Fleet, clearly failed to recognise the root
cause of the growing conflict between natives and settlers. Having stated
that both races would be regarded equally before the law, and that any
aggression would be punished 'with the utmost severity', it continued

'at the same time that His Majesty forbids any act of Injustice or
wanton Cruelty to the Natives, yet the Settler is not to suffer his
property to be invaded, or his existence endangered by them; in
preserving which he is to use effectual, but at the same time the most
humane, means of resisting such attacks.'[11]
Already, it seems, the assumption was being made at the highest level of
government that the natives had no rights to use and occupancy.

Reformist Views

Such a view did not go unchallenged. In 1837, the visiting English
Quaker, James Backhouse, wrote to the Governor of New South Wales:—

'It is scarcely to be supposed that in the present day any persons of
reflection will be found who will attempt to justify the measures
adopted by the British in taking possession of the territory of this
people, who had committed no offence against our Nation; but who,
being without strength to repel invaders, had their lands usurped,
without any attempt at purchase by treaty or any offer of reasonable
compensation, and a class of people introduced into their country,
amongst who were many ... who ... practised appalling cruelties
upon this almost helpless race. And when any of the latter have
retaliated, they have brought upon themselves the vengeance of
British strength, by which beyond a doubt many of the unoffending
have been destroyed, along with those who had ventured to return a
small measure of these wrongs upon their white oppressors.'[12]
In similar vein, Backhouse wrote to the chairman of the British House
of Commons' Select Committee on Aboriginal Tribes as follows:—

'The system of colonization that has been pursued by the British
Government has been upon principles that cannot be too strongly
reprobated and which want radical reformation. Aborigines have had
wholesale robbery of territory committed upon them by the Government, and settlers have become the receivers of this stolen property,
and have borne the curse of it in the wrath of the aborigines who,
sooner or later, have become exasperated at being driven off their
rightful possessions.'
Displaying a knowledge of the traditional Aboriginal attitude to the land
which gives the lie to the frequently expressed view that such knowledge
was not available until the twentieth century, Backhouse went on:—

'Though the mode of holding property differed among the aborigines
of Van Diemen's Land from that used among English people, yet
they had their property: each tribe was limited to its own hunting-
ground; and into such hunting-grounds the island was divided; and it
is said, the tenure on which the aborigines of New Holland hold their
country is somewhat more specific than that formerly used by the now
almost extinct race of aborigines of Van Diemen's Land.'[13]

The Select Committee, to which Backhouse addressed himself, issued its
report in 1837.[14] Introducing its report, the Committee noted the inconsistency with which Britain had acted in its colonies:—

'The duty of introducing into our relations with uncivilized nations
the righteous and profitable laws of justice is incontrovertible, and it
has been repeatedly acknowledged in the abstract, but has, we fear,
been rarely brought into practice; for, as a nation, we have not
hesitated to invade many of the rights which they hold most dear.

'Thus, while Acts of Parliament have laid down the general
principles of equity, other and conflicting Acts have been framed,
disposing of lands without any reference to the possessors and actual
occupants, and without making any reserve of the proceeds of the
property of the natives for their benefit.'

At this point, a footnote makes the following observation:—

'In the preamble of an Act passed August 1834, "empowering His
Majesty to erect South Australia into a British Province, etc." it is
stated that the part of Australia which lies as there described,
together with the islands adjacent, "consists of waste and unoccupied
lands, which are supposed to be fit for the purposes of colonization."
In the account of the proposed colony which appears to be
authorized by the Company who have purchased land under this Act,
it is stated that "great numbers of natives have been seen along that
part of the coast."'

The Select Committee continued:—

'Such omissions must surely be attributed to oversight; for it is not to
be asserted that Great Britain has any disposition to sanction unfair
dealing: nothing can be more plain, nothing can be more strong, than
the language used by the Government of this country on the subject.
We need only refer to the instructions of Charles II, addressed to the
Council of Foreign Plantations in the year 1670.'

Quoting at some length from Charles II, the committee notes that he
said, with respect to the Indians, that 'if any shall dare to offer any violence
to them in their persons, goods or possessions, the said governors do severely
punish the said injuries, agreeably to justice and right.'

'Nor', asserts the Committee, 'is modern authority wanting to the same
effect', and it goes on to quote from the Address of the House of Commons
to the King, passed unanimously July 1834:—

'His Majesty's faithful Commons in Parliament assembled, are deeply
impressed with the duty of acting upon the principles of justice and
humanity in the intercourse and relations of this country with the
native inhabitants of its colonial settlements, of affording them protection in the enjoyment of their civil rights, and of imparting to them
that degree of civilization, and that religion, with which Providence
has blessed this nation, and humbly prays that His Majesty will take
such measures, and give such directions to the governors and officers
of His Majesty's colonies, settlements, and plantations, as shall secure
to the natives the due observance of justice and the protection of
their rights, promote the spread of civilization amongst them, and
lead them to the peaceful and voluntary reception of the Christian
religion.'

On the question of land rights, the Committee went on to say,

'It might be presumed that the native inhabitants of any land have an incontrovertible right to their own soil: a plain and sacred right, however, which seems not to have been understood. Europeans have entered their borders uninvited, and, when there, have not only acted as if they were the undoubted lords of the soil, but have punished the natives as aggressors if they have evinced a disposition to live in their own country.'

Quoting, at this point, from the minutes of evidence in a clear reference to the Aborigines of Australia, the report goes on,

' "If they have been found upon their own property, they have been treated as thieves and robbers. They are driven back into the interior as if they were dogs or kangaroos." '

Under the heading 'New Holland', the Committee noted that the Aborigines,

'unoffending as they were towards us, have, as might have been expected, suffered in an aggravated degree from the planting amongst them of our penal settlements. In the formation of these settlements, it does not appear that the territorial rights of the natives were considered, and very little care has since been taken to protect them from the violence or the contamination of the dregs of our countrymen.'

Referring again to South Australia, the House of Commons Select Committee comments:—

'A new colony is about to be established in South Australia, and it deserves to be placed on record, that Parliament, as lately as August 1834, passed an Act disposing of the lands of this country without once adverting to the native population. With this remarkable exception, we have had satisfaction in observing the preliminary measures for the formation of this settlement, which appears, if we may judge from the Report of the Colonial Commissioners, likely to be undertaken in a better spirit than any such enterprises that have come before our notice. The Commissioners acknowledge that it is "a melancholy fact, which admits of no dispute, and which cannot be too deeply deplored, that the native tribes of Australia have hitherto been exposed to injustice and cruelty in their intercourse with Europeans" and they lay down certain regulations to remedy these evils in the proposed settlement.'

Having said that and much more, the Committee concluded with some fine rhetorical passages, which unfortunately seem to have done little to change the course of history. Consider, for example, the events of the next hundred years in the light of the following:—

'This, then, appears to be the moment for the nation to declare that, with all its desire to give encouragement to emigration, and to find a soil to which our surplus population may retreat, it will tolerate no scheme which implies violence or fraud in taking possession of such territory; that it will no longer subject itself to the guilt of conniving at oppression, and that it will take upon itself the task of defending those who are too weak and ignorant to defend themselves.'

Despite such seemingly empty rhetoric, the reformers in Britain did exert some influence, at least in theory, on the founding of South Australia. While largely ineffectual in practice, this may have laid an important foundation for legal recognition of Aboriginal land rights in the 1970s. Thus the Letters Patent issued to the South Australian Colonization Commission on 19 February, 1836, contained the proviso,

> 'provided always that nothing in these our Letters Patent contained shall affect or be construed to affect the rights of any Aboriginal Natives of the said Province to the actual occupation or enjoyment in their own persons or in the persons of their descendants of any Lands therein now actually occupied or enjoyed by such Natives.'[15]

The Commissioners, in their turn, informed the House of Commons that, of the land placed at their disposal, no portion which the natives might possess in occupation or enjoyment would be offered for sale until ceded to the Colonial Commissioner. Indeed, general instructions were issued to the Resident Commissioner containing provisions designed to implement this undertaking. Unfortunately, nothing was done about it.

Two years after the founding of the Province, the Secretary of the South Australian Association observed in a report, 'No legal provision by way of purchase of land on [the natives'] behalf or in any other mode has yet been made, nor do I think with proper care it is at all necessary.'

Despite the Letters Patent, South Australia's Aboriginal people were dispossessed, decimated, and pauperised in similar fashion to those in the other Australian colonies. Only the geographical isolation and inhospitable nature of the interior enabled sizeable areas to be reserved for the Aborigines, and indeed enabled them to survive.

It was not until the Aboriginal Lands Trust Act was introduced in South Australia in 1966, that a serious effort was made to honour the spirit of the Letters Patent,[16] which have since become a key link in the case to establish Aboriginal land rights through the courts.

Dispossession

Much more could be written of the intervening century, but little that even hints at respect for Aboriginal land rights, and much which demonstrates a callous disregard for the beliefs, economic independence, and lives of the Aboriginal people.

The Batman Treaty, referred to above by Baalman, and dated 6th June 1835, raised the central legal question as to whether the Aborigines owned the land in what was then the Colony of New South Wales.

Governor Bourke's prompt repudiation of the Treaty was clearly motivated by a desire to maintain control over the spread of settlement, as Port Phillip District lay outside the boundaries within which the Government had authorized the selection of land by settlers.[17]

Batman was, at first, inclined to challenge the Crown's right to disallow the Treaty. His agent in London, George Mercer, obtained a legal opinion from Dr. Stephen Lushington, which stated:

> '1. I am of the opinion that the Grants obtained by the Association are not valid without the consent of the Crown.
> '2 & 3. I do not think that the right to this Territory is at present vested in the Crown, but I am of opinion that the Crown might oust the Association; for I deem it competent to the Crown to prevent such settlements being made by British Subjects, if it should think fit.'[18]

Mercer had already acknowledged the jurisdiction, and by implication the sovereignty, of the Crown over the territory in question.[19] Thus Lushington's opinion that 'the right to this territory' was not vested in the Crown could only be based on the distinction between sovereignty and land ownership, and the failure of the Crown to purchase the land from the Aborigines.

In fact, no part of Australia had been, nor has yet been, purchased from the Aborigines by the Crown. On the contrary, Australia was, as the House of Commons Select Committee noted unfavourably in 1837, arbitrarily declared to be 'waste and unoccupied'. Such a patently false proposition formed, and remains to this day, the foundation of the Crown's claim to ownership of the land on a basis more substantial than the 'paramount title' which Baalman describes as 'little more than fiction' so far as land in nineteenth century England was concrned.

Writing on behalf of Lord Glenelg, who was then Colonial Secretary, Sir George Grey dismissed Lushington's opinion as follows:—

'Lord Glenelg is sensible of the great weight which is due to the deliberate judgement of Dr. Lushington on a question of this nature. As however the grounds, on which Dr. Lushington denies the title of the Crown to the Territory in question, are not explained; and as Lord Glenelg is not aware of any fact or principle which can be alleged in support of such a conclusion, *which would not apply with equal force to all the waste Lands in every other part of the Colony of New South Wales,* His Lordship must decline to acquiesce in this doctrine, and cannot but believe that it was advanced by Dr. Lushington under a misapprehension of some of the most material parts of the case.'[20] (My emphasis added, A.B.P.)

Grey thus advanced no arguments against Lushington's opinion other than the obvious inconvenience of its wider application to areas already alienated from the Aborigines. Unfortunately for the Aborigines, however, Batman and Mercer, seeing that the Treaty could not in any case be sustained, did not pursue the legal argument any further. And so the matter rested—a legal question of vital importance to the Aborigines had been raised, and allowed to subside again, unresolved.

Whatever Governor Bourke's intentions, his repudiation of the Batman Treaty neither protected the Aborigines nor ensured the controlled and orderly spread of settlement. Indeed, the settlement founded by the Port Phillip Association was officially recognised on 9th September 1836.

Such processes of unauthorised settlement and later de facto recognition by the Government, in fact, became the dominant pattern of Australian land settlement in the era of the squatters. The squatter's occupancy of land to which he had no legal claim, and certainly less claim than the Aboriginal inhabitants, gradually turned into a right; so much so that, by 1839, the squatter could claim the protection of the law for himself, his 'run', and his boundaries.

Mr. Chief Justice Stephen summed the matter up as follows:—

'A man passed into the interior and took possession of a tract of country, established his huts, sheep and shepherds in various directions, and the tract of country so occupied by himself and his establishment was said to be in his possession, and he could bring an action against any person who would intrude upon him. He was not bound to show his title.'[21]

The effect of this unauthorised invasion of so-called Crown land, apart from providing a large inheritance for many of the pillars of present-day white Australian society, was to undermine the theoretical paramount title of the Crown to which Baalman refers. As in England, this feudal concept was converted into little more than fiction in the more closely settled parts of Australia.

The new view, which gradually came to be upheld in Australian law, was that 'The territory of a country is in reality the property of its occupiers, which the nominees of the Crown administer advantageously only as they facilitate its settlement and culture.'[22] This, of course, was the view of the colonists, who did not pause to see how it reflected on the prior rights of the original occupants of the territory in question.

Throughout the intervening years, a few dedicated missionaries and government appointed 'protectors' worked to shelter the Aborigines from the worst forms of physical abuse and deprivation, and, in the classic phrase, 'to smooth the dying pillow'. Numbers declined drastically until the 1930s, when medical science, rations, and the resilience of the natives, led to a stabilisation of the pure Aboriginal population, and to the current rapid increase.

In many areas, Aborigines were encouraged, persuaded, or forced onto special Aboriginal settlements and reserves as closer settlement encroached on their traditional territory. As the white settlers' demand for land increased, the land reserved for Aborigines was whittled down. Naturally this process has gone furthest in south-eastern Australia, but it continues even today in the north and west at places such as Woomera, Weipa, Yirrkala, and Wingellina.

In Victoria, four of the six supervised Aboriginal stations and ten small reserves were revoked one by one. In the 1860s, 26,114 acres were set aside for Aborigines; now only some 4,000 acres at Lake Tyers and 548 acres at Framlingham remain.

The major government station, Coranderrk, was established in 1863, and by 1866, had been extended to 4,850 acres. The Aboriginal men were reported to be 'anxious to make the station self-supporting', and by 1870, the Aborigines had built neat houses of sawn timber, each family had its own garden, and some 120 acres had been cleared and planted. In that year, the secretary of the Board for the Protection of the Aborigines advised the Board that

> 'The men are still anxious and uncertain respecting the tenure of their land. They feel they may be turned away at any time, and I hope the Central Board will make an effort to get a grant of the land now reserved for the use of the Aborigines. This, more than anything else, would give contentment and ensure the happiness of these people.'

The original temporary reservation was made permanent in 1884.

In 1886, the Government legislated to exclude 'halfcaste' Aborigines from care, rendering them ineligible to reside on Aboriginal reserves, and thus forcing most of the able-bodied men to leave Coranderrk. In 1893, the Crown Lands Reserve Act excised 2,400 acres from the 'permanent' reserve for a village settlement. When the station was officially closed in 1924, all but a handful of aged Aboriginal residents were forcibly transferred to the Lake Tyers settlement in Gippsland. By 1927, another 78 acres had been alienated for a fauna reserve (which is now a well known tourist attraction), and 622 acres for other purposes. The last resident died in 1941, and the remaining land was revoked in 1948 by the Coranderk Lands Bill. Today only the cemetery and a memorial plaque remain.[23]

The Aboriginal Interest

Anthropologists began to play a significant role in Aboriginal affairs early this century, and, in 1911, Sir Baldwin Spencer visited the Northern Territory under the auspices of the Federal Government to study the Aboriginal population and report. Thus it was that the following passage appeared in the Annual Report of the Acting Administrator of the Northern Territory, for the year ending 30 June 1920.

'The greatest difficulty that confronts the Administration in dealing with the natives is the fact that they do not form themselves into settled communities, with individual possession as in New Guinea. . . . The aboriginals of the Territory are divided into a large number of tribes, each of which speaks a distinct dialect and occupies a well defined tract of country, the boundaries of which are well known to the natives. . . . The natives of Australia have never been recognised as having any legal title to their tribal lands. The whole of the lands of Australia were constituted Crown lands and under various Land Acts have been sold or leased by the various Governments to white settlers.

'In the Northern Territory long leases of large areas have been granted to pastoralists extending uninterruptedly in the aggregate over hundreds of miles of country, and many native tribes have not a square foot of land that they can call their own, although they are still living on their tribal lands that have been theirs from time immemorial.'

The Acting Administrator went on,

'I have given this problem of the Northern Territory the fullest and most anxious consideration, and I feel sure that the best solution of the question lies in the able and well considered recommendations of Sir Baldwin Spencer, who states, "There are two alternatives, either to allow them to wander about as outcasts, some of them doubtless working for the settlers but all of them practically dependent for their existence on promiscuous charity, or to establish a reserve for them under proper control. To be of any practical use, the reserve must be situated somewhere in their own district. To attempt to move them to some other part and place them amongst strange natives would be futile . . . . There is no other practicable policy but that of the establishment of large reserves, if the aborigines are to be preserved and if any serious effort is to be made for their betterment." '

The Report then lists the areas which Spencer recommended to be declared reserves, and the Acting Administrator states, 'I have endeavoured to carry out these proposals in their entirety.' He goes on to say,

'To insure that the natives are not dispossessed of their hereditary tribal hunting grounds and "made dependent for the existence on promiscuous charity" it should be laid down as the settled policy of Australia that in every district of the Territory an area must be reserved for the aboriginals which they will recognise as their own land, and on which they can live and hunt if they so desire. Each of these reserves should have permanent water and timber so that there is always available an adequate supply of their natural food—fish, animal life, yams, lily roots, seeds, etc.'

After reference to the practice of cattle station owners of supplying beef to old men, women, and children who are not employed by, but live on the stations, the Acting Administrator added,

'The conditions of employment of native labour may possibly, owing to legislature of the future, become so onerous that the station owner cannot continue the present patriarchal methods, and the lot of the aboriginals would then become pitiful if they were also deprived of lands set apart as aboriginal reserves.'

These last remarks take on a particular relevance since the introduction, in theory at least, of equal wages for Aborigines in the pastoral industry. Areas have not been excised from the huge pastoral leases, and Aborigines are being forced into over-crowded, highly institutionalised, and degrading settlements. This is one of the root causes of the current prolonged struggle by the Gurindji people to obtain recognition of their claim to 500 square miles of the 6,000 square mile Wave Hill Station, a property leased to the British Vestey group of companies which leases a total of nearly 17,000 square miles of the Northern Territory.[24]

Anthropologists have now documented, in detail, the traditional Aboriginal attachment to the land. Professor A. P. Elkin is important in this regard. In 1938, he wrote that 'the local group owns the hunting and food-gathering rights of its country; members of other groups may only enter it and hunt over it after certain preliminaries have been attended to and permission has been granted', a conclusion which supports the earlier observations of men such as Backhouse and other early missionaries and 'protectors'.

In the United States, evidence of anthropologists has played an important part in many of the claims brought before the Indian Claims Commission. In Australia, anthropological evidence has been presented recently in the case brought by the Yirrkala Aborigines before the Northern Territory Supreme Court over land on Gove Peninsula. Professor R. M. Berndt, who has a particular knowledge of the Gove area, wrote a long paper on the question of the Aborigines' relationship to the land and to sacred sites, with particular reference to the Gove dispute.

According to Berndt,

'In Aboriginal Australia generally, land was traditionally inalienable. ... Throughout most of Aboriginal Australia there were basically two kinds of small social group, each related to the land in a different way: one through descent, directly or otherwise, the other through occupancy and use. The first was an exogamous unit, such as a clan, associated with a site or combination of sites. ... This was a land-owning group: its focus was on these sites and the areas immediately adjacent to them. Their ownership was not a personal or individual affair, and territorial claims were not transferrable: the land was held in trust, collectively, in a time perspective which extended indefinitely back into the past and forward into the future. The other type of unit was what has usually been called a horde. ... This was a land-occupying and utilizing group, concerned predominantly with hunting and food-collecting.'

'These two kinds of unit reflected the two basic issues in social life —the religious and economic, viewed as interdependent. ... All Aborigines, male and female, were simultaneously members of both kinds of unit; but adult males had two distinct roles: in one, as land-owners, they were land-renewing or land-sustaining, in the sense of keeping the basic "machinery" going; in the other, with their women-folk, they were land-exploiting. To appreciate the question of land tenure in Aboriginal Australia these two facets must be taken into account.'[25]

The continuing historical process of dispossession has deprived the Aboriginal people, and their part-Aboriginal descendents, of both their cultural heritage and their economic independence. This is at the root of the present situation of Aboriginal poverty and alienation. The Aboriginal and part-Aboriginal people cannot be successfully integrated into an affluent twentieth century society unless they have some economic capital and bargaining power, and indeed a stake in the emerging multi-racial Australian community.

Characterizing the situation of part-Aboriginal people in country areas of New South Wales and South Australia in 1965 as typical of a 'culture of poverty', Professor C. D. Rowley wrote,

'The Aboriginal social and economic situation has resulted from expropriation, from "white settler" prejudice towards a coloured indigenous people; from the destruction of the basis of social order which gave legitimacy to Aboriginal leadership and custom, without compensatory attraction to, or entry into, the encroaching society and economy; and from a high degree of institutionalization, often with-out security, over long periods.'[26]

Commenting on the significance of the Yirrkala (Gove) land case, Professor Berndt asserts,

'The Yirrkala case has implications for the whole of Aboriginal Australia, whether people of Aboriginal descent are living on or away from what they consider to be their own land; whether they have come out of the large reserves to the fringe settlements; whether they work on pastoral stations (ranches), and occupy huts built on land which is said to be part of that pastoral property; and so on. ... Everywhere, throughout Australia, the only substantial asset the Aborigines possessed—the only commodity (besides their labour) required by the European intruder—was their land: and in every case, this has been arbitrarily taken over without any adequate compensation to the original owners.'

In January, 1969, the distinguished Australian economist and Chairman of the Commonwealth Government's own Council for Aboriginal Affairs, Dr. H. C. Coombs, spoke out about the situation on Gove Peninsula. Having commented on the 'human problem of frightening complexity' brought about by the mining development on the land of the Yirrkala prople, and on the need to involve the people beneficially, so as to avoid 'the Aboriginal com-munity deteriorating slowly into a depressed rabble of fringe-dwellers', Dr. Coombs continued,

'But haste is all to the mining venturer, and every day the facts of the intrusion are more apparent and the possibilities of benefit appear to the Yirrkala more and more remote.

'It is in this atmosphere that they have taken legal action against the Government and the company. In their eyes, this land is their property—occupied by them and their ancestors from the dreamtime of their ancestors, until recently undisturbed save for passing visitors and missionaries. What happened in 1788 on the shores of Sydney Cove is being repeated on Gove Peninsula—not a story in the history book, but a living event in our own time.

'It is in a way touching that they should appeal to the law—*to our law*. There are those who are inclined to dismiss this action as trivial, of neither domestic nor international significance. I wonder. I am no lawyer—but I understand that our law is intended as an expression of natural justice and that its very basis is the recognition and protection of rights and obligations, established in a time (as the lawyers say) beyond which the memory of man runneth not. It will be interesting to see what attitude it takes to rights and obligations of even greater antiquity, but derived from the needs and disciplines of a different society.'[27]

A Plural Society

The position of the Federal Government, headed by Mr. Gorton, was stated by the then Minister for the Interior, the Hon. Peter Nixon, in the House of Representatives on 3 September 1970, when he said,

'The Government believes that it is wholly wrong to encourage Aboriginals to think that because their ancestors have had a long association with a particular piece of land, Aboriginals of the present day have the right to demand ownership of it.'

The Minister went on to say that, in the Government's view, the Aborigines 'should secure land ownership under the system that applied to the Australian community and not outside it.'

The implication is quite clear. In the Government's view traditional Aboriginal society and customs lie outside 'the system'.

As we have seen, the squatters obtained their rights outside the system of their day, but the system soon bent to accommodate them.

We have also seen that it is at least arguable on historical and legal grounds, that the system of British common law which Australia has inherited does have room within it for recognition of traditional native land tenure, as is exemplified in Canada and New Zealand, as well as in the United States. The feudal concept of the paramount title of the Crown, and how it is to be understood today, are here of basic importance. In both the United States and Canada, the Government holds title to Indian lands essentially as a trustee, and there is an increasing tendency to hand over actual control and ownership to the Indian people themselves.

Indeed, this was the primary intention behind the 'Indian Reorganisation Act', passed by the United States Congress in 1934, the stated purpose of which was

'To conserve and develop Indian lands and resources; to extend to Indians the right to form business and other organisations; to establish a credit system for Indians; to grant certain rights of home rule to Indians; to provide for vocational education for Indians; and for other purposes.'

On June 25, 1969, the Federal Government of Canada presented to the Canadian Parliament an official statement on Indian Policy which foreshadowed an 'Indian Lands Act' which will grant full Indian control and ownership of reserve land. It reads, in part:—

'Under the existing system, title to reserve lands is held either by the Crown in right of Canada or the Crown in right of one of the provinces. Administrative control and legislative authority are, however, vested exclusively in the Government and the Parliament of Canada. It is a trust. As long as this trusts exists, the Government, as a trustee, must supervise the business connected with the land.'

'The result of Crown ownership and the Indian Act has been to tie the Indian people to a land system that lacks flexibility and inhibits development. If an Indian band wishes to gain income by leasing its land, it has to do so through a cumbersome system involving the Government as trustee. It cannot mortgage reserve land to finance development on its own initiative. Indian people do not have control of their lands except as the Government allows, and this is no longer acceptable to them. The Indians have made this clear at the consultation meetings. They now want real control, and this Government believes that they should have it. The Government recognizes that full and true equality calls for Indian control and ownership of reserve land.'

The statement goes on:—

'The Government is prepared to transfer to the Indian people the reserve lands, full control over them, and subject to the proposed Indian Lands Act, the right to determine who shares in ownership. The Government proposes to seek agreements with the banks and, where necessary, with the governments of the provinces. Discussions will be initiated with the Indian people and the provinces to this end.'

In Mr. Nixon's statement, which may be taken as representative of the established white Australian view, the Australian Minister went on to say that he had found that 'the land rights which were accorded to the Indian bands' in Canada 'had had the effect, in practice, of encouraging division between the Indian people and the wider Canadian community.'

In fact, as the Canadian statement implies, the real problem in Canada is not that the Indians' rights of use and occupancy were recognised, but rather that the Indians were unable to develop the land and obtain the necessary education, capital, and services, because of a too paternalistic and apathetic trusteeship role assumed by the Canadian Governments. As Canadians see it, the problem is not that Indian land rights have been recognised, but rather how to make those rights more effective in terms of Indian initiative and development. The question is not one of whether or not to recognise traditional Indian rights, but of how to embody these rights most effectively in modern Canadian society and law.

Commenting on the Canadian acceptance of more than one cultural and legal tradition within Canadian society, the Canadian Minister of Indian Affairs and Northern Development, the Hon. Jean Chrétien, said,

'We believe that a non-discriminatory society can accommodate different ways of holding and controlling land. Some people own land in their own names. Some hold land through corporations or partnerships. Some hold land in communal possession—such as the Hutterites. We believe that the Indian people can control their lands and ultimately own them without prejudicing their desire to have the lands remain Indian. The feeling Indian people have for their land is as strong as the French-Canadians' feeling for the French language. This feeling must be respected. The land must be protected. That is

why we propose to have an Indian Lands Act which will continue
and indeed enhance Indian control of their land by first transferring
it to them in law and adding special safeguards.'[28]

Here we see a crucial difference in approach vis-a-vis Australia.
Canadians accept that Canada is a plural society. Thanks to the French
presence, they can do no other and still survive as a nation. On the other
hand, Australians persist in denying the rights, and the current validity of
the cultural traditions, of the Aboriginal people. White Australians have not
yet come to terms with the fact that Australia, too, is a plural society.

Cook, and the settlers who followed him, found the Aboriginal people
relatively few in number, and for the most part not a serious threat. For
more than a century after that, white Australians were secure in the belief
that the Aborigines were a dying race.

Only gradually, in the last few decades, has it slowly dawned on the
non-Aboriginal population that the Aborigines are here to stay. Even more
recent, is the idea that Aborigines may not want to become dark-skinned
Europeans; so secure have we been in our belief in the self-evident material,
moral, and cultural superiority of the Anglo-European way of life. It is only
since 1965 that the official statement of the policy of Aboriginal 'assimilation'
has used the words 'will choose' rather than 'will' in describing the policy's
aim of ensuring that Aborigines conform to white standards.[29]

Realities and Responsibilities

Today, approximately one quarter of the total population of the north-
western half of Australia is of Aboriginal or Islander descent. Even allowing
for immigration, the coloured population is increasing more rapidly than the
white, and this despite one of the highest infant mortality rates in the
world.[30] The vast majority of these black Australians live in extreme poverty,
poorly housed and educated, in bad health and housing, and seriously under-
employed.

Aborigines, like French-Canadians, may not wish to be 'assimilated' into
a culturally 'homogeneous' Australian society. Nevertheless they do want,
and are increasingly articulate in demanding, their share of the economic
benefits of a technological age.

Whatever the merits or long-term realism of these cultural choices,[31] the
demands for material progress and economic equality bring us to consider
some sobering economic realities.

With an average annual increase in the Aboriginal and part-Aboriginal
population over the next twenty years of around 7,000, a capital expenditure
of around forty million dollars is needed to provide the necessary new jobs,
houses, schools, hospitals, and so forth, *every year*. In addition, a similar
annual expenditure is needed to overcome the poverty of the existing population of some 150,000 people of Aboriginal descent. Against this need, the
present total annual expenditure of all Australian governments on Aboriginal
affairs is about $30 million. It would seem unlikely that the balance will be
found from regular tax revenue in the near future.

Thus it is that the huge amount of capital available in the form of land,
which rightly belongs to the Aboriginal people, together with royalties and
compensation from the development and exploitation of Aboriginal land,
would seem to be the only realistic means to overall Aboriginal advancement.

This is not to say that recognition of Aboriginal land rights will be
sufficient on its own, or that it will necessarily work miracles. However, it

does seem clear that, without recognition of land rights, all the other positive measures which can and must be adopted will do little more than nibble at the edges of the problem. As in the American ghetto situation, conventional policies of assimilation cannot hope to even keep up with the growth in population. The problem of economic growth and social progress must be tackled where the people are and where they want to be, on their own land and in their own communities.

The present situation is remarkably unstable. There has been a revolution in communications and expectations which has forever ended the parochialism and isolation of Aborigines in their reserves, settlements, missions, and fringe-dweller shanty towns. Today, black Australians are increasingly articulate and impatient for progress. Already there is an increasing migration from the lands of their dis-inheritance into the slums and ghettos of the cities on the south-eastern seaboard. If Aborigines are forced off the cattle stations and reserves of the North-west, this trickle will turn into a torrent, and racial problems will have come to the cities with a vengeance.[32]

In the north-west, an average of one in four of the population is coloured. They could be a healthy and productive source of new enterprise and skilled labour, well adapted and at home in the harsh environment. On the other hand, if they continue to be treated as obstacles to progress or as a cheap pool of unskilled labour, they could well become increasingly alienated and troublesome to white administrations and enterprises.

Big business, much of it international in character, has a peculiar responsibility in the north-west, since most enterprise and employment in the area is highly capital-intensive and economic interests exert a powerful influence on government policy in the area. Preferential training and employment of local labour is clearly desirable in the interest of long-term social stability in the area, as is the deliberate creation of local, labour-intensive feeder industries and Aboriginal-owned enterprises.

Unfortunately, without some sort of economic bargaining power such as land rights or royalties, it appears from the record that big industry is most unwilling to make even marginal concessions.[33]

If big business continues to oppose Aboriginal land rights in the north-west, as NABALCO has done at Gove, it may well be acting against its own long-term interests.

The president of the American Oil Company put this in its proper perspective when he asked,

'Does management, in the exercise of its responsibility to its stockholders, have the right to invest time, effort, and money to help solve broad social problems? I don't lose much sleep over this one, nor should any other executive if he will really think through what it's all about.

'For while we are in business to make a profit, and profit motivation is a tremendous social force, we cannot abdicate our responsibility to help create and maintain a continuing society that will enable us to operate profitably. We neglect our obligation to our stockholders if we take refuge in the cliche that our duty ends with today's production and sale of competitive commodities.

'No segment of society, and no individual in it, can afford to sit placidly by while a horribly costly and utterly inhumane condition . . . goes from bad to worse.'[34]

Looking Ahead

The realities of politics and of competition for funds and resources have long led to Aboriginal affairs receiving low priority with Australian governments. If this situation is to be remedied, and growing racial conflict avoided, Aborigines must somehow gain a power to influence governments and events greater than their numbers and history would suggest possible.

Speaking of 'Aboriginal Power' at the opening of a national conference on Aboriginal and Islander advancement, Dr. Coombs suggested that,

> 'The greatest strength of the Aboriginal cause is that it stands squarely on the moral worth of its claims; it is in essence an appeal to standards of justice and humanity which all of us believe should underlie the structure of human society.'[35]

In the past, the moral worth of the Aboriginal cause has been proclaimed, usually from far off England, by the more idealistic sections of the white community. Australian legislatures, on the other hand, have been influenced more by the pragmatic materialism of the white settler and farming interests, and it is these which have prevailed. Whether white Australia has yet reached such a state of material security, social maturity, or civilisation that it can and will allow morality to prevail, remains to be seen. There are, in any event, other sources of Aboriginal power which offer at least some hope of progress.

Because of the peculiar distribution of the Australian population as regards colour, it appears that there are at least two, and possibly up to four, federal electorates where the Aboriginal vote could hold the balance of power as between the candidates of the major political parties. This is a situation which Aboriginal organisations and activists are bound to exploit, and ways and means of doing this are already being explored.

Appeals by people of Aboriginal descent for support and assistance from the United Nations and other bodies outside Australia are increasingly common, and becoming more sophisticated. These can be expected to exert some external pressure on Australian governments, although white Australians may well react against at least the cruder forms of external pressure in ways not helpful to the Aboriginal cause.

Probably the most fruitful form of external aid for the Aboriginal people will come in the form of encouragement, finance, and stimulus to Aboriginal leadership, organisation, and self-help. A big step in this direction was taken in 1970, when the World Council of Churches' Programme to Combat Racism made substantial grants to the two major Aboriginal advancement organisations in Australia, namely the 'Federal Council for the Advancement of Aborigines and Torres Strait Islanders', and the newly formed Aboriginal and Islander controlled 'National Tribal Council'.

As has already been implied, there is another potential source of Aboriginal power, namely the power to cause social and economic disruption, particularly in the North-West. In the immediately foreseeable future, it does not appear that Aborigines will deliberately seek to exploit this means of power, which in any case could well prove to be counter-productive. Nevertheless, frustration and idleness have already led to some mild examples, in some settlement situations, of the more or less pointless and spontaneous outbreaks of brawling and rioting which have been common in the American ghettos.

Taking a longer range view, it seems probable that unless considerable progress is made in the next few years, either through moral persuasion, external pressure, or the power of the ballot box, then the more radical tactic of deliberately fostering social and economic disruption may be adopted by some Aboriginal leaders.

The moral and practical arguments in favour of the recognition of Aboriginal land rights are overwhelming, but the task of winning a just and proper response from people and governments so late in Australia's history is a testing one. It involves a coming to terms with history, and a costly re-assessment of the role of the white man in Australia and the world. It also involves some powerful vested interests.

Hopefully, all that is necessary is to be able to expose the Australian public and governing elite to the full force of the case for land rights. Given, however, the current irresponsible attitude of the mining industry in particular towards this issue, and the fact that every major Australian newspaper and commercial television outlet is controlled by companies with mining investments, such a full exposure is problematical.

Whatever the courts decide on the legal issues, many important matters of principle and detail will remain to be resolved. How the courts, and Australia as a whole, responds to these issues, may well determine the future course of race relations in this country.

> Throughout this essay the words 'Aborigine' or 'Aboriginal' would, but for lack of space and awkwardness of expression, be accompanied by 'and Islander', since the people of the Torres Straits Islands, many descendants of whom reside on the mainland, suffer from many of the same injustices, including loss of land rights. Aborigines and Islanders work together, while maintaining their separate cultural traditions and identities, in both F.C.A.A.T.S.I. and N.T.C., and nothing in this essay is intended to detract from this unity in diversity. Cape Barren Islanders, who are partly descended from the obliterated Tasmanian Aborigines, also merit special mention.

REFERENCES

1 Written statement by the Prime Minister, Hansard, Senate, 12 September 1963, p. 488.

2 COHEN, FELIX S., in *The Legal Conscience* (Yale University Press, New Haven, 1960), pp. 230-252.

3 HARPER, ALLAN G., 'Canada's Indian Administration: The Treaty System', *America Indigina*, Vol. VII, No. 2, pp. 130-148.

4 COHEN, FELIX S., *op. cit.*, p. 291.

5 For an account of the operation of this Commission, see LURIE, NANCY O., 'The Indian Claims Commission Act', *The Annals of the American Academy Political and Social Science*, May 1957, pp. 56-70.

6 COHEN, FELIX S., *op. cit.*, pp. 280-281.

7 COHEN, FELIX S., *op. cit.*, p. 237.

8 BAALMAN, JOHN, *Outline of Law in Australia*, 2nd Edition, pp. 112-113.

9 Department of Territories, *Australian Territories*, Vol. 1, No. 1, pp. 12-15.

10 From *Captain James Cook in the Pacific*, selected extracts from his journals 1768-1779, edited by A. Grenfell Price.

11 *Historical Records of Australia*, Vol. III, pp. 592-593.

12 BACKHOUSE, JAMES, *A Narrative of a Visit to the Australian Colonies*, (Hamilton, Adams & Co., London, 1843), p. cxxxiv.

13 Quoted by TURNBULL, CLIVE in *Black War* (Lansdowne Press, Melbourne, 1965), p. 165.

14 'Report from Select Committee on Aborigines (British Settlements), 1837', Commons Papers, 1837, Vol. 7, 212 pp.

15 'Letters Patent Erecting and Establishing the Province of South Australia, 19 February 1836' (Libraries Board of South Australia, Adelaide, 1964).

16 See DUNSTAN, D. A., 'Aboriginal Land Title and Employment in South Australia', in *Aborigines in the Economy*, ed. SHARP, I. G. and TATZ, C. M., (Jacaranda Press, Brisbane, 1966.)

17 CLARKE, *Select Documents in Australian History*, pp. 225-227.

18 *Historical Records of Australia*, Series I, Vol. 18, p. 389.

19 *Ibid.*, p. 386.

20 *Ibid.*, p. 390.

21 Quoted in ROBERTS, S. H., *History of Australian Land Settlement*, 1788-1920 (Melbourne University Press), p. 168.

22 Quoted in ROBERTS, S. H., *op. cit.*, p. 215.

23 BARWICK, DIANE, 'A Little More Than Kin', Ph.D. thesis, Australian National University, 1963, and personal communication.

24 For an account of the Gurindji dispute see HARDY, FRANK, *The Unlucky Australians* (Nelson, Melbourne, 1968).

25 BERNDT, R. M., 'The Gove Dispute', *Anthropological Forum*, Vol. 1, No. 2, pp. 258-295 (University of W.A. Press, 1964).

26 ROWLEY, C. D., 'The Aboriginal Householder', *Quadrant*, Nov.-Dec., 1967, pp. 90-96.

27 COOMBS, DR. H. C., 'Guest of Honour', transcript of talk broadcast 5 January 1969, Australian Broadcasting Commission.

28 CHRETIEN, HON. JEAN, 'Indian Policy'—Where Does It Stand?', Speech at the Empire Club, Toronto, October 16, 1969 (Dept. of Indian Affairs and Northern Development, Ottawa, 13 pp.).

29 For an official discussion of this change, see 'The Australian Aborigines' (Department of Territories, 1967, 111 pp.), pp. 39-46.

30 For detailed documentation see LANCASTER JONES, F., *The Structure and Growth of Australia's Aboriginal Population* (Australian National University Press, 1970).

31 These are discussed more fully in the author's 'Toward a Multi-Racial Society', which appears in Volume III of this series.

32 Even in New Zealand, where the Maori people retain a considerable land-base, migration to the cities is raising new problems. See for example METGE, JOAN, *A New Maori Migration* (Melbourne University Press, 1964).

33 See for example *Aborigines in the Economy*, ed. Sharp & Tatz (Jacaranda Press, Melbourne, 1966), and STEVENS, FRANK, 'Weipa: The Politics of Pauperization', *The Australian Quarterly*, Vol. 41, No. 3 (1969).

34 MOORE, L. W. 'Urban Unrest: Whose Problem is it'? *Northwestern Business Reporter*, Winter 1968 (Northwestern University, Evanston, Illinois).

35 Address by COOMBS, DR. H. C., in *Kunmanggur*, No. 5, April 1970 (Office of Aboriginal Affairs, Box 477, Canberra).

BRUTALITY AND COMPASSION

14

BRUTALITY AND THE ABORIGINAL PEOPLE

J. Horner

Apologists for the current restrictive immigration policy in Australia sometimes argue that it prevents the (usually unspecified) horrors of racial conflict which they see erupting in other countries. The Republic of South Africa, Great Britain and the United States of America are commonly cited. This uneasiness is reflected in clause (d) of the Labor Party's policy on immigration. It declares the policy aims at achieving 'the avoidance of the difficult social and economic problems which may follow from an influx of peoples having different standards of living, traditions and cultures.'[1] What has been forgotten here, and in the occasional rhetoric of stable Australian government—'we have fought no battles on our soil, no revolutions, no glorious struggles for liberation, and ... no agonies of a turbulent history'[2] —is that a process of coercion and duress, both physically violent and more recently covert, is evident in Australian history since 1799 against the Aboriginal people.

In *The Destruction of Aboriginal Society*, Professor Charles Rowley quotes two first hand accounts of brutality, one from a settler, the other from an Aboriginal talking to Tom Petrie. There was much blood shed in establishing an Australian frontier.

The exasperated settler in 1839 found his first bullock speared while overlanding across the Murrumbidgee to South Australia, and reflected on the dilemma in his diary:

> 'A stockholder is in want of a fresh run for his stock, and therefore proceeds with them outside his neighbour's. He erects a hut and stockyard and takes up his residence. A day or two after his arrival, one or two blacks drop in, they are well received and entertained, get some meat and damper fare offered, a little tobacco, ... in a week or so the whole tribe is domesticated with the squatter ... Soon however they see an ox killed, cut and prepared for eating and they eat part of it themselves. That evening out of curiosity they kill one for themselves ... the blacks are remonstrated with, they then proceed to spear some every day. The squatter at length takes up arms, the blacks spear him or any of his stockmen when they find them with their blacks turned, and war commences and often continues for months and years.'[3]

The settler assumed, as Rowley comments, that non-Aboriginal land claims override the Aboriginal rights to life. He did not deny the existence of undeclared and unacknowledged war in the frontier; nor the certainty of the destruction of the Aborigines.

The Aboriginal account, of similar events near Brisbane in 1842, was related to Tom Petrie:—

'We were hunted from our ground, shot, poisoned, and had our daughters, sisters and wives taken from us . . . what a number were poisoned at Kilcoy . . . They stole our ground where we used to get food, and when we got hungry and took a bit of flour or killed a bullock to eat, they shot or poisoned us. All they give us now for our land is a blanket once a year.'[4]

In the war there were no treaties. For six months of 1824, martial law was proclaimed in the Mudgee-Bathurst district of New South Wales.[5] There were three ways of curbing the Aborigines—punitive expeditions organised by local settlers, poisonings directed by individuals, and sharp-shooting. Significantly, the Crown did not take up John Batman's attempt, in June 1835, to regulate land transfer by negotiated treaty; the Melbourne agreement with eight Aboriginals was disallowed by Governor Bourke. The Crown was more inclined, in the then current mood of the frustrated squatters and the determined resistance of the Aborigines, to encourage the sharp, short overwhelming engagement that taught natives a lesson, on the grounds that short victories saved lives. Of all the Governors, only Macquarie made a friendly exchange with the Aborigines.[6]

The earliest violent destruction of Aboriginal tribes was accidental . . . the introduction of smallpox, in 1789, devastating tribes up and down the coast for decades.[7] Phillip, in 1790, ordered the initial punitive expedition at Sydney Cove, for killing a gardener.[8] As the frontier advanced, the sudden spearing of stock, sheep or cattle, or of shepherds, was answered by the posse of neighbouring settlers with guns, concerned for swift revenge. There was no way of identifying the guilty party, so any group of black people was attacked. Some local histories, such as that between Grafton and Brisbane, have been documented regarding these expeditions;[9] but they spread to all colonies, including South Australia (where a policy of setting aside compensation quotas of land for Aborigines was begun, but dropped, under economic pressure of selling land to pay for migration).[10] A few pastoralists, notably Robert Christison of Lammermoor Station, North Queensland, Edward Ogilvie of Yugilbar, near Casino, New South Wales, and Patrick Durack in western Queensland, made firm verbal agreements with Aborigines that they were free to hunt, and even to kill some cattle for eating.

The Aboriginal oral tradition retains evidence of the poisonings. In 1961, Mr. Charles Leon, then President of the Aboriginal-Australian Fellowship in Sydney, gave me details of a mass soup meal, for the people of his tribe, the Worimi (between Port Stephens, Muswellbrook and Taree, on the central north coast of New South Wales, laced with arsenic and evidently prepared by a manager of a sheep station near Karuah. (Arsenic was a common weed killer or insecticide and a method of introducing it into food was developed, to rid properties of vermin.)

Documentary evidence for massacres is by no means fully collected, but the public reaction to the prosecution and execution of seven assigned servants, for the murders of Aboriginals at Myall Creek (1838), shows how commonly it was held to be just to kill Aborigines in cold blood in order to keep the peace. Since Aborigines could not give legal evidence, convictions were not easy to obtain.

The record for slaughter and stealthy murder must go to the armed Native Police Force. This was first recruited in Victoria, during the Protectorate (1838-49), made a northward path through the Riverina and north coast of New South Wales, and was established in Queensland in 1848. Evidently it had not occurred to Victorian colonial authorities that this native troop, though officered by Europeans, could easily assume control; its supreme skill in tracking and surrounding Aborigines, and its lack of loyalty for tribes outside its own kinship ties, made it an unshakeable and implacable force for reprisal by massacre. The theory was that Aborigines should be 'dispersed', since a gathering of tribes was considered dangerous—their social gatherings were not understood. As new frontiers opened, the Native Police accompanied pioneers: three Native policemen and a lieutenant landed with G. E. Dalrymple's exploring party at Cardwell, North Queensland, in January 1864 and supported settlers with the gun.[11] From two Parliamentary Select Committees (N.S.W. 1856,[12] Qld. 1861-2[13]) on the Native Police Force, it seems that the armed police also shot dogs, destroyed blankets, and abolished fishing rights. In 1880, Aboriginal resistance strengthened; along the Palmer River in Cape York a guerilla-type campaign (1875-82) stubbornly fought off miners and police; plantations and farms were constantly harried. However, by 1895, the peninsula supported cattle stations and the Native Police Force (of 100-200 men) was disbanded in 1897.

North of Geraldton, Western Australia, violence accompanied settlement from the beginning. Queensland overlanders brought their prejudices as well as their cattle to the Kimberleys, where labour and land were urgently needed. Cattle-spearing, constant reprisal, and forced labour produced a very violent frontier. In 1863, the Northern Territory was opened for settlement by South Australia,[14] and more Queenslanders overlanded there from 1872, when much Territory was still short of lawful control. There was a Protector in Darwin, part-time, from 1877, with a few sub-Protectors at important food depots. But sub-Protectors followed the settlers and, as policemen, they were 'dependent on the pastoralist for social acceptance and approval'. Opportunities to help Aborigines were not encouraged.

The Reverend J. R. Gribble, the Anglican missionary at Forrest River Mission near Wyndham, Western Australia, related in 'Dark Deeds in a Sunny Land' (1886):—

> 'At times the wild natives [were] really run down and captured, and taken to the stations, and if they [ran] away, which they were almost certain to do, a warrant was issued for their arrest and the police [were] set in motion and [ran them] down and ferretted them out'. 'Many natives [were] shot in the backs for no other reason than they were running away from their slave masters.'

This history of coercion was reflected in European attitudes to Aboriginal labour. The sealers who stole Tasmanian women in the 1800s and the mainland farmers who later stole lads for rural work, used physical force as circumstances demanded. Except for Boyd and Alexander Berry, who freely employed fishermen along the Shoalhaven river, the relation of victor to vanquished passed on to the employment relationship of the Aborigines who remained. The white men were masters and the blacks were assigned servants, in Victorian times, a strictly paternal bond. Tensions and mistrust continued after the 'peace', because the servants were bound to the masters for life, absconding Aboriginal servants often being returned by the police.

The Growth of Paternal Control

The violence of the nineteenth century led to pauperism for the remnants of Aboriginal tribes. Beginning with the Victorian Board for the Protection of Aborigines in 1860,[15] governments introduced policies of paternal protection, being convinced that the human inferiority of black people was a cause for their displacement by Europeans.[15a] Though these policies were concerned 'with how little violence to humanity this effacement could be attended' (as the Secretary of a W.A. Protection Board was to write in 1892),[16] this did not prevent harsh treatment coming to the Aborigines.

In Van Diemen's Land, G. A. Robinson's lonely haven for the last Tasmanians, at Gun Carriage Island (1831), was a model for later church missions and government Stations. The Victorian Aborigines' Protection Board, within ten years of 1860, owned seven isolated reserved lands, amounting to 22,000 acres, on which it segregated Aborigines, protecting them from 'injustice, imposition and fraud'. They gave rations and blankets as needed (and trained some children). In 1877, a Royal Commission on Aborigines concluded that absorption of Aborigines into the main community was impossible; until they died out, and were no more a claim upon the Government, they should be on such Stations, protected from degradation. But from 1884, people of mixed descent ('half-castes') in Victoria, under thirty five years of age, were forced to leave the Stations, though they were not trained for competitive work. These restrictions were rigidly enforced by police.[17]

As townships in New South Wales grew up around enclosed Aboriginal camps, disease and alcohol were the signs of a breakdown in social discipline. A restriction on liquor was made law in 1864. Three church missions were granted lands at Brewarrina, Maloga and Darlington Point. Many Aborigines had found employment in rural work, such as ring-barking and rabbitting; on the south coast, Berry and Boyd had created employment for fishermen. Nonetheless, the small reserve lands for Aboriginal groups, as in Victoria and South Australia, were provided for food and sanctuary. In 1883, a N.S.W. Aborigines' Protection Board in Sydney, set up (by Parkes) and chaired by the Inspector-General of Police, adopted the Victorian ideas to protect, segregate and disperse Aborigines. Some ninety reserves were gazetted, but in 1884, the Protection Board declared its opposition, on pragmatic grounds, to the Victorian view that part-Aborigines should live as Europeans do. The New South Wales politicians drew on Victoria's experience in drawing up their Aborigines' Protection Act in 1909, almost a full copy of the Victorian Act. It was not directly concerned with controlling Aborigines so much as attaining an *ad hoc* machinery, already tried and trusted, to contain an untidy situation.[18]

In southern colonies, missionary reserves closed down when governments were satisfied they had 'failed', and passed over to the Lands Departments: some became government reserves. Other reserves were leased to white settlers, especially in South Australia and Victoria.

The policy regarding Aborigines in southern States was meant to be benevolently restrictive.[19] To the missionary's zeal for the virtue of work, was added the squatter's experience as a paternal squire, dispensing food and offering cottage houses, blankets and possessive protection against sharp shooters in return for light and irregular rural work. The restrictions laid down in the N.S.W. Aborigines' Protection Act, 1909 (and carried out by an

Aborigines' Protection Board of six pastoralists and the head of the Police Force) were as follows:—

'All gift lands and reserves were vested in the Board; Aboriginal camps could be ordered well away from towns or reserves; Stations were to be controlled by a manager, local committees in nearby towns, or local [police] guardians. Europeans could not lodge or wander with Aborigines. Children were "apprenticed" to a master, and where possible the nearest relatives were charged with the infant maintenance. Europeans were absolutely barred from reserves.'

In practice, difficulties recurred in the institution and efforts to cut down costs and simplify administration tended to restrain Aborigines and to encourage their personal intimidation. Managers, for example, were also untrained teachers. From 1915, Inspectors were appointed who removed 'neglected' children from parents on reserves, to 'train' them in Homes for indentured work with employers; but their pay, most of it held 'in trust' by the Protection Board until they turned eighteen years of age, was so low as to be termed 'pocket money' (1/6 a week, rising to 5/- weekly). Four years later, New South Wales adopted the 1884 Victorian decision to disperse part-Aborigines from reserves: managers were empowered to deliver 'expulsion orders' to youths of lighter caste, to sink or swim in the community outside. This restriction in practice widened, to cover militant leaders, who were forced from reserves in this way.[20] During the lean years of widespread poverty, 1926-1941, some Managers also tried to control crowded Stations by withholding rationed food.[21]

Moreover, the decision to vest all reserves, whether donated to Aboriginal groups or surveyed by the Lands Department, as Crown land owned by the Protection Board, took away any social responsibility. People were daily dependent on European Managers, or police sergeants; seasonal work outside reserves, often at low rates of pay, left families in poverty and there was a marked tendency among efficient policemen to expect trouble on Aboriginal reserves.[22] Since Inspectors and managers were Board staff, and policemen were agents of the Protection Board, they collaborated in carrying out all the restrictions. For more than sixty years, the relations of Aborigines and the New South Wales police force were very strained (and in many ways still are). From 1936, New South Wales aligning itself with the other States, passed a law to prevent New South Wales Aborigines being employed in other States, ostensibly to stop exploitation, and magistrates were given greater powers over them.[23]

In Australia's northern half, since 1900, the Aborigines of full descent have been a high proportion of the population. Inevitable clash had occurred before that date where settlers took land and reprisals for speared cattle repeated themselves in the Northern Territory, as in the States. Conditions of labour were uncontrolled in the Kimberleys and, in northern Queensland, opium and the Native Police had brought appalling loss of life.

In response to an official report of unspeakable social conditions among Aborigines in North Queensland,[24] where shooting still occurred, the Queensland government enacted the Aborigines' Preservation and Protection Act in 1897, amended in 1902. It saved many lives, but unfortunately left a legacy of very strict institutional confinement for most of the Aborigines. To this day this coercive Act has changed very little. The Aborigines were placed in six large self-sufficient settlements managed by European Superintendents responsible to a Chief Protector in Brisbane, and ten small reserves near townships locally controlled by Protectors (usually police officers).

Restrictions under the Act and regulations were compulsive. A resident could be removed from one settlement or reserve to another, or to a penal reserve (Palm Island); he could only marry within the caste officially approved; he could not leave the settlement where he was employed; the Superintendent, or Protector, was also responsible for his orderly employment, wages, censoring of mail, apprenticeship and public behaviour and private property. Part of the wages were kept by a bank in trust, but the worker still paid taxes.[25]

A quasi-legal system on settlements, by which Native Courts dispensed justice, was a closed administration. The European Superintendent presided, and approved the judges. Minor misdemeanors were covered and it was possible for the same man (the Superintendent) to be the accuser, judge, advocate for the prosecution, court registrar and victim in his own case. As described by Professor C. Tatz,[26] the charges were petty and the sentences arbitrary. A threat of banishment to Palm Island was very real (until 1965).

Its remarkable results commended the Queensland administration to other States as a model to follow, and in 1905 the Chief Protector in Queensland, W. E. Roth, was invited to act as a Royal Commissioner into Aboriginal conditions in Western Australia.

From the Kimberleys district of Western Australia, where absconding Aboriginals were brought back by police to brutal working conditions, a practice spread all over the Northern Territory and as far south (in 1946) as Oodnadatta, South Australia. Cattle-spearing Aboriginals were walked to a courthouse behind a packhorse, initially handcuffed to a saddle but soon chained by the neck. The Roth Royal Commission deplored it, noting that men and and women were chained together; four witnesses or more might be chained together for weeks; but the neck-chain was a familiar method for many years, used by police on apprehended Aborigines over all Northern Australia, except in Queensland. The neck-chain was considered more humane than handcuffs, presumably because the Aboriginal was not jerked off-balance so much. Prisoners could be primed to plead guilty on the way, and witnesses were often chained to a tree, since there were only gaols at Broome and Darwin. The chain was a symbol, as much as a part of the strong element of coercion in native administration and, significantly, its retention was strongly defended, even by a Minister for the Interior, as late as 1949.[27]

Western Australia adopted much of Queensland's paternal authoritarian administration in the W.A. Aborigines' Protection Act of 1905-11; there were many restrictions on an Aboriginal's movement, employment and marriage rights. Labour legislation previously set down in 1886 had been largely ineffective and reserves were to be managed as in other States. The new Act gave policemen (Protectors) power to grant permits to employers, who were under no real obligation, however, to pay wages or to give rations, shelter or medicine. There were clauses to prevent inhumane conditions on pearl luggers (which were harsh also in the Torres Strait).

Clauses establishing segregation, similar to those in the Queensland Act were included in the 1911 S.A. Aborigines' Protection Act, prohibiting Aborigines from towns and other places. The Chief Protector was also named as the legal guardian of every child and could take over any Aboriginal property at his discretion.

In 1927, the traditional punitive massacre ended for good, when at Forrest River Mission, the Reverend E. Gribble (the son of J. R. Gribble) reported thirty Aborigines missing. The resulting magistrate's investigation showed that one European had been killed and, in retaliation, at least eleven Aboriginals, while chained, had been shot and burned. But the policemen involved were reinstated.[28]

The Northern Territory became a Federal responsibility in 1911 and followed the Queensland and Western Australian models of stern protection. People under the Act were categorised as either 'half-caste' or 'full-blood'; power was given by the Aboriginal Ordinance (1911) for the Chief Protector to take any Aboriginal into custody, to issue permits of employment and to name areas which Aborigines were prohibited to enter.

In every Australian administration, children could be removed from their parents for instruction, and the purpose was that they should not return. In the Northern Territory, for example, this was particular directed towards 'half-caste' children, who were sent to island missions far away. In Western Australia, any child could be sent to an open-air institution, authorised by the Chief Protector, but in New South Wales, where the child had to be 'neglected', the Inspector used his own discretion in choosing the child.

Three constant themes, in every State, during the years before World War II run through the history: the insecurity offered by the reserves (except Arnhem Land), the low wages which Aborigines and Torres Strait Islanders were forced to accept along with poor housing, and the mutual distrust between the police and Aborigines. In the southern States, the growing European population in isolated townships brought social discrimination with it . . . during the 1930s, for example, a number of New South Wales towns each asked for the removal of its Aboriginal community and on eleven separate occasions, a public outcry threatened to close primary schools rather than accept a high proportion of Aboriginal schoolchildren.

> 'In 1928, the Commonwealth Government asked Mr. Bleakley, the Chief Protector for Queensland, to report on the status and conditions of the Aborigines in the Northern Territory. He found that though the pastoral industry was absolutely dependent on the Aborigines for labour, the payment of wages to the workers was not insisted on; no attempt was made to house them or train them, though this would enhance their value; on many stations the old people were starving. They had been the original station hands, but all responsibility for them was disclaimed by the lessees.'[29]

Bleakley recommended better health facilities, especially at Alice Springs, protective laws and action against prostitution (rife in camps on account of low wages and resulting hunger), and a rule that Darwin's domestic servants be locked up at night in the compound (a curfew at that time excluded Aborigines from towns).

The Great Victorian Desert reserve was established in 1927, and that in Arnhem Land in 1932. But the administration could just as simply abandon a reserve, as they did when the gold miners moved to Tennant Creek, in 1934; the Warramunga people lost their land. In Victoria, all but one reserve was abolished, back in 1917. In New South Wales the new 'assimilation' policy was to provoke an administration to close down a number of reserves, from about 1940, having induced the last families to migrate to the cities by economic pressure.[30] Since the 1920s, part of the two largest stations in New

South Wales have been leased to local farmers, to raise money for the Department.

In the period between the wars, 'protection' became slowly and increasingly more coercive. In southern States, restrictive practices awoke Aboriginal resentment and in turn this provoked the police, as the agents of the Board, to take punitive action. For economic reasons Station Managers and Matrons were expected to teach as well as manage, tend the sick, issue orders and offer rations and some of them became increasingly arbitrary as their difficulties got worse. The panic flight of people from Cumeroogunga reserve, in January 1939, after years of neglect and hunger and arbitrary control, illustrates the social tensions which built up.[31]

Within the northern half of Australia, employment without pay was a strong form of compulsion. Only in Queensland was there an award wage, granted not as industrial law but by the Chief Protector; this was almost half the white man's scale of wages. Among trade unions, Aboriginal rights to wages, before World War II, were rarely supported and in the pastoral award, outside Queensland, station hands and domestics (the positions usually taken by the Aborigines on cattle stations) were rigorously excluded. In Darwin in 1938, 5/- a week was the standard Aboriginal payment. In the 1930s, the North Australian Workers' Union attempted to fix quotas on the employment of Aborigines in the cattle industry, favouring the Europeans.

In the Torres Strait, the Queensland Department of Native Affairs, in 1927, took control of the shelling and pearling fleets. Following its assumption of power, the D.N.A. exercised its authority through appointed Island agents. This control was directed not only at the Straits economy, but at the movement of individuals from island to mainland—wages in the pearling industry for Islanders were lower than those for Aborigines. A strike of Torres Strait Islanders began on New Year's Day, 1936, during which they refused to work on the boats for four months; it achieved greater autonomy for the islands' inhabitants.[32]

Social Services, including unemployment benefits, were barred from Aborigines living on reserves, in the belief that the Protection Board's welfare was as efficient as that of the Social Services Department.

Institutional Rule Since World War II

A new welfare policy announced in January 1939 by Mr. John McEwen, then Federal Minister for the Interior, was to liberalise the course of Aboriginal policies in southern states, but its effects in the north were nullified by the intrusion of World War II and the strong aversion of the great pastoral industry to any change. The idea of Native Courts was dropped, presumably because the Queensland precedent did not offer any flexibility. Welfare officers supervised Government stations in Arnhem Land, but they found that on cattle stations they were not encouraged, for the same conservative attitudes that disapproved of missions extended to the new Welfare Department, for fear of 'rocking the boat'. One of the basic objectives of the new policy was to prepare Aborigines for citizenship.

In the 1940s, two further influences brought change. The Australian Army offered Aborigines employment as labourers on equal terms in well-run Northern Territory Barracks, at ten pence a day. This resulted in a post-war industrial scale, rising to £1 a week in the fourth year of employment.[33] A strike of about 800 Aboriginal cattle stockmen, east of Port Hedland, Western Australia, in May, 1946, for a wage of 30/- a week and the insistence of these stockmen that a white man, Don McLeod, was their spokesman, affronted both the system of work without pay or adequate housing conditions and the strict segregation from Europeans.

The emphasis on achieving citizenship gave further power to bureaucratic control, though it was meant to be beneficial. Exemption certificates, suggested in 1939 by John McEwen, then Minister for the Interior, to release promising Aboriginal individuals from the restrictions of the State Acts, were adopted in Queensland and South Australia in 1939, and in New South Wales in 1943, and produced the W.A. Natives' (Citizenship Rights) Act in 1944. Since they could be granted, deferred, cancelled or renewed, conditional on good social behaviour, the exemption certificates caused much resentment, especially as the general Aboriginal distrust of the police force made them a useful way of achieving a liberty to drink liquor. They were also used to enable elderly people to gain old-age pensions. But one was expected to accept European social values, in most States, and not return to a reserve, even for a family visit.[34]

The policy adopted in 1938 was summed up in the word 'Assimilation', and in practice it meant that single families of Aborigines were being encouraged to live in the cities by all possible means. The integration of Aboriginal children in primary schools, from 1941—with the introduction of trained teachers on segregated Stations as part of this policy—awoke a very determined prejudice against Aboriginal children among the parents of white children attending school. They insisted upon the Board retaining the segregated schools for the Aboriginal children. An extreme illustration of this prejudice, common to most country towns in the southern states, was at Collarenebri in New South Wales, where, between 1941 and 1951, the Aboriginal class was forced to take its lessons on the stage of the neighbouring Town Hall; and even football was played on grounds separated by a high fence! In 1960, there were still fourteen segregated schools in New South Wales.[35]

Between August 1944 and April 1946, Drs. Ronald and Catherine Berndt made a survey of labour conditions of Aborigines in the Northern Territory, and detailed conditions on pastoral stations, Army settlements during the employment of Aborigines by the military authorities, buffalo camps, a civil compound and an 'uncontrolled' region.

The Berndts found that continued under-nourishment of local tribes was largely responsible for the low birth-rate, and high percentage of deaths among infants and young people; both food and clothing costs were cut to save expense. No adequate shelters were provided for the use of station employees or other natives during the wet season; no sanitation, educational facilities, nor organised training were provided, but there was evidently an excessively high degree of cohabitation between white men and native women. The Berndts found that 'violence and the threat of violence (was) considered by a large number of people in these areas to be the only effective means of exercising authority over natives'.[36]

In 1950, Mr. Paul Hasluck, then Minister for the Interior, tried to build an administration upon the 'assimilation and welfare' aim of John McEwen of 1939. Expenditure leapt from £63,486 (1946/47) to £175,094 (1950/51) and £495,510 (1956/57), but social conditions on most cattle stations did not change at all.

Mr. Hasluck did not support the 'policy of segregation for natives' and in reporting the first Native Welfare Conference in 1951 to the Commonwealth Parliament (October 1951), he asked for a 'clearer recognition of the claims of the Aboriginal as an individual'. 'The Coloured people should not be considered as a class but as a part of the general community . . . .'[37]

But on 15th February 1951, a protest strike, asking for fair wages and decent food, led by Fred Waters, was held in Darwin. Under Section 16 of the Aboriginals Ordinance, the Director of Native Affairs, with the power to arrest, deport and hold any Aborigines without a charge and without trial, detained Fred Waters (an Aboriginal employed on full pay by the North Australian Workers' Union) and had him deported to a Central Australian reserve. A public outcry and a writ of habeas corpus ensured his return to Darwin.

On 6th August 1952, Mr. Hasluck outlined to Commonwealth Parliament his new legislation for Aborigines.

> 'The Administrator, on the recommendation of the Director of Welfare, will formally declare that specified persons or groups of persons stand in need of special care and assistance. It is anticipated that those originally named will be the natives who are . . . on reserves or settlements, or in employment under permit.' So Aborigines . . . and *only* Aborigines . . . can become 'wards' and be 'put' under a system 'closely analogous to that customarily followed with regard to those of European race who need special care . . . for example, neglected children'.[38]

Section 17, Welfare Ordnance No. 16 of 1953, gave power to the Director to take a ward into custody and have him removed to a reserve or institution, or from one reserve to another, if he considered this to be in his own interests. Section 20 forbade the ward to leave, under penalty of three months' gaol. Settlements and missions became a major aspect of the Administration's policy, so that by the 1950s, taking Northern Territory and Queensland together, half the Aborigines were restrained in institutions.

Since Aborigines were able-bodied men and women, but without citizenship rights, the pastoralists demanded that they should be excluded from the European labour award.

When it became clear in 1962 that the prescriptive laws did not work, full citizenship rights in Northern Territory were granted. But, according to Professor Colin Tatz, a dual policy arose by which welfare work was carried out by the Administration for those Aborigines segregated from society on reserves, with army-type barracks, messroom and dormitories. Europeans were excluded but Aborigines had to live in this 'workhouse' environment.[39]

There is much documentary evidence of unofficial coercion and physical brutality in the 1940s and 1950s.

From Dr. C. Duguid, in *No Dying Race*, Adelaide, 1963, are quoted the following incidents:—

At an Adelaide Town Hall public meeting on 31st August, 1953, an eighteen year-old part-Aboriginal lad related that he and his friends had been refused the right to sit down with white people in the dining-car of the north-south railway train; and a young nurse said two friends had been turned away from an Adelaide hospital where they had applied to be trained.

In July, 1954, an Aboriginal Jimmy Gwiethoona, died at Merriden District Hospital, Western Australia, resulting from blows evidently given by a Constable two days before; despite the Coroner's verdict that 'R— K— L— unlawfully killed Jimmy Gwiethoona' (26th August, 1954), on November 12th of the same year the Crown Law Department announced it would not continue proceedings against L— because 'Gwiethoona had received his fatal injuries when he fell over when resisting arrest'. (The Minister of Justice subsequently declined to see a deputation.)

At Darwin, on 15th December 1954, two pastoralists, brothers aged thirty-two and twenty-nine, were each sentenced to six months imprisonment and each fined four hundred pounds for having whipped and assaulted four men and one woman. A drover aged twenty-five, was fined fifty pounds for wounding an Aboriginal with a horse-whip.

Evidence was given at Alice Springs Police Court (12 January, 1959) against a white aged thirty-two, a carpenter at Papunya native settlement, that he had gone to remove an Aboriginal, who was 'run down by a Land-Rover, thrashed with a pick handle and given a thorough hiding'. As the accused had left the Territory, no further action was taken.

In October 1959, at Alice Springs, a Melbourne woman witnessed the assault and arrest of a young part-Aboriginal drover, by a black tracker and two white policemen in a utility. A charge of drunkenness against the drover was dismissed by the Magistrate. When the police applied to withdraw the charge, the magistrate ordered the prosecutor to send the papers to 'the appropriate authorities'.

Of brutality on mission stations, there is the case of May, 1961, in which 'a young Aboriginal man, Jim Jacko, had been caned and transported from Hopvale Lutheran Mission, Cape York Peninsula, to Cooktown on the coast, there to await a steamer to take him via Cairns to the discipline of Palm Island'. At Cairns, he made contact with the Aborigines' Advancement League and, through this association, the local Member of Parliament found that no charge was placed against Jacko. It turned out, during the open magisterial inquiry into the caning under Justice J. O. Lee, whose findings were released in August, that the young man had left the Mission with his sweetheart without permission, but no charge was brought against him nor did he appear before a Court. Yet he was caned and sent to Palm Island.

In March 1950, a domestic quarrel in a tribe on the Church of England Edward River Mission, Cape York Peninsula, Queensland, ended in the death of a native policeman; 'As a reprisal, the hunting spears and woomeras of the entire tribe were piled high in a heap and, under the supervision of a Cairns police party, were smashed to pieces.' The noted anthropologist, Dr. Donald Thompson, who was present, described this as 'a reign of terror'. Nearly a fortnight later, a constable forced two handcuffed Aborigines, with four women and four children, fifty miles in heavy rain to Coen, without food or sleep, for trial. The case collapsed when Dr. Thompson gave evidence.

Frank Stevens has reported a gaoling of five Aboriginals from the same Mission some fifteen years after the above incident. On July 24th, 1966, they were sentenced at Coen Court each to five days' gaol and were later removed to Palm Island by the Department of Native Affairs Director, for 18 months, without trial and in defiance of the new (1965) Act.

Cases of brutality or coercion on settlements or Stations are more difficult to confirm for lack of evidence. (European people are not allowed on to Government stations, unless they are either on the Staff or are 'official' Chaplains.)

On 15th November, 1963, eleven Aboriginal residents at Mapoon, until that July part of the Presbyterian mission extending to Weipa, North

Queensland, were moved by force by five policemen, despite promises to the contrary, and their cottages burned. 'The policemen said that the people might run away and they will lose their job. They didn't give the people time to have a bath or eat their supper'. The reason given was that these families 'were exercising an undue influence over a number of the remaining people and were apparently precluding them from exercising a free and impartial judgment to the benefit of their families.'[40]

Restraint on settlements has been continuing in Queensland since the Act was passed in 1905. In Queensland, 'many of the charges against individuals were recorded simply as unsatisfactory conduct subversive to good order of the settlement and incarceration was frequently at the Director's pleasure'.[41]

In Western Australia, the practices of coercion were directed in respect of labour requirements in the North, and towards the education of children in the South. Until 1962, a fictitious line of demarcation running North-West to South-East, between Port Hedland and Broome, popularly called 'The Leper Line', was strictly maintained by police officers, ostensibly to limit the spread of leprosy to the Kimberleys, but apparently directed to restraining the movement of Aboriginal stockmen from this district. A case of restraint upon children learning at school occurred at Carrolup, when, in 1952, a Mrs. Rutter attempted to create commercial markets in London for the children's excellent crayon drawings; the Department of Native Welfare, apparently embarrassed, closed Carrolup School. In September 1956, the Department wished to 'remove all children of school age from the Warburton Ranges area, without the consent of the parents, and take them 400 miles away across an area most of which is barren, waterless country, to Cosmo Newbery, the parents being left in the Ranges.' The purpose was to educate the children away from the parents . . . a policy many years old, evidently pursued by the Department for nearly twenty years.[42]

The minimum wage rates on Queensland settlements, low as they are, have never approached parity with European workers. In 1965, the Department opposed the granting of equal wages to Aborigines and refused to pay equal wages to their own Aboriginal employees. In practice, all the trade union activity has been suppressed. The Trust Fund of Aboriginal wages, inaugurated by Mr. Bleakley in 1927, was still loosely administered, so that the wage earners were being credited in bank accounts kept within the Department with smaller amounts than those to which they were entitled. This opened the possibility of embezzlement to any Protector, who could refuse a permit of employment, fix the wages to be paid and the nature of food and accommodation, direct the employer to pay the whole or portion of the wages to the Aboriginals or to himself. If a native leaves a job to which he has been sent by the authorities, action may be taken against him to force him to return.[43]

Unofficial action in cities against Aborigines was still likely in the 1960s. In Sydney, on the eve of Good Friday, 1961, a police squad raided the Redfern streets and arrested at least twenty-seven lads returning from football practice. The ostensible reason was to stop a wave of petty pilfering; but it closed weekly dances run by the Aboriginal-Australian Fellowship and a youth club. Consequently further arrests of Aboriginal youths, many on fictitious charges, were challenged in Court by the Aboriginal-Australian Fellowship and the arresting stopped. Two cases made (1962) against K. Brindle, an Aboriginal leader, involving a charge of assaulting an officer and found to be groundless, are well documented by the Council of Civil Liberties in New South Wales.

There are cases recorded by F. Stevens, in 1965, of police officers in North Queensland allegedly assaulting Aborigines; and of one man who was sent to hospital for three years and whose wife was never informed by the authorities that he was there.[44]

The Evidence of Continuing Brutality

'Men who had once been proud, hunting for food in support of their families now sat around idle, or dragged rakes over yards which did not require raking . . . because it was said they could not just be given food without earning it. Even their food, which was good before it reached the kitchen, was cooked and handed to them. More homes are built to house the ever-increasing white staff, while a village for the Aborigines has been planned by white men and a contract let by white men to do the building. The situation has occasionally been explosive; work is what the discontented need, not punishment.[45]

The above description of life on a Northern Territory Government settlement, suggests not simply official neglect of Aborigines, but the enforcement of institutional life from above, without consultation. If Government officials have a conviction that no change is possible, it follows that no change is at all likely. Civic committees are not encouraged on reserves or settlements; and there is no encouragement for Northern Territory Aborigines to live in an urban environment. Northern Territory Aborigines, with the one exception of the mixed-descent people dispersed to Darwin in 1969 from Croker Island Mission, were fixed in a system of bureaucratic controls. 'When such a system of control is devoid of any consultative machinery and responsible organisation is discouraged, the human personality becomes depressed and his community more malleable. In this way the administration of Aborigines through coercion has had a real part to play in policy. With the removal of the people from the normal avenues of economic incentive, through the failure to pay wages which had any relationship to the skill and energy applied, the coercive basis of the system was reinforced. In the absence of payment for labour there is little alternative but to force a person to work.'[46]

Three policies of the Northern Territory Administration tend to confirm this. The first prevents people from outside the Administration entering Aboriginal reserves. This had also been strictly adhered to in *all* States, until 1969, when the N.S.W. Aborigines' Act No. 7 of 1969, although vesting reserve lands in the authority, declared them 'public places'. In social terms, an Aboriginal reserve in New South Wales is now a neighbourhood, a community, not an enclave. Anthropologists, journalists, research scientists, Legislative Council members, political candidates have all been refused permission to travel to Northern Territory Aboriginal reserves.[46a] Aborigines were not allowed to hold a public meeting at Bagot, 1965; Davis Daniels, an Aboriginal trade union organiser, was arrested in 1968 at Roper River (his birthplace) for vagrancy (though he had cash). But prospectors employed by mining companies may explore likely commercial mineral deposits on reserves. Segregation, except for the purpose of exploiting a profitable enterprise, is virtually complete.

The second policy may be stated negatively. Not a single pastoral company has been prosecuted for breaches of industrial regulations, on housing, pay or food, in Northern Territory since the Native Welfare employment regulations (1959) and the Pastoral award became law in 1968.[47]

The third policy concerns the lack of any Aboriginal rights to traditional land. Late in 1962, an area was excised from Arnhem Land, near the Yirrkala Mission Station, without consulting the Aboriginal people. The same land areas have since been bought by another mining consortium and added to their concession at Gove, where building is now in progress. Mining concessions at Oenpelli were won by a European firm, Union Carbide Ltd. in September, 1970, when a similar application by Goulburn Island Aborigines was declined for technical reasons. In that month, the Minister for the Interior, Mr. P. Nixon, debating the Gurindji claim to Wattie Creek, made it plain that 'the government believes it is wholly wrong to encourage Aboriginals to think that because their ancestors have had a long association with a particular piece of land, Aboriginals of the present day have the right to demand ownership of it.'[48]

The law in Queensland remains virtually unchanged since 1893, apart from the right to marry. The amendments of 1965 included the election of councillors on settlements, and the transfer of Protectors' powers to the Court of Petty Sessions. Since 1965, commentators have remarked that the Clerk of Petty Sessions is usually the same police officer who was previously the Protector; and in 1970, the Conference of Councillors held at Cairns, upheld the Queensland Government's view that the Aborigines' Act be *not* changed, except for a provision for local option of licensing wet canteens on settlements. In short, the Councillors, like the Native Courts, and Native Police, appear to be another form of control ultimately deriving their importance from the Department of Aboriginal and Island Affairs itself.[49]

Historically, race relations in Australia since 1788 have been distorted by much brutality in fact. It later changed to the segregation of Aborigines, hardening into a practice in all States (and the Northern Territory) of coercion. This survived the beneficial changes of policy to welfare in the 1940s, and it was not until the adoption by the Southern states, in the late 1960s, of a policy aimed at voluntary racial associations . . . with an open choice offered to Aborigines . . . that the legacy of political indiscriminate force lapsed there. The voluntary aspect including elected Aboriginal Advisory Councils assumes a policy of representative, but not responsible, self-government. Future legislation banning social discrimination, upholding land rights and empowering participatory self-government by Aboriginal communities, is the logical extension of the trend.[50] Whether it will be accomplished in this lifetime remains to be seen.

REFERENCES

1 Australian Labor Party, Federal Platform, 1969 Immigration Policy.

2 *The Sunday Australian,* 25 April 1971. Editorial, p. 10.

3 ROWLEY, C. D., *The Destruction of Aboriginal Society,* Canberra, 1971, pp. 153-4.

4 *Ibid.,* p. 158. Quoting from CONSTANCE CAMPBELL PETRIE, *Tom Petrie's Reminiscences of Early Queensland,* pp. 162-3. Dalaipi is the speaker.

5 SALISBURY, T., *Wyndradine of the Wiradjuri: Martial Law at Bathurst in* 1824, Sydney, 1971.

6 Parramatta Peace Conference, 1814. See SALISBURY, T., *ibid.,* and ROWLEY, *op. cit.*

7 DOCKER, E. G., *Simply Human Beings*, Brisbane, 1964, p. 52, citing 'medical historians of the nineteenth century'. Also CUMPSTON, J. H. L. 'The History of Small-pox in Australia, 1788-1908', quoting *H.R. of N.S.W.*, Vol. 1, No. 2, p. 299.

8 STANNER, W. E. H., *After the Dreaming*, Sydney, 1968.

9 DOCKER, E. G., *op. cit.*, PETRIE, *op. cit.* See also RYAN, S. S. *The Land of Ulitarra*, Grafton, 1964.

10 ENGEL, F., *Turning Land into Hope*, Sydney, 1968, quoting DUNSTAN, D. A., 'Aboriginal Land Title and Employment in South Australia', in SHARP, I. G. and TATZ, C. M., *Aborigines in the Economy*, Melbourne, 1966.

11 DALRYMPLE, G. E.: Legend on commemorative cairn at Cardwell.

12 Report from the Select Committee on the Native Police Force, N.S.W. V. and P. (L.A.), 1865-67, Vol. 1, pp. 1157-216.

13 Select Committee on the Native Police Force and the Condition of Aborigines generally, Q. V. and P., 1861.

14 On W.A. frontier: BISKUP, P., 'Native Administration and Welfare in Western Australia,' Thesis, University of W.A., 1965; also HOLTHOUSE, H., *And Up Rode the Squatter*, Sydney, 1971.
The formal separation of N.T. was by authority of a 1863 Imperial Act, so that N.T. was no longer part of N.S.W. but became a part of South Australia.

14a See 'Aborigines—Slaves or Citizens' in this volume.

15 Victorian Aborigines Act, 1860.

15a See Mr. Justice Blackburn's rationalisation of the Europeans' right to displace Aboriginal landholders in P. Tobin's article, 'Aborigines and the Social System' in this volume.

16 Secretary of the A.P.B. of Western Australia, 1892, in a letter to the Governor of W.A., Sir William Robinson, quoted by STEVENS, F., 'The Aboriginal Contribution to Australian Society' in *Australian Society*, Davis and Encel Eds.), Melbourne, 1970.

17 FELTON, P. E., 'Methods Adopted by the Aborigines Welfare Board in Victoria', in *Proceedings of Conference on Welfare Policies for Australian Aborigines*', Adult Education Department, University of New England, 1960. The words quoted appear in both Victorian and N.S.W. Aborigines' Protection Acts.

18 FELTON, P. E., *ibid.*; BELL, J. H., 'Some Aspects of the New South Wales Situation', *ibid.* Also DOCKER, E. G., *op. cit.*

19 N.S.W. Aborigines Protection Act, No. 25 of 1909, amended 1915 and 1918 and Regulations. The structure of the A.P.B. quoted here did not change in N.S.W. until 1916, when it comprised representatives of Government departments. See Reports of N.S.W. Aboriginal Protection and Welfare Boards, 1884-1967.

20 N.S.W. Aborigines' Protection Act, Regulations to 1915 and 1918 amending Acts.

21 N.S.W. Select Committee on Aboriginal Protection Board, Proceedings, in N.S.W. Parliamentary Papers, V. and P. (L.A.), 1937-38.

22 N.S.W. Public Service Board Report on Aborigines' Protection Board, August, 1938, N.S.W. Parliamentary Papers, 1937-38, immediately following Reference No. 20.

23 N.S.W. Aborigines' Protection (Amendment) Act, No. 32, 1936 and Regulations.

24 Report of Roth Royal Commission on the Conditions of the Natives, 1905. MESTON, ARCHIBALD *Report on the Aboriginals of Queensland*, Brisbane, 1896.

25 CAMPBELL, A. H., *et al.*, *The Aborigines and Torres Islanders of Queensland*, a short history and a criticism of the Queensland Preservation and Protection Act, 1939-46. Brisbane, 1958.

26 TATZ, C. M., 'Queensland Aborigines: Natural Justice and the Rule of Law', *Australian Quarterly*, Sydney, September 1963.

27 Documentation for neck-chaining: Roth Royal Commission on Conditions of the Natives, Brisbane, 1905; Caledon Bay arrests, 1933, newspaper reports; DUGUID, C., *No Dying Race*, Adelaide, 1963, of Oodnadatta case, 1946; HORNER, J., biography of W. Ferguson (not yet published), of interview with M. Sawtell concerning neck-chaining at Derby, W.A. in 1908. JOHNSON, HON. H. V., Commonwealth Minister for the Interior, 1945-49, M.P. for Kalgoorlie, W.A. since 1940, State Secretary 1935-40 and General President 1942-48 of the Australian Workers' Union. He defended the current use of chains before a deputation of Aborigines led by W. Ferguson, at Canberra, June 1949. See HORNER, J., *op. cit.* and *Dubbo Dispatch*, 6 June 1949.

28 Report of the Royal Commission of Inquiry into the Alleged Killing of Aborigines, etc. W.A. V. & P. No. 3, 1927.

29 BENNETT, M. M. *Human Rights for Australian Aborigines*, Brisbane, 1957.

30 FELTON, P. E., *op. cit.*, on Victorian reserves abolition. Reports of N.S.W. Aborigines' Welfare Board from 1941 for N.S.W. reserves. See also, HORNER, J., 'List of Acreage Leased from N.S.W. Aboriginal Stations (1938-1964), from the N.S.W. Public Service Report 1938 and the N.S.W. Aborigines' Welfare Board Report 1964'. This shows that between those years, Reserves in N.S.W. gained 620 acres; lost 2958 acres; Stations gained 151 acres and lost 10,576 acres. A total of 771 acres gained, 13,534 acres lost. Published by Aboriginal-Australian Fellowship for use at State Conference, October 1965, and subsequently by F.C.A.A.T.S.I.

31 N.S.W. Parliamentary Select Committee Proceedings, on Aborigines, 1937-38, generally, *op. cit.* For Cumeroogunga exodus, see *The Age*, Melbourne, 7 February 1938.

32 BECKETT, J. R., Current Affairs Bulletin, Sydney, 1962. *Torres Strait Islands;* also PEEL, G., *Isles of the Torres Strait*, Sydney, 1946. On the strike, see Queensland Parliamentary Inquiry, 1936.

33 N.T. Aboriginals (Pastoral Industry) Regulations, 1949, No. 5.

34 Exemption Certificates were authorised by:—
   1. N.S.W. Aborigines Protection Act, Act No. 13, 1943 (s. 36).
   2. Queensland P. and P. Act, 1939 (s. 5 (3)).
   3. W.A. Natives Citizenship Rights Act 1944.
   4. S.A. Aborigines Protection Act 1934-39.

35 DUNCAN, A. T., M.A., Thesis on 'Aboriginal Education in N.S.W.,' University of Sydney, 1970.

36 BENNETT, M. M., *op. cit.*, p. 26.

37 HASLUCK, P., speeches, *Native Welfare in Australia*, Canberra, 1951.

38 Commonwealth of Australia, Parliamentary Debates, No. 12, 6 August 1952.

39 TATZ, C. M., Ph.D. Thesis, 'Aboriginal Administration in the Northern Territory of Australia, Australian National University, 1964.

40 'On Aboriginal Affairs', Parkville, Melbourne, No. 11, February-June 1964. Quoting a press statement of the Cairns Aborigines' Advancement League of 26 November 1963.

41 Quotation from STEVENS, F., 'Aborigines and the International Convention on Human Rights', commenting on Tatz. Paper to N.S.W. Human Rights State Conference, Sydney, 9 December 1968.

42 BENNETT, M. M., *op. cit.*, p. 22. W. A. Parliamentary Debates, 1956, 1st Session, p. 1105.

43 See STEVENS, F., 'Lawful Injustice: The Trust Accounts System in Queensland', *Aboriginal Quarterly*, Winter, 1969.

44 STEVENS, F., 'Protection or Persecution?', *Dissent*, Winter, 1969.

45 KETTLE, E., *Gone Bush*, Sydney, 1967.

46 STEVENS, F., 'Aborigines and the International Convention of Human Rights', *loc. cit.*

46a See STEVENS, F., 'Encouragement and Control of Aborigines in the Northern Territory', Sydney, 1967, for details of these cases.

47 TATZ, C. M., *op. cit.*

48 Commonwealth Parliamentary Debates, second session, 1970, 3 September 1970 at p. 968.

49 The Aborigines' and Torres Strait Islanders' Act of 1965, No. 27, of 1965, assented to 10 May 1965. See TATZ, 'Aborigines: Equality or Inequality', *The Australian Quarterly*, March, 1966, for detailed criticisms of this Act.

50 See TATZ, C. M., 'Aborigines: Law and Political Development', in this volume for a development of the idea of participatory self-government among Aborigines and their current awareness of the fact that the Advisory Councils to the N.S.W. and Victorian governments ('toy telephones' is their colourful and descriptive phrase) are not participating in government, nor properly representative of Aboriginal discussion 'at the grass-roots'.

15

TASMANIA: THE ULTIMATE SOLUTION

Clive Turnbull

Put him in gaol, Mata Guberna! You take it him own country,
take it him black woman, kill 't right out, all him litta child—
den you put him in your gaol. Ah, Mata Guberna, dat a very
good way. 'Pose you like dat way—'pose all same dat black un.
I nebber like dat way. You better kill it right out.

—Black Tom to Lieutenant Governor Arthur.[1]

Black Tom's advice has been accepted both in Tasmania and in Victoria. The
last full-blood Tasmanian aborigine in her native land died in 1876, less than
seventy-five years after its colonisation by Europeans, although mixed blood
descendants survive in the islands of Bass Strait. The last full-blood aborigine
of Victoria died (I am told) only a few years ago although, again, mixed
bloods may be seen wandering forlornly about the slums of Melbourne; it is
embarrassing to have confrontation in the streets with these mournful people,
in the words of Mary Gilmore in another context, 'looking for pity where pity
was none'.

Some people would like to forget the old sad story of the Tasmanian
aborigines. It was all a long time ago, they say, nothing can be done about
it now—why bring that up? The tragedy was inherent in the circumstances
of the time. But, if the Tasmanian and the Victorian Aborigines long since
passed the point of no return, are there not similar circumstances in
other parts of Australia in which kindred peoples are living and perhaps
also preparing to die? The Tasmanian story is not an isolated story. Some,
but not all of the factors, are economic. Others relate to the perversion of
the human heart and they range through the American Deep South from
slavery to the present day, through the Germany of Hitler to, so we are
told, Vietnam. Holier than thou! we cry to the Americans and South
Africans; and with no justification.

Such is the propensity for rationalisation and self-justification that, in
1852, Mrs. Charles Meredith, an educated, intelligent and, no doubt, wholly
worthy woman, was writing that the early settlers of Tasmania

> 'were neither pirates nor robbers . . . but British farmers and country
> gentlemen, not usually considered a desperately ferocious and blood-
> thirsty class, nor by many means disposed to commence hostilities
> against quiet unoffending people . . . . The enmity exhibited by the
> natives . . . was in the first instance unprovoked by the white
> population.'[2]

Perhaps, if one were sitting in an agreeable Tasmanian country house,
practising a little sketching while one's daughter played the piano and one's
husband was out about the pursuits of a squire, it was possible to believe

this; but it is nonsensical and untrue. The colonists of earliest Van Diemen's Land were not farmers and country gentlemen but the outcasts of the British social system in a brutal era, and their gaolers. In this overspill from the prisons of New South Wales—colonisation began in Tasmania in 1803— were not only people whose principal offences were poverty and rebels for causes which may now seem good but the scum of the English rookies, brutalised persons whose activities were to range through shooting, bashing out brains, burning alive, and slaughter of Aborigines for dogs' meat to cannibalism among themselves.[3]

A grossly inefficient penal system allowed such people to escape into the bush to become 'bushrangers', killing the natives' game and, when the natives resented it, the natives themselves. The bushrangers and the convict stock keepers who perpetrated atrocities were not the overt agents of European society—their activities sometimes called down the vengeance of the Aborigines upon the free settlers who came later (*c.f.* Mrs. Meredith)— nevertheless they served the purpose of a society eager to acquire the native hunting grounds as pastoral ranges and to impose a foreign system of land ownership on once wild domains.

As such, these criminals, by circumstance or choice, may be said to have 'pacified' the country, just as countries with malcontent indigenes are 'pacified' today; and although people sitting behind comfortable desks certainly did not endorse emasculation or the cutting off of hands in traps, and perhaps, indeed, deplored them, they no doubt said, 'Such things are unfortunate but human experience shows that they are bound to happen in the circumstances.'

So we find a wide range of opinion, from those who believe that the 'blacks' were sub-human vermin, to be destroyed like foxes and rabbits (and as they have been destroyed in other parts of Australia by rifle and poison), to those humanitarians emerging from the brutality of the Georgian world who were indeed shocked and ashamed by such inhumanity to people who, they felt, were men and women also. Others felt, and no doubt with justification in the circumstances, that the processes set in motion would move inevitably to a final resolution. In 1836, the Reverand Thomas Atkins, a visitor to Van Diemen's Land, wrote,

> 'Indeed, from a large induction of facts, it seems to me to be a universal law in the Divine government, when savage tribes who live by hunting and fishing, and on the wild herbs, roots and fruits of earth, come into collision with civilised races of men, whose avocations are the depasturing of flocks and herds, agricultural employments and commercial pursuits, the savage tribes disappear before the progress of civilised races ... Indeed they have not complied with the conditions on which "the Lord of the whole earth" granted to the first progenitors of our race this habitable world. "For God blessed them, and God said unto them, be fruitful and multiply, and replenish the earth and subdue it ... ." By these statements, however, I do by no means justify the avaricious and unjust, the inhuman and murderous conduct of many of the original settlers and colonists of Tasmania. A day of retribution will come, when the righteous Judge of the whole earth "will make an inquisition for blood." '[4]

Thus, even Mr. Atkins who, as a Christian, was we have no doubt, genuinely revolted by cruelty and injustice, thought that there was an inevitability about the whole business—the end, if not the means to the end,

Divinely approved. Why indeed, then should the layman, looking at his lush acres, entertain doubts? For by this time we are in the era of Mrs. Meredith's traditional English settlers. The shootings and spearings and 'black wars' are over. My own ancestors have left occasional references to seeing Aborigines but I am sure that they never shot any; nor did they have occasion to. People could no longer scream, as did the *Colonial Times,*

> 'We make no pompous display of Philanthropy—we say unequivo-cally—*self defence is the first law of nature. The Government must remove the natives—if not, they will be hunted down like wild beasts and destroyed!*'5

But if they were no longer regarded as devilish marauders, menacing every lonely white man or woman, the Aborigines were considered a nuisance who should be corralled and got out of the way, if possible, with the belief that it would be for their own good anyway. So, with many fanfares and pious protestations, they were rounded up—such of them as were left—and put in concentration camps. If you want to get rid of some-one, the most convenient place to put him is on an island and there have been many such islands—St. Helena, Norfolk Island, Devil's Island, Alcatraz and, of course the biggest island of all, Australia, and its dependant island, Van Diemen's Land, or Tasmania.

The colonial Tasmanians were fortunate in having their own potential prison islands, a whole host of them in Bass Strait. Swan Island was tried, but the lack of water was considered a disadvantage. In turn, Gun Carriage Island proved a 'miserable little place'. The Aborigines were profoundly affected by their removal from their own lands. They began the process of dying from deficiency diseases—they were frequently cheated of their rations —tuberculosis and what we may romantically term broken hearts, for Bonwick, the historian, was assured by an old hand that, 'they died in the sulks, like so many bears', an illusion to the koala, or native 'bear', which rarely survives its capture.6

From Carriage Island, the Aborigines were in turn transferred to Flinders Island, where all but a remnant were to die; the few survivors were returned to the mainland to die in circumstances sordid or macabre. On Flinders Island, which I have compared elsewhere to Swift's Academy of Lagado, they were submitted to the control of a succession of boobies, some ramming fundamentalist religion down their throats, others cheating them or neglecting them. For the colonists as a whole, they were happily out of sight and out of mind. Even Governor Arthur could now afford to be honest, not only with himself, but with others; he wrote:—

> 'for undoubtedly the being reduced to the necessity of driving a simple but warlike, and as it now appears, noble-minded race from their native hunting grounds, is a measure in itself so distressing that I am willing to make almost any prudent sacrifices that may tend to compensate for the injuries that the Government is unwillingly and unavoidably made the instrument of inflicting.'7

But there was a little face-saving even in this death-bed repentance (the Aborigines' deathbed). The Aborigines had to have been warlike, other-wise there could be no justification for anything. Yet the many records of the pre-colonial navigators show that the Aborigines were friendly unless provoked; and, even if they were provoked, their weapons of spears and stones were scarcely a match for the eighteenth century musket. These early navigators were often men of science and humanity; some of them chose to find noble savages. Others, at least, found human beings. But, to many of the early colonists, the natives were black crows.

Their origins are matter for argument among anthropologists. How many there were at the time of colonisation, we can only try to guess—estimates in the past have varied from 700 to 8,000. They were nomadic, living on fish and game, their clothing a few skins; how they survived the Tasmanian winter we may wonder.

Out of all the Aborigines who inhabited Tasmania when it was first occupied by Europeans, about 200 remained in the 1830s, all at Flinders Island, excepting five or six boys who had been placed in the Government Orphan School at New Town near Hobart. The headmaster of the school reported that, with some exceptions, the Aboriginal children were not inferior in capacity to the European children in his charge. One, George Walter Arthur, read fairly well and wrote a good hand.[8] By bureaucratic intervention, these children were returned to Flinders Island.[9] In time, George Walter Arthur married Mary Ann, the half-caste daughter of an Aboriginal woman by a sealer. He survived the miseries of Flinders Island, to die in the degraded settlement of Oyster Cove in southern Tasmania. 'Here we are thrown upon the scum of society,' said Mary Ann bitterly to Bonwick. 'They have brought us among the offscoring of the earth.'[10]

The Aborigines on Flinders Island died because they had little to live on and little to live for, their own culture suppressed and replaced at times by a mumbo-jumbo of nineteenth century fundamentalist religiosity. They ceased to breed, and pined away. By 1842, 150 of the original 200 were said to have died. The survivors, however, were adept in hymn singing and it was even thought that a few understood what the words meant.[11] The monotony was occasionally relieved when, in religious anger at their moral offences, the 'catechist' flogged the girls.[12]

The scandal of Flinders Island caused the removal of the remaining forty-four people to Oyster Bay—twelve men, twenty-two women and ten young people (some half-castes). Six of the children were placed at the Orphan School where they died. Existing in misery, pursued or persecuted by low-life Europeans infected with veneral disease, some of the Aborigines found solace in drink, and ultimate peace in the waters of the Rivert Derwent. By 1854, there were only sixteen left at the Oyster Bay station.

A few had been kept as pets by Europeans. Such a one was Mathinna, adopted as a child by Lady Franklin, bringing with her a kangaroo skin, a rush basket, a shell necklace and a pet opossum. Soon, dressed in a short scarlet frock, she was to be seen with Lady Franklin in her carriage. 'There she stood and stands now in my mind's eye like a queen,' says a contemporary, '. . . black, bright, glossy and oh so beautiful!' When Lady Franklin left Tasmania, Mathinna, said to be tubercular, was left behind. In due course, she recovered sufficiently to be sent to the infamy of Oyster Cove, to end, like George Walter Arthur, in the river.[13]

Says Edward Stephens,

'The beautiful Mathinna, after being petted and admired in the drawing rooms of Government House under the regime of Sir John Franklin and then allowed to drift in Hobart dens of infamy and vice, was, in her own person, a picture of the possibilities and destiny of the Tasmanians themselves.'[14]

William Lanney, the last Aboriginal man, survived Oyster Cove to become a whaler. He drank like a European and was ridiculed with the nickname of King Billy. In 1869, he returned ill from a whaling voyage and died in his room at the Dog and Partridge public house.

> 'O Dog and Partridge, thou hast cause to mourn,
> Thy favourite son is from they bosom torn!'

wrote a humorous versifier.

As the last Tasmanian man, Lanney possessed a cadaver of anatomical interest, and what appear to have been rival parties of body-snatchers reduced it to masses of blood and fat, making off with the bones.[15]

Truganini, the last woman, lived on in apprehension. Her uncle had been shot by a soldier, her sister had been stolen by sealer, her mother stabbed. Her man had had his hands cut off in life and her last compatriot his hands cut off in death. My own father remembered her as a grizzled old woman in Hobart, a bright kerchief bound about her head. 'Don't let them cut me up,' she said to the doctor as she lay dying, 'bury me behind the mountains.' In 1876, she died, and was buried with great precautions against the body-snatchers.[16] But they dug her up and re-articulated her skeleton and put it on display in a glass case in the Museum, like the skeleton of a baboon or any other 'curiosity'. As a child I often saw it. When, in 1948, I told the story of this obscene display, I received a letter from an old Tasmanian who told me that when, after many years, he revisited the Museum and saw Truganini's bones he was consumed with rage, made a great scene and, shaking his stick, threatened to smash the case. Perhaps this had some effect; for the bones are no longer there to be gaped at.

So that was the end of the story of the Tasmanians. What has it to say to us?

We no longer shoot Aborigines (so far as I know), poison flour or set mantraps. But we practise the averted gaze as proficiently as the white Tasmanians of bygone years. The Aborigines do not frighten us, despite some pathetic statements about Black Power. But we do not really believe that they 'own', or ever did own, Australia. We go a good deal of the way with the Reverend Mr. Atkins, hereinbefore cited. The Aborigines do not spear us between the shoulder blades when we are looking at the football or at the girlie magazines in the shop windows. All they do is what they did in Tasmania when they were, as it were, moved on, or what they did in New South Wales when the sharpshooter (sniper) described by Mary Gilmore, honoured among men, stealthily stalked them and picked them off one by one.

What, then, did they do? They got in the way—in the way, first, of sheep, now of bulldozers, in places where the only other inhabitants were totemic animals. Nearer home, they exhibit their poverty in degraded humpy settlements; and these receive neither charity nor the hymn books which served instead of fresh meat at Flinders Island.

Is the problem 'settling itself', in other words, will we reach the final solution because all the Aborigines are dead? Denied adequate nutrition they will cease to breed, but perhaps it is easier to get handouts of food in the outback of the Australian mainland, for we are told that in remote places the population is increasing.

The economic problem no longer exists; we do not have, and have never had, job competition between Aborigines and poor whites. Miscegenation, so profitable a subject for pornographic novelists of the American Deep South, is not a problem. Nor are worldly possessions in dispute, for we have already taken from the Aborigines all that they had.

It is not the function of this paper to enunciate a policy which might save the bodies of the Aborigines or the souls of us white folk. But the lesson of the old Tasmanian tale is surely that we should examine our motivations. To Tasmanians of the early years the Aborigines were dirty, degraded, barbarous creatures, treacherous and engaging in carnal rituals. This picture was based upon a lie. In the very few cases where they were given a chance to prove their merit and intelligence, as George Walter Arthur and his wife proved theirs, they showed themselves no less able than any others of the human species. If the dowry of the beautiful Mathinna was a kangaroo skin, a rush basket, a shell necklace and a pet opossum, then the dowry that we returned to the Aborigines was pox, clap, grog and death, the Four Last Things of their early sojourn.

Because we ill-used and destroyed them, it was necessary for us to vilify them; just as Arthur had to find them 'warlike' if he was to retain the last fragment of self-justification.

This vilification did not die with Truganini but has flourished, and flourishes in our own time. Degraded Aborigines begging—'Gibbit tickpen' —are part of what passes for national humour. They are pictured as being compulsive drunkards, shiftless worthless people, and hence impossible to help.

People selling buttons in Melbourne streets for an Aborigine cause not long ago were astounded by the savagery of the answers given by some of those asked to buy—'I'd rub the lot out,' 'Give 'em a bait,' and so on, and these from people who had probably never seen an Aborigine and who certainly had no reason to fear one. Their rage welled up from some dark springs of hate for all that is different, rage which can most safely be vented on what is weakest.

Tasmania is the picture of Dorian Gray in our national attic. The nonsense dished up by Mrs. Meredith is now easily exposed for what it is. Very few of us now wish to 'give 'em a bait.' But *laissez faire*, as in the case of the Tasmanians, can be just as effective a killer. Out of sight, out of mind, out of life itself. The concept of conservation is new, whether it be conservation of water, or scallops, or hairy-nosed wombats. Can Aborigines come under this umbrella or should they go the way of the dodo, the passenger pigeon, the stands of cedar?

Did anyone in Tasmania really believe that what was being done was for the benefit of the Aborigines? I do not think so. It was done because it was politically expedient and if the Aborigines died of the treatment, well, the Reverend Atkins had surely explained all that.

Nobody had told the Tasmanian colonists that no man is an island; that even Tasmania itself, in the larger ecological sense, is not an island, and that all of life is diminished by the loss of any part of it. The Victorians were fond of citing scripture and we may claim the devil's privilege and do likewise. Of the Aborigines, we may say that they hungered and were given no meat; they were thirsty and given no drink; they were naked and not clothed (with the cloak of charity at any rate); they were sick, and in prison, and were visited not. And, as one of the less popular verses of Matthew, addressed to those who failed to give those things, has it: 'Inasmuch as ye did it not unto the least of these, ye did it not to me; and these shall go away into everlasting punishment.' With that Mr. Atkins would have agreed.

REFERENCES

1 *The History of the Island of Van Diemen's Land from the Year* 1824 *to* 1835. by Henry Melville. 1835. P. 80 *et seq.*

2 *My Home in Tasmania During a Residence of Nine Years* by Mrs. Charles Meredith. 1852. Vol. 1, p. 191.

3 There is a large number of references to these atrocities, e.g.: Arthur to Murray, 15 April 1830 (House of Commons paper—*Military Operations* etc. 23 September 1831): Kelly's evidence, *Military Operations;* Stewart to Campbell, 28 September 1815, *H.R.A.* Series III, Vol. II, pp. 573-4; *Discoveries in Australia* by J. Lord Stokes, 1846, Vol. I, p. 278, Vol. II, p. 459; Roderick O'Connor, in *Military Operations; Six Years Residence in the Australian Provinces,* by W. Mann, 1849, p. 56; *The History of Tasmania* by John West, Vol. II, p. 9; Gilbert Robertson's evidence, *Military Operations.*

4 *The Wanderings of the Clerical Eulysses, Described in a Narrative of Ten Years' Residence in Tasmania and New South Wales,* by the Rev. T. Atkins, N.D., pp. 13-14.

5 *Colonial Times,* 1 December 1826.

6 *The Last of the Tasmanians, or The Black War of Van Diemen's Land* by James Bonwick, 1870, is invaluable.

7 Arthur to Goderich, 14 April 1832. House of Commons paper—*Aboriginal Tribes,* 14 August 1834.

8 *Early Tasmanians* by J. B. Walker, 1902, p. 281.

9 Robinson's recommendation in the Tasmanian Archives.

10 Bonwick, p. 247, *et seq.*

11 Stokes, Vol. II, pp. 465-469.

12 Bonwick, p. 269.

13 The story of Mathinna is told by *Old Boomer* in *The Mercury,* 7 June 1869.

14 Stephens to Walker, Tasmanian Archives.

15 The death and burial of Lanney, his resurrection and mutilation and the proceedings which followed are described in detail in *The Mercury* of 8 March 1969 and succeeding issues.

16 *The Mercury,* May 1876.

ADDITIONAL REFERENCES

A bibliography of books, periodicals and other documents relating to the Aborigines is given in *Black War: The Extermination of the Tasmanian Aborigines* by Cliver Turnbull, 2nd edition, Cheshire-Lansdowne, 1965. Since that list was compiled there has appeared N. J. B. Plomley's monumental *Friendly Mission: The Tasmanian Journals and Papers of George Augustus Robinson,* 1829-1834: Tasmanian Historical Research Association, 1966.

16

THE HEALTH DISADVANTAGES OF ABORIGINES

Peter M. Moodie

A great many Aborigines of all ages suffer disadvantages in their physical health when compared with white Australian standards and expectations. Both full-blood Aborigines in the north and part-Aborigines throughout Australia have been shown to have high death and disease rates from the communicable diseases, malnutrition and its consequences, and diseases of early infancy such as prematurity, and to suffer permanent disability due to disease and injury which has been untreated or not treated early enough. The impact of disease is noticed among the young children in particular— partly because young children form a greater proportion of the Aboriginal population, but basically because Aboriginal children, individually, face greater risks of disease or death.[1] The high proportion of children in the Aboriginal population is partly the outcome of a relatively low expectation of life, although the major factor operating to produce this age distribution is the high Aboriginal birth-rate. Large families of young children, as found particularly in the part-Aboriginal communities, incur health as well as economic penalties, for those who belong to them do not fit readily into the Australian 'average' requirements for housing, health care and medical services.

There may be certain causes of disease or death, in certain age-groups, where Aborigines may have an apparent advantage (one can think of road accident rates for young adults, for instance) but, generally speaking, these advantages with respect to single causes do not noticeably affect the overall disease and death rates within any age-group. There is little evidence to suggest that present-day Aborigines are less prone to heart disease, cancer, diabetes or any other disease which causes concern in the white Australian population.

It is not the writer's intention here to list, compare and analyse Aboriginal disease statistics. The pattern of disease is not remarkable, in that nearly identical patterns may be found among the populations of the developing countries, and also among many indigenous or immigrant ethnic minorities in the developed countries. Aborigines in northern Australia are at some advantage over their counterparts in other tropical areas in that North Australia is currently free of most of the 'tropical' scourges such as malaria, cholera, smallpox, plague and the disabling parasitic diseases such as filariasis, schistosomiasis and trypanosomiasis. On the other hand, they are at a disadvantage where, because of living in isolated and widely-scattered small communities, access to health and medical services and skilled nursing may be restricted.

In the field encompassed by race relations and Aboriginal health, there are two important questions which should be examined. The first is whether ill-health among Aborigines (restricting the term here to physical ill-health) is created, encouraged or maintained by anti-Aboriginal policies on the part of governments, or anti-Aboriginal attitudes and behaviour on the part of health and medical personnel—both private and departmental.

The second question is whether the status of Aboriginal health, as conceived in the stereotype of a 'disease-ridden' Aboriginal community, is creating or reinforcing white prejudices and intolerance. If the answer to both these questions is 'yes', there exists another of those vicious circles which are apparent in most situations of social or economic conflict, and a stronger argument for attacking Aboriginal health problems the more vigorously and urgently for being causes, as well as effects, of under-privileged status.

When considering 'racism' in relation to the health of Aborigines, it would appear to be unrealistic to restrict the term to blatant racist attitudes and behaviour such as may be exhibited by neo-Nazi political groups. There is a more subtle form—a sort of 'racism-by-omission', wherein the special problems and cultural peculiarities of an ethnic minority are ignored or discounted in offering them facilities and services geared to the white middle-class social and economic situation, on a take-it-or-leave-it basis. Believing that the term 'racism' is too strong in this context, the writer prefers to label it ethnocentrism, but does not discount it as a very potent influence on race relations as well as on health status.

Is racism influencing Aboriginal health?

It is not justifiable to assume that all the health disadvantages of Aborigines are attributable to either racism or ethnocentrism on the part of non-Aborigines. Any group of people who are not fully acculturated into what might be called 'progressive Western technological and material society' will be at a health disadvantage in some respects, although almost certainly at an advantage in others. This applies to the Aborigines now and prior to white settlement of Australia, and applies equally to communities yet to be contacted by the outside world—if there are any—and to communities of cultural minorities who are otherwise fully 'integrated'. It is also not valid to assume that the presence in Australia of a technologically advanced Western society should guarantee the indigenous inhabitants—and their descendants—advanced Western standards of health.

It is not only the organizational, economic and technical resources of the highly developed societies which have allowed them to mount such effective attacks on communicable and many other diseases; they are equally dependant upon the values and behaviour patterns of their respective communities. The community's values, of course, largely determine official health priorities, so that health activities initiated 'by popular request' have an inbuilt tendency to succeed, provided that the money, manpower and skills are available.

All such resources in Australia brought to bear on, say, the high Aboriginal infant mortality are unlikely to bring it very close to the white Australian level so long as Aborigines retain their present cultural differences, and the different values and goals that go with it.

So there appears to be a paradox. If Aboriginal (or part-Aboriginal) cultural differences are tolerated fully, as would be the case if other Australians exhibited no ethnocentrism, then health disadvantages within certain parameters must be tolerated also. If Aborigines must have the same health status as other Australians, then there is no alternative to complete social and economic assimilation, with complete loss of Aboriginal identity.

Having made this point—and it is an important one—it is better perhaps to rephrase the question: Is there any evidence that Aborigines have been denied good health because of either active or passive racism? Are Aborigines obstructed in achieving their health goals by racist policies or by the behaviour of racist individuals?

The writer believes that the best answer to such questions can come only from the Aborigines themselves, but they are a 'silent minority', particularly on this subject. Whether this silence, in itself, is a symptom of past or present racial injustice cannot be judged here, but in the absence of Aboriginal opinion expressed on the matter of racism in health, the best the writer can do is to piece together his personal impressions and findings, hearsay evidence, and some deductions from the known circumstances of Aborigines. The result is an entirely personal view.

Racism and the Aboriginal environment

The domestic and community physical environment is generally acknowledged to be an important determinant of physical (and mental) health, being very much concerned in the epidemiology of communicable diseases, accidents, stress disorders, and in the ease with which established disease may be treated or personally compensated for. In the settled parts of Australia, this environment is bought rather than personally created, and the servicing of the environment—water, sanitation, garbage disposal, lighting, power and heating—is also bought. Economic status, through its effect on the quality of the environment, influences exposure to disease. Those who condemn Aborigines for the domestic squalor in which many of them live, and their high rates for many communicable diseases, are also condemning them for being poor.[2] Where economic poverty is contributed to by racial intolerance, there will always be ill-effects on health which can also be attributed to the same attitudes through resultant defects in the domestic and community environment.

A related matter is the location of Aboriginal dwellings, and it is here that the evidence for frank discrimination is strongest. In the past, Aboriginal settlements were established in out-of-the-way locations for a variety of reasons, but the result was that the occupants were placed beyond the reach of local community facilities and services, including not only health, medical and hospital services but also public transport to reach them. Fringe-camps, although usually lacking basic facilities for hygiene (water and sanitation) are usually within walking distance of a local doctor and hospital, and situated where the older settlements *should* have been sited. Although local and State authorities are now endeavouring to house Aboriginal families within town boundaries, there are still instances of moves to keep Aborigines isolated from townships. The writer heard of an instance a few years ago, where a local service club in New South Wales was erecting houses for Aboriginal families then living in shanties near an isolated rubbish tip. The new houses were to be six miles out of town. There may have been economic considerations involved, such as the price of land nearer town, but one suspects that had the people concerned been white pensioners, for instance, every effort would have been made to house them in the town itself for their physical convenience, social needs, and access to public utilities and services.

Current town housing policy, with improved environment and access to services, should have a marked impact on Aboriginal health from the preventive aspect. But what of Aboriginal access to medical treatment?

Medical discrimination against Aborigines

Whereas preventive measures in public health and related fields tend to be rather impersonal—and, therefore, less conditioned by the personal feelings of either the subject or the health personnel involved—medical and hospital treatment is an intensely personal matter for the patient. He is more likely to be sensitive to the attitudes and behaviour of the nurse or doctor who treats his illnesses than the nurse or doctor who administers a vaccine or operates a mass chest X-ray unit. The doctor or nurse who is openly intolerant of, or hostile to, Aborigines, is unlikely to be consulted until the need is great and outweights a strong wish to avoid a personal confrontation —and often this is too late. A doctor who is tolerant, but tactless or brusque, will be interpreted as being intolerant and find himself in the same position. A doctor should be aware that most Aborigines still regard him with the same awe and apprehension as the ordinary 'man-in-the-street' of fifty years ago, and act accordingly. The writer has encountered several instances of doctor-avoidance (based on fear and lack of self-confidence) among Aborigines known to him personally, and believes it is responsible for a large number of cases where delayed treatment, neglected follow-up, or no treatment at all, has been responsible for serious permanent disability and sometimes death. In the cities and larger towns, Aborigines can be selective in whom they consult, and the most tolerant and gentle doctors and nurses will bear the major brunt of the treatment of sick Aborigines in their area—often at considerable financial loss for doctors in private practice.

There is, no doubt, considerable economic discrimination by some doctors against Aborigines exists in settled Australia, because of the many who cannot pay or who do not belong to medical benefits funds. The same doctors may discriminate equally against white patients who do not pay, but the Aboriginal patient is more likely to attribute the discrimination to his Aboriginal identity—which, of course, is permanent even though his financial situation may improve. His confidence in seeking medical advice, once destroyed, will not be fully restored by an improvement in his economic status.

Because of the economic factor in relation to medical and hospital care for non-pensioners, cases of outright racial discrimination by individual private practitioners would be hard to prove, even if complaints were made known—which does not seem to happen. It is only when Aborigines are not handicapped economically in making use of private and 'public' medical services that remaining difficulties can be safely attributed to other factors.

There are two areas where racist attitudes may be identified with more confidence because the income of the personnel involved is not a factor: in Government policy, and in the behaviour of salaried health personnel.

There have been a number of allegations of discrimination, in the field of health, against Aborigines by Governments. Two instances that come to mind from the medical literature were allegations by Christophers[3, 4] that laws restricting the travel of Western Australian Aborigines south of the 20th parallel (the 'Leper Line'), and the restriction of blood transfusions for Northern Territory Aborigines with anaemia to those with very low haemoglobin levels, were discriminatory. Both these allegations were defended by health authorities, largely on the grounds that the measures referred to were for the benefit of Aborigines—as they were in the strictly medical and public health sense—but there is no doubt that the 'Leper Line' legislation was discriminatory both in concept and in method in the way in which it attempted to limit Aborigines' freedom of movement. The most important objection that can be raised against such legislation is that Aboriginal psychological handicaps are so great already that any measure which adds to them should be avoided, even at the cost of added risks to their physical health. In the inter-relationships between physical and mental health, community health problems can more often be attributed to community psychological problems than *vice versa*. Furthermore, we tend to hand our psychological handicaps, but not our physical handicaps, on to our children. The slightest nuance of official discrimination in medical services, based on Aboriginal identity is likely to have much more severe, prolonged and irremediable consequences to both physical and mental health than the health problems which gave rise to it.

There has been some demand from Aborigines for special consideration —for favourable discrimination in a sense—but, as far as the writer is aware, few such demands have been made with respect to health. Aborigines have not been in the habit of demanding anything until quite recently, so that it is difficult to judge the extent to which Aboriginal wishes or fears have been overridden. Most complaints have been made for Aborigines by white Australians, some of whom appear to have looked at the 'Aboriginal Problem' from an entirely ethnocentric viewpoint. There is thus a pressing need for Aborigines to speak up and identify their problems in their own way, and one would expect that, if this occurred, many discriminatory laws or practices objectionable to Aborigines in the field of health could be identified and removed before they have the opposite effect to that intended.

Apart from the policies of assimilation or integration as expressed by governments—which are basically 'racist' in concept although intended to be favourable to the Aborigines—there seems to have little evidence now for what might be called active anti-Aboriginalism in Government policy. At the local government level, there are many councils who are trying hard to remove obstacles to better health, housing and economic status for Aborigines, and are enlisting the co-operation and counsel of local Aborigines in their projects. In the view of the writer, racism in health services, where it occurs, is more likely to be an error of omission than commission, and more likely to result from the behaviour of local personnel adopting local attitudes. Where governments may be at fault is in not laying down clear rules of conduct, and in not explaining the dangerous consequences of even unconscious racism in the very personal matter of health and medical treatment.

One still hears stories of blatantly racist behaviour by local health and medical personnel. One such story, now some years old, highlights the physical, as well as psychological, dangers, inherent in discriminatory behaviour; the story of the country hospital where Aborigines attending the outpatient's clinic were seen after the white citizens irrespective of when they arrived. When the clinic closed for the day, Aborigines not seen were told to come back next day, when they again had to join the end of the queue. Another story, from an impeccable source of the writer's acquaintance, is of the Baby Clinic sister who carried out a public clean-up of her clinic after Aboriginal mothers had consulted her—admitting the purpose was to reassure the white mothers in the waiting room. Instances such as these may still be common in some parts of Australia. They can be attributed to ignorance and lack of sensitivity as well as to racism, but are highly anti-Aboriginal, particularly in their effort of discouraging Aborigines from using available community health services.

With both public and private opinion moving, albeit slowly, away from the racist concepts of the past in relation to Aboriginal health and health needs, there would appear to be a danger that the vigorous condemnation of Australian society as 'racists', by individuals with academic status and influence may not only harden the attitudes of the real racists in Australia; it may also create an unwarranted sense of guilt among the uncommitted on this issue. Guilt is a bad motivator, in that it leads to rationalization, suppression or misdirected action to get rid of it. In connection with this, the writer deplores the tendency by many Australians—including some Aboriginal opinion-leaders—to harp upon the past misdeeds of citizens and governments in the treatment of Aborigines. So long as the past wrongs occupy the minds and activities of those concerned for Aborigines, present conditions will appear so much better by comparison that present Aboriginal handicaps will not be apparent, and will have less impact on the public mind. It is, after all, the public mind, and pressures generated by public opinion which can best counter racist tendencies of individuals, or governments of the future. It would be a psychological catastrophe for both Aborigines and other Australians if non-Aboriginal opinion were to be based on a feeling of collective guilt, as it would if Aboriginal attention was focussed on past injustices.

The physical health of the Aboriginal community is more a reflection of social, economic and psychological factors than of the routine activities of health departments and the medical profession. Any steps taken to avoid psychological trauma in the pursuit of physical health will be of great benefit to the whole Australian population in the long-run. Perhaps the health and medical services—both public and private—have as great a role to play in the area of community 'psychotherapy' as they can ever have in the area of physical health.

As far as the utilization of health, medical and hospital services by Aborigines is concerned, the writer believes that the most effective step that governments and local authorities can take is the extensive employment of Aborigines and part-Aborigines as health and medical auxiliaries *in the field.* Experience in the developing countries has shown that the educational qualifications of such personnel are almost irrelevant: what counts for far more is integrity and application to the job on the part of the field worker, and the ability of the community being served to personally identify to some extent with the field-worker (and *vice versa*). The conscious service and educational roles of Aboriginal health auxiliaries (and later, professionals) is no more important that their hopefully unconscious roles as Aboriginal status-boosters and stimulators of Aboriginal 'public opinion' on health matters.

Both Aboriginal populations and Australian governments have a poor record in the establishment of a cadre of Aboriginal field workers—for different reasons in each case—and a change in attitude seems to be necessary for both sides. Governments must change their attitudes with respect to qualifications necessary for effective field work, but at the same time Aborigines must change their attitudes and accept the role of community aide and advisor. There is reason to expect that the latter change will follow the former, rather than the other way round, so that the onus is more upon the governments to amend their educational and technical requirements for such jobs.

Does Aboriginal ill-health lead to discrimination and prejudice against Aborigines?

Without any doubt the answer to this question is 'yes'. People with racist views almost invariably include the prevalence of communicable diseases amongst Aborigines as a reason for excluding them *en masse* from white society and the use of public facilities—as evidenced by the various public swimming-pool controversies in country towns. It is not so clear whether the status of Aboriginal health gives rise to discriminatory attitudes or prejudice amongst otherwise uncommitted people, but it is likely that it does. The interesting observation here is that the diseases which communities appear to have the greatest fear of contracting from Aborigines (ringworm, headlice, worm infestations) are generally regarded as trivial by the medical profession and are not often regarded very seriously by health departments. In the strictly medical sense, such diseases are trivial, in that they are rarely threats to life and limb, are not frequent in the overall population, and *can* be cured without the intervention of a doctor or a hospital.

However, the social effects of these conditions, as far as Aborigines are concerned, are out of all proportion to their physical effects. For this reason, they warrant greater attention from the health and medical services. Because of the psychological climate in which the visible sufferers from these complaints find themselves (in a mixed community), and the prejudices against Aborigines in general which appear to be generated by them, every possible effort should be made to eliminate them as a matter of *social* urgency. Such diseases should be regarded as seriously as are tuberculosis, gastroenteritis or malnutrition—but as threats to social rather than physical viability. The writer believes that appropriate advice and treatment for ringworm, headlice and worms at least should be completely free for all sufferers (Aboriginal or otherwise) for this reason.

Free treatment will not, by itself, eliminate these diseases from the community, but at least it will create a set of physical and psychological circumstances favourable to their elimination. One way in which this can happen, in southern part-Aboriginal communities, is to draw the attention of the members of the community to the 'importance' of these diseases. Free worm treatment, which used to be generally available to Aborigines on settlements in New South Wales has certainly—in the writer's experience—made settlement populations more aware of and concerned about the 'worm problem'. The fact that such treatment alone is relatively ineffective in eradicating worm infestations from the community (because of prolonged reinfection from heavily polluted soil) is not relevant.

It is not difficult to postulate discriminatory repercussions for many other diseases common amongst Aborigines—growth stunting, runny noses, suppurating ears, severe dental caries (all being visible abnormalities) and any chronic or recurrent condition which tends to interfere with some Aborigines' ability to hold a steady job. Again the social consequences of such diseases (through the reinforcement of discrimination and prejudice) are likely to exceed the physical consequences.

Unfortunately, it is true that there is some threat to non-Aboriginal communities from the pool of communicable diseases present among Aborigines living in the same area or attending the same schools, but the threat is much less than is commonly supposed and—again for psychological reasons—should not be used as an incentive for attacking communicable disease problems among Aborigines.

The pool of medically minor communicable diseases is an ideal first target for Aboriginal health auxiliaries—they are important for the reasons discussed, they are easily and safely treated, and visible cure will be appreciated by the affected individuals.

Conclusions

The general conclusions which the writer has reached after this brief examination of the racial implications in Aboriginal health are that, firstly, there is a vicious circle involving ill-health and ethnocentrism or prejudice; secondly, that while governments and the majority of health and medical personnel are rarely blatantly racist in policy and behaviour, there are many highly ethnocentric aspects of government health policy, and ethnocentric or unconsciously racist individuals harming race relations with Aborigines and exerting psychological pressures which Aborigines should not have to face in this so-called enlightened age; thirdly, governments have both the responsibility and the opportunity of breaking the vicious circle at two points—the removal of remaining discriminatory practices by themselves or by health and medical personnel, and mounting a more vigorous attack on those diseases which reinforce discrimination and prejudice on the part of the white population.

Both governments and Aborigines can contribute greatly to these objectives by working out a formula for the employment of greatly increased numbers of Aboriginal (and part-Aboriginal) health auxiliaries.

REFERENCES

NOTE. The writer is a medical officer engaged in research and teaching within a government department. The views expressed in this article are the writer's own personal views, based on personal experience in Australia and overseas, and not necessarily those of any government or government department.

1 MOODIE, P. M. (1969) 'Mortality and Morbidity in Australian Aboriginal Children', *Med. J. Aust.* 1: 180-185.

2 The exterior appearance of an Aboriginal dwelling is not a particularly good guide to the hygiene of the occupants. There are many Aborigines living in decrepit shanties who nevertheless keep them as neat and as clean as could be expected of anyone in similar circumstances, and who follow the principles of good hygiene to the best of their knowledge and ability. The dwelling's appearance and location, however, is usually a reliable guide to the sort of services available to it, and the 'mod cons' without which optimum hygiene cannot be achieved.

3 CHRISTOPHERS, B. E. (1961), *Med. J. Aust.* 1:147 (Correspondence).

4 CHRISTOPHERS, B. E. (1962), *Med. J. Aust.* 1:25 (Correspondence).

17

THE MISSIONS AND RACE PREJUDICE

E. A. Wells

> If a splinter is flaked off from one culture and is introduced
> into a foreign body social it will tend to draw in after it the
> component element of the social system in which the splinter
> is at home. In cultural intercourse one thing leads to another.
> No wonder that the victim's normal attitude towards an
> intrusive alien culture is a self defeating attitude of opposition
> and hostility.
>
> —Toynbee[1]

In September of 1914, the Reverend Joseph Bowes, of Ipswich, Queensland,
an expert on Aboriginal affairs, contributed an article to the documentary
record; 'A Century in the Pacific'. This remarkable work listed over one
hundred sources in the bibliography and indicated that scholars had already
established the four and eight sub-class system found in the Australian
Aboriginal kinship system. Roth, Spencer and Gillen, together with other
very early investigators dating from and including F. Peron of 1800 A.D.,
were included in this missionary work. Accordingly, it might be shown that,
early in the colonization of Australia, the Church had access to an inspired
source of information on the Australian Aborigines, terminating in Bowes'
day with the perceptive, conclusion that:—
> 'The Aborigine must be regarded as a being with a spiritual
> conception.'
> 'There is to him a spiritual universe.'
> 'Their ritualistic and sacerdotal rites represent their faith and their
> hope.'[2]
The dialect had been mastered, catechism, Bible portions and hymn book
verses had been printed in the vernacular, but all ended in failure.

In 1913, the total Aboriginal population was thought to be some 90,000
and Mr. Bowes regretfully comments, 'the Methodist Church is not represented by any agent in this work'. The question must be asked then, 'why
was the Methodist Church, historically so exhuberantly missionary minded
and having recorded outstanding success in the Pacific, unable to evangelise
the Australian Aborigine?'

Professor Stanner[3] points to a possible source of negative influence,
when he instances 'a relentless denial of Aboriginal religious capacity' which
developed within the Australian community generally in the mid 1850s.

This view of the Aborigines, as either too archaic in the social sense or
too debased in the moral sense to have veritable religion, made it possible,
for example, to attend gravely to the egregious nonsense spoken by
C. Stanisland Wake, a director of the New Anthropological Institute, when
he wrote, in 1871 A.D., that the Aborigines 'possessed hardly any of what are

usually understood as phenomena of intellect', and that 'any idea of abstract morality or even a true instinct of moral propriety' seemed absent from their minds. How could such people, he questioned, 'representative of humanity itself', be capable of religion?[4]

Subsequent events in the Australian attitude to the Aborigines appear to indicate that, as Stanner says,[5]

> 'this view came to prevail in both Church councils and the legislative bodies of various States ... and that the particular biases of the new science designed as if to fit in with the particular blind spot in lay and clerical outlooks in Australia'.

Thus, when Arnhem Land was opened up in 1916, the scholarship of the early 1800s was simply not used. The Church is still paying a great price for this oversight, to say nothing of the Aborigines whose interest the missions serve in the Northern Territory.

One of the serious consequences of the present day rejection of early investigation is seen in the way missionaries feel it necessary to analyse the people they go to serve. Among the missionaries sent to Arnhem Land, where great personal devotion and extraordinary tenacity towards the goal of religious evangelism has characterised so many Christians, a pronounced and significant number are so very sure of their vision that, as Stanner points out: 'they were genuinely unable to see, let alone credit, the facts that have convinced modern anthropologists, that Aborigines are a deeply religious people'.[6] Many modern missionaries manage to reject what little of the new discipline manages to emerge in popular religious literature. Lay missionaries in particular, not having undergone special reading courses in sociology and anthropology, tend to regard the modern attitudes as contrary to the rather fundamental theological interpretation of the Word of God to which most subscribe. Some, indeed, regard anthropology as definitely anti-Christian as did a missionary motor mechanic at one outpost with which I have been associated.

This modern blindness, coupled with the inherited mental attitudes from the 1850s, fits neatly into the racial mental scheme which comes to have deep psychological influence over the whole sphere of operations of the Church in its missionary and evangelical activities amongst indigenous people.

In the realm of indigenous art, I had serious difficulty with the mission staff at Yirrkala. Following a devotional meeting one night, a missionary introduced the question of the Aboriginal art, which was said to be in preparation as a gift for the new Church then nearing completion. 'Was it true, that as superintendent, I had agreed to allow the finished work a prominent place within the new Church?' he enquired. I had to agree that this was so.

The art boards in question represented sectional legends of the Dua and Yirritja moieties. They had been executed with extreme care and it had taken sixteen men some four to seven weeks to complete them. The exquisite work had been allocated a place to the side and the rear of the communion table in the Church and represented a marvellous 'gift of the ancients' to the Church, revealing for all to see some of what the old men were prepared to give up as exclusive knowledge. So hard does prejudice die, that the staff of the mission tried desperately to force my hand and have the consent to include them in the Church withdrawn. One of the sentences used in the fierce confrontation which followed it provided a clue to the thinking of the committed: 'They were', they claimed, 'perpetual reminders of evil times and still in the mind'. The art boards were reminders, certainly, but I preferred to think of them as carrying poetry of a very high order, land ties, ancestral heroes and all that goes to remind a people of a homeland. And even, for those finishing the journey, there was the shade tree—an important point of symbolism for those reaching out for a new spiritual experience.

Not only in art has racism fierce echoes in the mission field, but all aspects of economic experience as well.

Although educationalists believe 'that any subject can be taught effectively in some intellectually honest form to any child at any stage of development',[7] so great is racial bias in Australian missionary work that this hypothesis does not hold good for the teaching of even common arithmetic to an Aborigine.

Teachers appear to start with an assumption: 'the Aborigines are no good at numbers'. One of the strategically placed headmasters in the Aboriginal Schools section was one day explaining this to a group of visiting politicians and went on to illustrate; 'you see they never had to count beyond five before we came'. This was patent rubbish!

'You mean to say that a man with ten wives could only count up to five in the vernacular. Early Australian sheep farmers used Aborigines to count sheep and Dame Mary Gilmore records a very early report of an Aboriginal system of counting the stars using a multiple of three',[8] I retorted.

The conflict, to my mind, clearly showed that the work of the specialists is slow to penetrate the missionary field. It is regretable that the contribution of Dr. Donald Thompson,[9] a distinguished anthropologist, has not had a greater hearing. In his work, he noted cycles covering thousands of miles of territory which, set in a sacral order, could form the basis of an economic pattern reasonably easy for men to follow. Baler shell and pearl shell exchanges illustrated by Mulvaney[10] as covering almost the entire continent do not belong to a people who could not add up in simple form.

Aborigines being regarded as indispensable labour in Australian frontier conditions and even on mission stations, the racist attitude governs what it is permissible for them to possess by way of possible educational adaptation. The need to exploit Aboriginal labour has tied the Aboriginal people down with mental and geographical restriction so geared to European work motivation that a psychological stunting of vast proportion has resulted. Work on mission stations in the early years of establishment was more geared to institutionally orientated settlement requirements than to economically satisfying conditions for the Aborigines themselves.

It used to be said that the Aborigine did not like to work with the soil; this, of course, is true of many other people as well. However, the introduction of community type farming at Milingimbi, which shared out the results in actual consumption of the crops by the workers who toiled to produce them, resulted in a dramatic rising annual return. On the other hand, the first house building programme at Milingimbi with adobe bricks and for which wages were paid at the general station level, gradually slowed down until the number of bricks per week made the experiment a doubtful economic proposition. We had a meeting about this and it was explained to me that brick making was the hardest work they had ever done. I pointed out that some men did work hard and that it was a pity they had to share the wages with those who were not really contributing much to the operation. A system was worked out whereby they could work as they liked, but that they would be paid so much per brick, and each man could count his own bricks. The increase was astronomical. The lesson in 'numbers' was quickly mastered by the adult population.

How grievous it was to hear the layman who took my place at Yirrkala and became acting superintendent say, 'I treat all Aboriginal adults as fourteen year olds; as far as I am concerned they never progress beyond that point'. This denial of responsibility is one source of the failure of Aborigines to respond to the incentives which might be otherwise placed before them. Under-achievement in actual life situations, where the rewards for work are so obviously appreciated by white men, also encourages rejection of the work situation by Aborigines. In these circumstances, the Aborigine hides his seeming ignorance in a moody silence. The attitude is particularly evident before strangers when a white person is most anxious to have the Aborigine prove himself. This is particularly so in the discussion of abstract subjects.

The resultant harm of rejection and avoidance by Aborigines comes, in these situations, to play a significant part in the grouping of small socially disadvantaged minorities. This grouping within an environment of poverty stunts both intellectual and economic growth. This, coupled with lowered vitality, creates the forerunner of the fringe society we know so well in Australian urban conditions. The elite groups emerging among the Aborigines make little impression on the adults once the racist syndrome has done its deadly work. Any person with leadership capacity is treated as belonging to white society and a little under suspicion as being 'maybe for some white man idea'.

The creation of the mental ghetto into which the unhappy Aborigines can slide through racist views, is also responsible for the lack of interest some of them display in political affairs. Starting from the popular racist statement, 'how can he possibly understand?' low level participation is anticipated and usually in evidence. But political debate, to a few of the Aboriginal population, is the same exciting duel of wits and words that it is with his European counterpart.

After Aboriginal Garmali had been struck down in a tribal affray and was dead, one of the missionaries let me know, and added, 'if anyone had to die it was a good thing it was Garmali ... he was a trouble maker'. Of course he was! But I came to regard his trouble as part of the emergence of the whole man in a position of social change; and what a man!

A master wood carver, the first Aboriginal to introduce the chain system to lightning outline drawing on timber so that others could fill in the detail and thus produce more of this work, which was much sought after. The man who electrified the Commonwealth Committee of Enquiry at Yirrkala, by producing a common Shell map of the area in dispute and proving how he could read it in detail, then went on to deliver a fine speech indicating how deeply he felt about the attempt to rob him 'of his land for his children'.

The idea that the Australian Aborigine is not capable of becoming politically aware suits the people who desire what the Aborigines still believe to be their own—their land.

Racism and the Problems of Australian Polygyny

The question of admitting polygynists to the membership of the sections of the Christian Church operating amongst the Aborigines is a very difficult one indeed. The major denominations, the Anglican and the Roman Catholic, are bound on the one hand by the decision of the Lambeth Conference which makes it impossible, and on the other, by traditional attitude which makes it quite unthinkable. However, the Protestant sections of the Church give a very confused picture of the continuing debate and many *ad hoc* decisions are made on the field outside of policy decision. The unpublished thesis of Mrs. Mabel Wyllie[11] contains some very interesting material on this subject and reflects a strikingly contrary view to that held by various denominational bodies on this issue. Some are generous and some are dogmatically overbearing, as if a primitive society was of very necessity living in sin, or, as Mr. Long of the Baptist oriented Aboriginal Inland Mission would put it, 'living in a state of heathendom'.[12]

One of the most surprising aspects emerging from a study of the material available is that the Commonwealth Government has consistently allowed religious denominational interpretations of social ethics to add to the inevitable conflict arising from European-Aboriginal culture contact. Bishop Gsell, writing to Mrs. Wyllie in 1949,[13] mentions patience as a governing principle: 'The attitude of the Church is one of patience and expectation. The mentality of the natives must be raised and purified before any attempt at conversion can be started'. In actual fact, 'patience' was strained a little by hastening the breakdown of the basic cultural pattern of the Aborigines by sudden and traumatic interference with the institutional convenience of gathering boys and girls in dormitory systems. This ruthlessly broke down the traditional kinship system.

Father Docherty of Port Keats in a reply to the questionnaire gave as a reason why the Aborigines preferred polygyny as a form of marriage, as 'Concupiscence, Pride and the Devil'.[14]

Running through the whole of the literature by missionaries and some prominent educationalists, is the insistence that the 'power of the old men must be broken'. Granted that the old men are the depositories of ancient law and custom, it must be conceded that the greatest objection to Aboriginal culture has centred around this custom of a plurality of wives. However, objectionable polygyny may be to European interpretations of the Church in the twentieth century, we could do well to remember that the Gospel in Europe was content to accept the form of marriage existing amongst the pagans of Western Europe. European racialism had no right whatever to undermine the Aboriginal cultural sytem by removing a pivotal element until such time as economically viable substitutes could have restored the balance created by the enforced removal of a part.

Pope Paul, during his recent visit to Australia, commented:—[15]
'the Catholic Church respected Aboriginal culture. Like all other ethnic minorities you have human and civic rights equal to those of the majority. We would like to stress that the common good can never be used legitimately as a pretext to harm the positive values of your particular way of life'.

Falkenberg, in his magnificent scholarly appreciation of the kinship structure of the Aborigines at Port Keats, gives an indication of how the total life cycle of the Aborigines cultural system is actually broken down by massive onslaughts on its central features whilst supporting it in minutiae.[16]
'In 1947 the mission (Roman Catholic) at Port Keats established a dormitory where boys from the age of 7 to 8 years live permanently under supervision from the missionaries. In the same way the young

girls some years earlier were collected at a convent where they also
reside permanently. At the same time the children go to school until
they are fourteen years of age. Thus easily was the complete dis-
continuation of the boy's initiation ceremonies assured.'

I recall building the first day-school premises at Milingimbi in 1952.
The long structure built to take some one hundred students did not meet
with the approval of the tribal elders. Enquiries, which proved difficult and
had to be conducted over a long time, brought to light the views that 'the
length of the structure and its distance from the camps of the people
indicate that it is intended for a dormitory for the girls.' This incident was
the first 'go slow' type of organised resistance I had met. The elders took a
lot of convincing that this building was not a dormitory of some kind,
intended for 'shutting up the children'.

Education used with deliberate intent to separate the young of a
cultural system from their elders in order to introduce an alien system is
foreign to the general appreciation of our democratic processes and needs
revision. As an illustration of racism, it has echoes in South Africa.

Falkenberg points out that the dormitory system was introduced at Port
Keats[17] 'on the theory that children are most receptive to new ideas and can
learn most easily . . . .' In actual field practice it means that this system
removes them from the influence of 'Dad'. The charismatic values associated
with 'Dad', or, in more general terms, with Aboriginal leadership at the time
of the experiment in dormitory practices, presented both the Commonwealth
Government and the various Boards of Mission with a most potent vehicle
of thought for the transmission of new ideas to the whole Australian
Aboriginal community. All the valuable associations of traditional sanctions
could have been brought to bear on a programme of 'Total Family Education
for the Aborigines'. But the racist belief that there is nothing to save or
encourage in the Aboriginal culture if it slows down the process of assimilation, has meant that education was only for the young.

The very small amount of financial aid available for adult education
within both Welfare and Mission finances can only illustrate this attitude of
secondary values in educational encouragement to any but the young.
Australia's attitude and deliberate policy of separatism in education has
broken down tribal life, divided the young from their elders and contributed
greatly to mass frustration within the Aboriginal community.

Another emerging people present a different picture. It is a pity that
Australia has been so slow to heed the lessons of Ghana, where tremendously
successful mass appeal experiments have brought incentives to learning to
whole villages in outback situations and enabled fathers and mothers to
appreciate what was meant by the education of their children.[18]

However, it is true in Australia, as it has been through the long years
of the Church's history that, amongst some who felt called to serve their
Lord in the Mission field, are those of humble heart whose devotion to the
Gospel is so individually remarkable that affectionate response is a reward
transcending legal definitions of purpose within any of the many orders
operating.

I believe that Aborigines will eventually achieve both the intellectual
and spiritual sophistication with all of the best that is inherited within the
core of Christ's consciousness.

However, to ensure the permanent transfer from the Aborigines to the
Europeans of all that Aborigines have possessed, economically, religiously,

and particularly in land ownership, it has appeared necessary for the white usurper to totally denigrate every cultural trait.

The acknowledgement that the Aborigine is the inheritor of a sensitive capacity for spiritual discernment found in the cumulative value of the leaderly group system amongst them, will become the corner stone of the psychological structure necessary for his social acceptance amongst Europeans. Only recognition of this need will lead to the intellectual security on which it is necessary to base a well ordered society designed to exploit the genius of both races.

REFERENCES

1 TOYNBEE, A. J. *The World and the West*. London 1953, p. 75.

2 BEALE, W. H. *A Century in the Pacific*. The Methodist Book Room. First Edition 1914.

3 BERNDT, R. M. and C. H. *Aboriginal Man in Australia*. Angus & Robertson 1965, p. 209.

4 STANNER in R. M. and C. H. BERNDT, *ibid.*, p. 209.

5 *Ibid.*, p. 212.

6 *Ibid.*, p. 208.

7 BRYNER, J. S. *The Teaching Revolution*. Methuen 1969, p. 36.

8 GILMORE, DAME MARY. *Old Days—Old Ways*. Angus & Robertson 1934.

9 THOMPSON, D. *Economic Exchange Cycle of Arnhemland*. Macmillan 1945.

10 MULVANEY, D. J. *The Pre-History of Australia*. Thames & Hudson 1969, p. 96.

11 WYLLIE, MABEL. 'A Study of Polygynous Marriage', M.A. Thesis, University of Sydney, 1950.

12 *Ibid.*, p. 92.

13 *Ibid.*, p. 88.

14 *Ibid.*, p. 76.

15 *The Australian*, Sydney, 3 December 1970.

16 FALKENBERG, JOHANNES. *Kin and Totem*. Oslo University Press 1962, p. 19.

17 *Ibid.*, p. 19.

18 DU SAUTOY, PETER. *Community Development of Ghana*. Oxford University Press 1958.

THE SEARCH FOR ALTERNATIVE POLICIES

18

EDUCATION AND LAND RIGHTS: AUSTRALIAN AND SOUTH AFRICAN IDEOLOGIES

C. M. Tatz

> The last temptation is the greatest treason:
> To do the right deed for the wrong reason.
> T. S. Eliot, *Murder in the Cathedral.*

Most people would contend that the approach of a democratic state to any social, economic, political, legal, religious or cultural problem must differ from the approach of a totalitarian state. They would assert that ideas, institutions and mechanisms originating in Portugal, South Africa and Soviet Russia on the one hand and Australia, Canada, New Zealand and the U.S.A. on the other, must and do reflect their differing ideologies. Hence, any adoption or adaptation of antithetical ideologically-based values would be neither desirable, conceivable nor possible.

Many western social scientists have joined with sociologist Daniel Bell in his 'anti-ideologism'. 'Today we witness the end of an ideological era', he wrote, 'and are witnessing the birth of totally non-ideological sociology—of unbiased, objective, and passionless social research.' The Russian sociologist, F. Konstantinov, says this is nonsense.[1] Each generation of human beings finds itself caught up in the clash of ideological systems and the struggle of social ideas. The idea that sociology—or any other social science 'ology'—can exist in some 'non-ideological' sphere, he adds, is one of the myths furthest removed from reality. I agree.

The main concern of this paper is not with the subjectivity of social science, but with the possible adoption and adaptation for the advancement of Aborigines of well-established techniques and models, in spite of their unacceptable ideological origins or their practice by a totalitarian regime. Given the divergent premises underlying South Africa's and Australia's race philosophies, I contend that 'ideological justice' can be done to techniques and mechanisms derived from apartheid philosophy: that what doesn't work in South Africa for bad or wrong reasons can be the right deed in Australia for good reasons. In short, if the vehicle is sound, it will transport one from Goal A to Goal B, irrespective of the manufacturer's or driver's world outlook.

There is obvious value in comparative study. It provides a yardstick for measurement of one's own actions; it broadens perspectives; it enables adaptation, modification and accommodation of other successful ideas and programmes; if often obviates years of local expenditure and evolutionary experiment. At worst, it can point to the disaster areas to be avoided.

South Africa's self-described image as 'the polecat of the world' has led to an almost universal dismissal of all that country says or does, at least in the field of human relations. Such disavowal is often accompanied and assisted by dogmatic insistence on the 'uniqueness' of the Australian racial 'problem' and confident assertion that we will solve our own problems in our own way—or better, that we can come to guide the world. 'I see no reason why Australia's attack on the problem of moving a minority group into a different but dominant culture should not become a model for other areas of the world', wrote one Australian educationist.[2]

Association of Australia with South Africa will produce instant emotional rejection in most people. They will cite the obnoxious parallels that already exist, or which existed until very recently: the closed reserve system, grossly unequal wages, the wide and arbitrary powers delegated to officials, the separate and punitive system of justice on Queensland reserves, the prohibitions on liquor and sexual relations; in fact the whole Australian concept of wardship, tutelage and guardianship which is so very close to earlier South African notions of 'Christian trusteeship' for the black man who, as Prime Minister General Hertzog once put it, 'stands as an eight-year old child next to a man of greying experience—a child in religion, a child in moral conviction, without art and without science, with the most primitive requirements and a most rudimentary knowledge of how to supply these needs.'[3]

This understandable desire for disassociation from South African attitudes and practices has nevertheless led to some monumental stupidities (or perhaps *post-hoc* rationalisations). For example, for some time now, both federal and state health and education departments in Australia have stated that separate figures are not kept for Aborigines—'as a matter of policy'. One department, Queensland Education, has said that such statistical information 'may be of general interest but its value for educational planning is doubtful'.[4] This sort of policy is clearly a political and social one, not an educational one. Two assumptions underlie this rationalisation: first, that assimilation, in the sense of absorption, is the desired objective, and is the antithesis of apartheid; secondly, the inference that separate numbers are a form of apartheid and must be avoided at all costs.

While avoidance of 'segregation', 'discrimination', or 'apartheid' may be politically admirable, *the keeping of statistics for Aborigines is not in itself a form of apartheid*. It is not difficult to identify Aboriginal pupils or patients. And this seems to be imperative, because if governments and other agencies are to conduct effective social, economic and educational programmes they must know what numbers are involved. (I sometimes uncharitably suspect that the 'avoid-apartheid-at-all-costs' attitude is consciously used as a justification for declining to provide comparative statistics in certain socio-economic situations.)

*   *   *   *

In my view, there are several aspects of South African practice which Australia could well adapt or even emulate. Two are dealt with in this paper: education and land rights for the indigenous populations. A third, which I have no space for, is South Africa's recognition of what is there called a code of native law and custom, a separate segment of law but one recognised and upheld in special courts.

Serious consideration of adaptations is only feasible if we undertake two primary steps: first, that we appreciate the subtle but very real divergence between assimilationist ideology and accommodationist ideology;

secondly, that we reject, once and for all, what can be called a sociocentric view of Aboriginal life in Australia.

A sociocentric view is one which assumes that Aboriginal (or any other similar group's) realities can be taken as constant. Astonishingly, no less an eminence in race relations than Robert Ezra Park once wrote:[5] 'We can only know the minds of peoples, as we know a work of art, in so far as *we* are able to recreate, in our own minds, the experiences which have made them what they are.' This seems to me to be the epitome of the ethnocentric position in race relations: it implies a passive and static indigenous people whose life-style and outlook have to be clinically recreated and analysed, jigsaw-puzzle fashion, by us. It assumes that the administered people have no positive or dynamic viewpoint; or, if they have, then little or no heed need be paid to it. Casting Aborigines or Africans in this passive role dooms the assimilationists and their programmes—which they view as the product of their own disinterested generosity—to failure. To my knowledge, the only Australian who foresaw the dangers of such a stance was Sir Paul Hasluck. In 1952, when enunciating his thoroughly assimilationist philosophy, he warned administrators to heed constantly what he called 'the changing mind of the native'.[6]

Assimilation as a policy has an ideological base.[7] It can be defined as a process of generalization, inwardly or ethnocentrically orientated, incorporating new situations into existing frameworks of thought and action. It involves the generalization of strategies developed in metropolitan institutions and their duplication in rural (or overseas) contexts. To be successful, assimilationist practices require that indigenous people abandon traditional methods of interaction and analysis, and hence accommodate to the white models.

Accommodation also has an ideological base. It involves a process of specification; it is outwardly oriented, modifying existing schemes of thought and action in order to fit them to a new situation. In effect, it means adopting strategies that depart, often radically, from pre-existing metropolitan norms. A successful accommodationist policy reflects the degree to which administrators modify their strategies in view of Aboriginal realities, especially changing realities.

Before administrators affirm that they always accommodate Aboriginal realities, let it be clear that such taking into account does not mean, for example, abandoning Aboriginal thirteen- or fourteen-year olds because the 'reality' is that they all lose interest in education at that age. Negative accommodation is not accommodation when it takes the form of abolishing an entire social or educational programme on the ground that the recipients of it are seen, variously, as beyond the pale, beyond tuition, genetically cussed and perverse, and worse, ungrateful.

*   *   *   *

There was much that was wrong with African education before 1953. The state's financial contribution was inadequate and management was inefficient. There was understaffing, overcrowding and buildings were sub-standard. Teacher qualifications were generally low and in many instances African teachers were unqualified.

In 1950, the average school life of African children was only four years. The majority did not reach the third year of schooling. In 1925, the proportion of pupils in post-primary classes was as low as 1.5 per cent; by 1949, it was only 2.62 per cent. Each province controlled its own African education; each had a special primary curriculum, but in every case the secondary syllabus was the same as for white children.

Until 1953, there were three main features of African education. The first was the niggardliness with which successive governments financed it. The second was the recognition that tribalism and traditional values were dying out and that the bulk of the African population had accommodated to many white values. The third feature was that the education system did not attempt to inculcate in African children a different set of values and outlook on life. There was no attempt to instil in African children, ideas of separateness or of their being an independent 'race' with special abilities, qualities and aptitudes.

In 1951, the Report of the Commission on Native Education[8] announced two fundamental premises for the future. First, for the whole of African society, education was to be the development of a 'modern, progressive culture', with social institutions which would be in harmony 'with the evolving conditions of life to be met in South Africa'; secondly, for the individual African, the aim was the development of 'character and intellect, and the equipage of the child for his future work and surroundings'.

Six guiding principles were suggested. Sufficient schools 'with a definite Christian character' should be provided: the central government should therefore control African education. There should be greater emphasis on the education of the mass of Africans. Mother-tongue education was necessary, at least in the primary stage. Parents should share in 'the control and life of the schools' and schools should educate parents 'in certain social values'. Africans should shoulder a proportionately heavy share of financing education. Finally, schools should provide for 'the maximum development of the Bantu individual, mentally, morally and spiritually'. On the face of it, as a general policy, there is not too much to quibble at to this point.

But what were the ideological purposes and motives of Bantu education? In the debate on the *Bantu Education Act* in 1953, Dr. Verwoerd said:—[9]

'Racial relations cannot improve if the wrong type of education is given to the Native. They cannot improve if the result of Native education is the creation of frustrated people, who, as a result of the education they receive, have expectations in life which circumstances in South Africa do not allow to be fulfilled immediately, when it creates people who are trained for professions not open to them ... Education must train and teach people in accordance with their opportunities in life, according to the sphere in which they live.'

Till then, he added, the African had been 'subject to a school system which drew him away from his own community and misled him by showing him the green pastures of European society in which he is not allowed to graze'. Thus, Bantu education was designed to equip Africans for the inferior role in life which Nationalist ideology prescribed.

But why so equipped? Because a basic tenet of South African race policy is the artificial re-creation of dead and dying tribalism among the wholly and partially detribalised Africans outside the reserves (7.97 million in number).

In 1925, General Hertzog announced his solution of the race problem: separate development on a territorial segregation basis. There was, he said, when referring to the African as an eight-year old child, a difference in national characteristics and habits. There would therefore always be a difference in racial needs 'and for that reason separate treatment shall be meted out not only as regards legislation, but also in regard to the administration of the law'.[10]

The fact that the African, particularly in urban areas, was rapidly becoming more westernized as a result of white contact was beginning to weaken the argument of African 'primitiveness'. There was an urgent need to find a differentiating factor. The answer was tribalism. Both Hertzog, in the 1930s, and Verwoerd, in the 1950s and 1960s, passed legislation to resurrect tribalism, and then used this very 'tribalism' as conclusive proof of African primitiveness and difference. In this way it soon becomes clear that there is an unbridgeable gap between the two 'civilizations'. The justification for separate treatment becomes simple: with his blanket of tribalism the African is so different from the white man that he cannot be accepted as a member of the common political society. The principle behind the *Bantu Education Act* then is that African civilization, tribally-rich, prestige-filled, is unsuited for association with or participation in the richly-endowed, wholly-different white civilization.

In the end we have an educational nightmare. The social studies syllabuses bear this out. In history, African children are told of the 'wars of extermination' they waged against the Boers, and of the 'ravages' committed by their people. White aggression is nowhere mentioned. Textbooks state that 'these tawny people (Egyptians) are the descendants of Canaan, the son of Ham, who was cursed by his father Noah'. And so on.

It will be questioned how any of this can be relevant, adaptable or acceptable in the Australian context. Ideologically, all Australian governments are now saying three significant things: first, that Aborigines shall have a right of choice in their life-style and in all matters affecting them; secondly, that Aborigines should participate in decision-making; thirdly, that as much as possible of their traditional life will be encouraged. A fourth principle was declared by the Director of the Commonwealth Office of Aboriginal Affairs in May this year, namely, that his Office has no intention whatever of trying to assimilate Aborigines.[11]

Accepting these policy principles as serious-minded and honest ones, I am seriously advocating that if modified aspects of the Bantu education system are applied here, they will go much further than existing ideology and practice towards achieving first, what Aborigines are asking for, and secondly, what governments are seeking on their behalf.

Let us look briefly at some principles and techniques that could be applied:—

(i) The resurrection and re-imposition of tribalism in South Africa has been attempted for objectionable reasons, especially when it is applied to third- and fourth-generation urban-born Africans who have adopted western goals and values. But maintenance and perpetuation of traditional values is required here, by Aborigines who resist change, by Aborigines experiencing an identity crisis, and by whites perceptive enough to recognise these Aboriginal reactions.

Most field staff in Australia have met with stolid resistance to social change programmes. What many do not see, is that rejection of their innovations is strongest where the new ideas have no correspondence to the institutions and values of the traditional culture. Their consequent frustration then takes refuge in stereotypes of Aboriginal uneducability, perversity and biological predestination to the mysterious darknesses of the primitive mind.

South African's resurrection of tribalism has one notable feature so
strikingly absent in our context: armed with relevant ethnographic data,
administrators have studiously sought to introduce innovations that have
strands of thought equivalent to African cultural assumptions and which
underlay their traditional institutions. For example, the chieftainship concept
has not been replaced by participatory-democracy type political institutions,
but has rather been resurrected, re-shaped and reinforced. In Australia we
have not accommodated the tribal elders' educational processes for their
children. We have placed their children in *schools*, assuming or pretending
that the traditional relationships between teacher and taught and between
'pupil' and 'pupil' never existed; whereupon western assumptions about such
relationships have been imposed from without, most often to the total
exclusion of parents and kin.

Evangelism offers another example. With perhaps one or two exceptions, missionaries have neither sought nor thought to use the spiritual
content and symbolic mechanisms of Aboriginal religion as a vehicle for the
transmission of Christian theology. Mostly it has been derision of 'olden time
law' and demand for instant acceptance of Christian lore.

Identity crisis is not uncommon in ethnic minorities. South Africa rigidly
insists that every shade of pigmentation must inexorably be accompanied by
a specific set of folkways, and each set of folkways is seen to have distinctive
characteristics as well as meaning for each racially classified individual. ('I
am black but comely' in the Song of Solomon becomes, incredibly, 'I am
suntanned but comely' in the Afrikaans translation.)

Assimilationist outlooks here tend to judge 'Aborigines' or 'Aboriginality'
externally, by skin colour, with the palest approximating closest to white
'civilization'. There is evidence that 'the pale ones' suffer acutely from lack
of identification with either white or tribal society. For years in Melbourne I
gave, on request, extra-lessons to Aboriginal teenagers, lessons in
'Aboriginality'. It was both ironic and pathetic. These young people wanted
to identify as Aborigines, but felt that they had no cultural, religious,
historical or ritualistic bases for a satisfying or genuine identification.

Culture is not a static phenomenon. Reinforcement of certain cultural
configurations can produce a valid and meaningful biculturalism, emotionally
and psychologically satisfying. It does not mean what unthinking critics will
absurdly claim it to be: sub-incision rituals in the streets of Redfern and
Fitzroy. (Jews stopped sacrificing paschal lambs a thousand years ago, but
they still retain a meaningful, symbolic ritualism in that connection.)

(ii) In Africa, assimilation of and into most white models was desired
by Africans. Instead, segregation, separate development and retribalization
were imposed upon them from above. In Australia, assimilation has been
dictated from above, but *voluntary separatism on a bicultural basis* is being
sought from below by many Aborigines. This is probably the crux of the
whole matter: that there is a world of difference between segregation
imposed by the dominant society and voluntary separatism actively sought
by the dominated. Aborigines will doubtless have a tough battle trying to
transmit the message that grass-roots separatism is *not* synonymous with the
worst excesses of the South African system. Even if the message does come
across, they will still be faced—despite the arguments of this article—with
a host of emotional blockages that the South African word *apartheid* inspires.

(iii) South Africa has rarely been guilty of a sociocentric approach. It
has been only too aware of the 'changing mind of the native', despite occa-

sional protestations to the world that Africans are 'the happiest of all nature's children'.

(iv) There is much talk, in both policy and legislation, of the need for political and economic development and cohesion in Aboriginal communities. Yet assimilation has destroyed the decision-making mechanisms in Aboriginal society[12]—and turned their open society into an institutionalised one. South Africa's accommodation or re-accommodation, if adopted in Australia, is much more likely to encourage such development.

(v) The Bantu education system has stressed the development and perpetuation of both modern and traditional African culture. Australia's assimilationist practices have, as many anthropologists note, undermined respected traditions and institutions. It will be claimed that several missions still actively foster traditional craft. The Australian Council for the Arts is fostering Aboriginal visual and performing arts for the right reasons. Missions often still tend to foster them because of the exigencies of mission budgets. (For nearly twenty years, one particular mission banned craft works on the ground that such activity 'strengthened their religion'.)

(vi) Bantu education has consciously related education to local institutions, whether political, legal, economic, social or religious. Aboriginal education has borne no such relationship, even where on settlements and missions there could be a very close link with the white sector of the institutions as well as with the traditional institutions of Aboriginal life. Where syllabuses do relate, it is to metropolitan institutions of which the students can have little conception or interest.

(vii) In Africa there is a definite, if over-emphasised, relationship between education and the child's future and his milieu. We make virtually no attempt in this direction. Where it is made, it is by inference of a future life in the institution, in a perceivably low-grade occupation ('I'm work houseboy for my maluka, rakeim up, cuttim grass, cartim way rubbish'), at perceptibly lower wages; or, if envisaged outside of the reserve, as seasonal labourers.

(viii) The South African emphasis on mass literacy and adult education has been remarkable. Elsewhere I have described Australian inadequacies in this field.[13] A senior Australian administrator—noting that Commonwealth Aboriginal education programmes began seriously in the Northern Territory in 1951—pointed out that the first Aboriginal matriculants could be expected only in 1975.[14] Incredible as it may sound, South African teenagers have been moved from total illiteracy to literacy in less than a month by the use of special techniques. Whatever South Africa's economic motives for these programmes, the fact is that their techniques have been tried, tested and proved. They are available—from such bodies as the Witwatersrand Native Labour Association, the National Institute for Personnel Research and the Bureau of Literacy and Literature.

(ix) Both before and after Bantu education, there was consistent recognition of the value of the vernacular in education, at least at the primary level. In Australia, missionaries such as Reverend Bill Edwards of Ernabella Mission and Miss Beulah Lowe of Milingimbi Methodist Mission have fought hard battles to achieve official legitimacy for their vernacular methods.[15] There is a fairly strong movement among part-Aborigines to re-learn an Aboriginal language. Many young Aborigines today are asking why they, and white children, cannot study an Aboriginal language in a school curriculum. Indeed, why not?

(x) Regarding parental involvement in the life of the school, South Africa has gone too far, in this sense: government has pegged expenditure on African education and African parents have to meet costs in excess of the pegged sum; uniquely, parents pay dollar for dollar for capital costs. That is one extreme. Australia represents another. White Australian teachers are known to be generally hesitant about approaching parents. Where Aboriginal parents are concerned, however, there is generally no approach and less interest—even where the teachers believe that they recognize the especial problems and social pathologies of the Aboriginal child.[16] This is more understandable in the urban and town contexts: on settlements and missions it borders on the incredible.

(xi) In history, geography, religion, civics and the like, African syllabuses are a distortion. In the fields of animal husbandry, agriculture, domestic science, horticulture, commerce, secretarial practice, and the like, they are first-rate. Considerable refinements of text-books and teaching methods have taken place in these areas over the past eighteen years. It is regrettable that we are embarking on our own laborious experiments without reference to these available techniques.

*   *   *   *

Limitation of space prevents a full exposition of the attempts made in the past ten years to secure land rights for Aborigines and to prevent further incursions into and excision of 'their' land. 'Their land', unlike the land of indigenous peoples in Canada,the U.S.A., New Zealand and South Africa, is Crown Land, set aside temporarily as an area of occupancy for Aborigines. As Crown Land, the reservation in favour of Aborigines is revocable by the federal or state authority—and such revocations have been numerous.

Apart from carefully prepared agitation by Aborigines and private advancement organizations, several significant governmental developments have occurred in the past eight years. The first was the 1963 petition of the seventeen Yirrkala clans in Arnhem Land protesting at the Commonwealth government's decision to lease approximately fifty square miles of Yirrkala territory to an overseas bauxite company. This resulted in the appointment of a select committee of federal parliament to investigate the grievances of the Yirrkala people. Their report was effectively shelved.[17]

The second development was South Australia's enactment of the *Aboriginal Lands Trust Act* in 1966. The aim is to give Aborigines specific title to reserves, to give them mineral rights beyond those normally consequent on freehold title and to provide compensation machinery. Another aim is to 'atone' for failure to carry out the Letters Patent in 1836.[18] The statute created an Aborigines Land Trust Board, consisting wholly of Aborigines. To the first three nominated trustees, have been transferred all unoccupied reserve lands and all occupied but unstaffed reserves—where the residents indicate that they want their land held by the Trust. The Trust has power to deal with Aboriginal lands by developing them, leasing them or even selling them—but only with Ministerial consent.[19]

The third development was the refusal of the Gurindji tribesmen at Wave Hill station in the Northern Territory to work for wages for the Vestey's company. Their strike and claim for 500 square miles of that vast cattle station has elicited strong sympathy and support in Australia and abroad.[20] Their claims have not been successful, and a countervailing force against them has been the Department of the Interior which, since 1968, has been responsible, through its Welfare Branch, for the control of Territory Aborigines, and which insists that its guided assimilationist policies are the only ones that can lead the Gurindjis to 'fruition' as a people.

A fourth but minor episode, was the Victorian government's belated investment of the title to the Lake Tyers 4,000-acre reserve and the 500-acre Framlingham reserve in designated Aboriginal share-holders in 1970. Of the 26,114 acres ever gazetted for Aborigines in Victoria—made up of six stations and ten small reserves—only Lake Tyers and Framlingham remain for Aboriginal occupancy.

The most critical event has been the Yirrkala Land Rights Case, decided in April 1971 by Mr. Justice Blackburn of the Northern Territory Supreme Court.[21] The Yirrkala Aborigines, urged and assisted by a group of Methodist ministers and former missionaries, brought suit against the Commonwealth government and Nabalco Pty. Ltd., an aluminium company, for recognition of their title to the Gove Peninsula land area, and for compensation for lands leased to and exploited by the company. Before judgment was given, and while the case was in effect *sub judice*, the then Minister of the Interior informed Parliament that 'recognition of land rights would not help the Aboriginal people of the Northern Territory', and that it was not Government policy to recognize traditional ownership of Aboriginal land.[22]

Before the judgment, I had speculated that the Commonwealth could not afford to lose this case which, if won, would have legally recognised traditional occupancy and therefore communal native title to this land. Others joined this speculation. Counsel for the Yirrkala Aborigines expressed the view that had the government lost, it would undoubtedly have legislated to expropriate the land for mining purposes.[23]

The judgment against the Aboriginal plaintiffs endorses a hitherto widely-held view: that the absence of treaties with the Aborigines in 1770 and the actions of Governor Phillip in 1788 in claiming political sovereignty over land, thus vesting it in the Crown, meant that Aboriginal ownership of land was never considered. Though Aborigines were defined in law as British subjects, in practice they had the effective status of wards, meriting special protection. In short, there were only moral but no legal obligations to them. (The injunction in the Letters Patent [Reference 15] seems to me to border more on the legal than the moral.) The court has taken British Common law as its basis for decision: that a 'civilised' government had the right to occupy a territory without a civilised government, that is, an organized government. And Aborigines had no organized administrative authority at the time of exploration and settlement. 'The claim is that the plaintiff clans, and no others, have in their several ways occupied the subject land from time immemorial as a right, that the right of the plaintiff clans are proprietary rights, that these rights are still in existence and that Nabalco's activities are unlawful in that they are an invasion of such proprietary rights'.[24] After examining the laws of various jurisdictions, the judge's opinion was that the doctrine of communal native title had no place in any of them. Aborigines, he said, could not point to any grant from the Crown in the basis of the title they claimed. They could not, therefore, succeed unless they could show that there was a doctrine in their favour, co-existing with the rights of the Crown. (The clan, he said, had not been shown to have a significant economic relationship to the land, though the spiritual relationship was well proved.)

In this case, Aborigines have argued in vain that culturally they do not conceive of land as a contractable commodity, as something subject to individual freehold which can be leased, mortgaged, bought or sold. A spiritual relationship with land, a sense of collective, communal and tribal possession as a natural order of things is clearly alien to our commercial and legal ideology. But not so in South Africa.

A week after the judgment,[25] the Prime Minister announced 'the establishment of a seven-man committee of Federal Ministers to enquire urgently into Aboriginal land rights in the Northern Territory.' The committee will examine whether changes or developments in Territory policy are needed in relation to:—

  (i) '*Protection* of lands *reserved* for the *use and benefit* of Aborigines';
  (ii) 'The *making available* to individual Aborigines, and groups of Aborigines, the land necessary for commercial enterprises';
  (iii) 'Setting up an Aboriginal land fund to acquire land coming on the market in the Northern Territory which can be *made available* to Aboriginal groups for commercial enterprises';
  (iv) 'Ensuring that, *subject to the requirements of national development,* Aborigines on lands reserved for their use and benefit will be given *reasonable preference* in mineral prospecting and exploration'; and
  (v) 'Supporting commercial enterprises which have reasonable prospects of success on land *held* by Aboriginal communities by grants from the Aboriginal advancement trust account and loans from the capital trust fund for Aboriginal enterprises'.

The judgment went against the Aborigines and they have decided that, rather than appeal, they will campaign for a change in the law. Two Yirrkala leaders presented a five-point petition to the Prime Minister on the 6th May 1971,[26] namely, that the people of Yirrkala want:—

  '(1) ownership of the land;
  (2) a direct share of the royalties paid by Nabalco;
  (3) no other economic ventures in the Aboriginal reserve without the permission of the Yirrkala Aboriginal Council;
  (4) royalties from all other economic enterprises established on the Aboriginal reserve;
  (5) land to be returned to our title as Nabalco is finished mining.'

It is clear that the Aboriginal plaintiffs are arguing for proprietary rights, not for financial backing for mineral entrepreneurship; and for recognition of the doctrine of communal native title, not for setting up economic competition with such consortium partners as Colonial Sugar Refining Co. Ltd., the A.M.P. Society, the Commercial Bank of Sydney and Elder Smith Goldsbrough Mort Ltd. Aborigines are talking about 'ownership', 'direct shares', 'land returned', and 'our title'. In the matters listed for Ministerial investigation, there is a pre-judged and pre-determined economic-assistance emphasis which makes no mention whatever of proprietary rights: only such phrases as 'protection', 'reserved land', 'making land available', 'use and benefit', and 'land held' by Aborigines—all, inevitably, 'subject to the requirements of national development'.

It is in the South African context that the Ministerial committee could well find a model, although—as with Bantu education—the motives for setting up land-ownership machinery are obnoxious.

In 1913, the South African government passed the *Native Land Act*, the underlying principle of which was that the bulk of the African and white groups should live on, occupy and acquire land in separate areas.[27] The 'indiscriminate acquisition of land' by Africans had to be stopped. The Act, intended as a temporary one, froze the free purchase of land by Africans. Except with the Governor General's permission, an African could not acquire from a non-African, or a non-African from an African, any land in any area outside of the 'scheduled African areas'. In somewhat typical fashion, the Act was promulgated *before* a commission was appointed to define the further scheduled areas where Africans could acquire land.

At that stage, Africans owned 10,729,433 morgen (one morgen = two and one-ninth acres) of land in Scheduled Native Areas. The Beaumont Commission was appointed in 1913 to 'lay down lines of permanent terri- torial segregation' by delimiting once and for all the extent of African land acquisition in areas outside these Scheduled areas.

From 1852 onwards, African land was inevitably tied to the question of non-white political rights. In the Cape Province only, *all* non-whites enjoyed a common-roll franchise, based on educational, income or property qualifica- tions. To deny land rights to Cape Africans was to interfere with their franchise rights, rights 'entrenched' in the Constitution and safeguarded by the requirement of special amending machinery. Beaumont was accordingly frustrated in his desire to apply the Land Act to the Union as a whole, and his Report in 1916 to Parliament was generally found unacceptable.

Thereafter, a series of Local Committees—for the Cape, Natal, Orange Free State, Eastern Transvaal and Western Transvaal—were appointed to draw the magic maps of black and white areas. They fared no better than Beaumont. Of the witnesses who gave evidence, Professor Edgar Brookes wrote: 'A large body of entertaining fools all over the Union suggested that the driest, or alternatively the most fever-stricken, areas in their Province were the most suitable to be set apart for Natives'.

Nothing further was done until the advent of General Hertzog as Prime Minister in 1924. He then set about his solution: separate development on a territorial segregation basis. For twelve years he laboured to achieve what no one at Union in 1910 thought was possible: obtain the necessary two- thirds majority of both Houses of Parliament sitting together in order to amend the Constitution and so disfranchise the Cape African voters.

The *Representation of Natives Act* of 1936 disfranchised Cape Africans, created a Natives Representative Council as an advisory body, and allowed Africans throughout the Union to elect four whites to represent them in the Senate and three whites to represent them in the Assembly.[28] Hertzog's main *quid pro quo* for this disfranchisement was the *Native Trust and Land Act* of 1936.

The government, said Hertzog, was now in a position to fulfil its pledge: to grant Africans the 'substance' of the land—where they could live and develop along their own lines—in place of the 'shadow' of the vote. The land programme was also to be compensation for the restrictions placed on land purchases in 1913. The Act set out a schedule of Released Areas, areas in which Africans could acquire further land, on a quota basis: that is, a total of 7.250,000 morgen was to be released for further purchase. Together with the already held 10.7 million morgen, the 17.97 million would amount, forever more, to no more than 12.59 per cent of the country's total land space. In 1936, Hertzog pledged that the government would acquire the 7.25 million within five years. By 1971 the full quotas have not yet been acquired: the government has yet to purchase another 1,382,000 morgen.[29]

From Australia's point of view, the important concept was the Act's establishment of a corporate body known as the South African Native Trust, with the Governor-General as trustee, to be administered for the settlement, support, benefit and material and moral welfare of Africans. The Governor-General was authorised to delegate his power and functions as trustee to the Minister of Native Affairs in consultation with the then existing Native Affairs Commission.

The Act not only vested in the Trust all of the established Crown land reserves, but all the Crown land in the released areas. At the same time, it empowered the Trust to acquire additional land for Africans, under leasehold tenure and under supervision, until the 7.25 million morgen quota was reached. The Trust was also empowered to develop and repair existing reserves: 'It is notorious (said a White Paper) that the existing native locations and reserves are congested, denuded, over-stocked, eroded and, for the most part, in a deplorable condition'. The Trust did, however, make provision to assist Africans in buying land from the Trust or from private owners in released areas. *It never envisaged non-Africans acquiring Trust or African-owned land in these areas.* Finally, land ownership was recognised as taking three forms: individual, group or collective, and tribal.

For all its ideological shortcomings, it seems to me that this model could well be adapted and modified for Australian conditions. If the courts can't change the law, say Aborigines, then government can. The Commonwealth has concurrent power to legislate for State Aborigines: it could establish an Australian Aboriginal Land Trust, a corporate statutory body, with responsibility to Parliament and delegation to a Minister acting in direct consultation with the Office of Aboriginal Affairs. If declared policy means anything, it would certainly mean not only consultation with Aborigines, but direct Aboriginal decision-making in the functions of any such Trust. Among other functions, it could invest *all* Crown land temporarily reserved for Aborigines in the Trust, and it could assist Aborigines to acquire, by purchase or grant, such trust land with a view to individual, group or tribal *ownership*. It could incorporate the existing Aboriginal capital enterprises fund and make loans or grants available for land development. It could make funds available to Aboriginal communities to enable their access to the best legal counsel in their dealings with the Trust on land matters. It could regulate mineral exploitation, royalties and shareholdings on such land. In this way, all existing Aboriginal reserves could vest in Aborigines through the Trust, making the revocations, excisions and cessions of reserves to non-Aborigines impossible. It could, and should, also function as a Land Claims Commission, to arbitrate on claims by Aborigines who consider they have been dispossessed of land.

*   *   *   *

I have argued that what South Africa has set out to do, for the wrong reasons, has considerable potential use for Australia, and that South African experience may have valuable lessons for us.

Concentration on the two seemingly disparate elements of education and land rights has been deliberate: in my view there is a direct relationship between them. One cannot reconcile governmental concentration on occupation, possession or ownership of land in areas of Aboriginal population—with the explicit corollary that Aborigines wish to or will occupy such land—with simultaneous governmental encouragement of educational programmes that bear no relationship whatever to life and living on such land.

For two decades now, education policy has been predicated on assimilationist social change programmes, programmes which for the most part have taken place in almost total isolation from the metropolitan values and institutions which form so much of the spirit and content of the curricula. Recognition or intended-recognition, whether willing or otherwise, of Aboriginal attachment to traditionally-occupied land suggests a serious need to re-think approaches to other aspects of Aboriginal life.

Assimilationist ideology is inconsistent with such policy aspirations as Aboriginal participation in decision-making, Aboriginal choice in matters affecting them and encouragement of traditional life and culture. The former Prime Minister's determination to achieve an urgent breakthrough in the field of land rights is equally inconsistent with education for a life-style many Aborigines may never choose to want or do not in fact want. Unless ambiguities and inconsistencies of this kind are clarified very soon, Aboriginal requests will change rapidly into demands, demands to frustration, frustration to withdrawal and alienation, and alienation to violence.

REFERENCES

NOTE. This paper was presented at the 43rd ANZAAS Conference, Brisbane, 28 May 1971.

1 KONSTANTINOV, F. 'Sociology and Ideology', *Transactions of the Sixth World Congress on Sociology*, 1966, Vol. 1, pp. 3-20, esp. at pp. 7-10.

2 GALLACHER, J. D., 'Some Problems Facing an Educator in a Programme of Social Change', in *Aborigines and Education*, eds. DUNN, S. S. and TATZ, C. M. Sun Books, 1969, at p. 104.

3 Speech at Malmesbury, Cape, May 1926: quoted in TATZ, C. M., *Shadow and Substance in South Africa*, Natal University Press, 1962, at p. 40.

4 *Op. cit., Aborigines and Education*, pp. 59-62.

5 PARK, ROBERT EZRA, *Race and Culture*, Glencoe Press, 1950, at p. 30.

6 HASLUCK, PAUL, 'The Future of the Australian Aborigines', presidential address to Section F (Anthropology) of the 29th Meeting of ANZAAS, Sydney, 22 August 1952.

7 For a full exposition of assimilation and accommodation concepts in colonial educational policies in Africa, see CLIGNET, REMI, 'Inadequacies of the Notion of Assimilation in African Education', *The Journal of Modern African Studies*, Vol. 8, No. 3, 1970, pp. 425-444.

8 *Report of the Commission on Native Education*, 1949-1951, U.G. 53/1951, Government Printer, Pretoria.

9 *House of Assembly Debates*, Vol. 83, 17 September 1953, column 3575.

10 *Op. cit., Shadow and Substance in South Africa*, pp. 38-52.

11 DEXTER, MR. B. G., as reported in *The Australian*, May 1971.

12 For example, Peter Coffin—a fully tribalized part-Aboriginal leader of the independent Mugarinya Aboriginal group in the Port Hedland-Marble Bar area—has shown what can be done by strong Aboriginal leadership in the day-to-day life of an Aboriginal community. Had he been living in the Northern Territory, the assimilationist legislation and administration would have classified him as an 'honourary white', and thus separated him from his people.

13 *Op. cit., Aborigines and Education*, pp. 66-67.

14 *Op. cit.*, GIESE, H. C. p. 95.

15 There is, I believe, considerable significance in the following viewpoint, one expressed not by academics but by a black newspaper in Johannesburg, *The World*, on 13 April 1971:
'The good matriculation results in the African schools last year is attributed to the use of the mother-tongue medium in the primary schools . . . Last year's matric results were better than ever before. Five schools obtained more than 90 per cent passes'.

16 In Armidale the organisers of the homework centre for Aboriginal children have now agreed to re-think their whole approach, one which hitherto excluded the parents from consideration. In essence, they have found that the Aboriginal children use the scheme as an opportunity 'to take the mickey out of us', with the parents largely ignorant of what the whole scheme is *really* about.

17 House of Representatives: *Select Committee on Grievances of Yirrkala Aborigines*, Arnhem Land Reserve, October 1963.

18 These stated: 'Provided always that nothing in these our Letters Patent contained shall affect or be construed to affect the rights of any Aboriginal natives of the said province to the actual occupation or enjoyment in their own persons or in the persons of their descendants of any lands therein now actually occupied or enjoyed by such natives.'

19 See Don Dunstan's account of this legislation in his chapter, 'Aboriginal Land Title and Employment in South Australia', in *Aborigines in the Economy*, eds. SHARP, I. G. and TATZ, C. M., Jacaranda, 1966, pp. 314-344.

20 See *The Aborigines of Australia*, a report to the Anti-Slavery Society for the Protection of Human Rights by its Secretary on his visit to Australia in 1970, published in 1970.

21 Millirrpum, Mungurrawuy, Daymbalipu and others v. Nabalco Pty. Limited and Commonwealth of Australia, Supreme Court of the Northern Territory, No. 341 of 1968.

22 *The Age*, Melbourne, 4 September 1970.

23 See the special report entitled: 'Plight of a People that the Law Forgot' in *The Sunday Australian*, 2 May 1971, at p. 11.

24 See *The Australian's* front-page account of the judgment, 28 April 1971.

25 *The Australian*, 7 May 1971, at p. 3.

26 *The Canberra Times*, 7 May 1971.

27 The summary following is dealt with in detail in Chapters II, III, IV, V and VI of my *Shadow and Substance in South Africa*.

28 This representation was abolished by Dr. Verwoerd in 1959, in a piece of legislation perversely entitled *The Promotion of Bantu Self-Government Act*.

29 *A Survey of Race Relations in South Africa 1970*, South African Institute of Race Relations, Johannesburg, 1970, at p. 130.